IRINIT

SOUTH COU

ILLUSTRATOR   AUTHOR   CHARACTER DESIGN   VOLUME
KIYO KYUJYO   SUNAO YOSHIDA   THORES SHIBAMOTO   NINE

Trinity Blood Volume 9
Story By Sunao Yoshida
Art By Kiyo Kyujyo
Character Designs by Thores Shibamoto

Translation - Beni Axia Conrad
English Adaptation - Christine Boylan
Retouch and Lettering - Star Print Brokers
Production Artist - Vicente Rivera, Jr.
Graphic Designer - James Lee

Senior Editor - Jenna Winterberg
Pre-Production Supervisor - Vicente Rivera, Jr.
Print-Production Specialist - Lucas Rivera
Managing Editor - Vy Nguyen
Senior Designer - Louis Csontos
Senior Designer - James Lee
Senior Editor - Bryce P. Coleman
Associate Publisher - Marco F. Pavia
President and C.O.O. - John Parker
C.E.O. and Chief Creative Officer - Stu Levy

A ⚙ **TOKYOPOP**® Manga

TOKYOPOP and ⚙ are trademarks or registered trademarks of TOKYOPOP Inc.

TOKYOPOP Inc.
5900 Wilshire Blvd. Suite 2000
Los Angeles, CA 90036

E-mail: info@TOKYOPOP.com
Come visit us online at www.TOKYOPOP.com

TRINITY BLOOD Volume 9 © Kiyo KYUJYO 2007
© Sunao YOSHIDA 2007 First published in Japan in 2007
by KADOKAWA SHOTEN PUBLISHING CO., LTD., Tokyo.
English translation rights arranged with KADOKAWA SHOTEN
PUBLISHING CO., LTD., Tokyo through TUTTLE–MORI
AGENCY, INC., Tokyo.
English text copyright © 2009 TOKYOPOP Inc.

ISBN: 978-1-4278-0884-4

First TOKYOPOP printing: February 2009
10 9 8 7 6 5 4 3 2 1
Printed in the USA

TRINITY BLOOD™

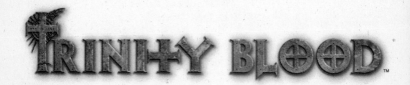

VOLUME 9

WRITTEN BY
SUNAO YOSHIDA
ILLUSTRATED BY
KIYO KYUJYO

TOKYOPOP®

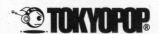

HAMBURG // LONDON // LOS ANGELES // TOKYO

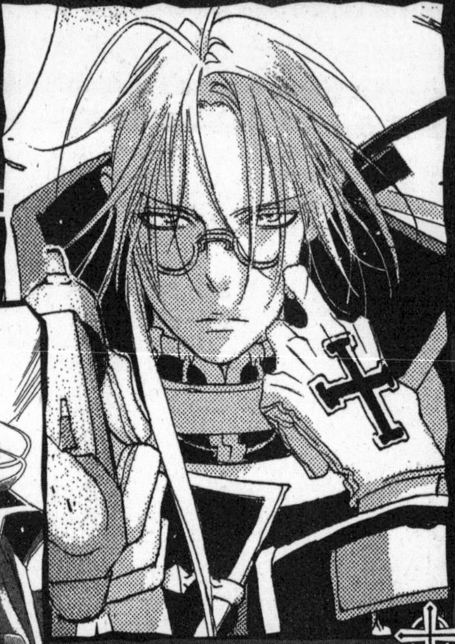

Abel Nightroad

An absentminded, destitute traveling priest from the Vatican's secret AX organization. His official title is AX enforcement officer. His job is to arrest law-breaking vampires. And he takes 13 spoonfuls of sugar in his tea.

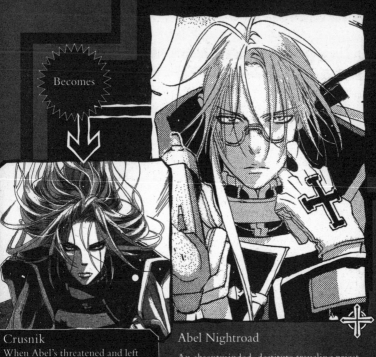

Becomes

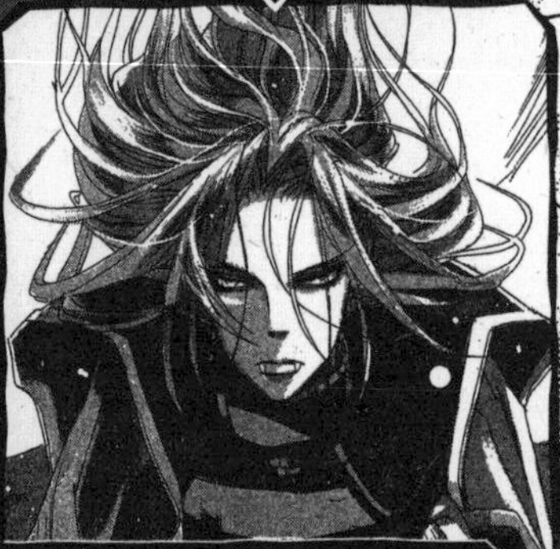

Crusnik

When Abel's threatened and left with no other means of escape, he transforms into a Crusnik, a mysterious vampire who drinks the blood of other vampires and possesses great power.

Story

In the distant future, civilization has been destroyed by a catastrophe of epic proportions. Mankind is at war with vampires, an alien life form that appeared when the Earth changed. Falsely accused of an attempt to murder the Emperor, Esther and Ion are held in custody. There, Ion is seized by a vampiric thirst and attacks Esther. Ion tries to commit suicide to save Esther, but Father Abel stops him. Meanwhile, Suleyman of the radical faction attempts to assassinate the Emperor Vladica of the Tzara Methuselate. The Emperor reveals herself to be…Seth! A defeated Suleyman dies in Seth's arms. Now...the battle between Dietrich of the Rosenkreuz Orden and the Crusnik begins...

Characters & Story

Ion Fortuna

The Earl of Memphis of the Tzara Methuselate; the vampire sent as a messenger of the Empire, who has strong affection for Esther. After returning home, he was framed for the murder of his grandmother.

Esther Blanchett

A novice nun with a strong sense of justice. After she lost her church and friends in a battle with vampires, she chose action over despair and followed Abel when he said, "I am on your side."

Seth

A medical student who works part time as a tea seller in town. Though possessed of a keen knowledge and confidence, she says she's "just your average pretty girl." Her true identiy is Emperor Vladica of the Tzara Methuselate!!

Radu Barvon

The Baron of Luxor of the Tzara Methuselate. He was Ion's "tovarăş," but betrayed him and joined the Rosenkreuz Orden. After a battle with Ion, Radu was believed dead, but he has recently reappeared, intending to assassinate the Emperor.

Astharoshe Asran

The Marquis of Kiev of the Tzara Methuselate; she considers Abel a true "tovarăş," since they worked an investigation together in the past. She's known as a "Terran Lover" in the Empire.

CONTENTS

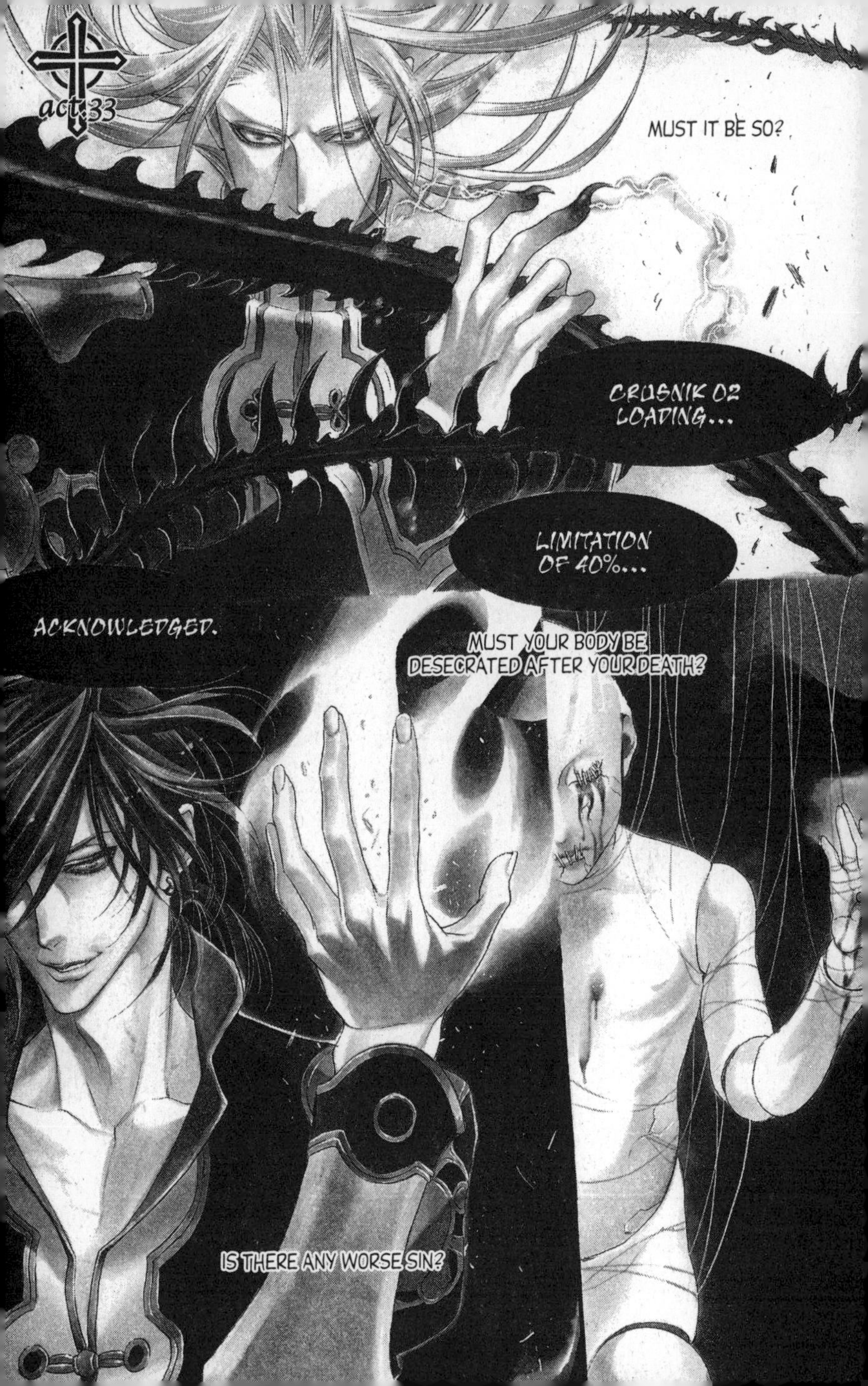
act.33
MUST IT BE SO?
CRUSNIK 02 LOADING...
LIMITATION OF 40%...
ACKNOWLEDGED.
MUST YOUR BODY BE DESECRATED AFTER YOUR DEATH?
IS THERE ANY WORSE SIN?

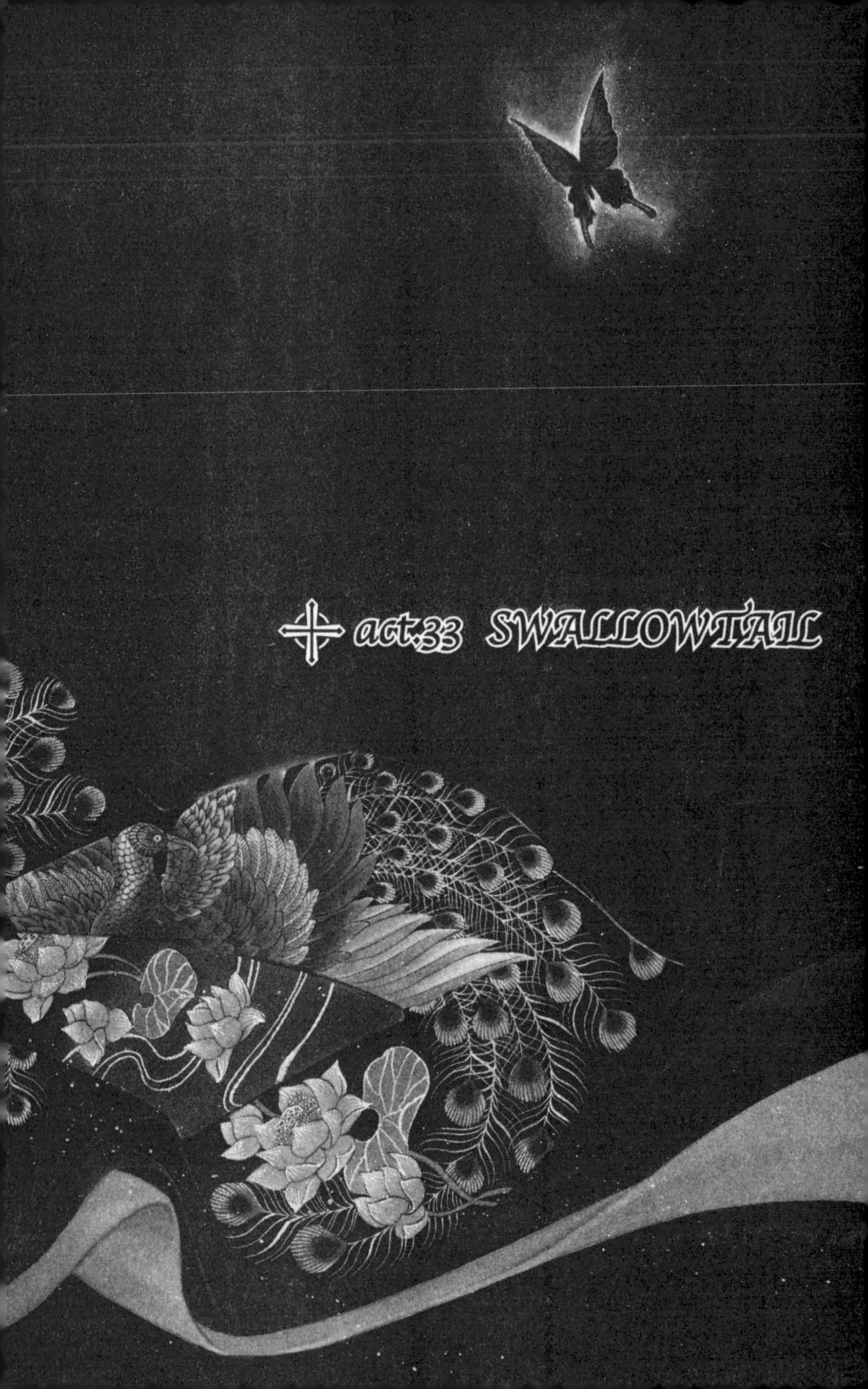
act.33 SWALLOWTAIL

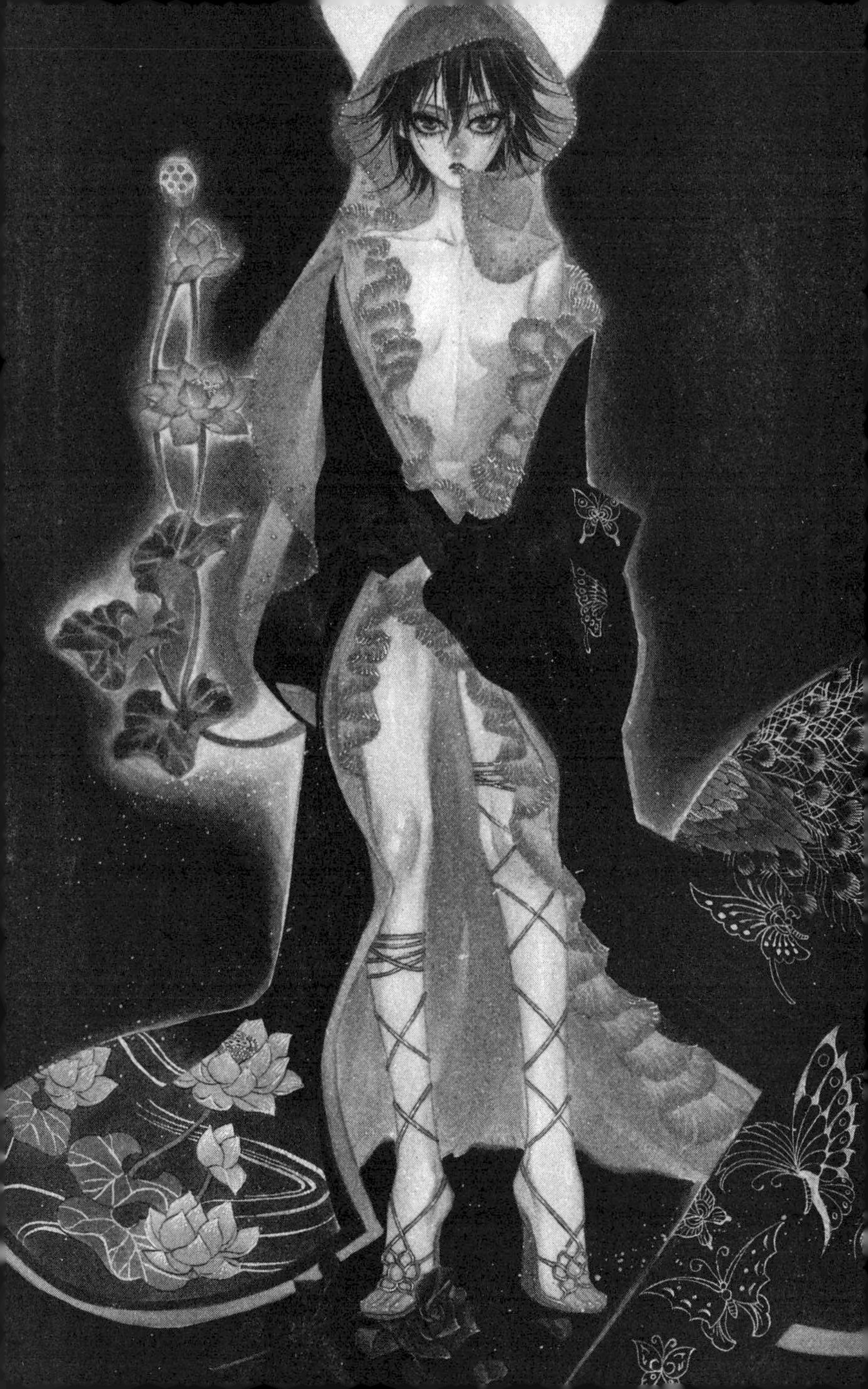

TRINITY BLOOD

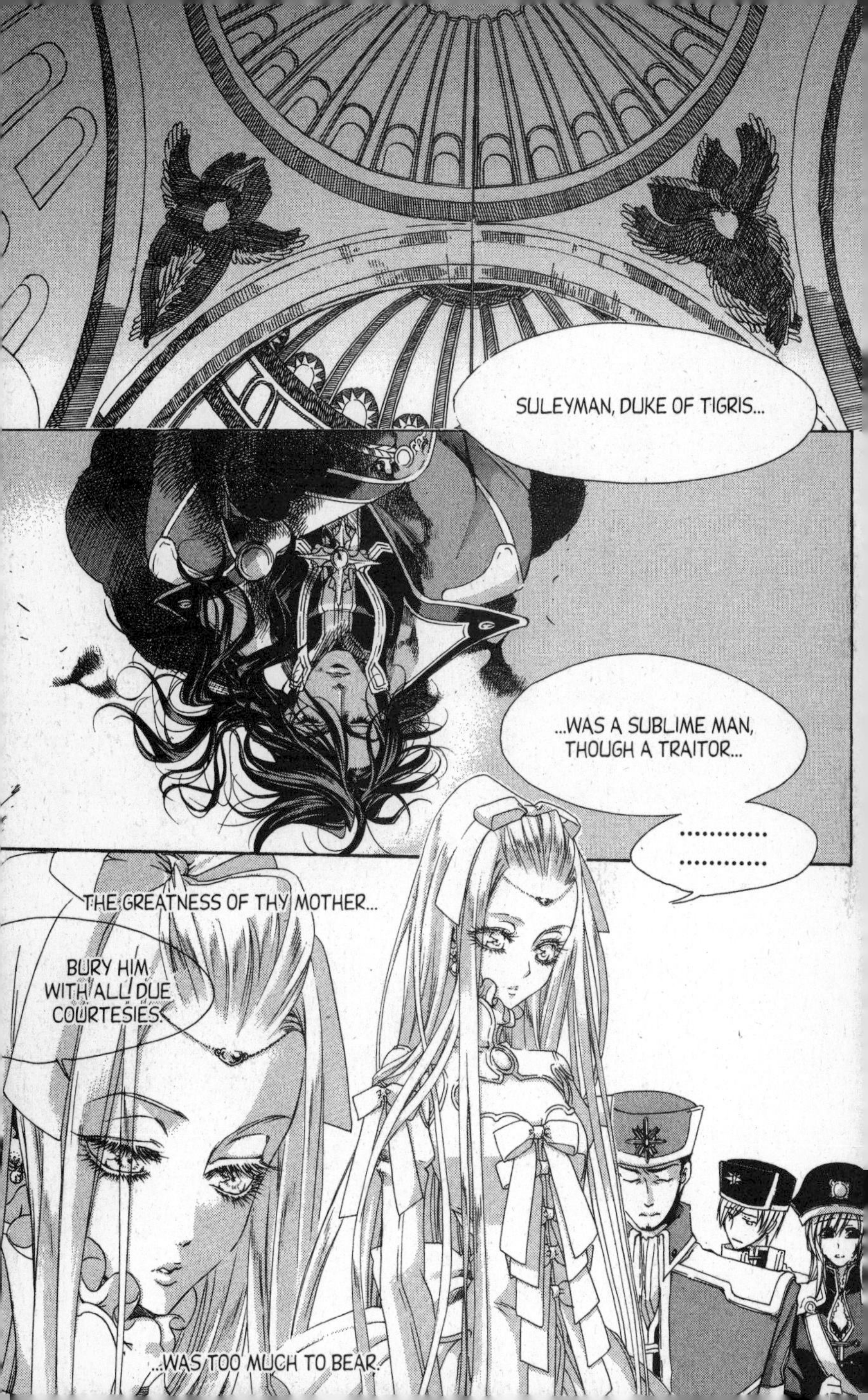
SULEYMAN, DUKE OF TIGRIS...
...WAS A SUBLIME MAN, THOUGH A TRAITOR...
....
THE GREATNESS OF THY MOTHER...
BURY HIM WITH ALL DUE COURTESIES.
...WAS TOO MUCH TO BEAR.

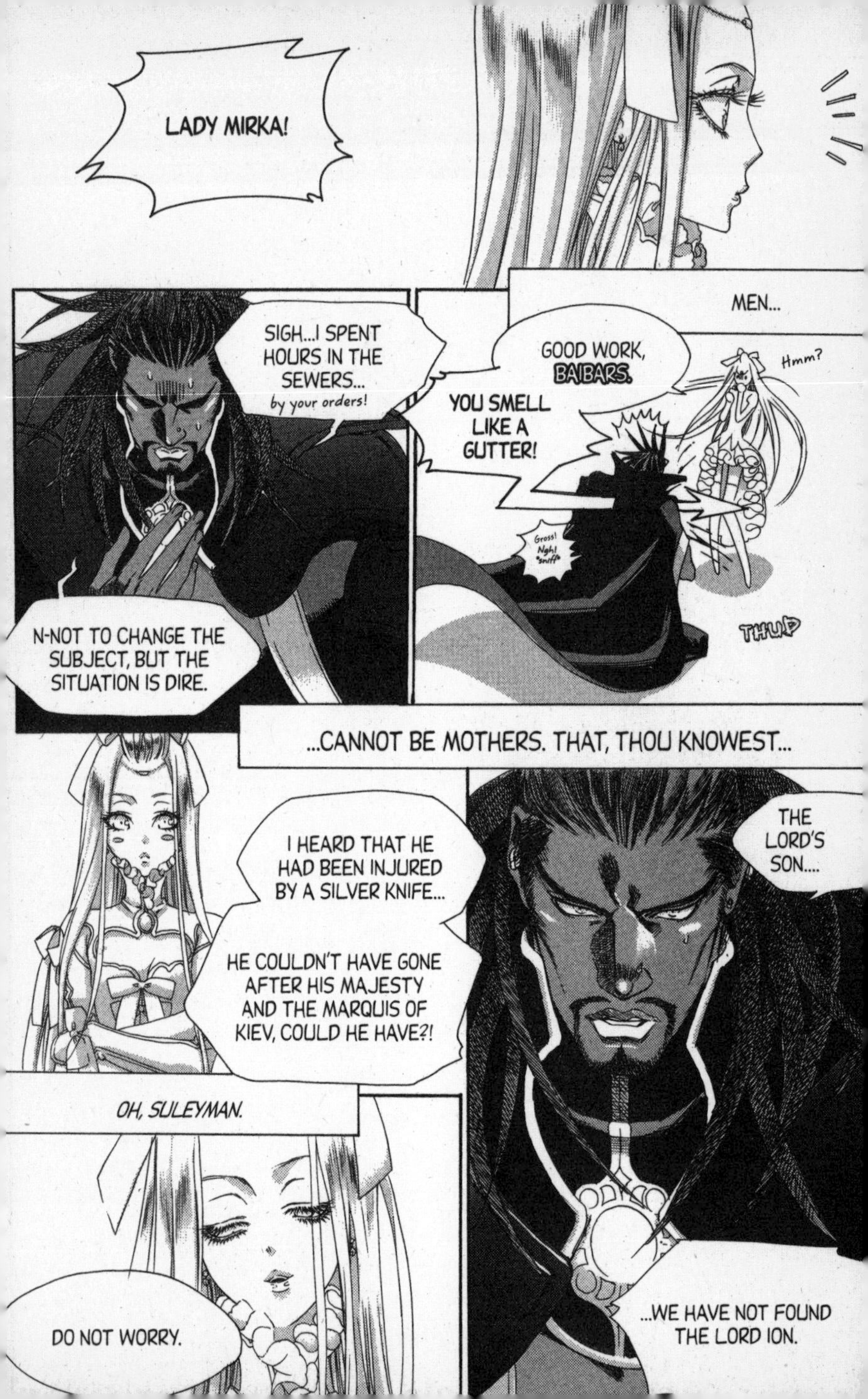

LADY MIRKA!
MEN...
GOOD WORK, BAIBARS.
Hmm?
YOU SMELL LIKE A GUTTER!
Gross! Ngh! *sniff*
THUD
SIGH...I SPENT HOURS IN THE SEWERS... by your orders!
N-NOT TO CHANGE THE SUBJECT, BUT THE SITUATION IS DIRE.
...CANNOT BE MOTHERS. THAT, THOU KNOWEST...
THE LORD'S SON....
...WE HAVE NOT FOUND THE LORD ION.
I HEARD THAT HE HAD BEEN INJURED BY A SILVER KNIFE...
HE COULDN'T HAVE GONE AFTER HIS MAJESTY AND THE MARQUIS OF KIEV, COULD HE HAVE?!
OH, SULEYMAN.
DO NOT WORRY.

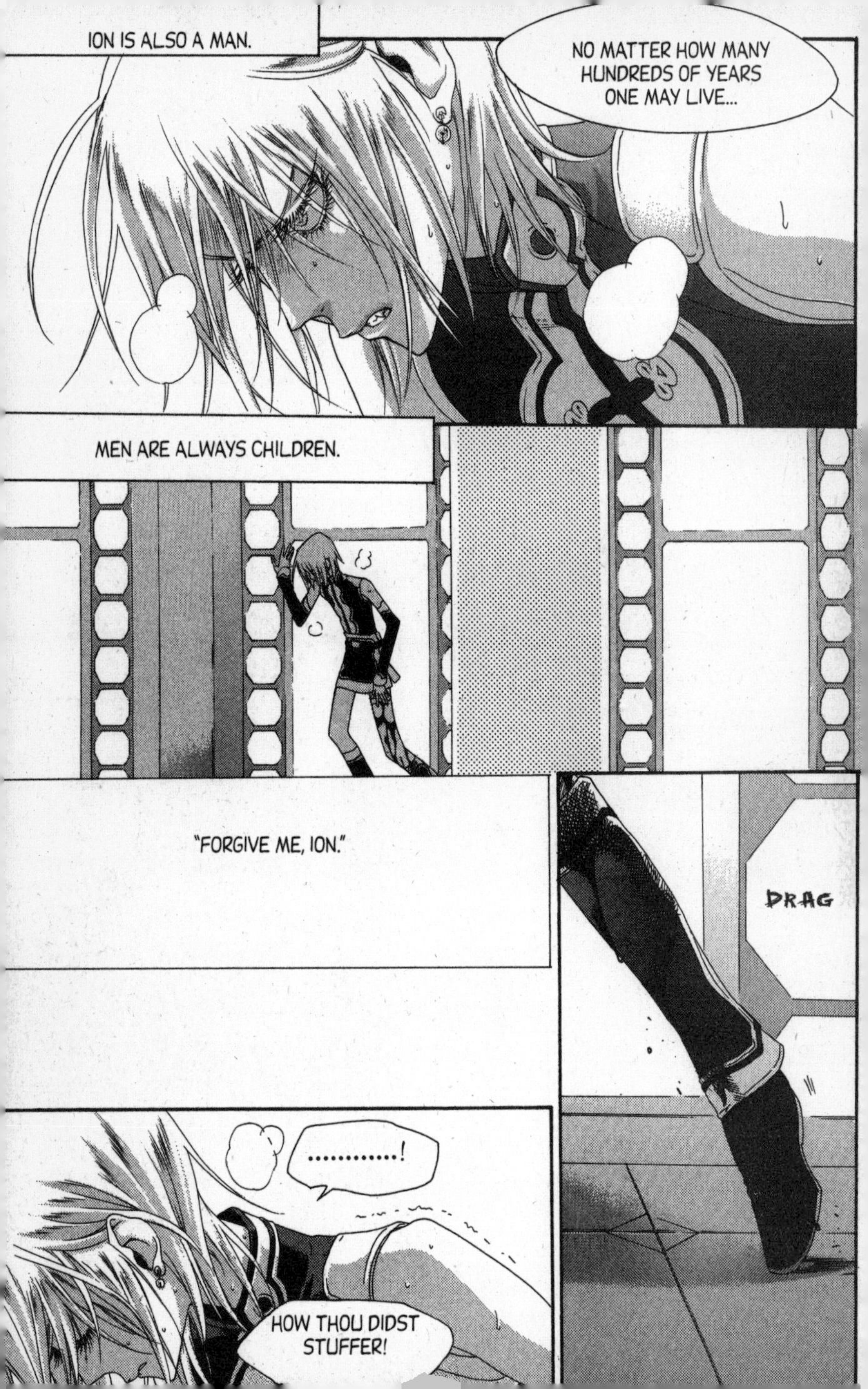
NO MATTER HOW MANY HUNDREDS OF YEARS ONE MAY LIVE...
ION IS ALSO A MAN.
MEN ARE ALWAYS CHILDREN.
DRAG
"FORGIVE ME, ION."
.............!
HOW THOU DIDST STUFFER!

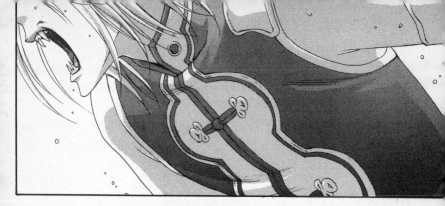

RADUUU!!!

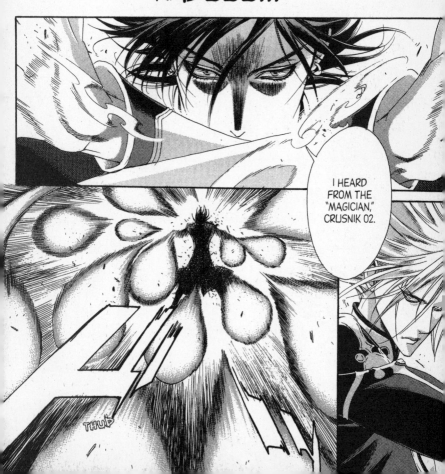

I HEARD FROM THE "MAGICIAN," CRUSNIK 02.

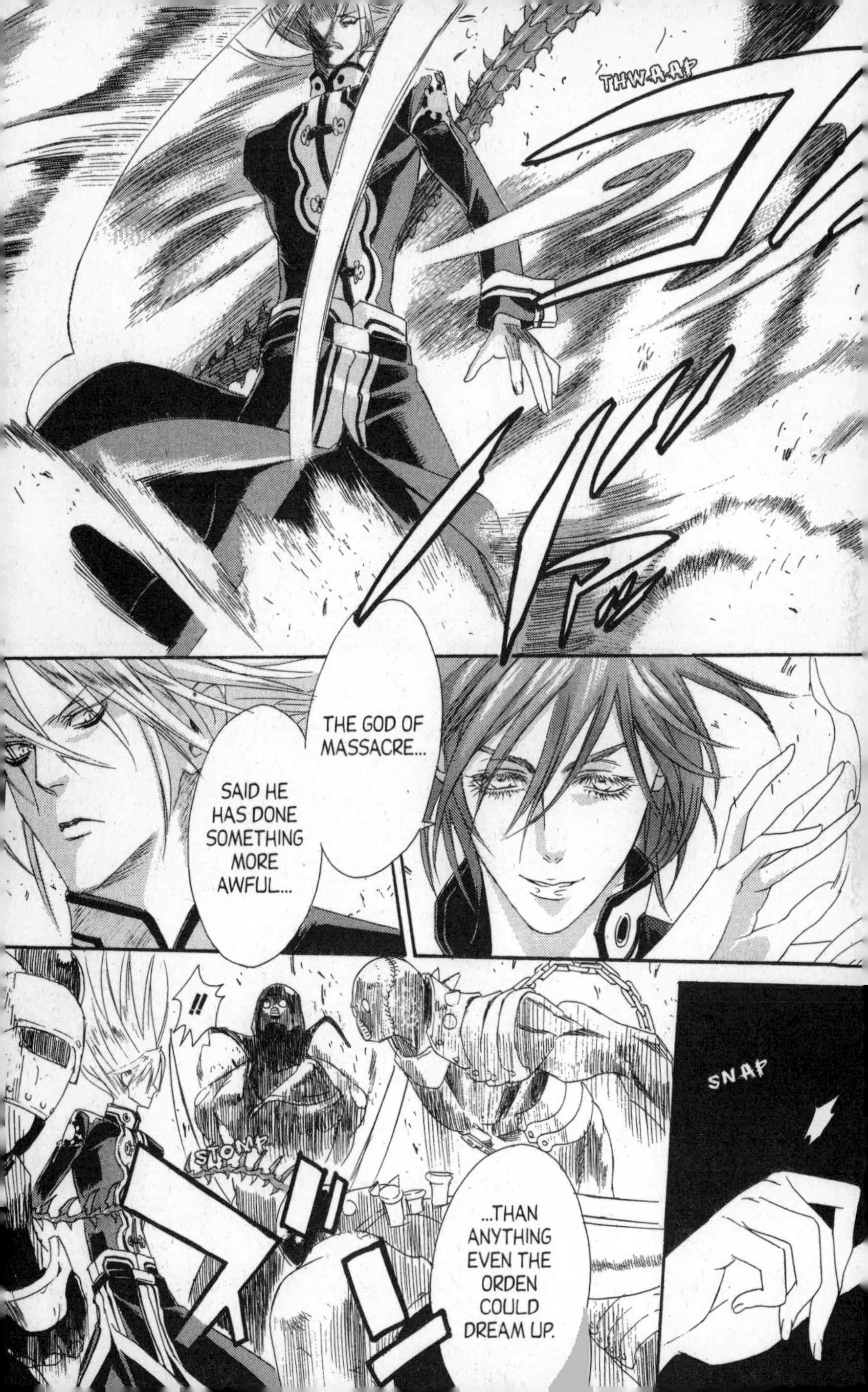
THWAAAP
THE GOD OF MASSACRE...
SAID HE HAS DONE SOMETHING MORE AWFUL...
SNAP
!!
STOMP
...THAN ANYTHING EVEN THE ORDEN COULD DREAM UP.

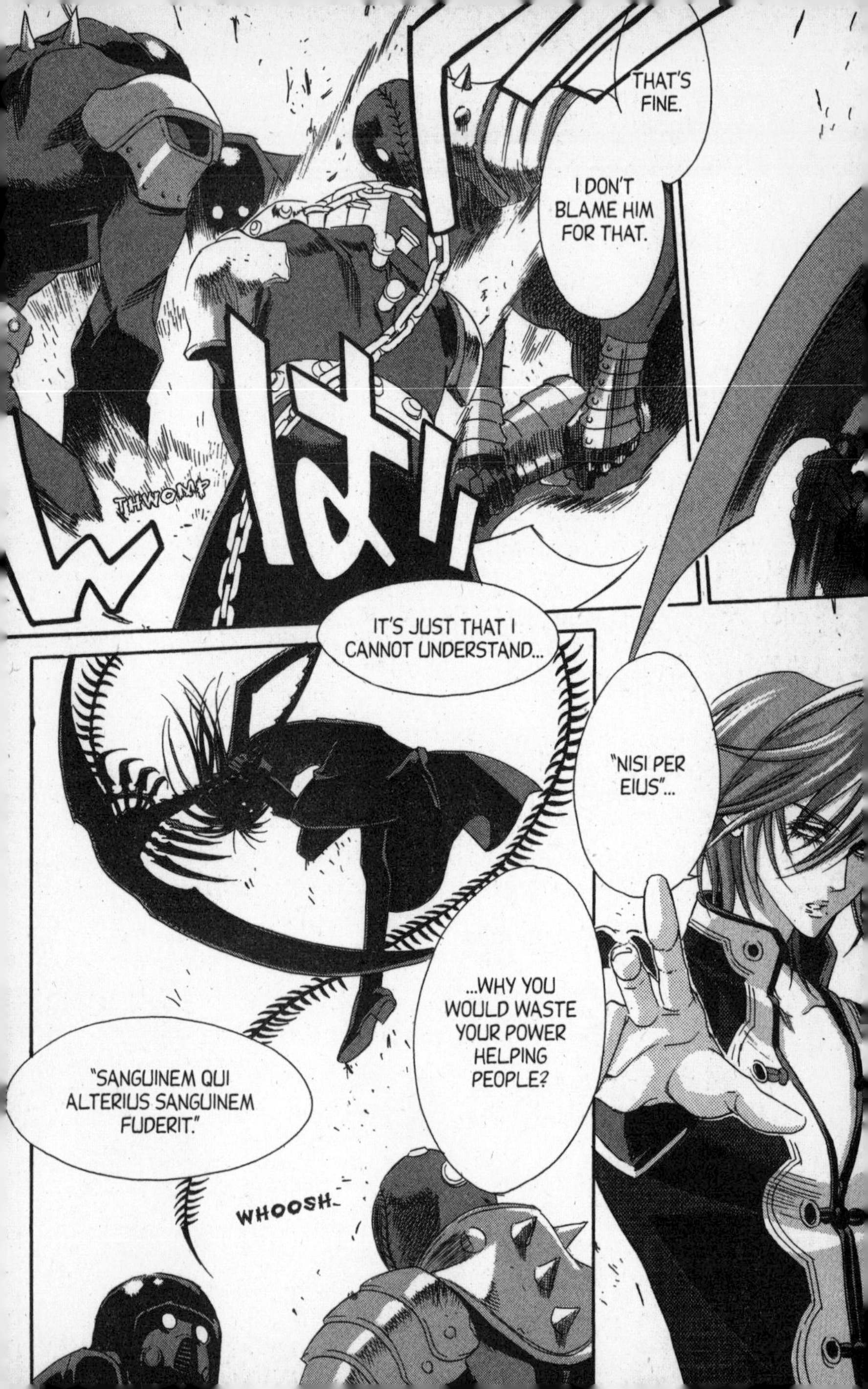
THAT'S FINE.
I DON'T BLAME HIM FOR THAT.
THWOMP
IT'S JUST THAT I CANNOT UNDERSTAND...
...WHY YOU WOULD WASTE YOUR POWER HELPING PEOPLE?
"NISI PER EIUS"...
"SANGUINEM QUI ALTERIUS SANGUINEM FUDERIT."
WHOOSH

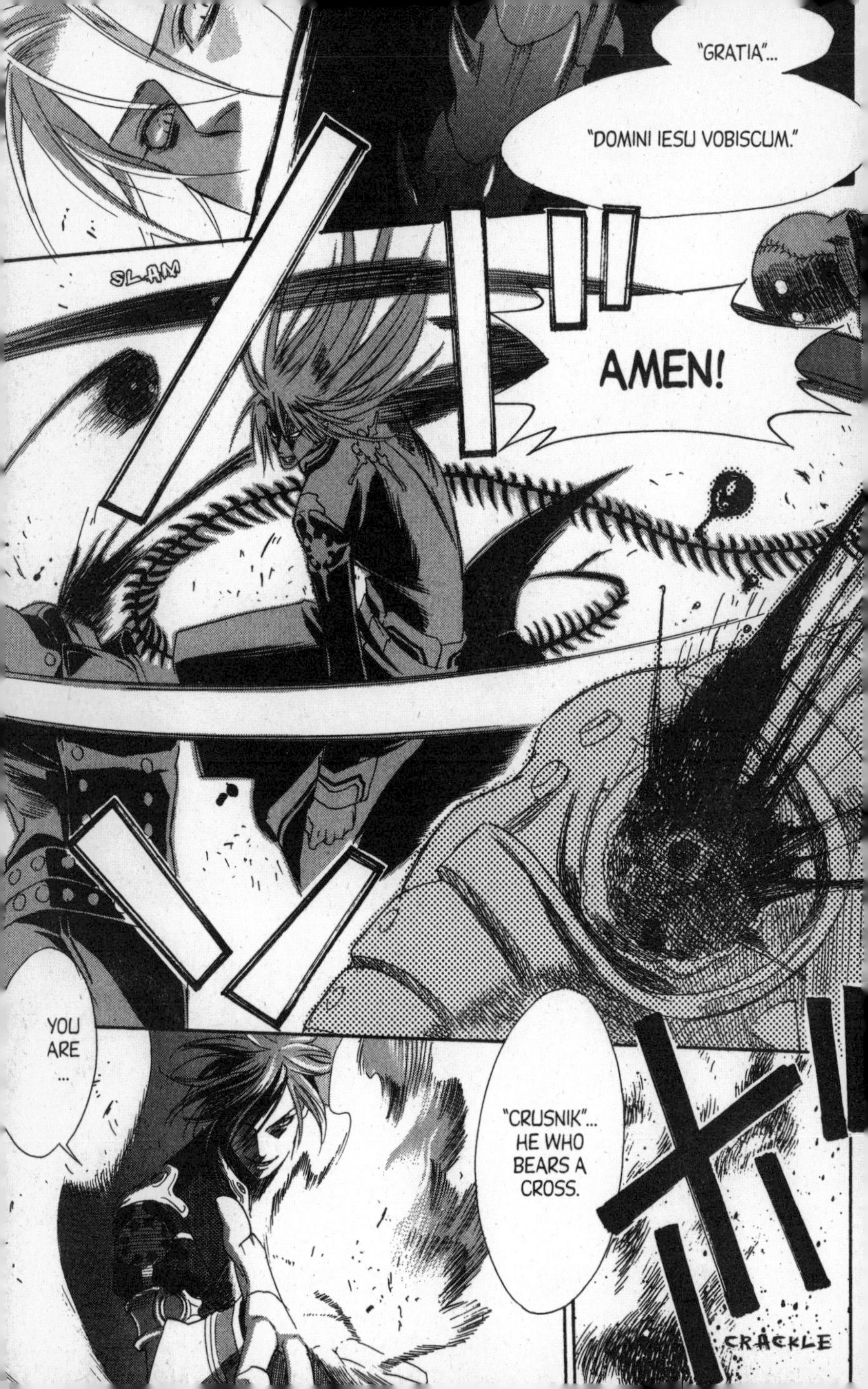
"GRATIA"...
"DOMINI IESU VOBISCUM."
SLAM
AMEN!
CRACKLE
"CRUSNIK"... HE WHO BEARS A CROSS.
YOU ARE ...

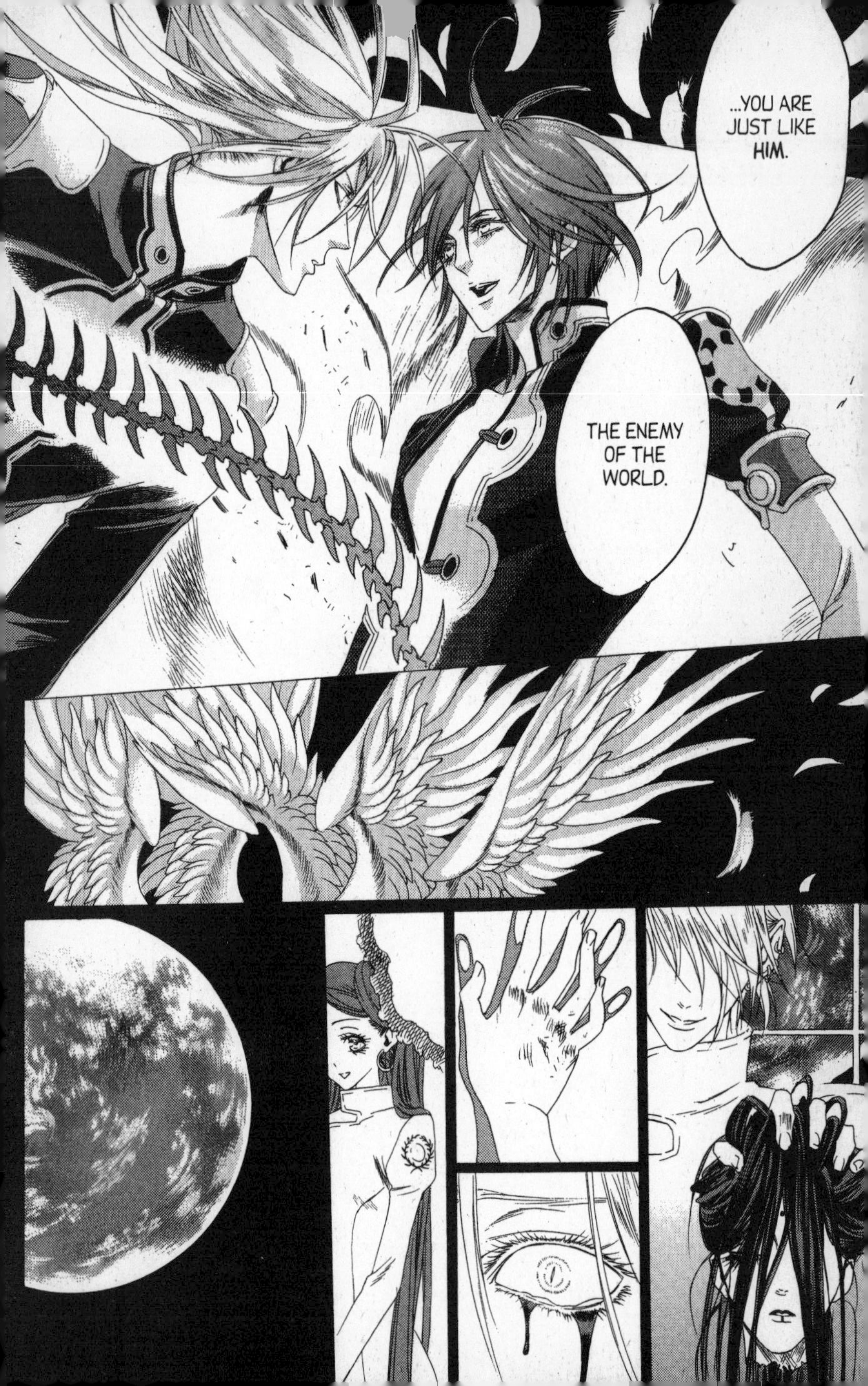
...YOU ARE JUST LIKE HIM.
THE ENEMY OF THE WORLD.

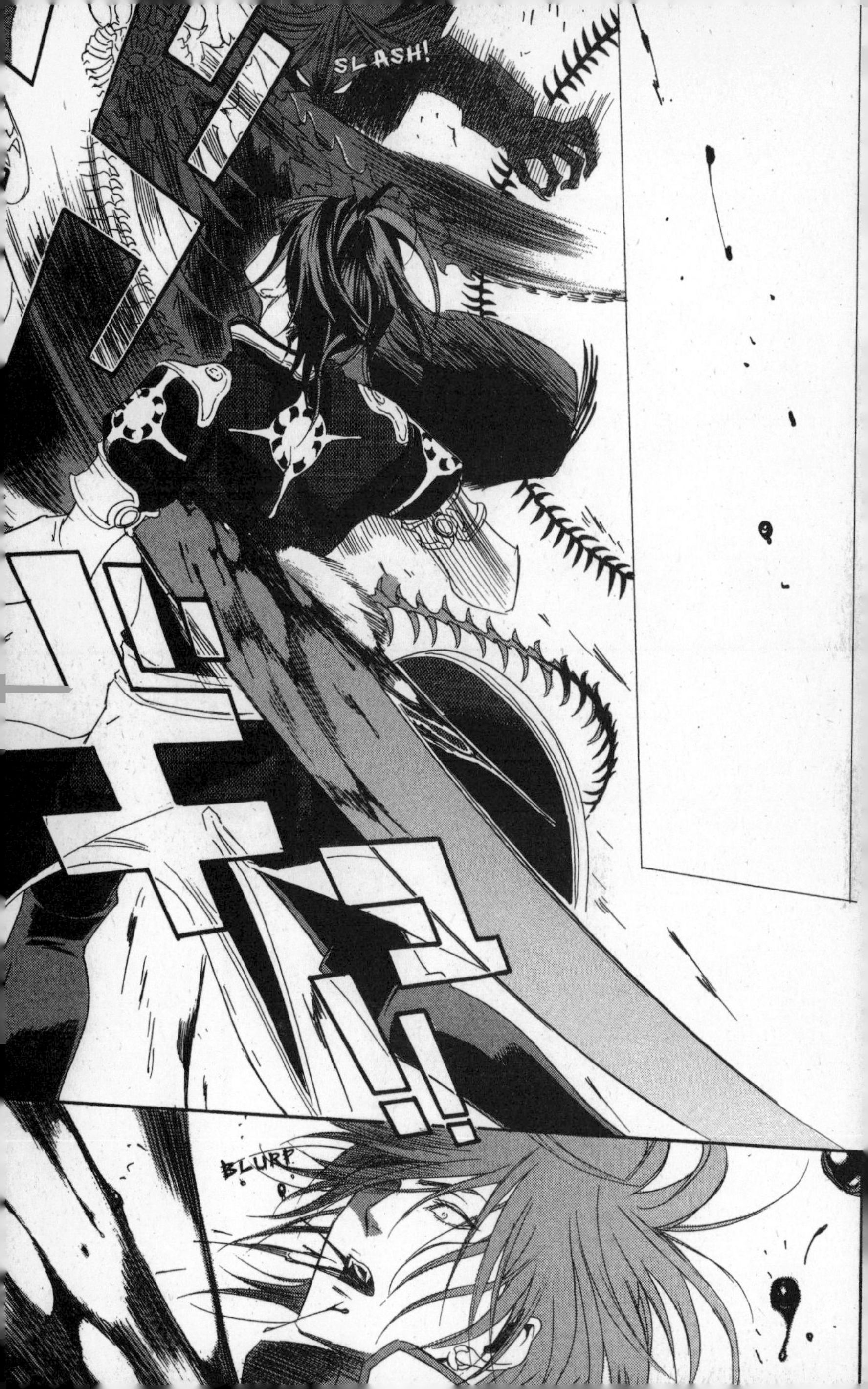
SLASH!
BLURP

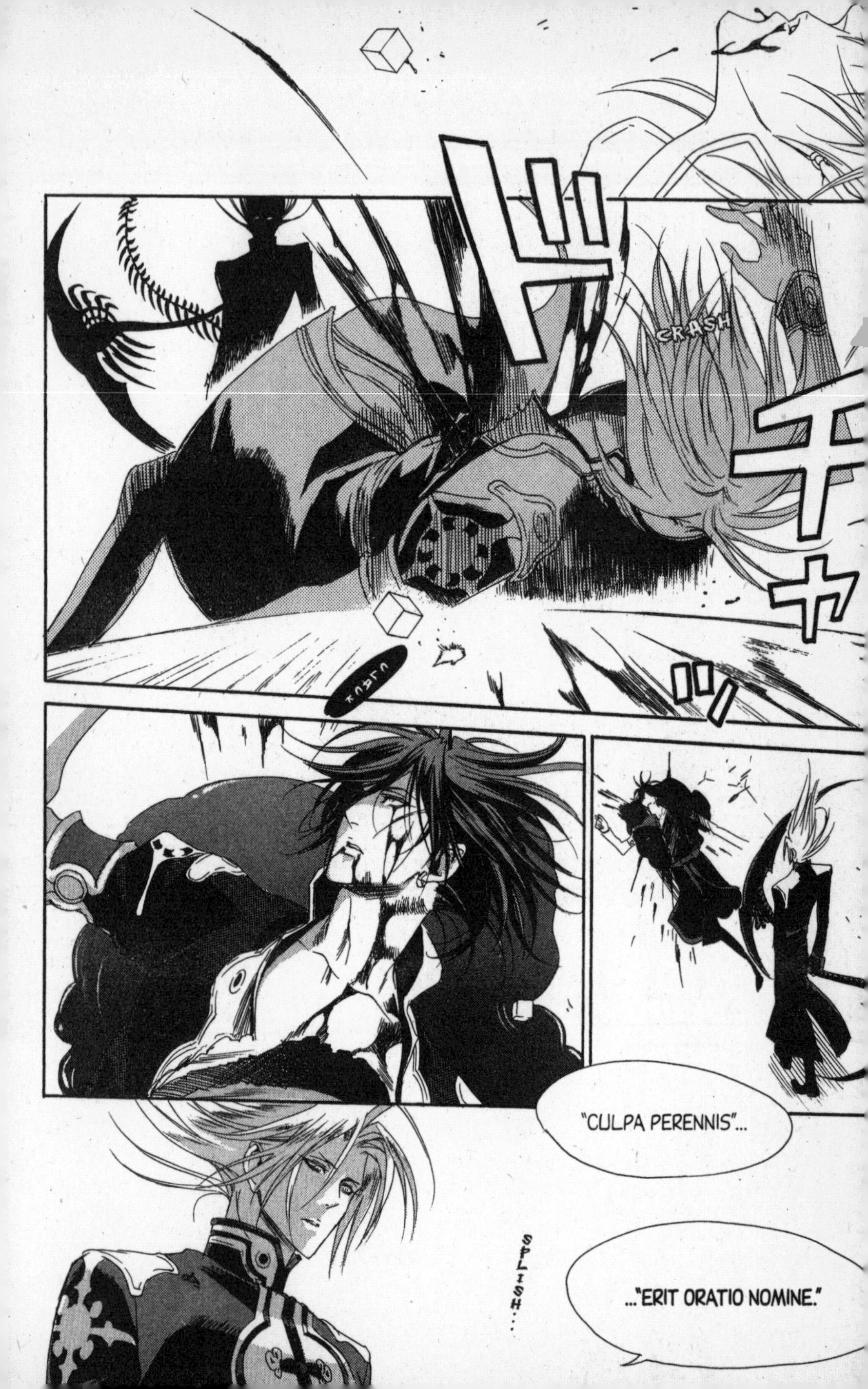
CRASH
"CULPA PERENNIS"...
SPLISH...
..."ERIT ORATIO NOMINE."

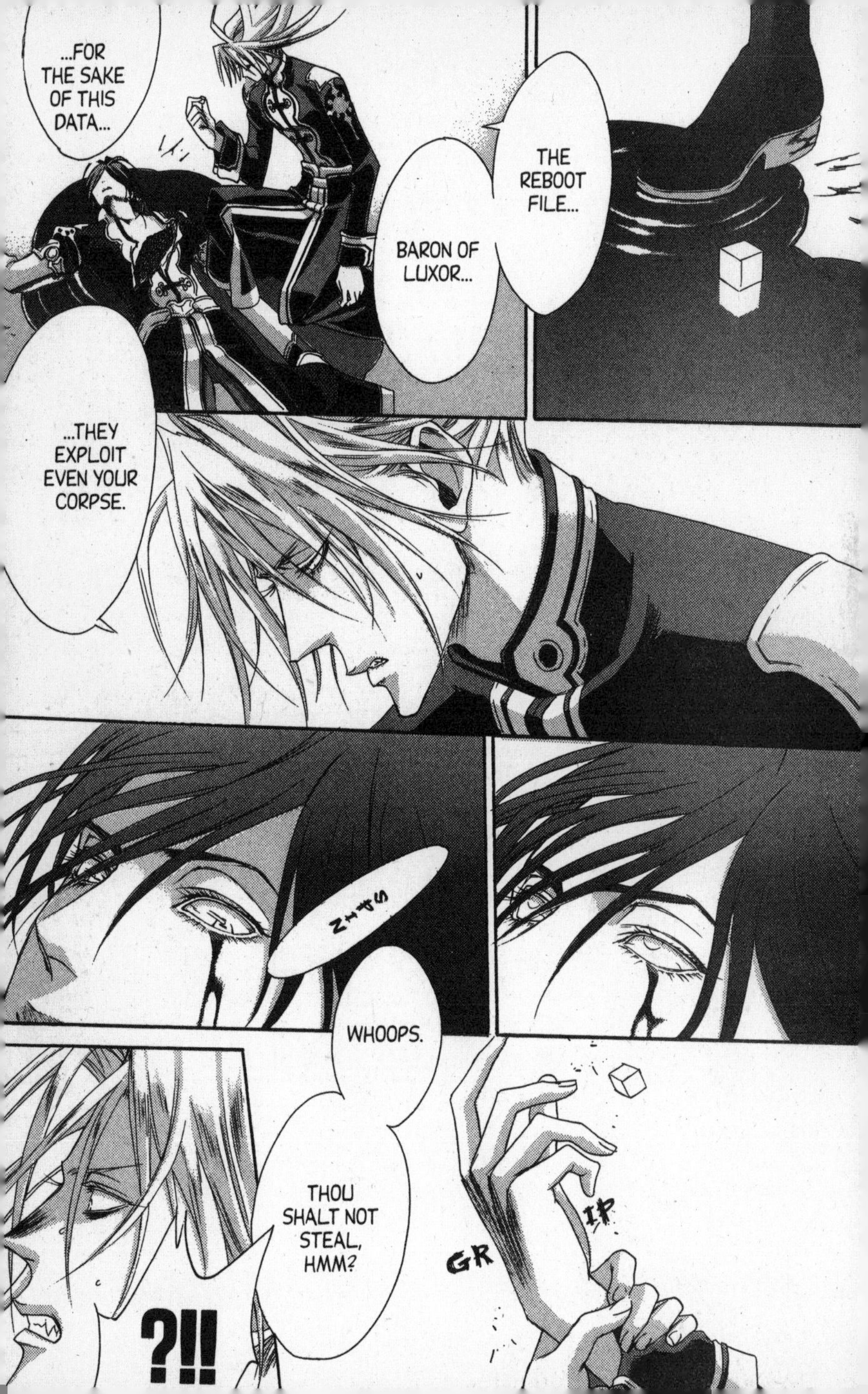
THE REBOOT FILE...
BARON OF LUXOR...
...FOR THE SAKE OF THIS DATA...
...THEY EXPLOIT EVEN YOUR CORPSE.
SPIN
WHOOPS.
GRIP
THOU SHALT NOT STEAL, HMM?
?!!

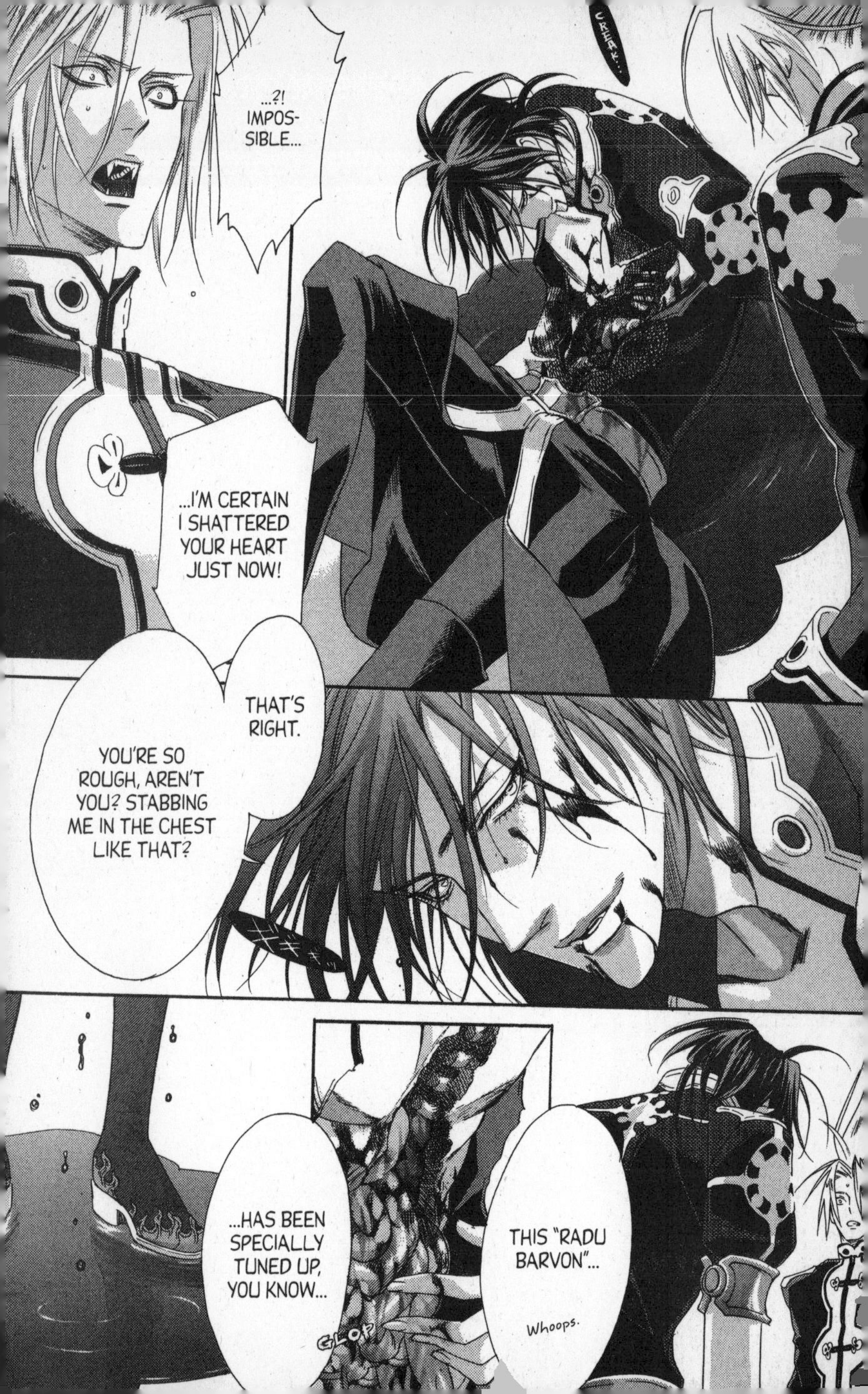
CREAK...
...?! IMPOS-SIBLE...
...I'M CERTAIN I SHATTERED YOUR HEART JUST NOW!
THAT'S RIGHT.
YOU'RE SO ROUGH, AREN'T YOU? STABBING ME IN THE CHEST LIKE THAT?
THIS "RADU BARVON"...
Whoops.
...HAS BEEN SPECIALLY TUNED UP, YOU KNOW...
GLOP

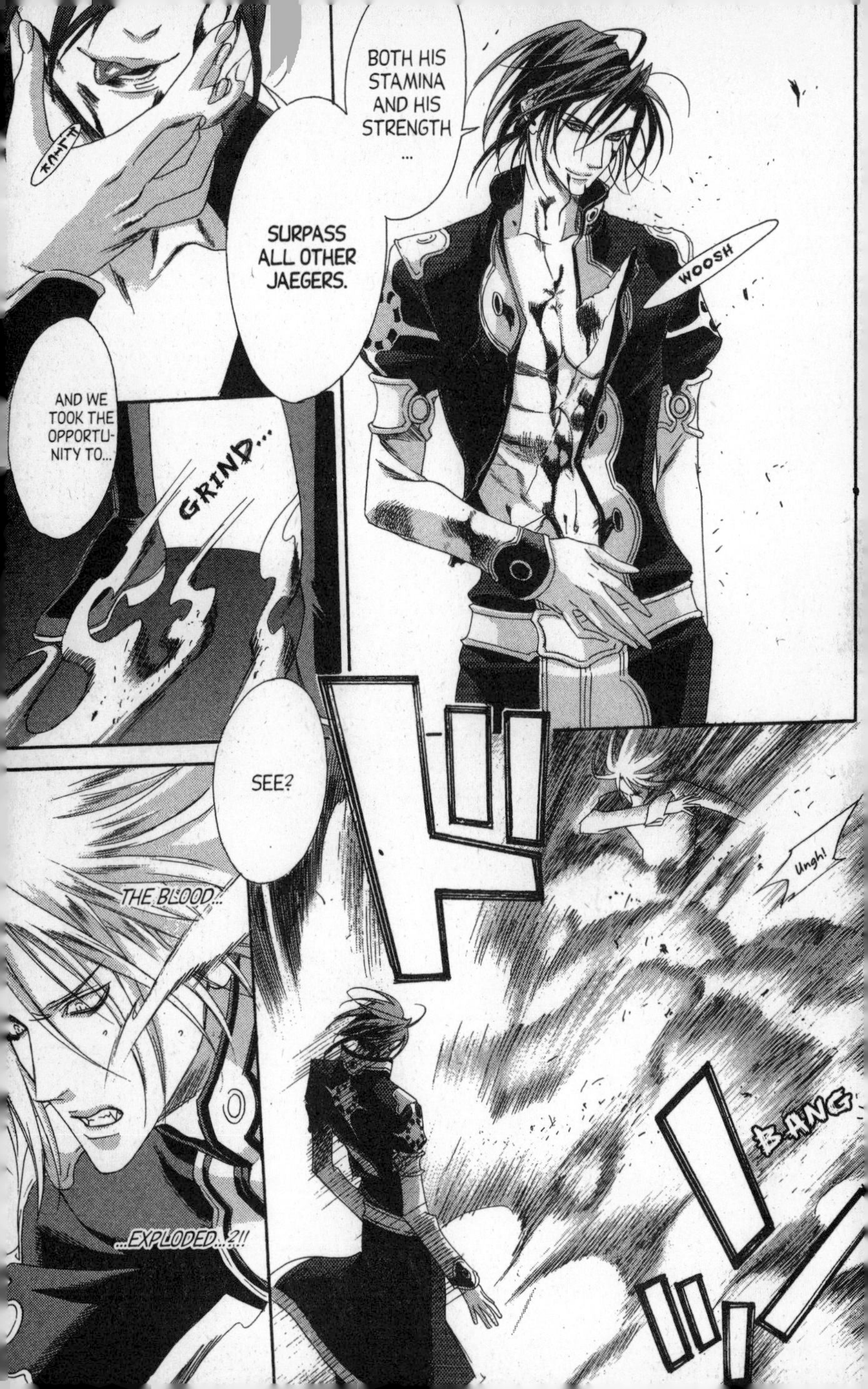
BOTH HIS STAMINA AND HIS STRENGTH ...
SURPASS ALL OTHER JAEGERS.
WOOSH
AND WE TOOK THE OPPORTU-NITY TO...
GRIND...
SEE?
Ungh!
BANG
THE BLOOD...
...EXPLODED...?!!

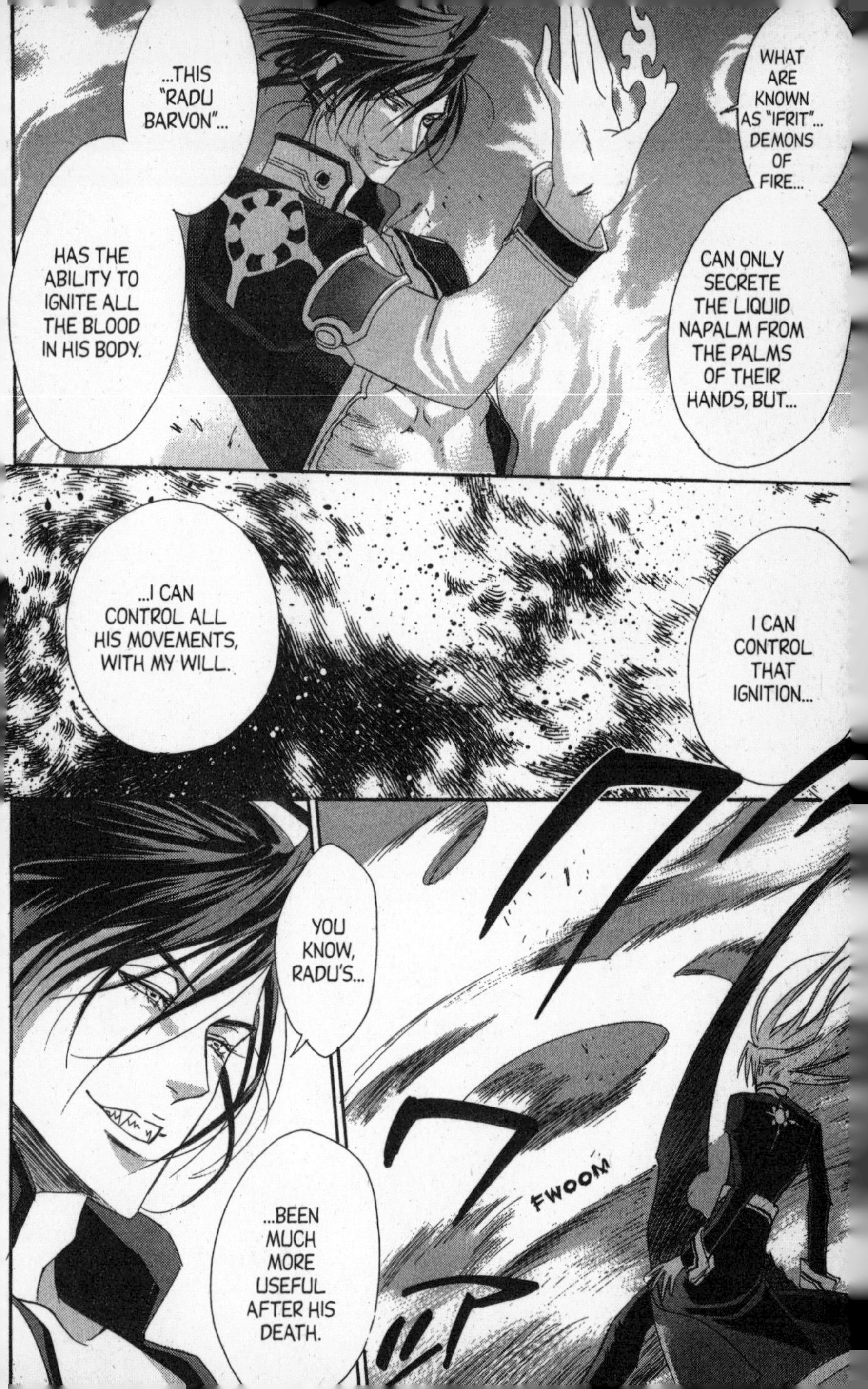
WHAT ARE KNOWN AS "IFRIT"... DEMONS OF FIRE...
CAN ONLY SECRETE THE LIQUID NAPALM FROM THE PALMS OF THEIR HANDS, BUT...
...THIS "RADU BARVON"...
HAS THE ABILITY TO IGNITE ALL THE BLOOD IN HIS BODY.
I CAN CONTROL THAT IGNITION...
...I CAN CONTROL ALL HIS MOVEMENTS, WITH MY WILL.
FWOOM
YOU KNOW, RADU'S...
...BEEN MUCH MORE USEFUL AFTER HIS DEATH.

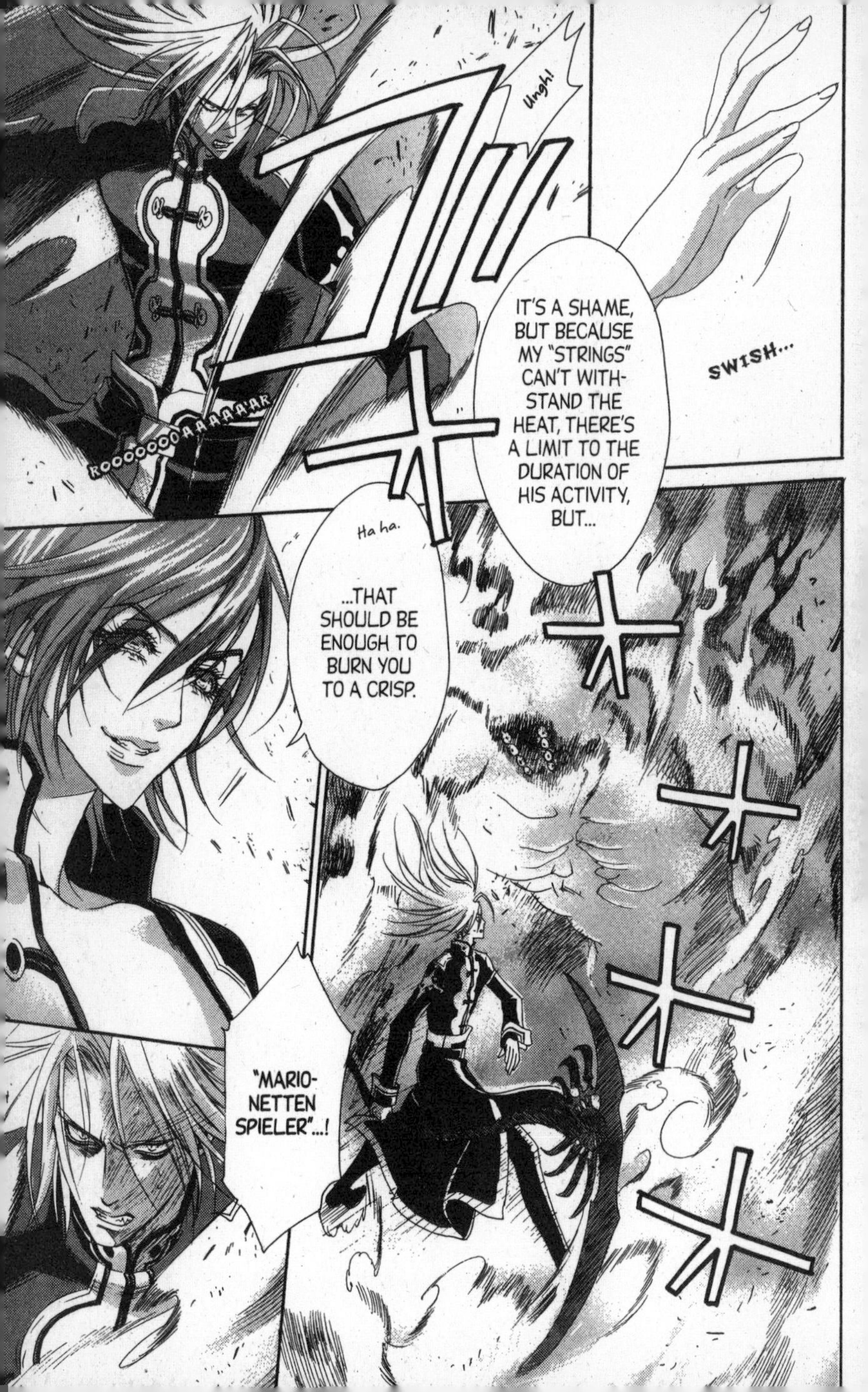

SWISH...
Ungh!
ROOOOOOOOAAAAAA'AR
IT'S A SHAME, BUT BECAUSE MY "STRINGS" CAN'T WITH-STAND THE HEAT, THERE'S A LIMIT TO THE DURATION OF HIS ACTIVITY, BUT...
Ha ha.
...THAT SHOULD BE ENOUGH TO BURN YOU TO A CRISP.
"MARIO-NETTEN SPIELER"...!

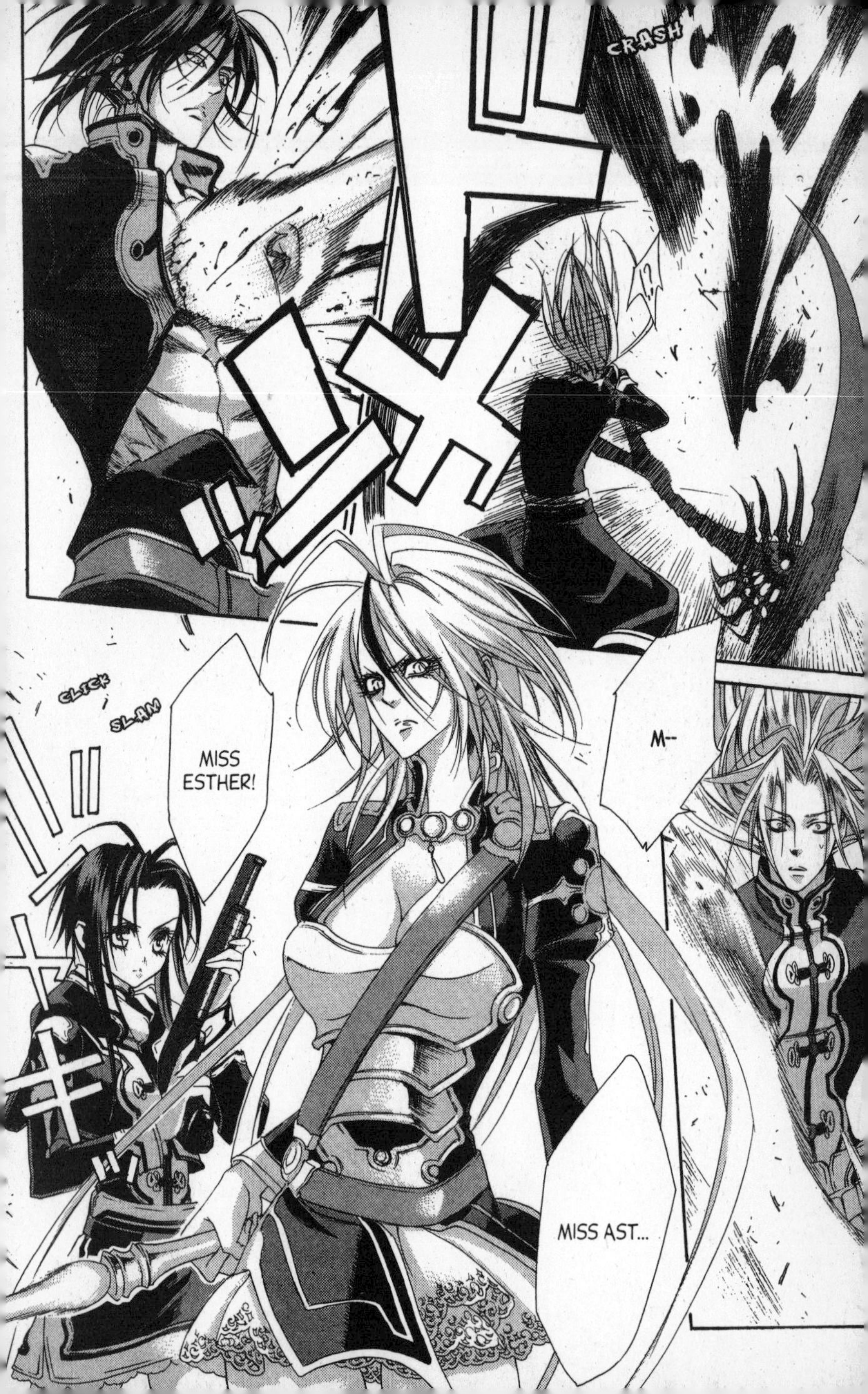
CRASH
!?
M--
MISS AST...
CLICK
SLAM
MISS
ESTHER!

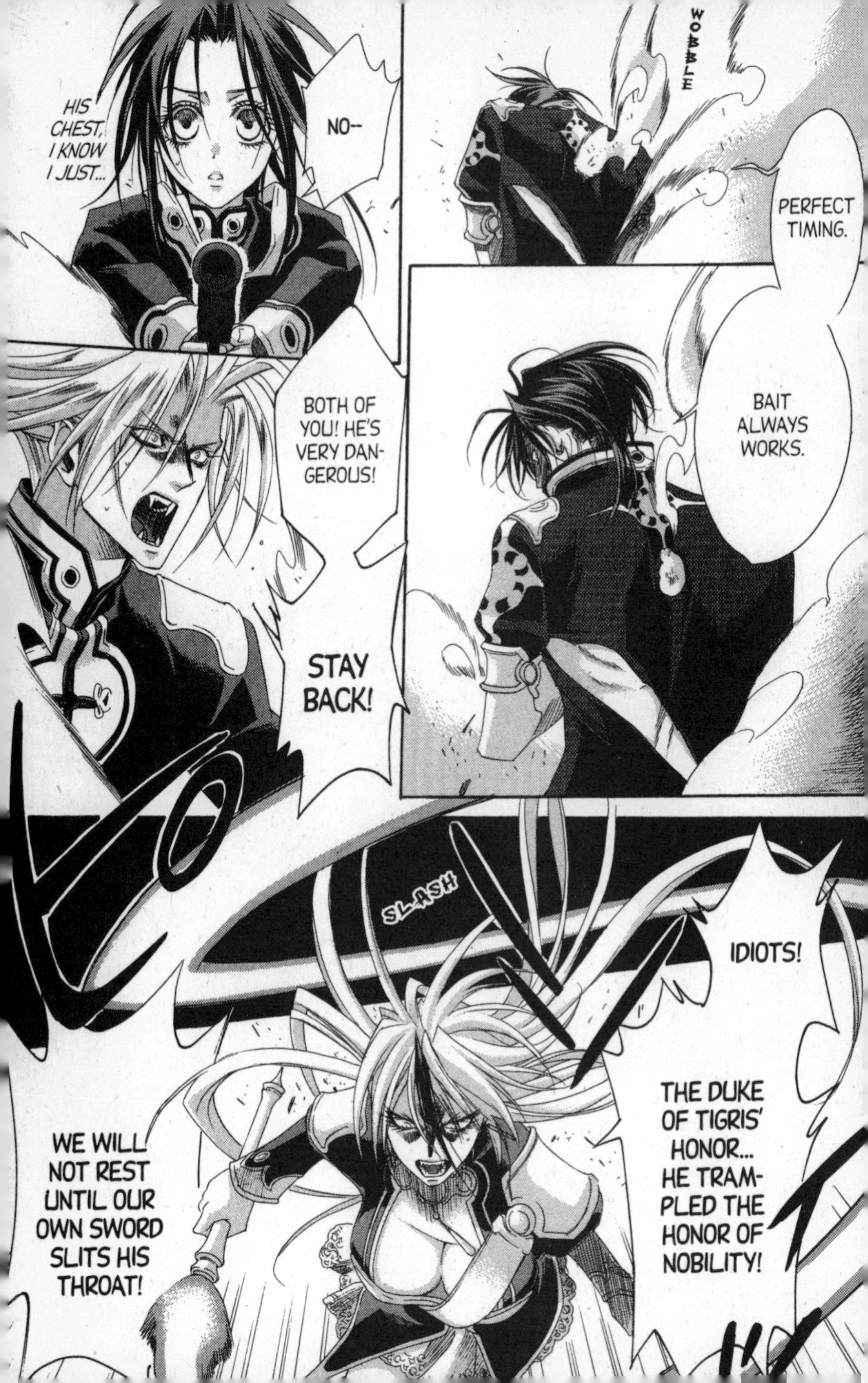
WOBBLE
PERFECT TIMING.
NO--
HIS CHEST, I KNOW I JUST...
BAIT ALWAYS WORKS.
BOTH OF YOU! HE'S VERY DAN-GEROUS!
STAY BACK!
SLASH
IDIOTS!
THE DUKE OF TIGRIS' HONOR... HE TRAM-PLED THE HONOR OF NOBILITY!
WE WILL NOT REST UNTIL OUR OWN SWORD SLITS HIS THROAT!

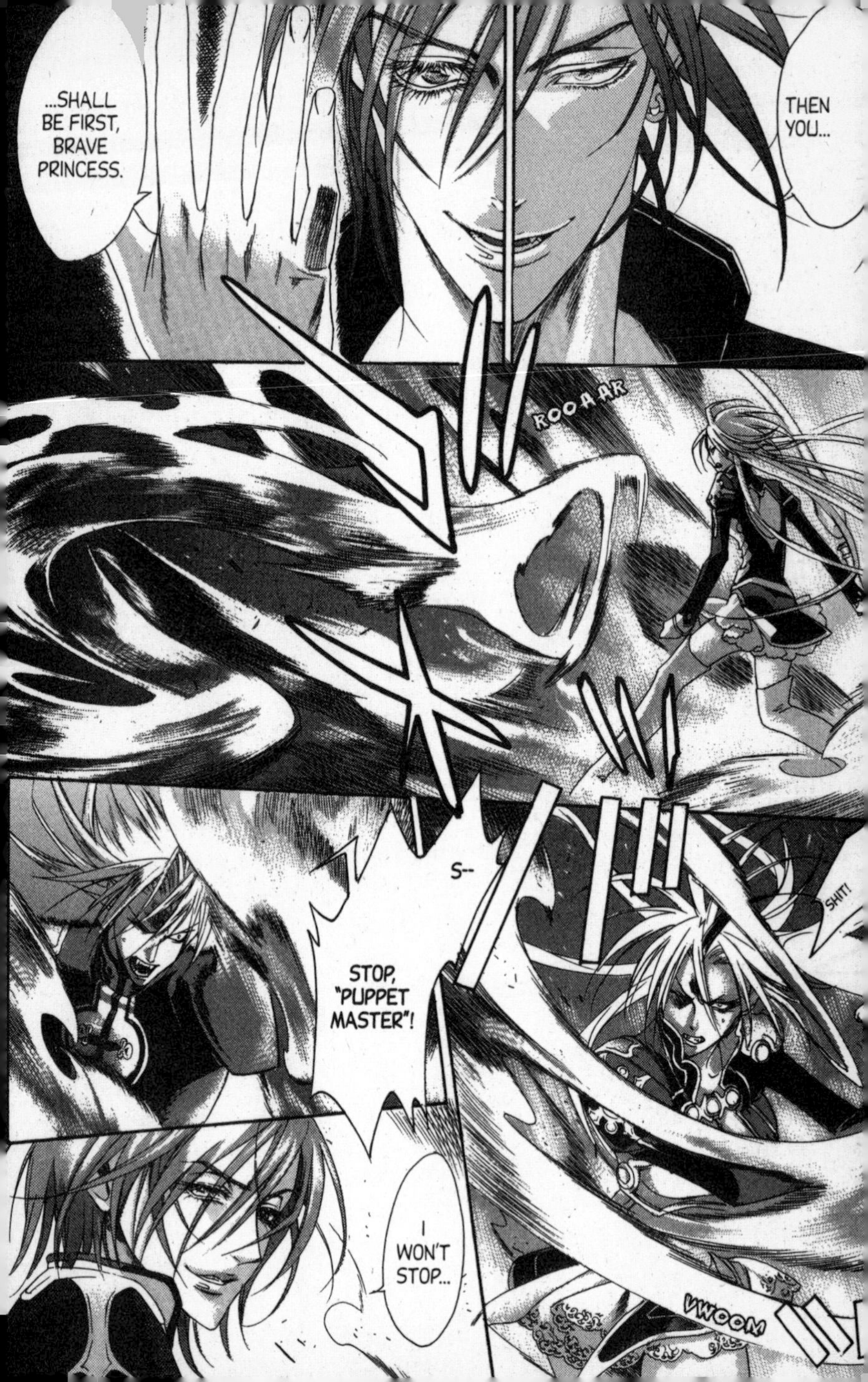
THEN YOU...
...SHALL BE FIRST, BRAVE PRINCESS.
ROOAAR
SHIT!
VWOOM
S--
STOP, "PUPPET MASTER"!
I WON'T STOP...

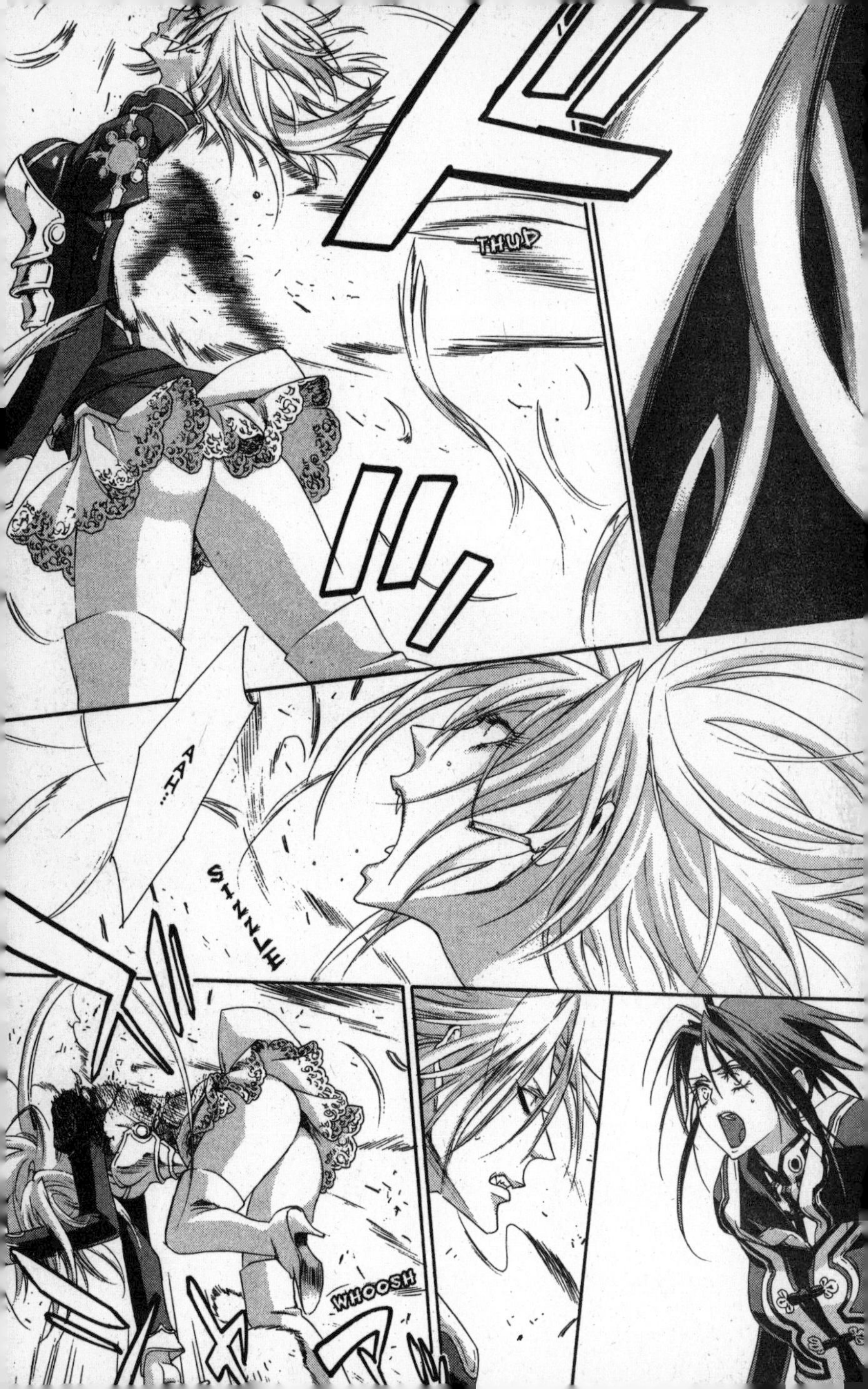
THUD
AH...
WHOOSH

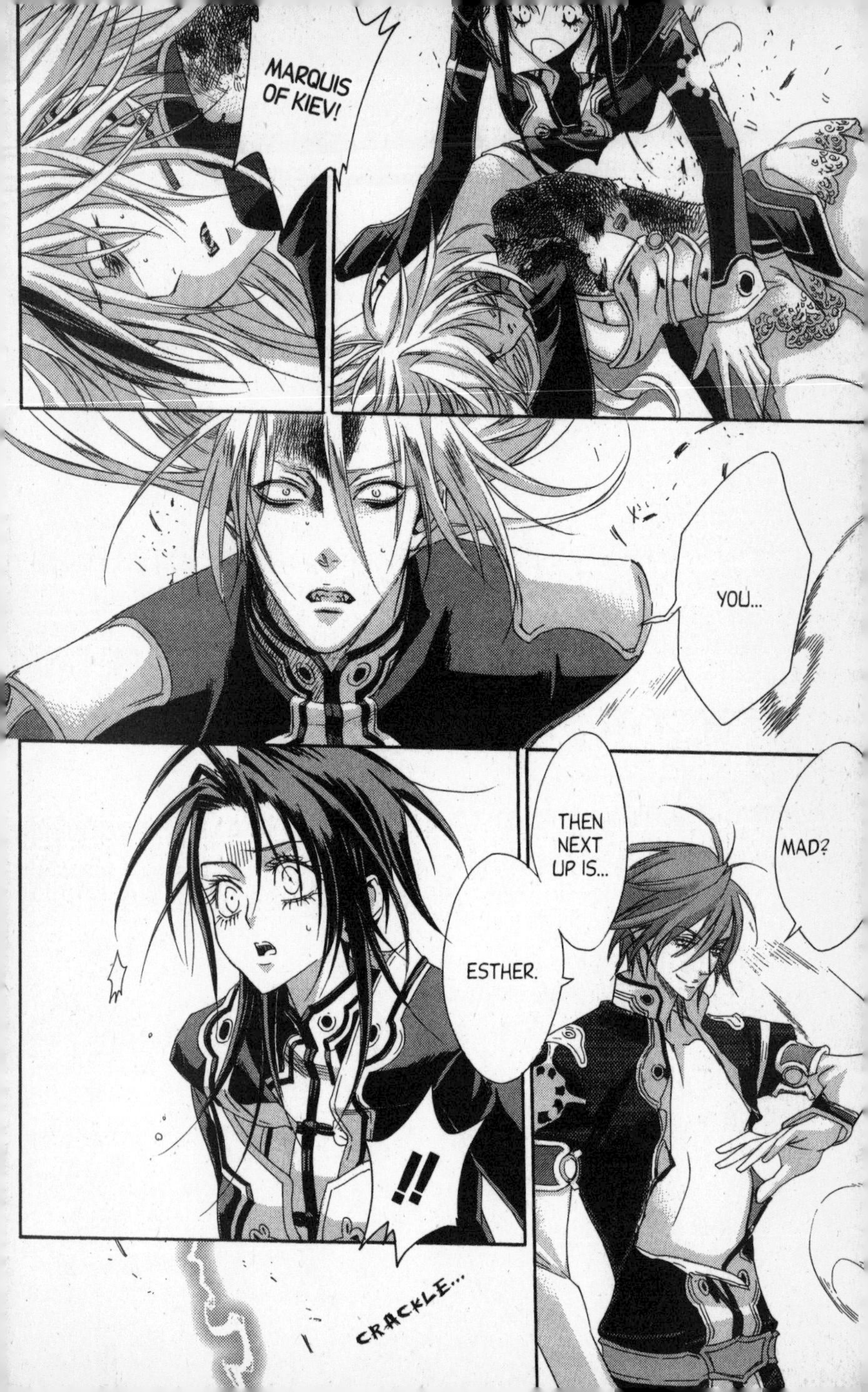
MARQUIS OF KIEV!
YOU...
MAD?
THEN NEXT UP IS...
ESTHER.
!!
CRACKLE...

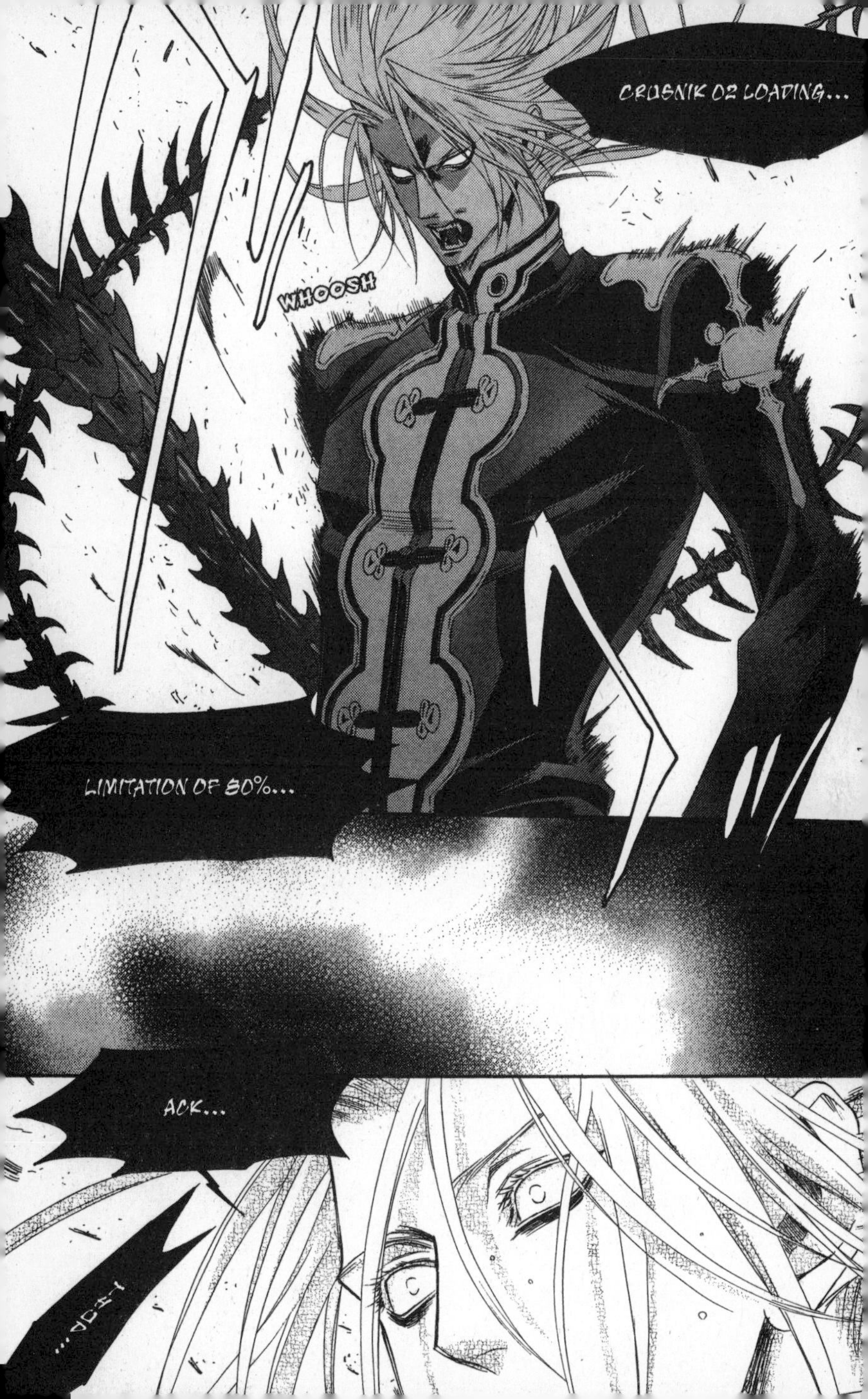
CRUSNIK 02 LOADING...
WHOOSH
LIMITATION OF 80%...
ACK...

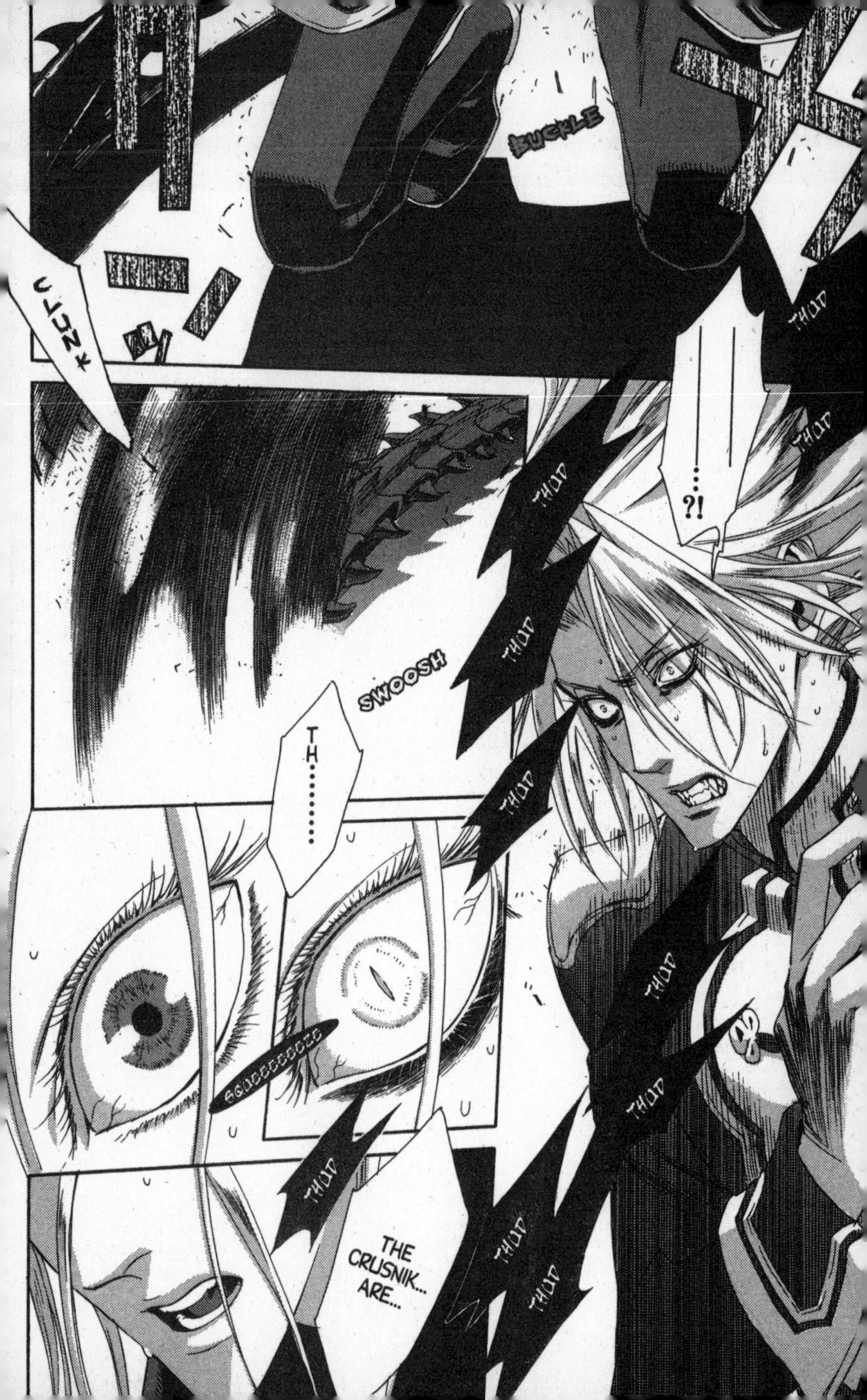
BUCKLE
CLUNK
THUD
...?!
THUD
THUD
THUD
THUD
THUD
THUD
SWOOSH
TH.......
SQUEEEEEEEZE
THUD
THUD
THUD
THE CRUSNIK... ARE...

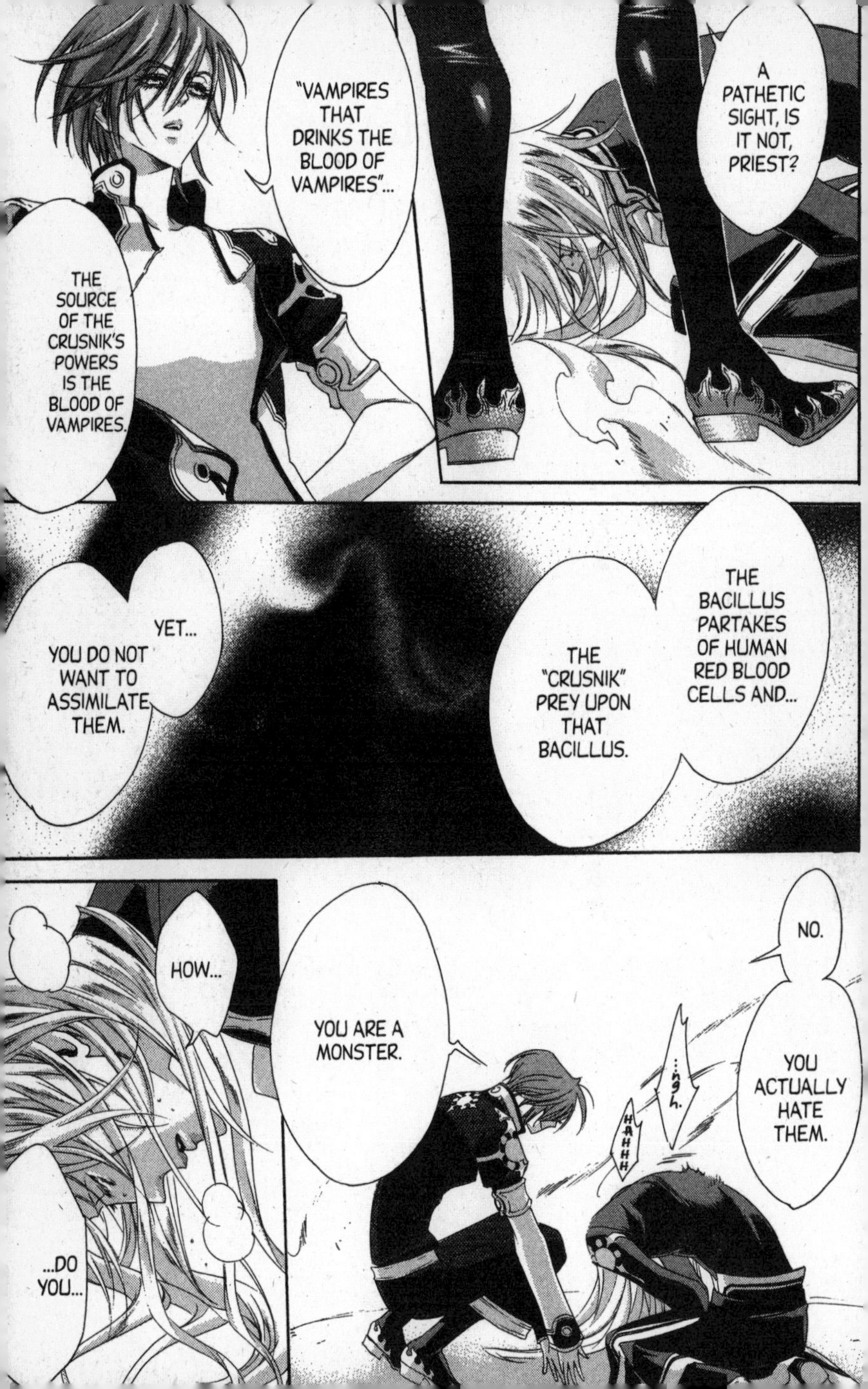
A PATHETIC SIGHT, IS IT NOT, PRIEST?
"VAMPIRES THAT DRINKS THE BLOOD OF VAMPIRES"...
THE SOURCE OF THE CRUSNIK'S POWERS IS THE BLOOD OF VAMPIRES.
THE BACILLUS PARTAKES OF HUMAN RED BLOOD CELLS AND...
THE "CRUSNIK" PREY UPON THAT BACILLUS.
YET...
YOU DO NOT WANT TO ASSIMILATE THEM.
NO.
YOU ACTUALLY HATE THEM.
...ngh.
HAHHH
YOU ARE A MONSTER.
HOW...
...DO YOU...

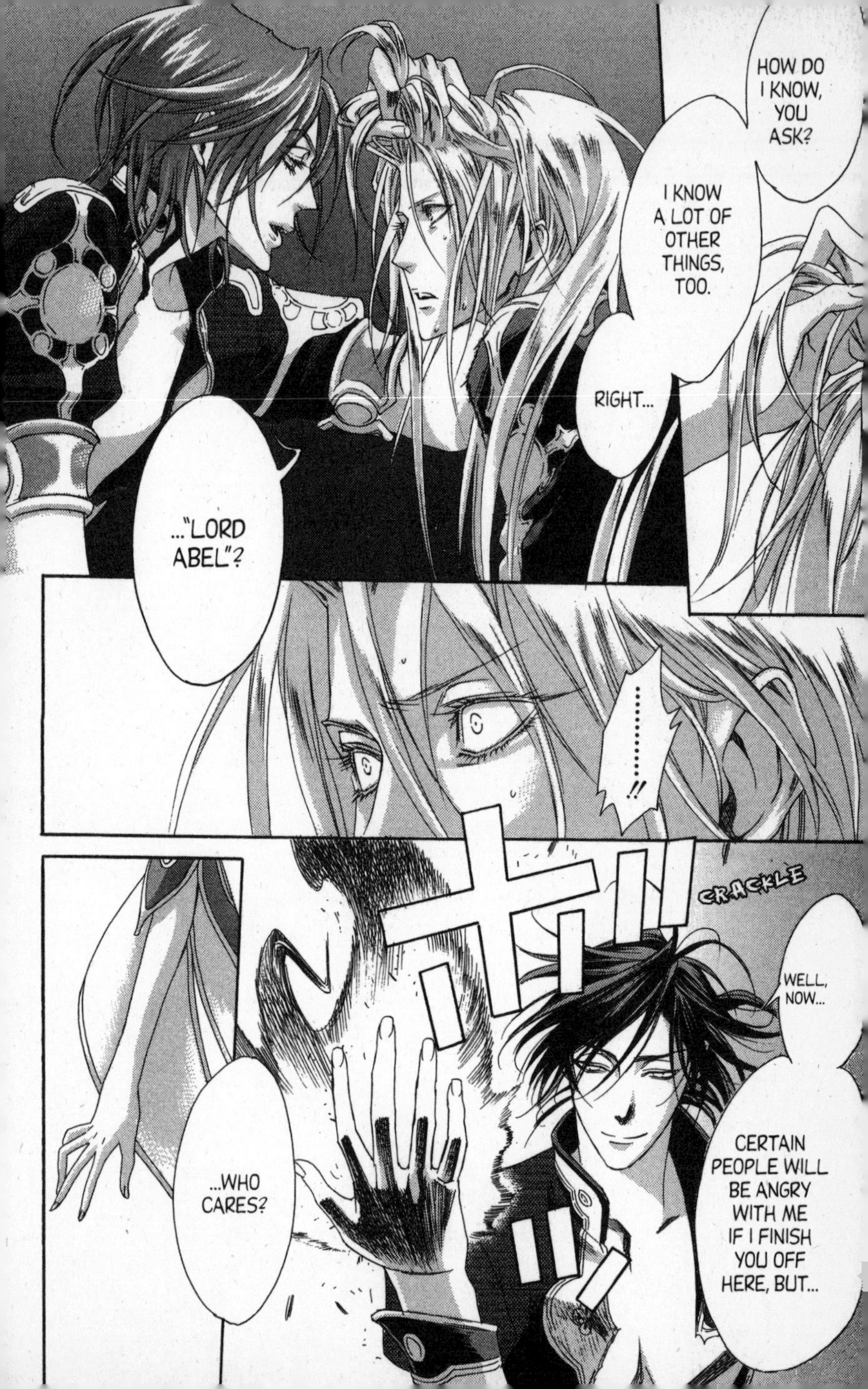
HOW DO I KNOW, YOU ASK?
I KNOW A LOT OF OTHER THINGS, TOO.
RIGHT...
..."LORD ABEL"?
........!!
CRACKLE
WELL, NOW...
CERTAIN PEOPLE WILL BE ANGRY WITH ME IF I FINISH YOU OFF HERE, BUT...
...WHO CARES?

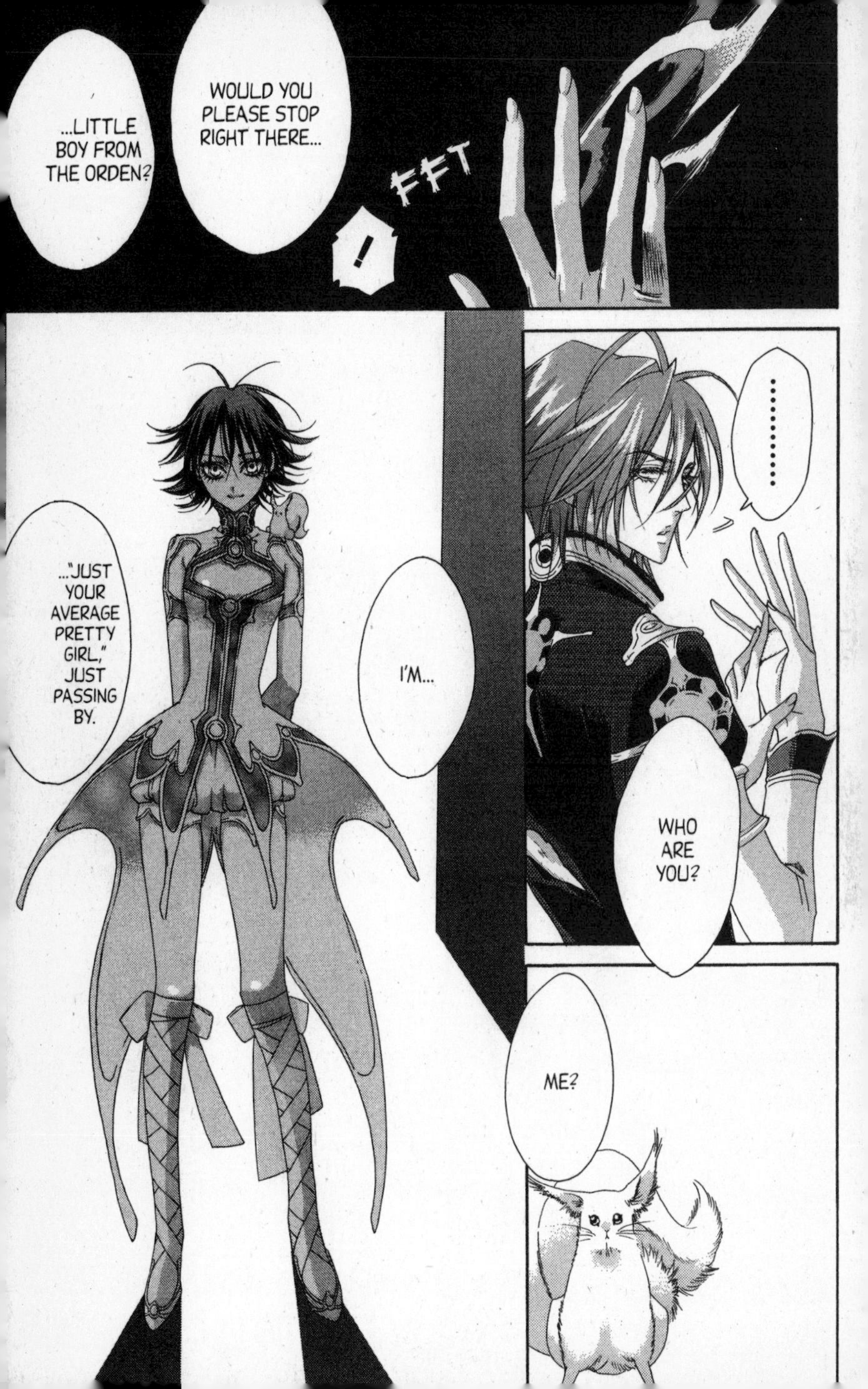
FFT
!
WOULD YOU PLEASE STOP RIGHT THERE...
...LITTLE BOY FROM THE ORDEN?
....
WHO ARE YOU?
ME?
I'M...
..."JUST YOUR AVERAGE PRETTY GIRL," JUST PASSING BY.

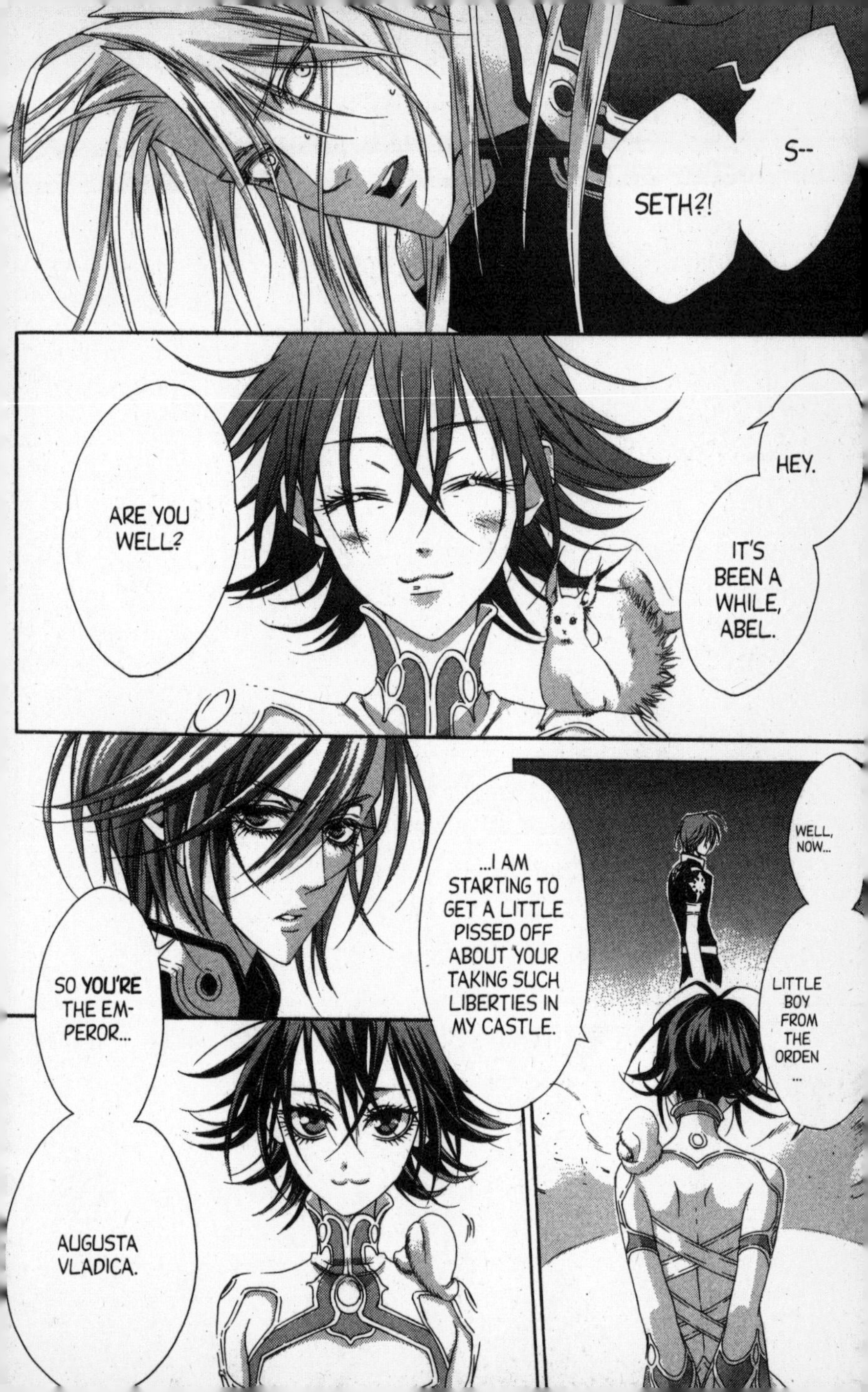
S--
SETH?!
HEY.
IT'S BEEN A WHILE, ABEL.
ARE YOU WELL?
WELL, NOW...
LITTLE BOY FROM THE ORDEN ...
...I AM STARTING TO GET A LITTLE PISSED OFF ABOUT YOUR TAKING SUCH LIBERTIES IN MY CASTLE.
SO YOU'RE THE EM-PEROR...
AUGUSTA VLADICA.

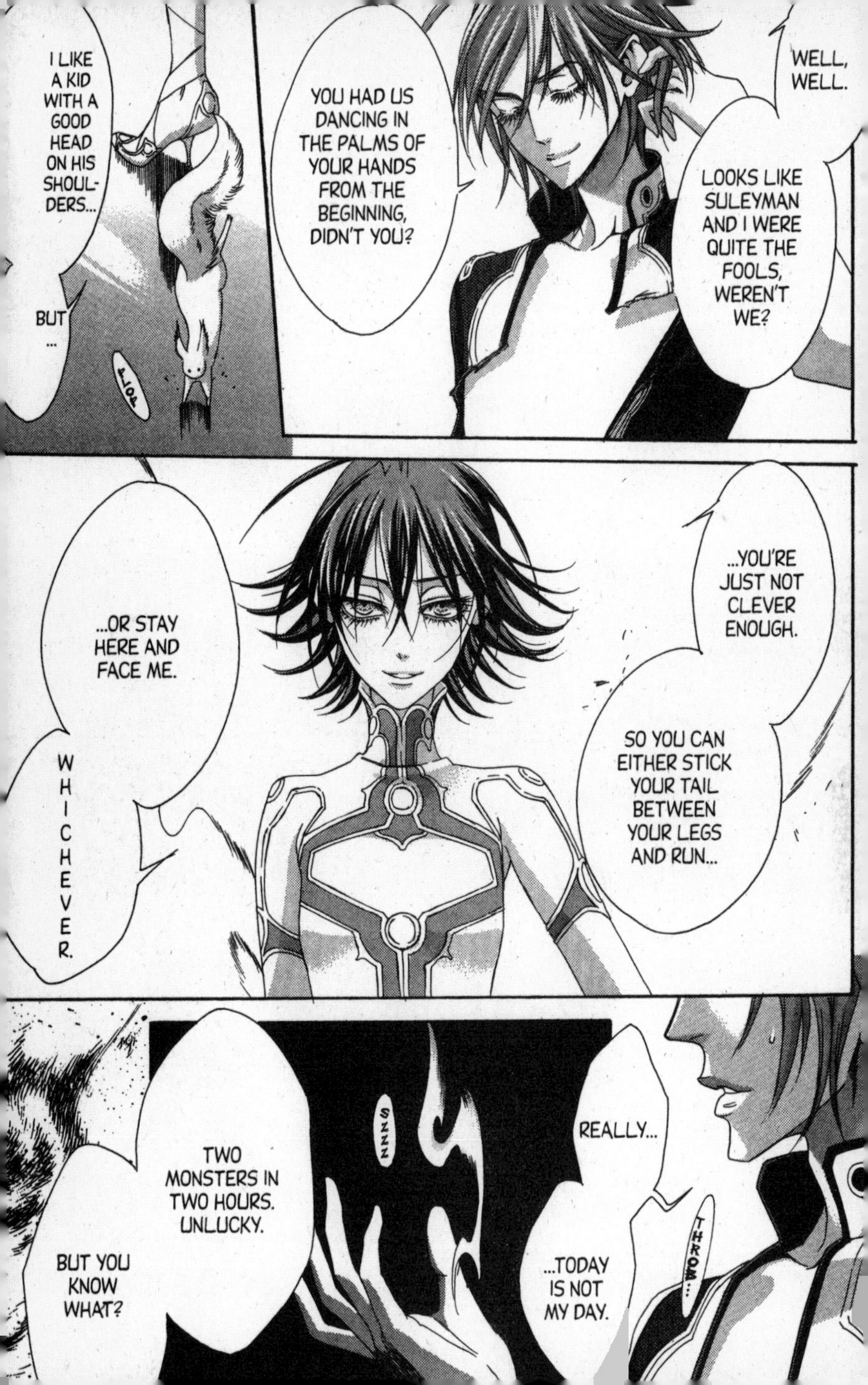
WELL, WELL.
LOOKS LIKE SULEYMAN AND I WERE QUITE THE FOOLS, WEREN'T WE?
YOU HAD US DANCING IN THE PALMS OF YOUR HANDS FROM THE BEGINNING, DIDN'T YOU?
I LIKE A KID WITH A GOOD HEAD ON HIS SHOUL-DERS...
BUT ...
...YOU'RE JUST NOT CLEVER ENOUGH.
SO YOU CAN EITHER STICK YOUR TAIL BETWEEN YOUR LEGS AND RUN...
...OR STAY HERE AND FACE ME.
WHICHEVER.
THROB...
REALLY...
...TODAY IS NOT MY DAY.
SZZZ
TWO MONSTERS IN TWO HOURS. UNLUCKY.
BUT YOU KNOW WHAT?

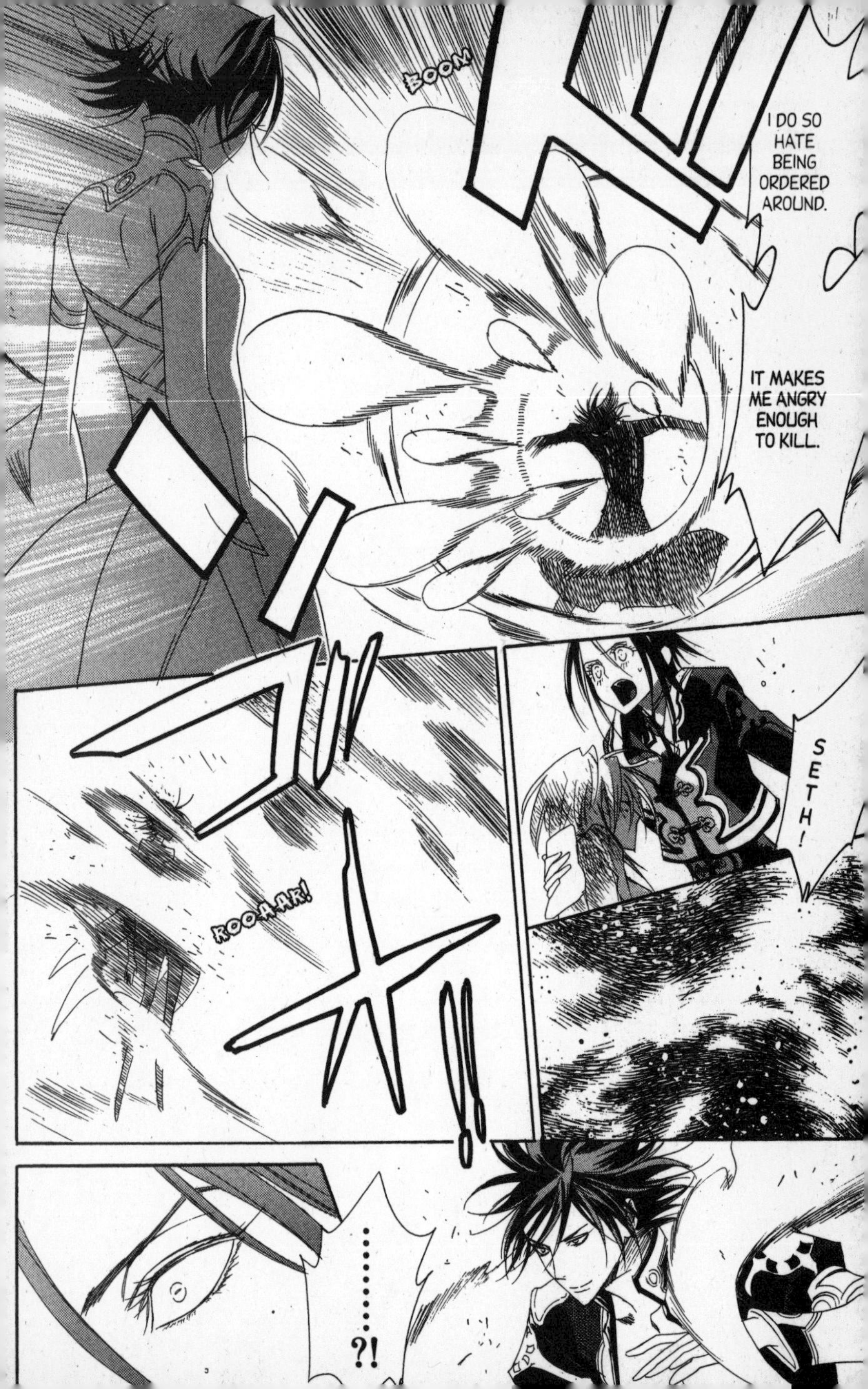
BOOM
I DO SO HATE BEING ORDERED AROUND.
IT MAKES ME ANGRY ENOUGH TO KILL.
SETH!
ROOAAR!
......?!

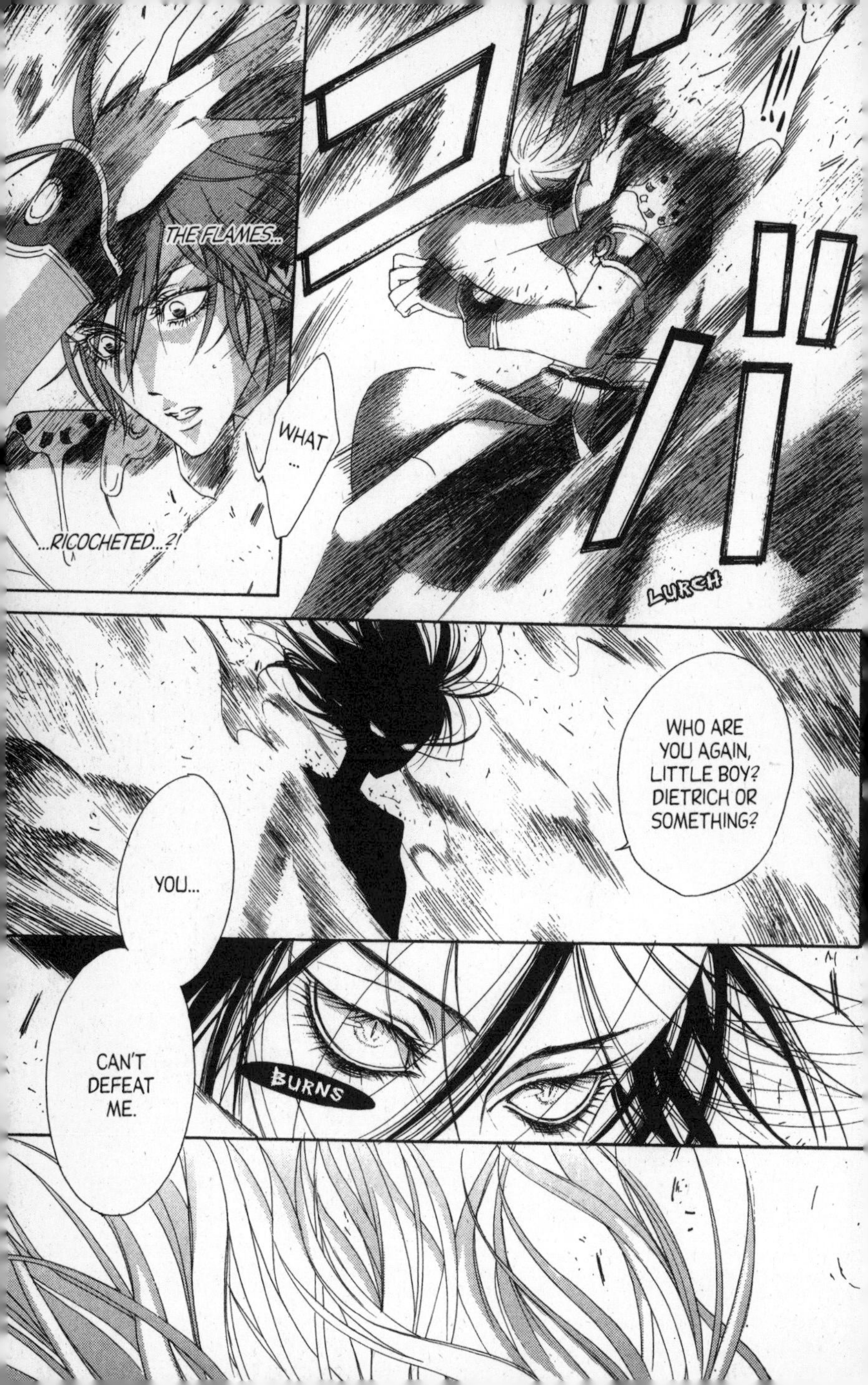
LURCH
THE FLAMES...
WHAT...
...RICOCHETED...?!
WHO ARE YOU AGAIN, LITTLE BOY? DIETRICH OR SOMETHING?
YOU...
BURNS
CAN'T DEFEAT ME.

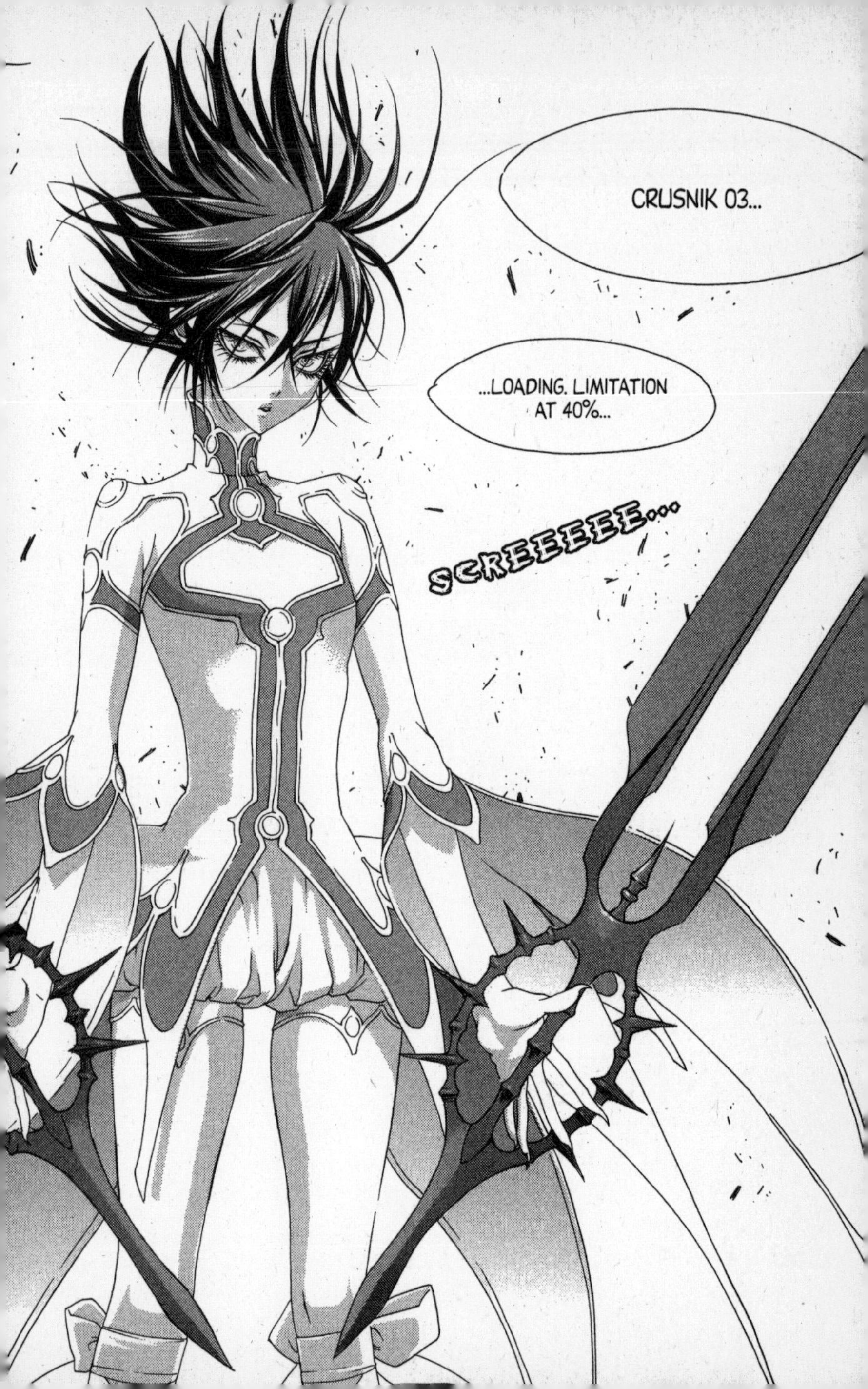
CRUSNIK 03...
...LOADING. LIMITATION AT 40%...
SCREEEEEE...

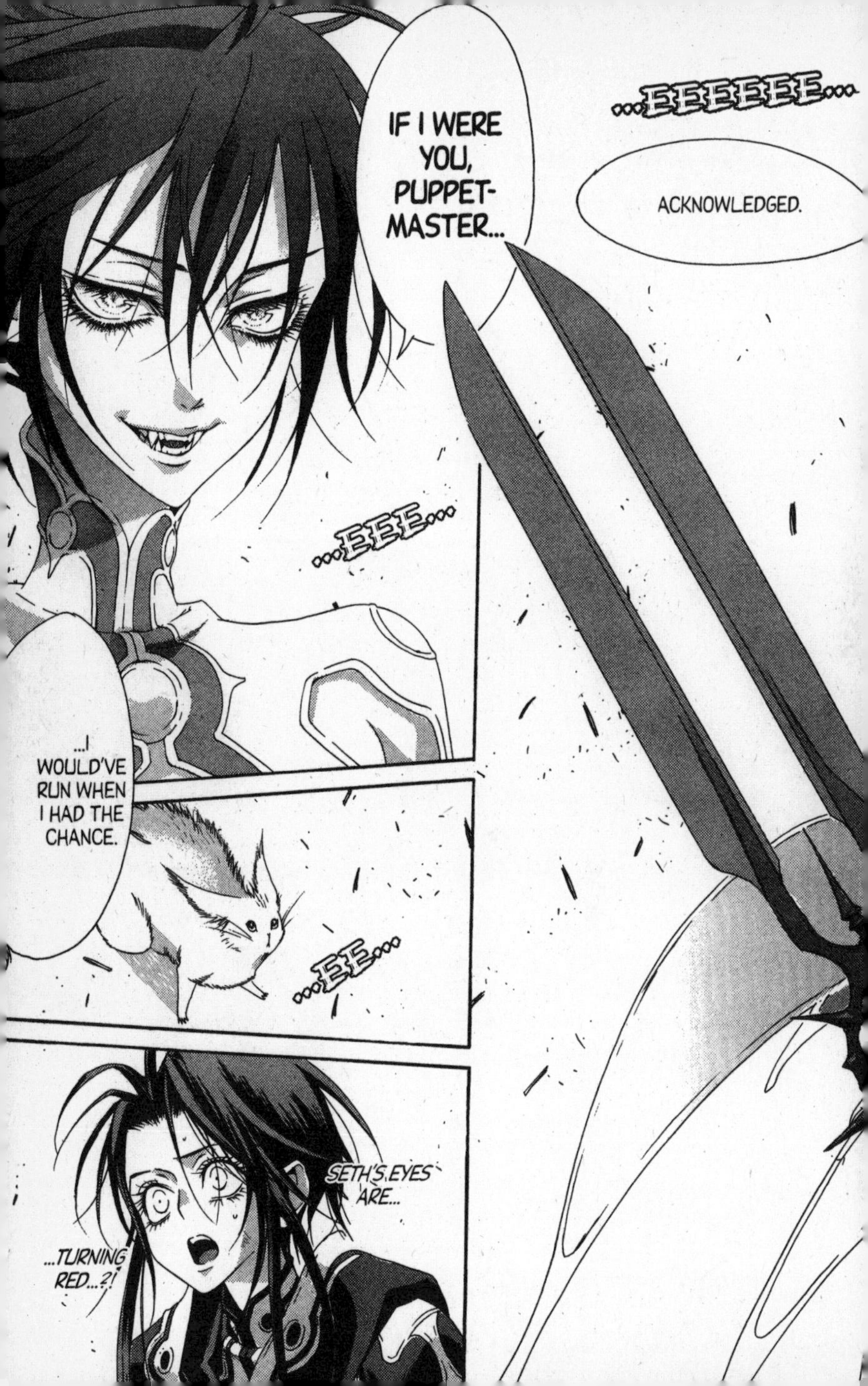
...EEEEEE...
ACKNOWLEDGED.
IF I WERE YOU, PUPPET-MASTER...
...EEE...
...I WOULD'VE RUN WHEN I HAD THE CHANCE.
...EE...
SETH'S EYES ARE...
...TURNING RED...?!

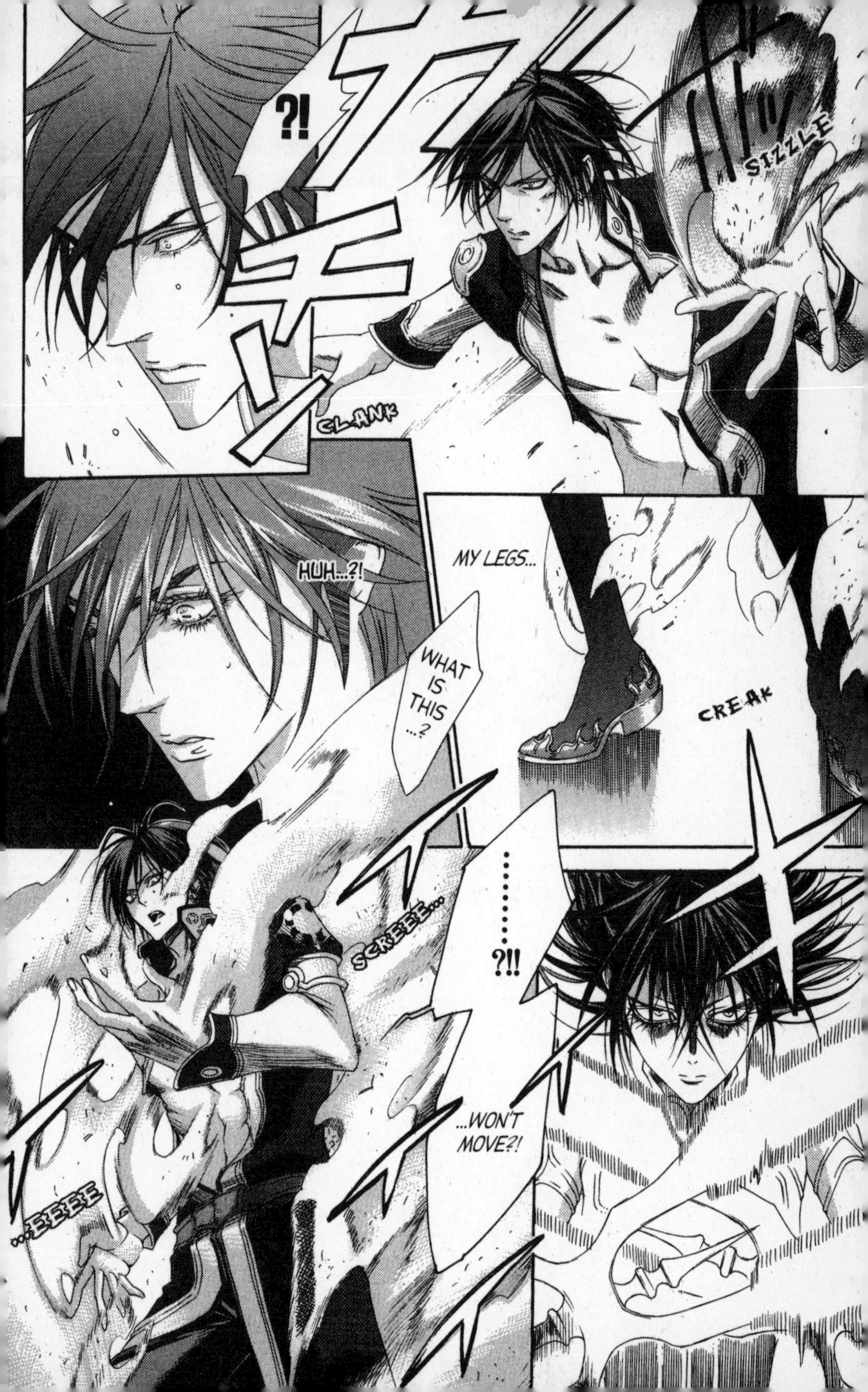
SIZZLE
?!
CLANK
MY LEGS...
CREAK
HUH...?!
WHAT IS THIS ...?
......
?!!
...WON'T MOVE?!
SCREEE...
...EEEE

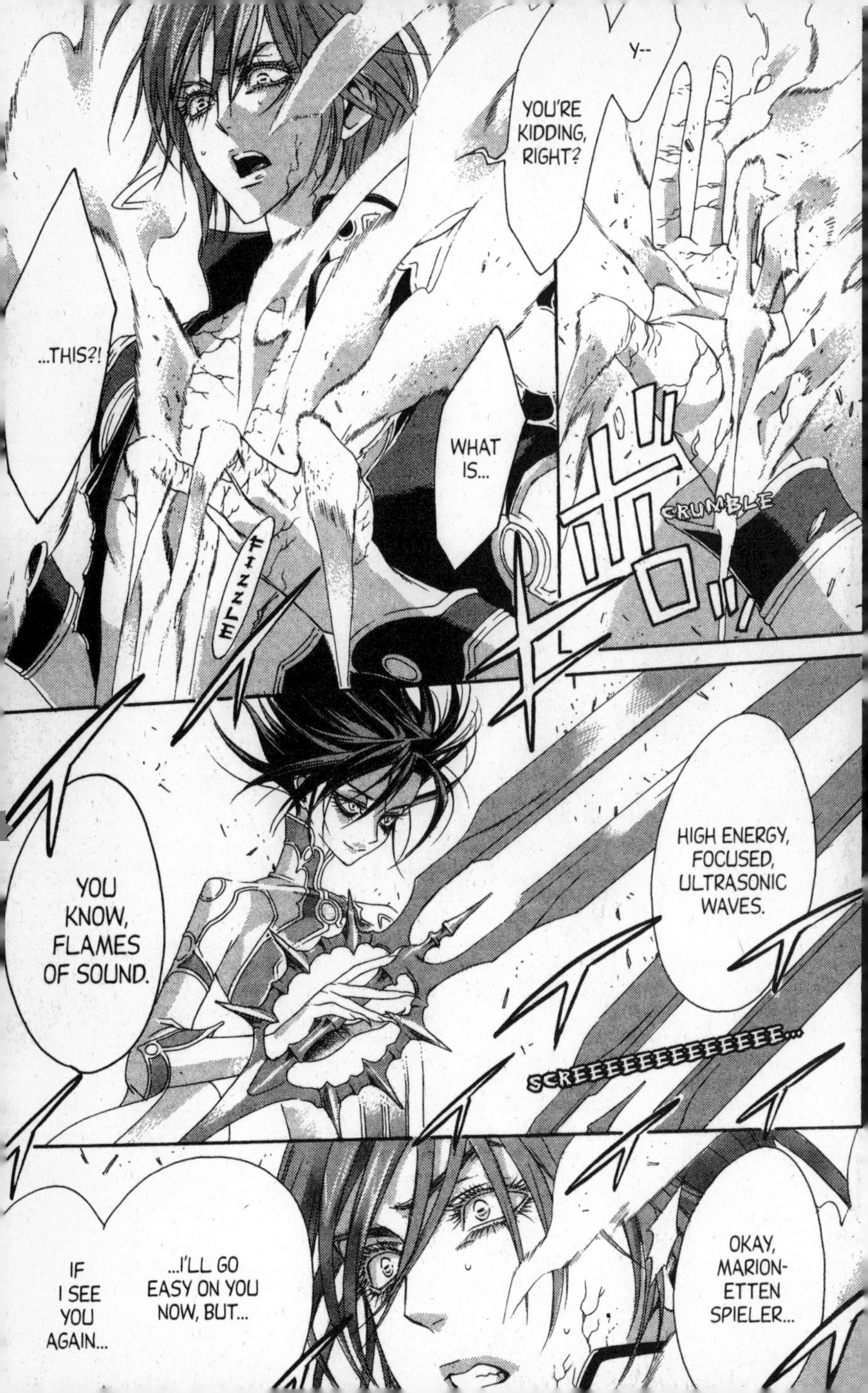
Y--
YOU'RE KIDDING, RIGHT?
CRUMBLE
WHAT IS...
...THIS?!
FIZZLE
HIGH ENERGY, FOCUSED, ULTRASONIC WAVES.
YOU KNOW, FLAMES OF SOUND.
SCREEEEEEEEEEEEEEE...
OKAY, MARION-ETTEN SPIELER...
...I'LL GO EASY ON YOU NOW, BUT...
IF I SEE YOU AGAIN...

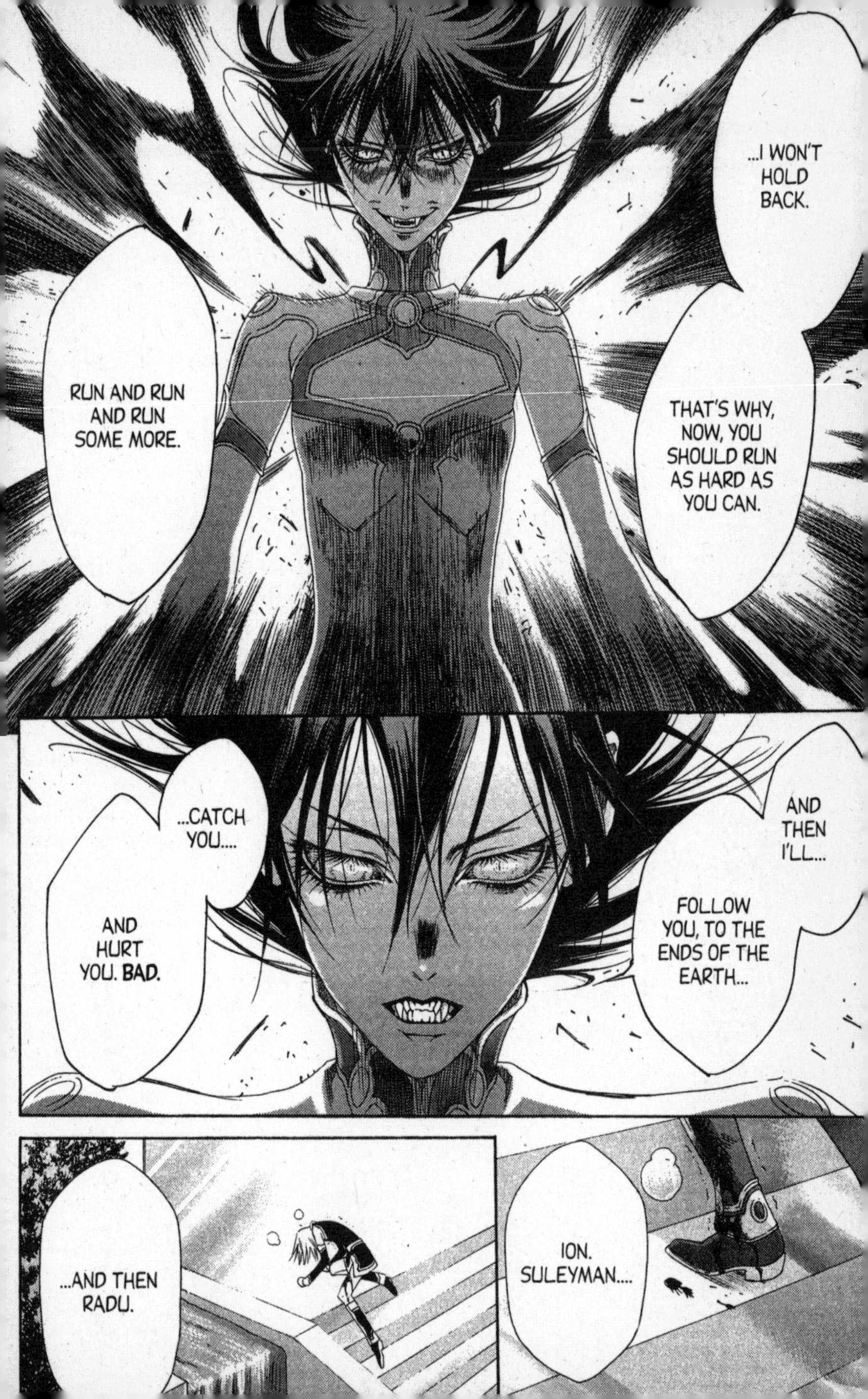
...I WON'T HOLD BACK.
THAT'S WHY, NOW, YOU SHOULD RUN AS HARD AS YOU CAN.
RUN AND RUN AND RUN SOME MORE.
AND THEN I'LL...
FOLLOW YOU, TO THE ENDS OF THE EARTH...
...CATCH YOU....
AND HURT YOU. BAD.
ION. SULEYMAN....
...AND THEN RADU.

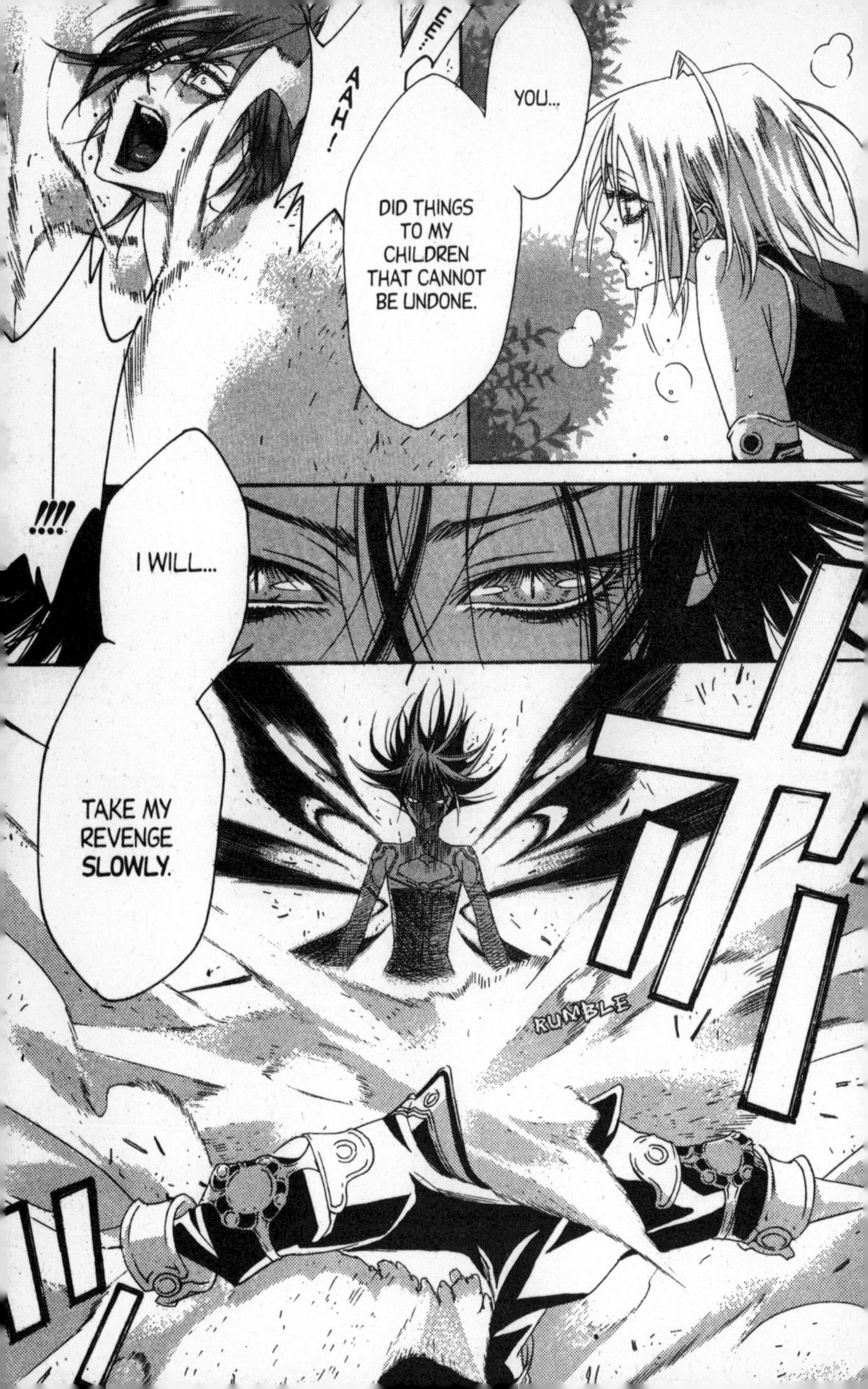
YOU...
DID THINGS TO MY CHILDREN THAT CANNOT BE UNDONE.
...EE AAH!
!!!!
I WILL...
TAKE MY REVENGE SLOWLY.
RUMBLE

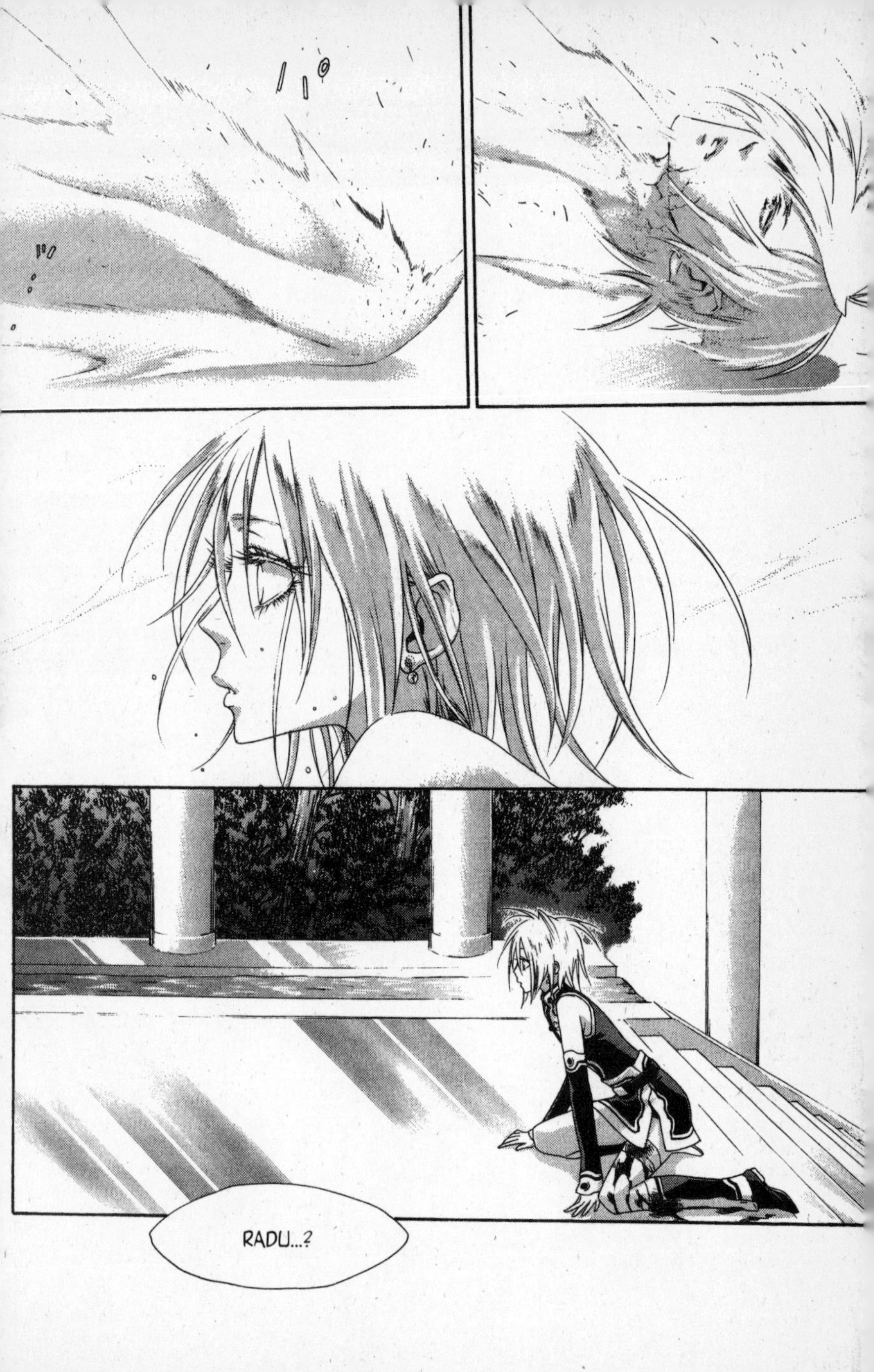
RADU...?

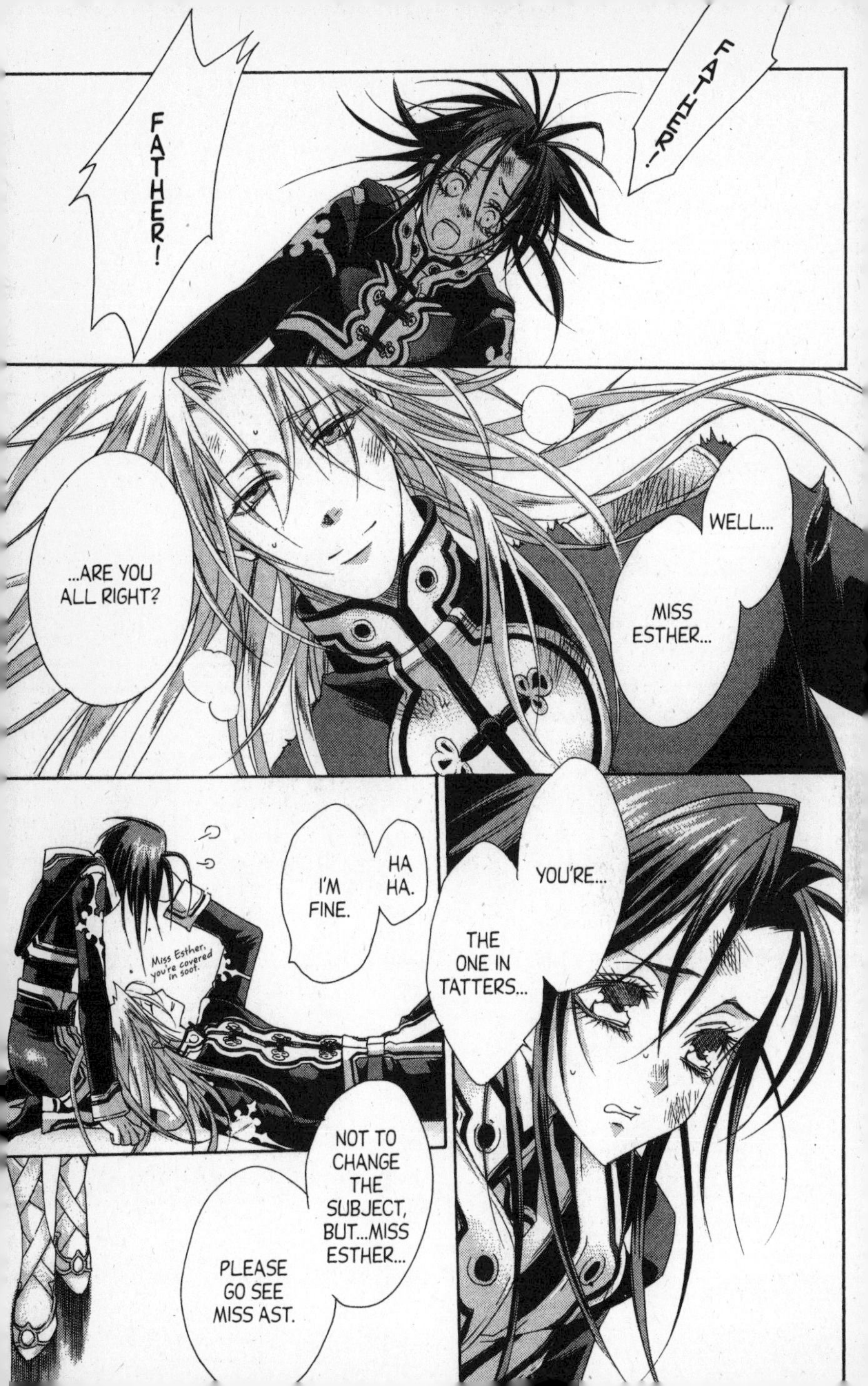

FATHER!
FATHER!
WELL...
MISS ESTHER...
...ARE YOU ALL RIGHT?
YOU'RE...
THE ONE IN TATTERS...
HA HA.
I'M FINE.
Miss Esther, you're covered in soot.
NOT TO CHANGE THE SUBJECT, BUT...MISS ESTHER...
PLEASE GO SEE MISS AST.

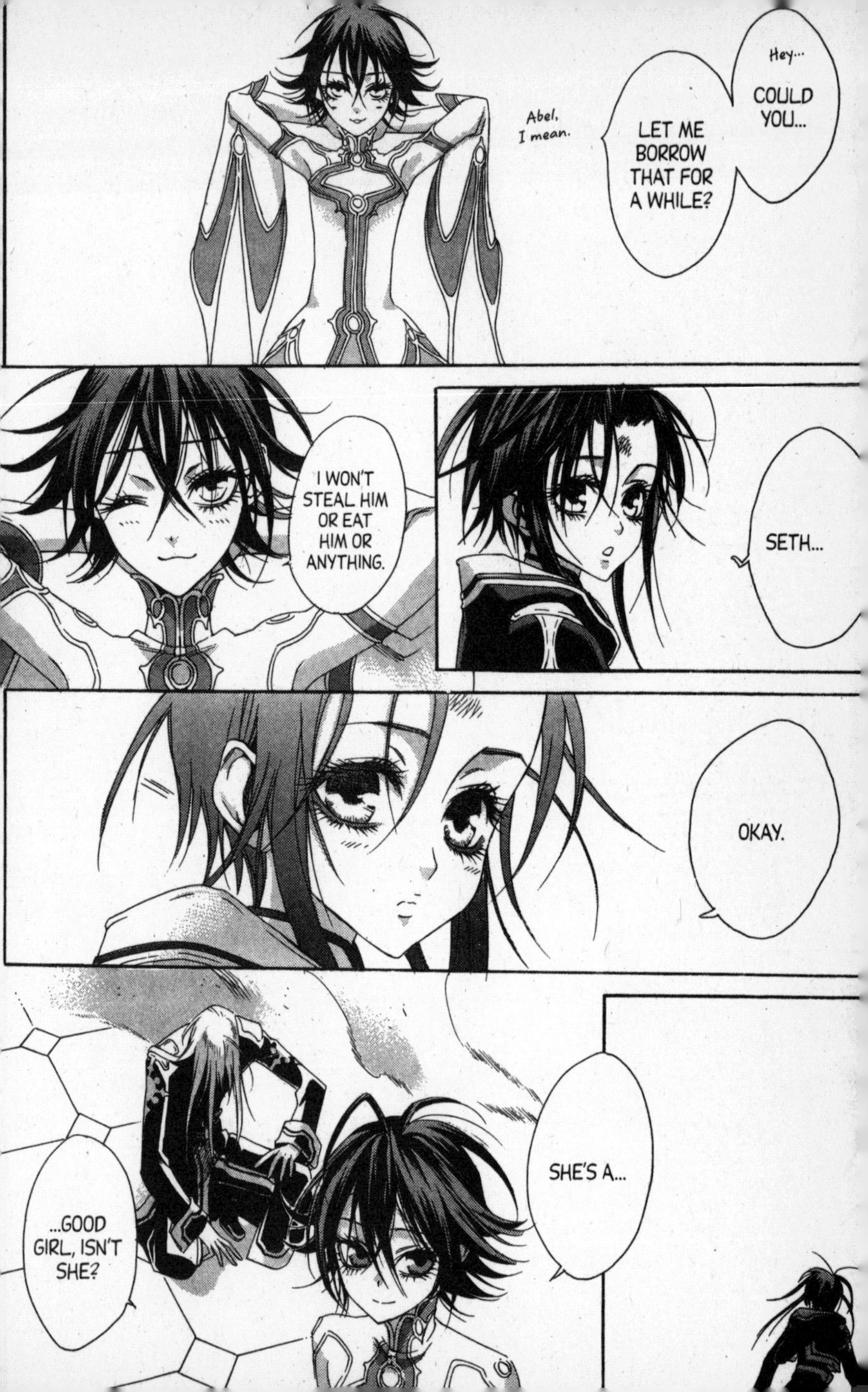
Hey... COULD YOU...
LET ME BORROW THAT FOR A WHILE?
Abel, I mean.
SETH...
I WON'T STEAL HIM OR EAT HIM OR ANYTHING.
OKAY.
SHE'S A...
...GOOD GIRL, ISN'T SHE?

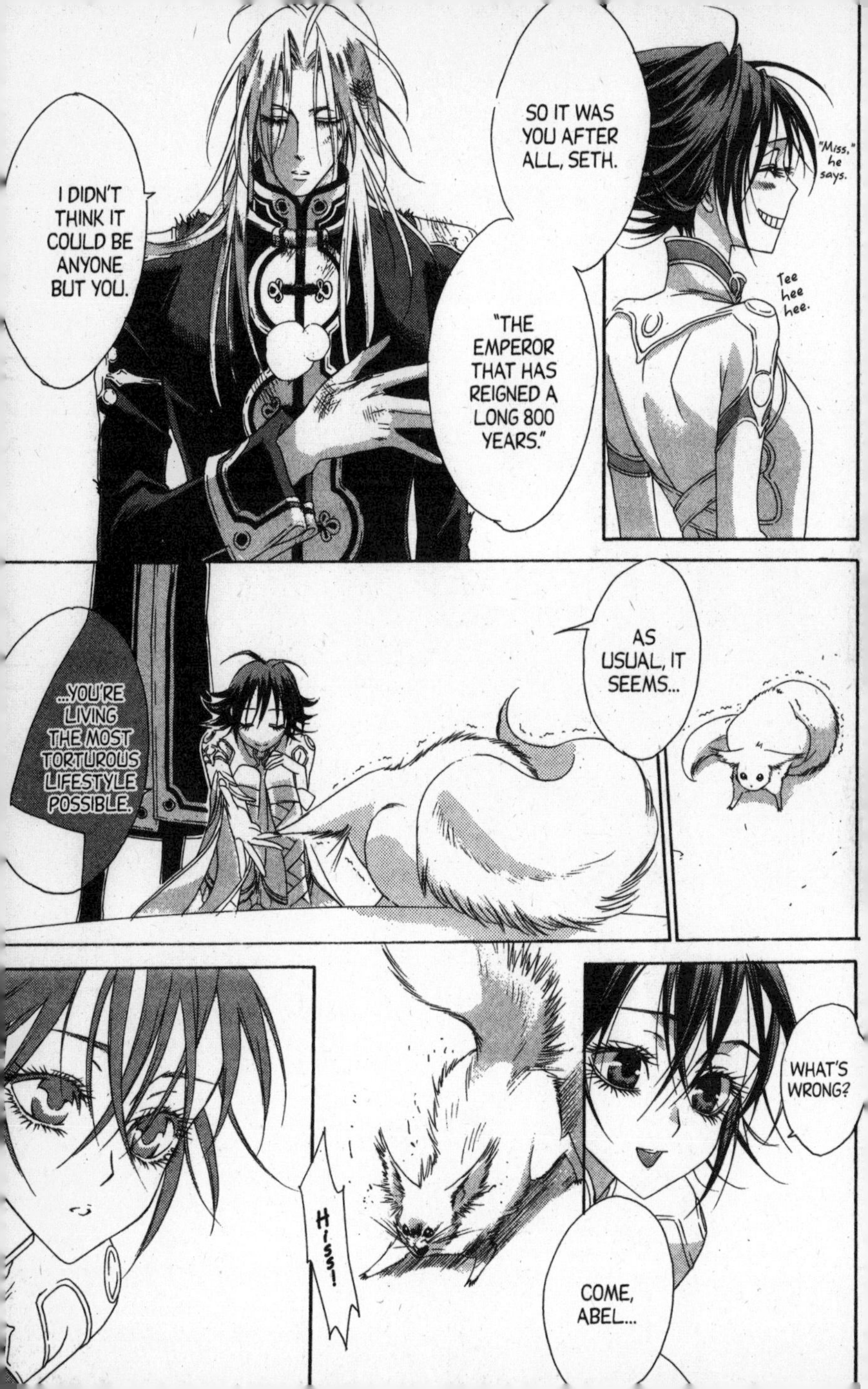
"Miss," he says.
Tee hee hee.
SO IT WAS YOU AFTER ALL, SETH.
"THE EMPEROR THAT HAS REIGNED A LONG 800 YEARS."
I DIDN'T THINK IT COULD BE ANYONE BUT YOU.
AS USUAL, IT SEEMS...
...YOU'RE LIVING THE MOST TORTUROUS LIFESTYLE POSSIBLE.
WHAT'S WRONG?
COME, ABEL...
Hiss!

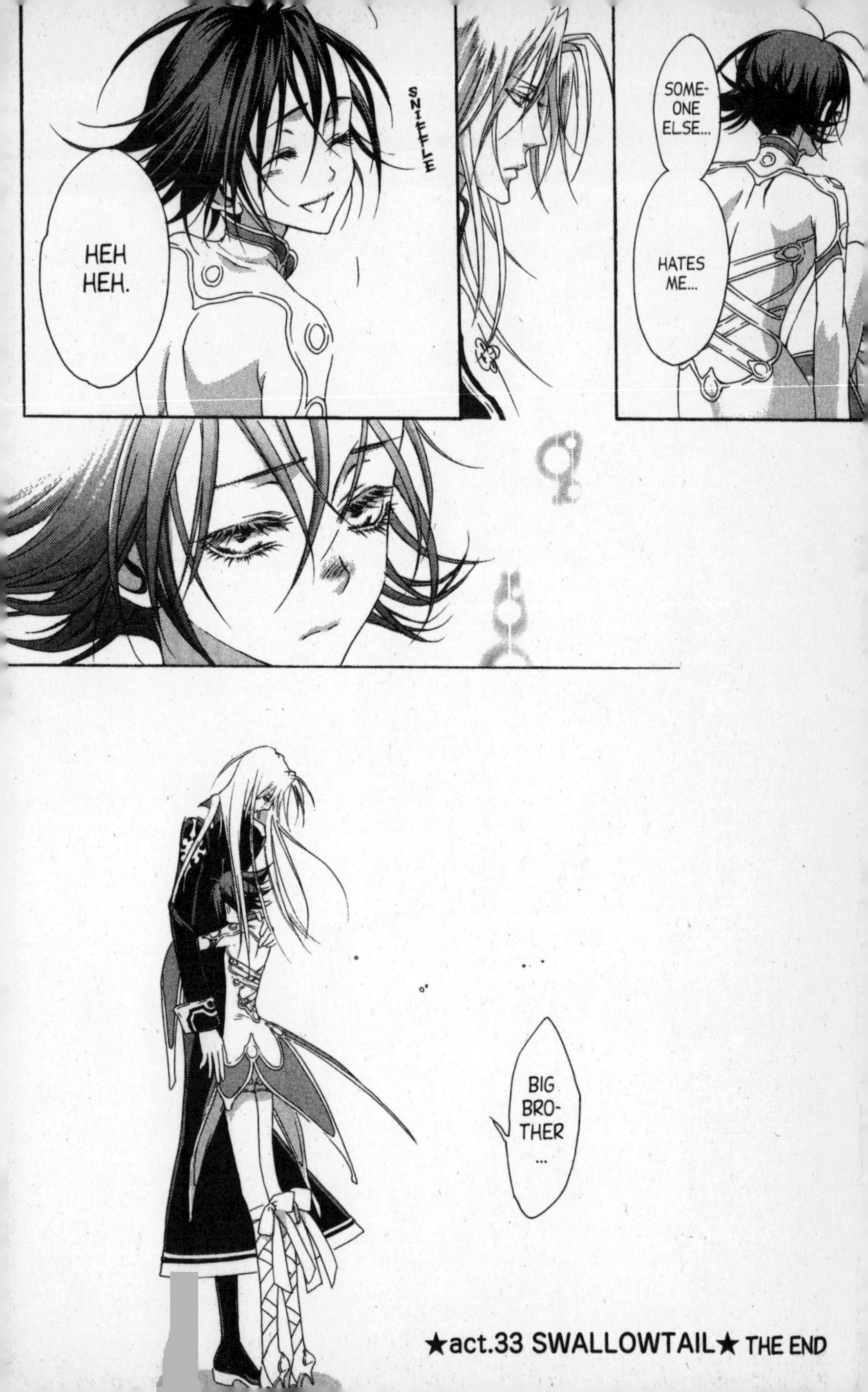
SOME-ONE ELSE...
HATES ME...
SNIFFLE
HEH HEH.
BIG BRO-THER ...
★act.33 SWALLOWTAIL★ THE END

act.34 The Never Ending Story

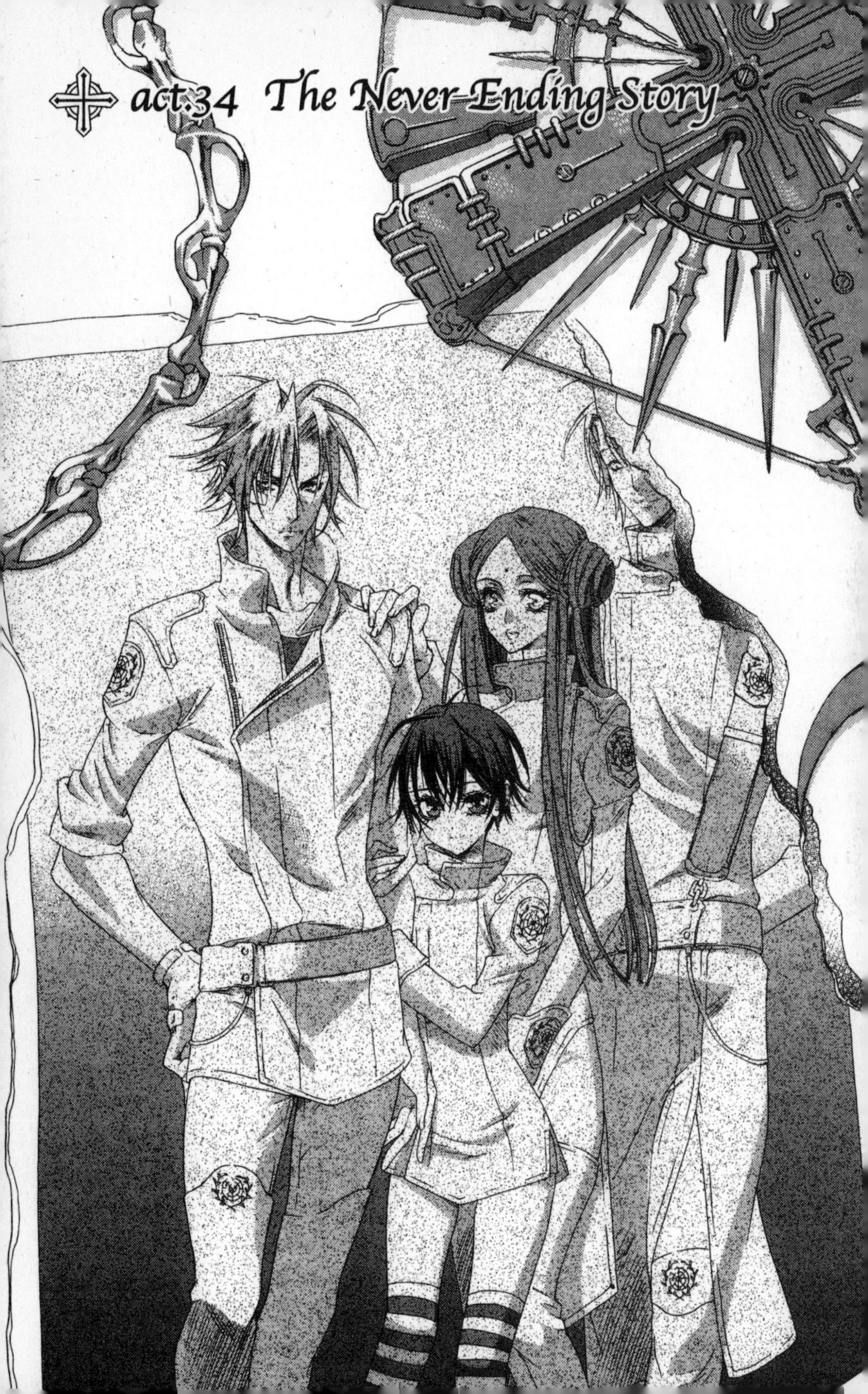

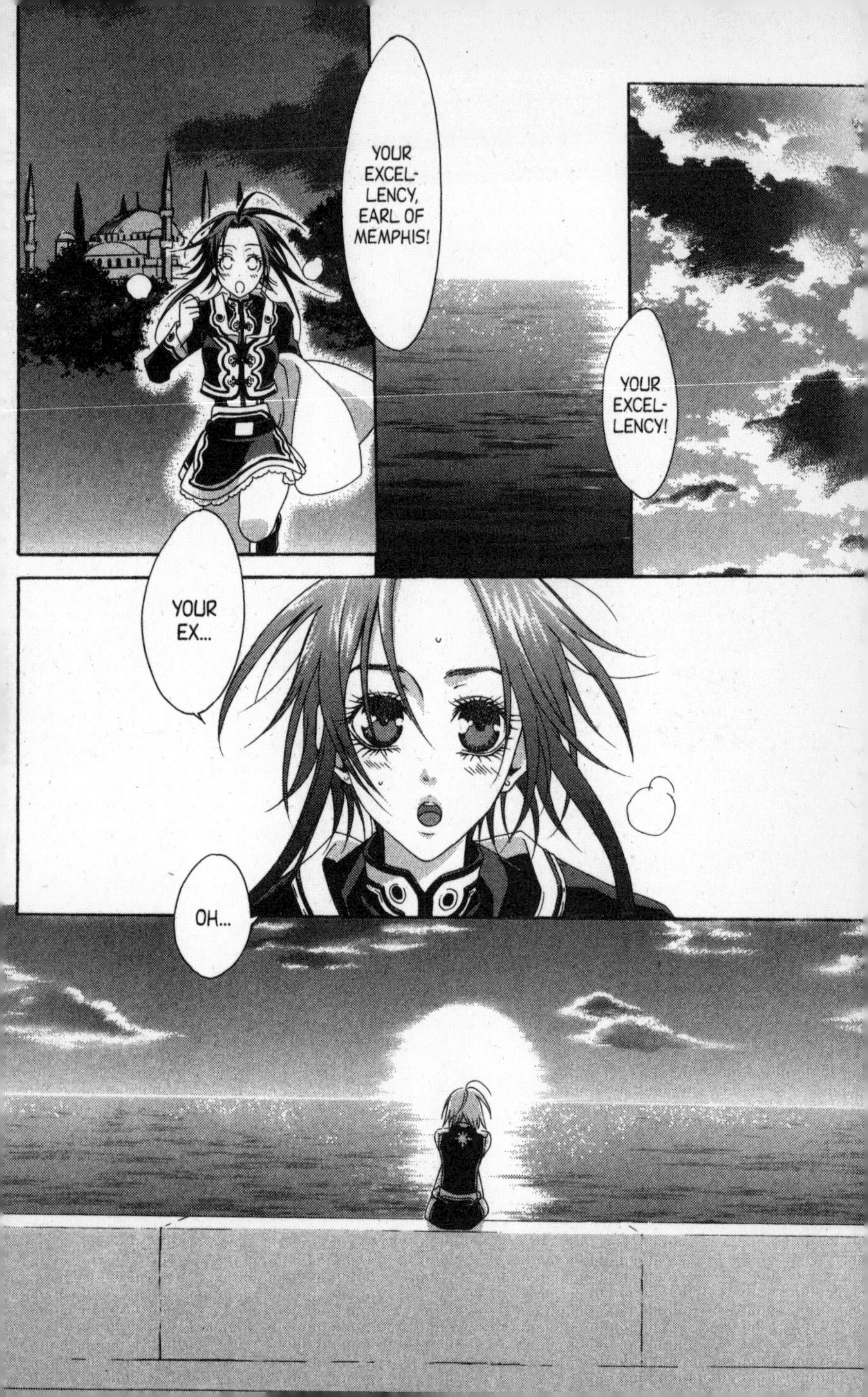
YOUR EXCEL-LENCY, EARL OF MEMPHIS!
YOUR EXCEL-LENCY!
YOUR EX...
OH...

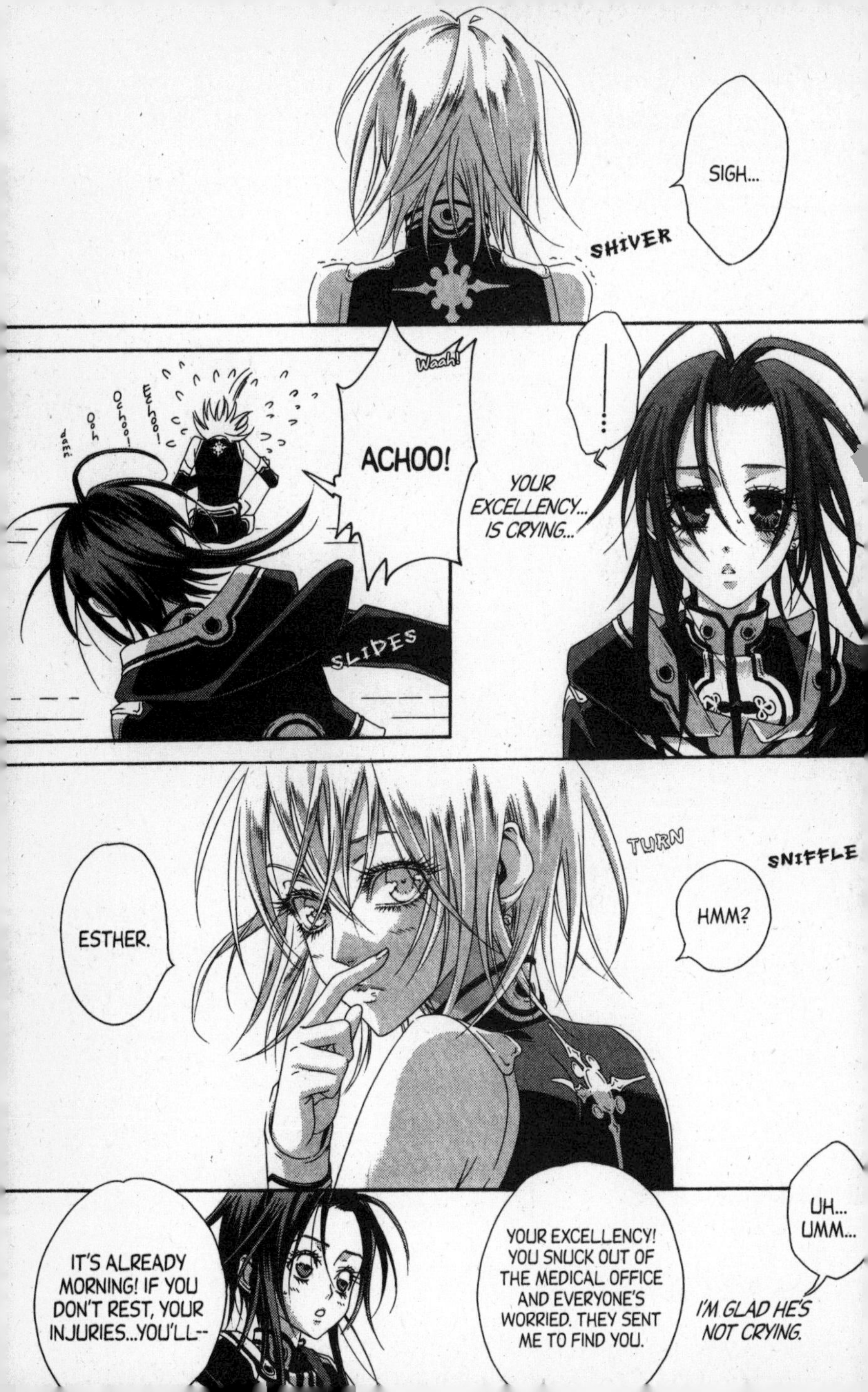

SIGH...
SHIVER
!...
YOUR EXCELLENCY... IS CRYING...
Waah!
ACHOO!
Echoo!
Ochoo!
Ooh
dam!
SLIDES
TURN
SNIFFLE
HMM?
ESTHER.
UH... UMM...
I'M GLAD HE'S NOT CRYING.
YOUR EXCELLENCY! YOU SNUCK OUT OF THE MEDICAL OFFICE AND EVERYONE'S WORRIED. THEY SENT ME TO FIND YOU.
IT'S ALREADY MORNING! IF YOU DON'T REST, YOUR INJURIES...YOU'LL--

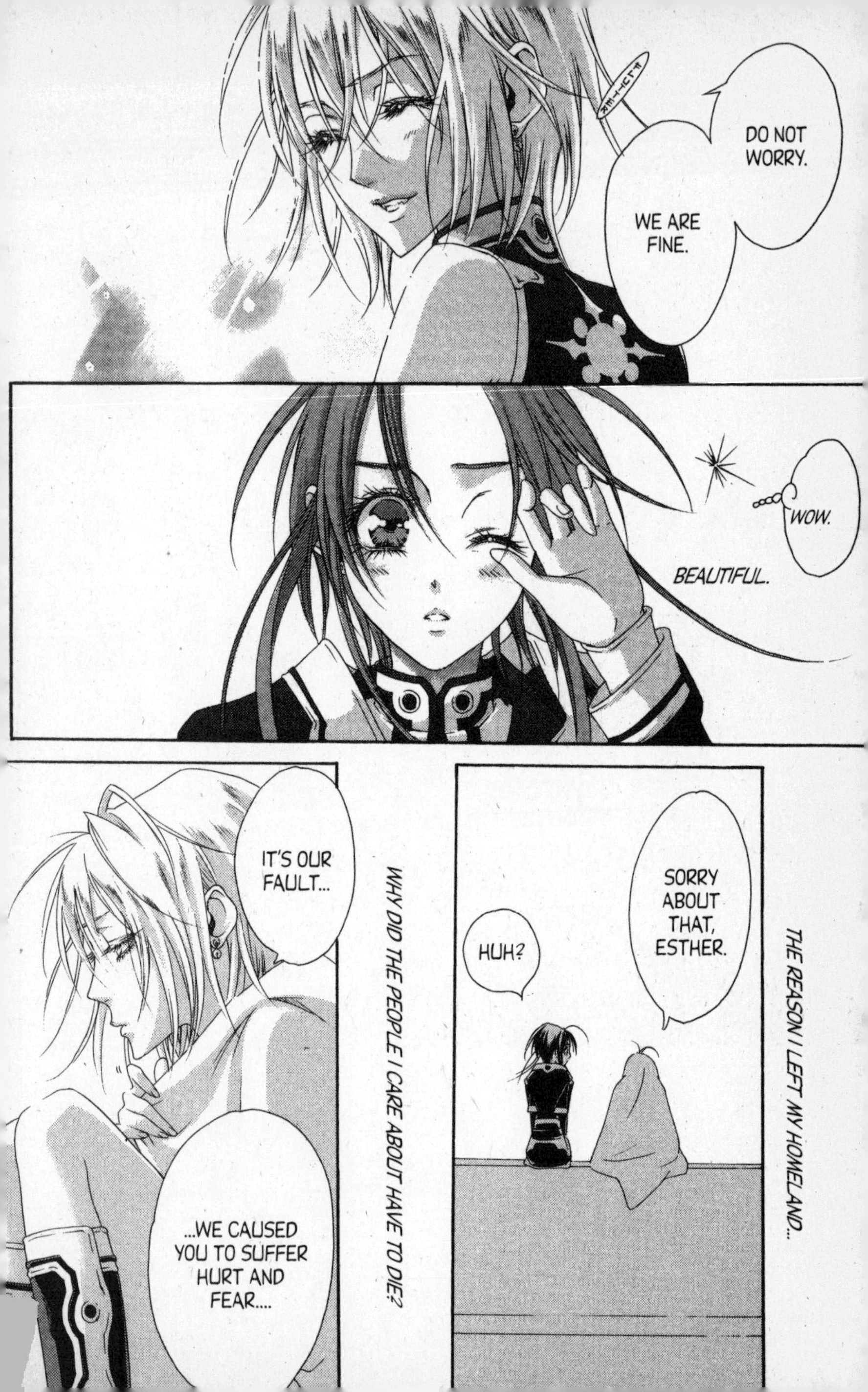
DO NOT WORRY.
WE ARE FINE.
WOW.
BEAUTIFUL.
THE REASON I LEFT MY HOMELAND...
SORRY ABOUT THAT, ESTHER.
HUH?
WHY DID THE PEOPLE I CARE ABOUT HAVE TO DIE?
IT'S OUR FAULT...
...WE CAUSED YOU TO SUFFER HURT AND FEAR....

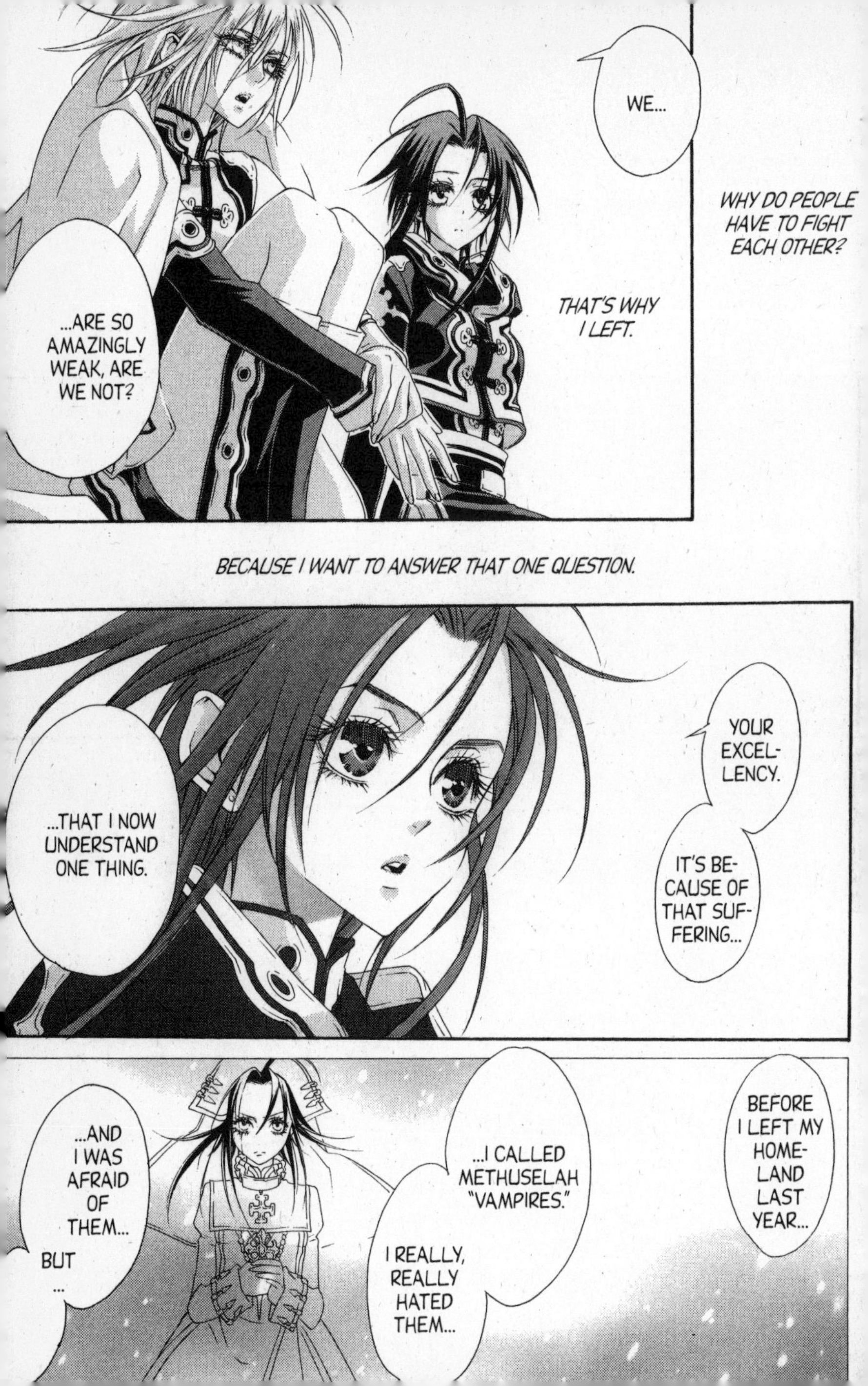
WE...
WHY DO PEOPLE HAVE TO FIGHT EACH OTHER?
THAT'S WHY I LEFT.
...ARE SO AMAZINGLY WEAK, ARE WE NOT?
BECAUSE I WANT TO ANSWER THAT ONE QUESTION.
YOUR EXCEL-LENCY.
IT'S BE-CAUSE OF THAT SUF-FERING...
...THAT I NOW UNDERSTAND ONE THING.
BEFORE I LEFT MY HOME-LAND LAST YEAR...
...I CALLED METHUSELAH "VAMPIRES."
I REALLY, REALLY HATED THEM...
...AND I WAS AFRAID OF THEM...
BUT ...

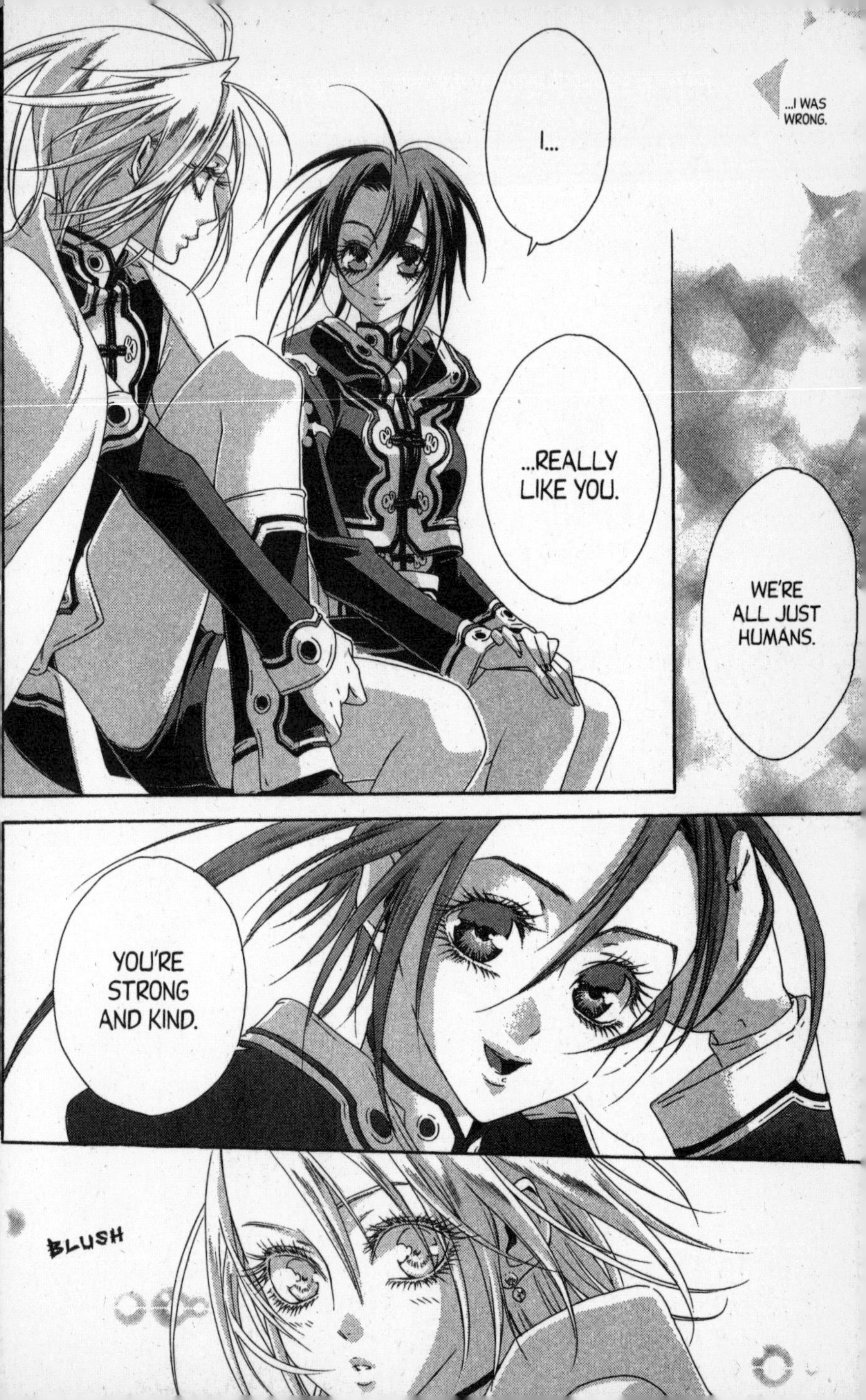
...I WAS WRONG.
WE'RE ALL JUST HUMANS.
I...
...REALLY LIKE YOU.
YOU'RE STRONG AND KIND.
BLUSH

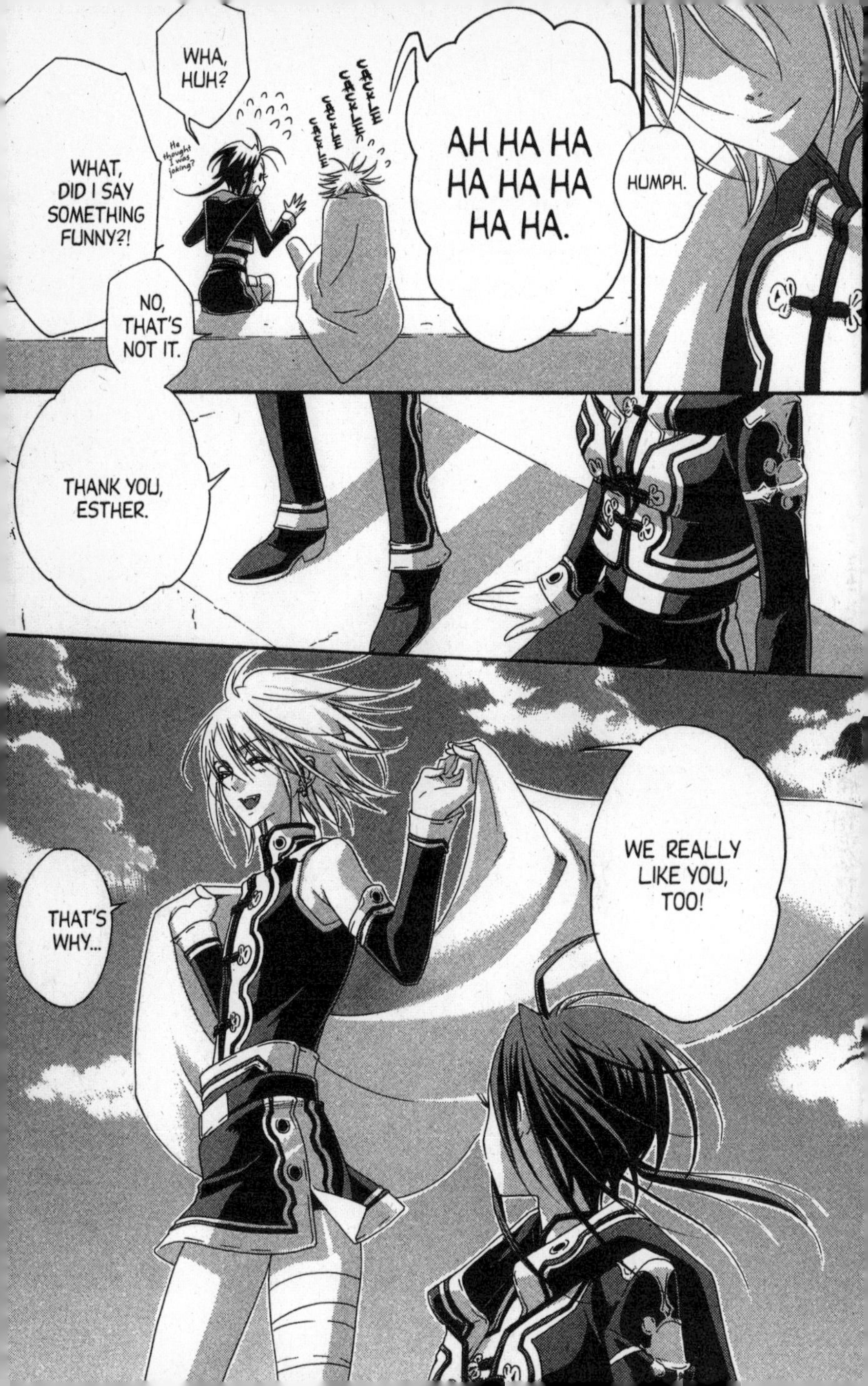
HUMPH.
AH HA HA HA HA HA HA HA.
CACKLE
CACKLE
CACKLE
CACKLE
WHA, HUH?
He thought I was joking?
WHAT, DID I SAY SOMETHING FUNNY?!
NO, THAT'S NOT IT.
THANK YOU, ESTHER.
WE REALLY LIKE YOU, TOO!
THAT'S WHY...

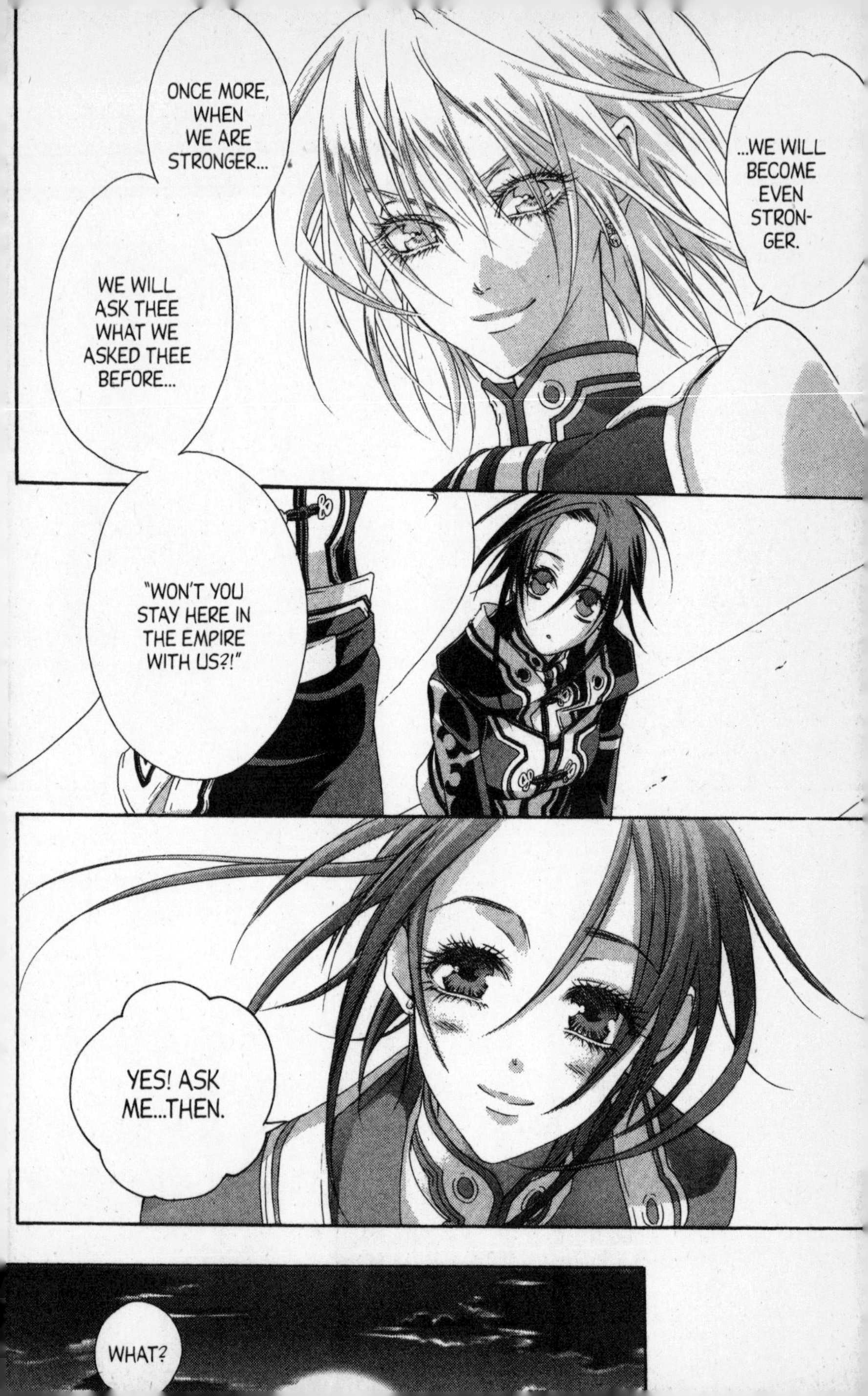
...WE WILL BECOME EVEN STRONGER.
ONCE MORE, WHEN WE ARE STRONGER...
WE WILL ASK THEE WHAT WE ASKED THEE BEFORE...
"WON'T YOU STAY HERE IN THE EMPIRE WITH US?!"
YES! ASK ME...THEN.
WHAT?

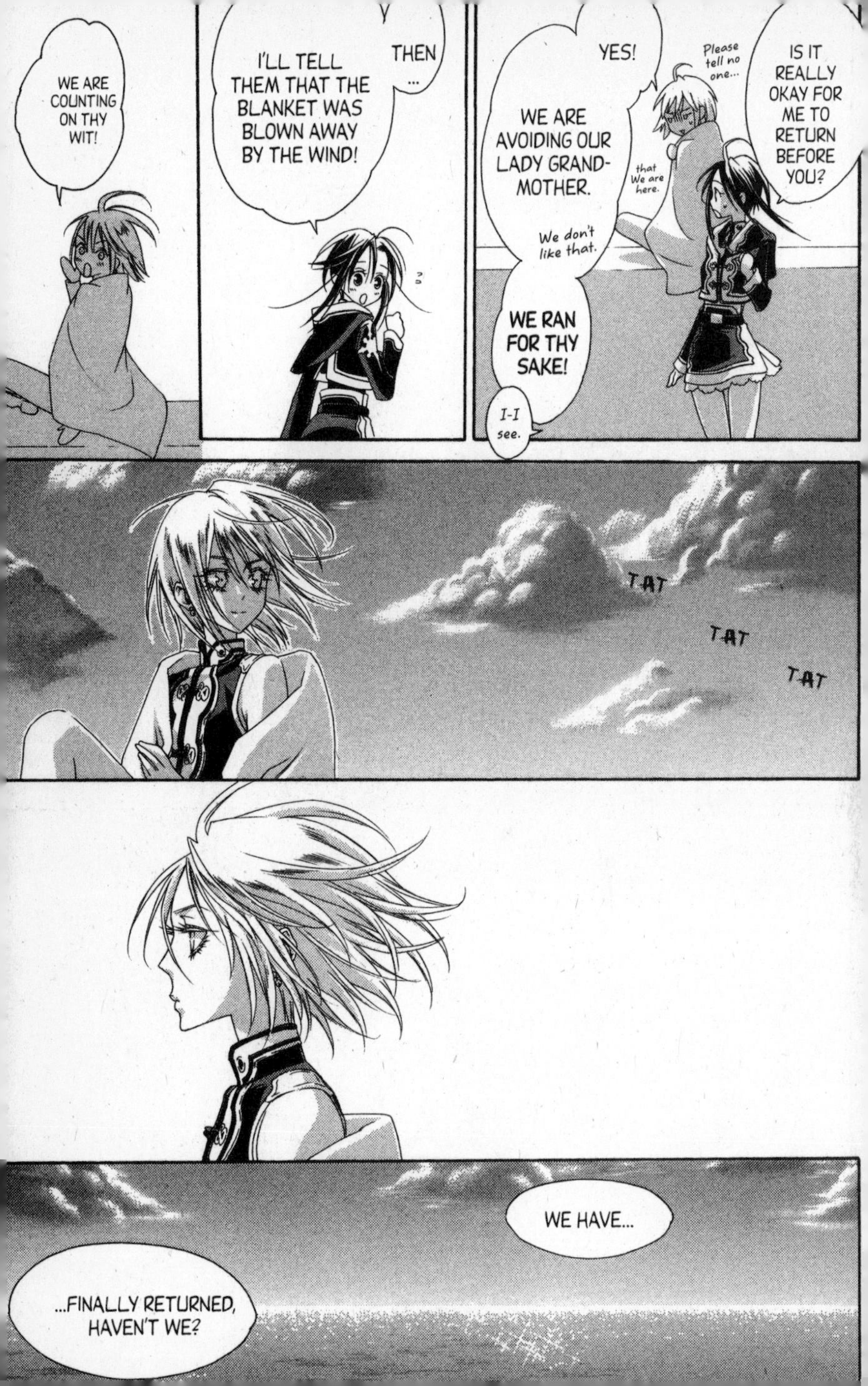
IS IT REALLY OKAY FOR ME TO RETURN BEFORE YOU?
Please tell no one... that We are here.
YES!
WE ARE AVOIDING OUR LADY GRAND-MOTHER.
We don't like that.
WE RAN FOR THY SAKE!
I-I see.
THEN ...
I'LL TELL THEM THAT THE BLANKET WAS BLOWN AWAY BY THE WIND!
WE ARE COUNTING ON THY WIT!
TAT
TAT
TAT
WE HAVE...
...FINALLY RETURNED, HAVEN'T WE?

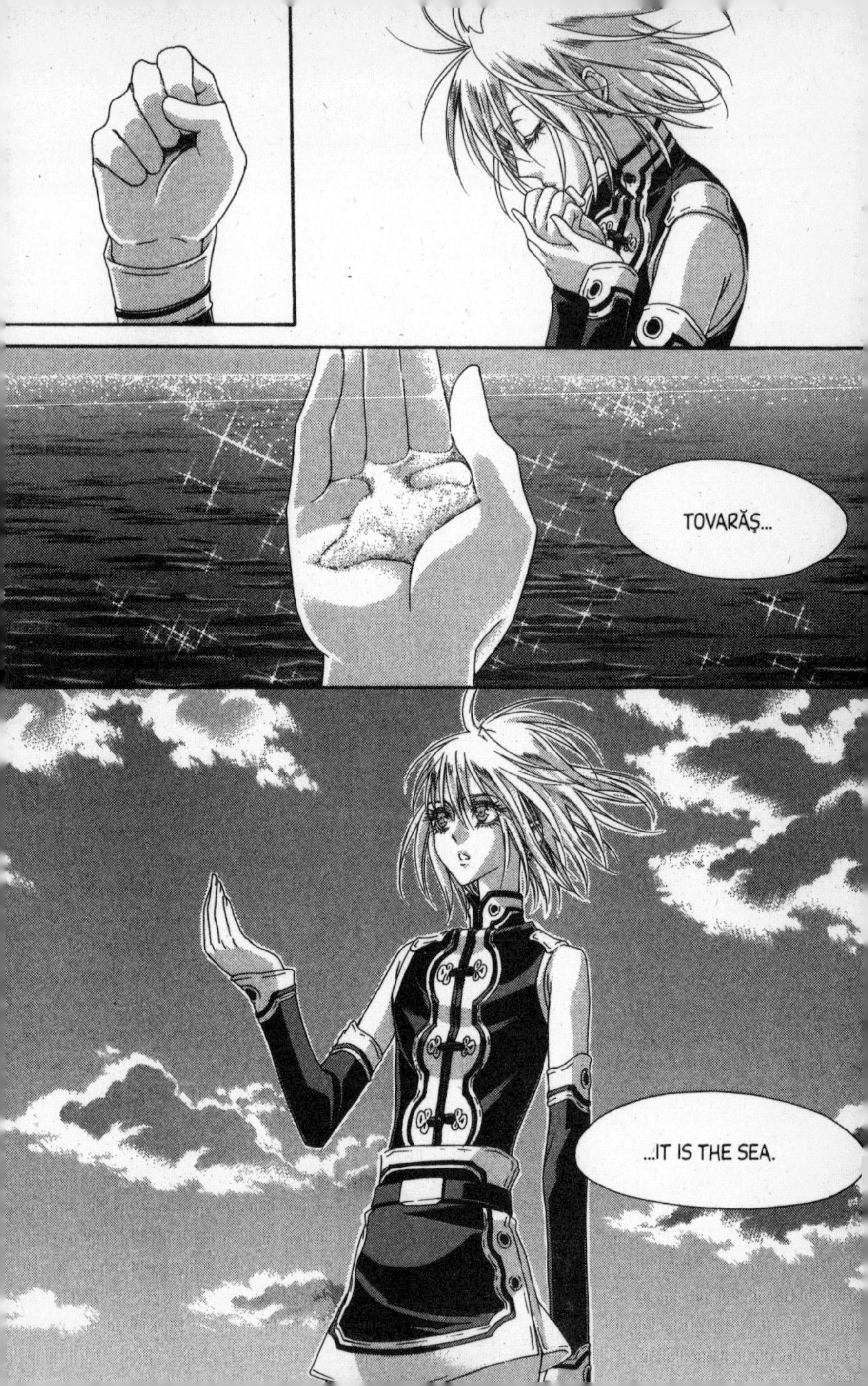
TOVARĂŞ...
...IT IS THE SEA.

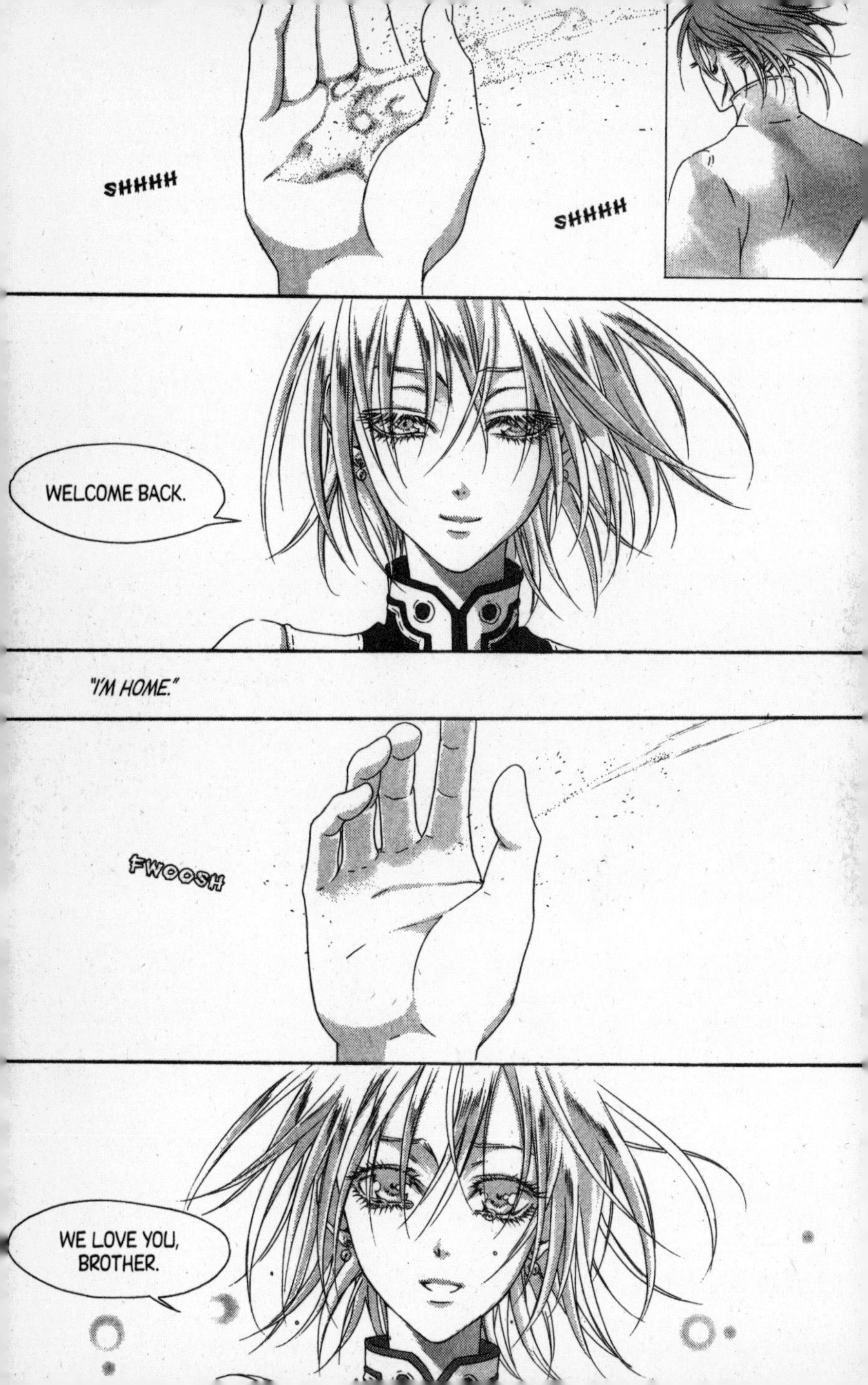
SHHHH
SHHHH
WELCOME BACK.
"I'M HOME."
FWOOSH
WE LOVE YOU, BROTHER.

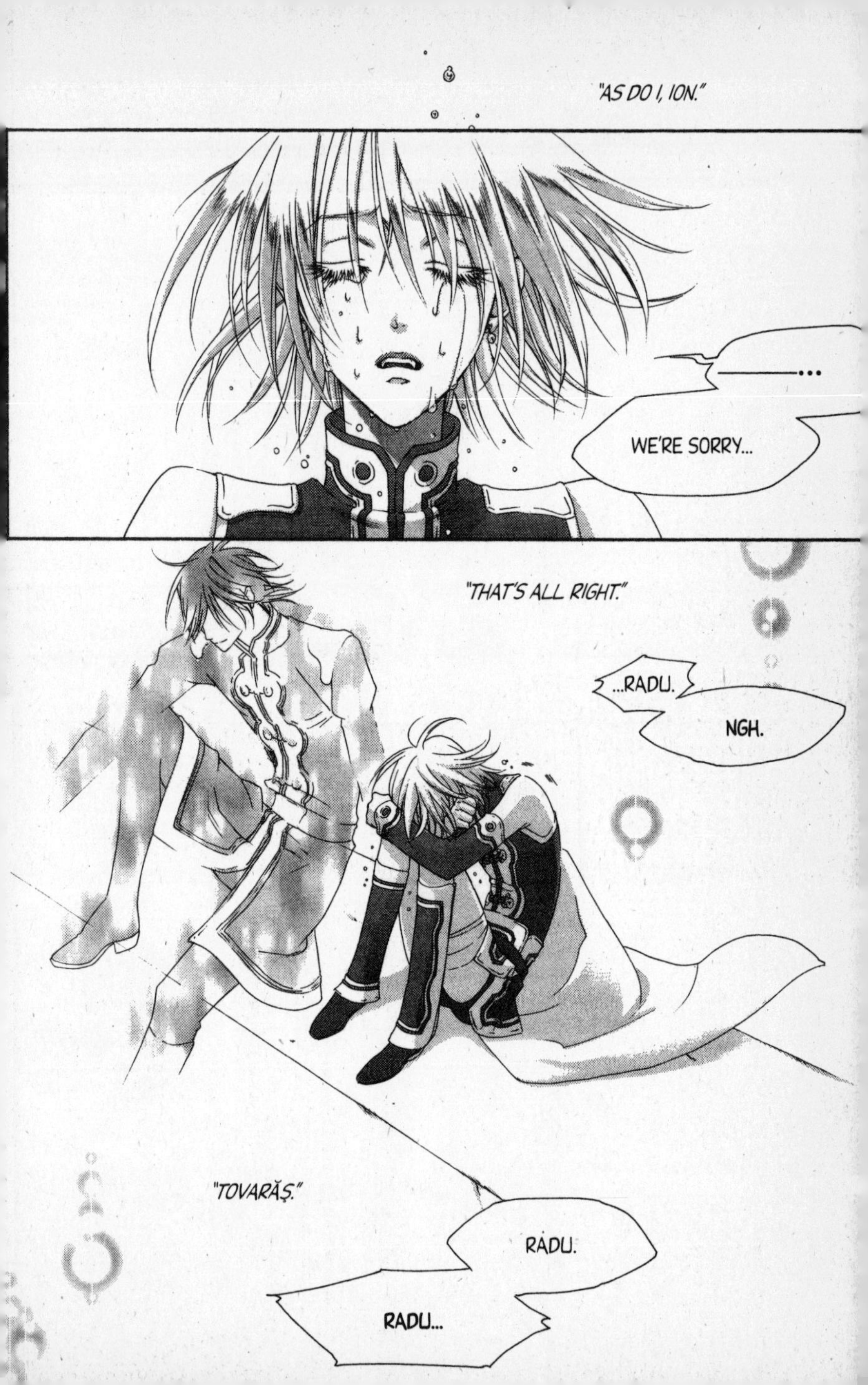
"AS DO I, ION."
———...
WE'RE SORRY...
"THAT'S ALL RIGHT."
...RADU.
NGH.
"TOVARĂŞ."
RADU.
RADU...

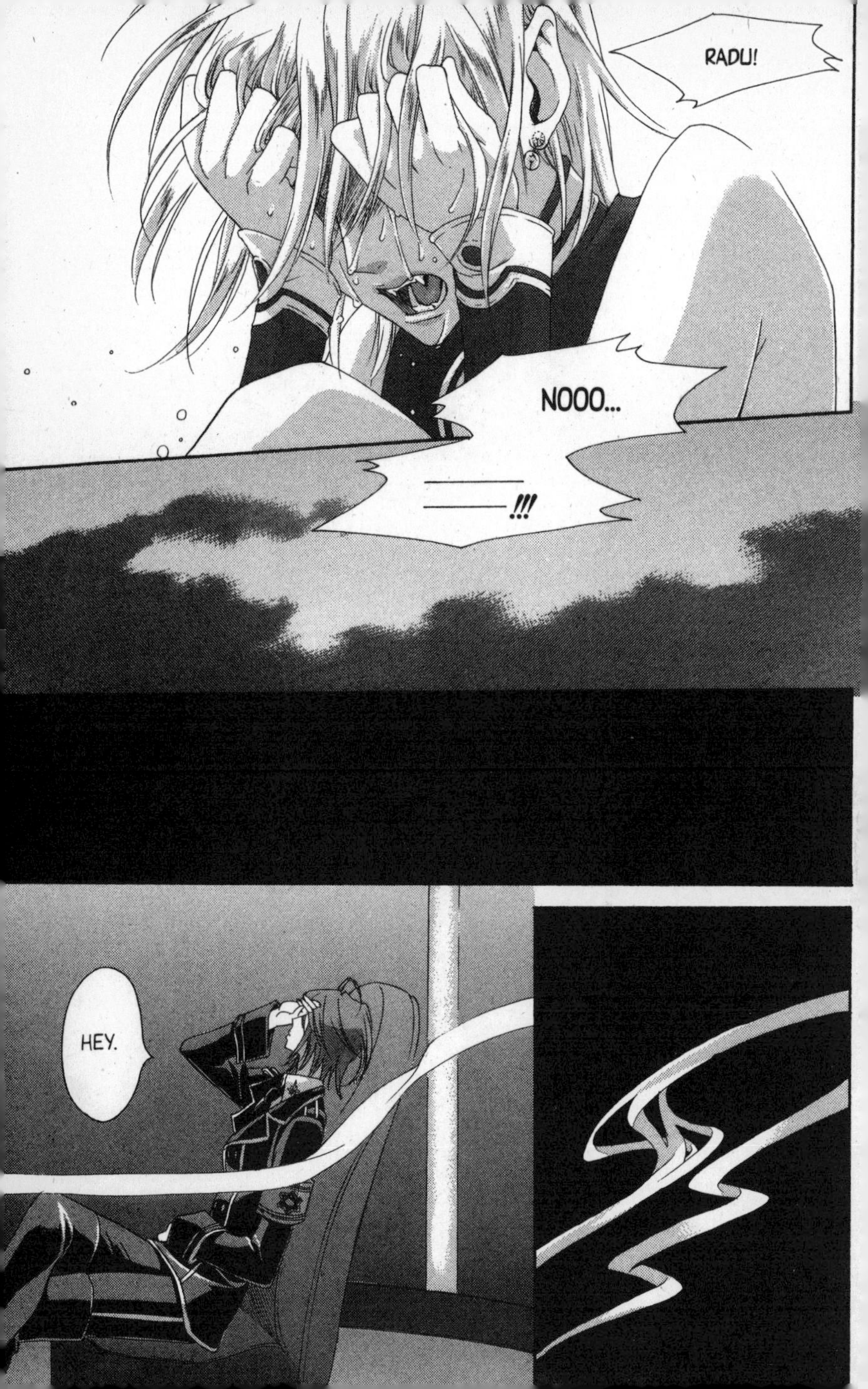
RADU!
NOOO...
———
———!!!
HEY.

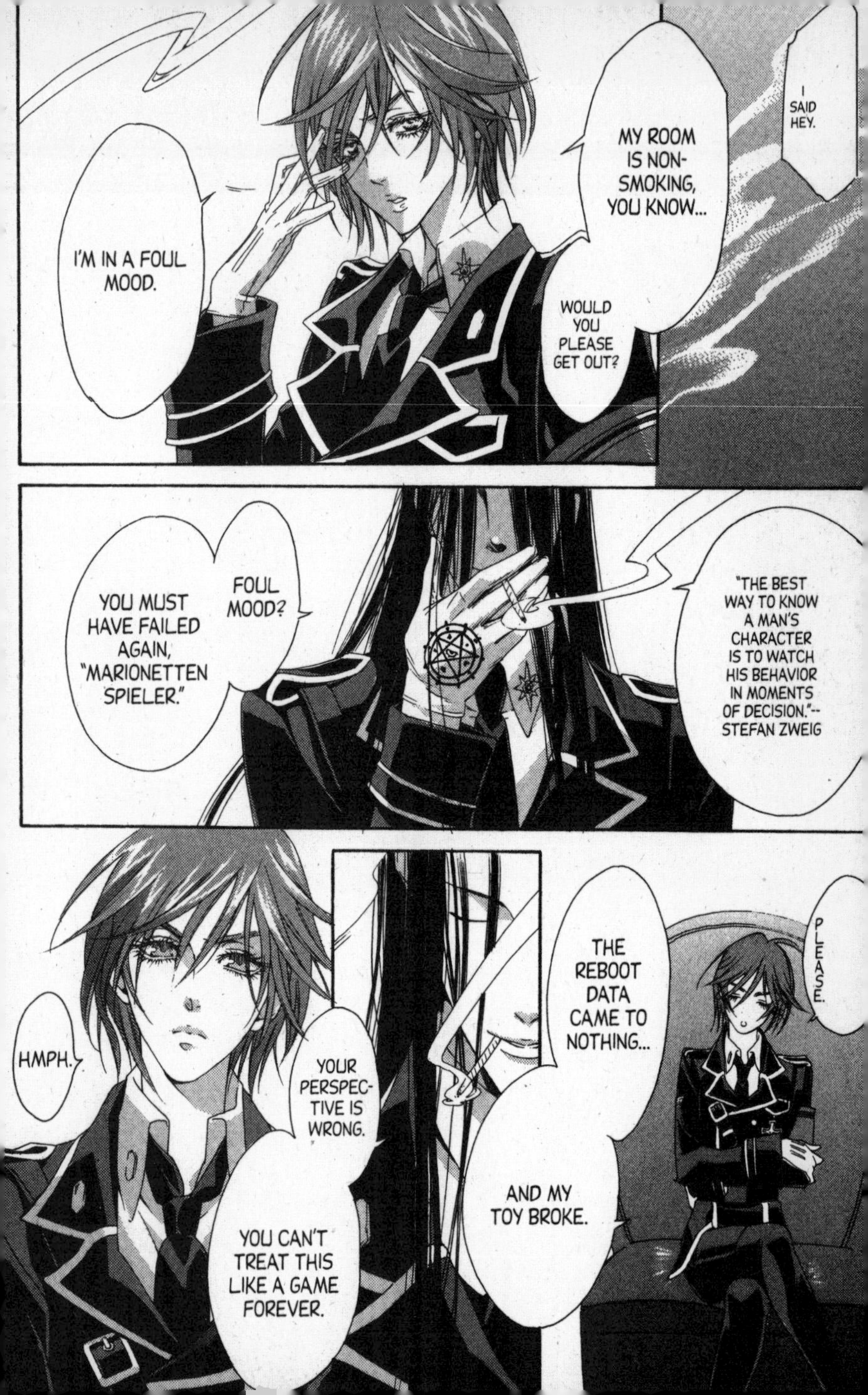
I SAID HEY.
MY ROOM IS NON-SMOKING, YOU KNOW...
WOULD YOU PLEASE GET OUT?
I'M IN A FOUL MOOD.
"THE BEST WAY TO KNOW A MAN'S CHARACTER IS TO WATCH HIS BEHAVIOR IN MOMENTS OF DECISION."-- STEFAN ZWEIG
FOUL MOOD?
YOU MUST HAVE FAILED AGAIN, "MARIONETTEN SPIELER."
PLEASE.
THE REBOOT DATA CAME TO NOTHING...
AND MY TOY BROKE.
YOUR PERSPECTIVE IS WRONG.
YOU CAN'T TREAT THIS LIKE A GAME FOREVER.
HMPH.

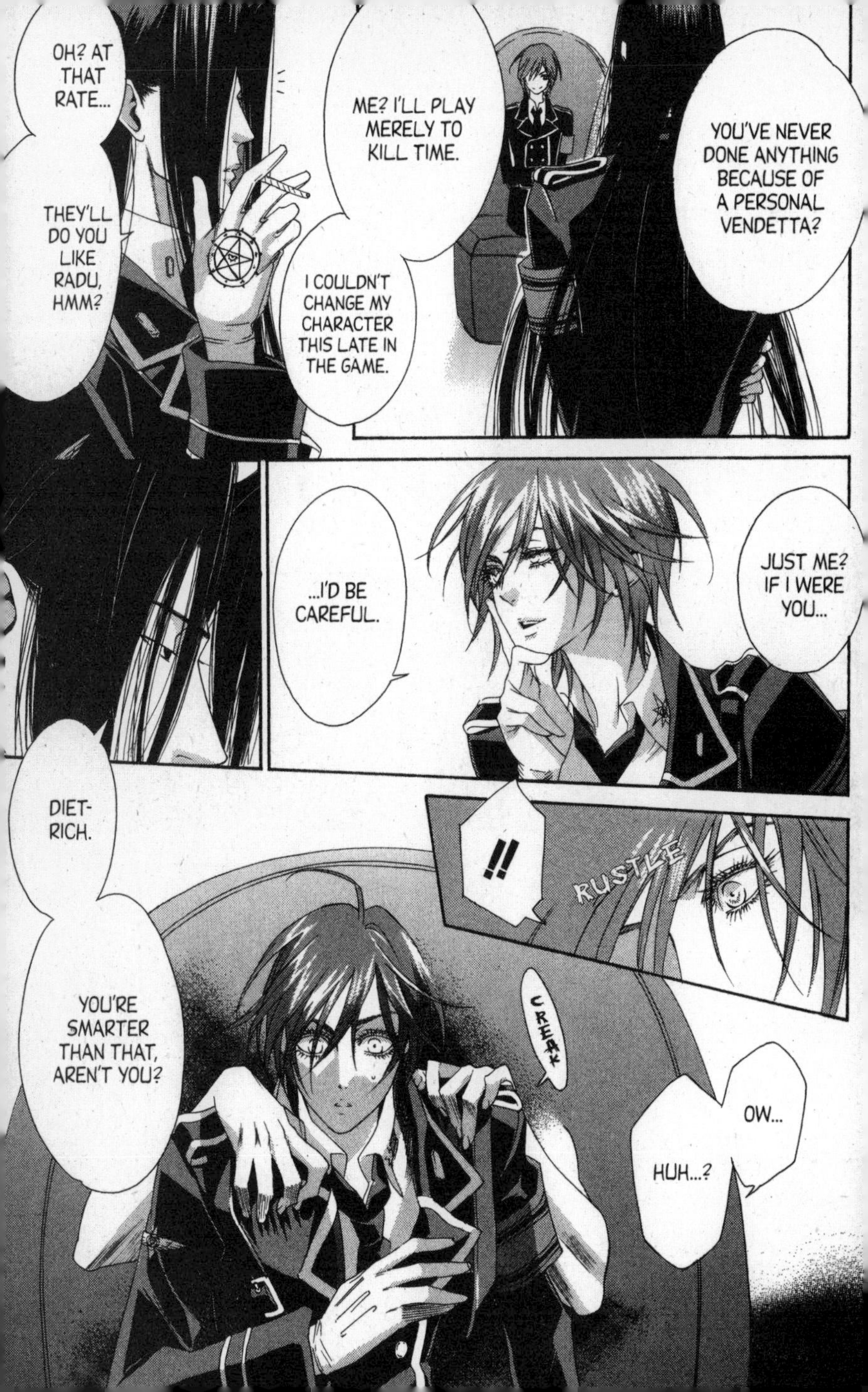

YOU'VE NEVER DONE ANYTHING BECAUSE OF A PERSONAL VENDETTA?
ME? I'LL PLAY MERELY TO KILL TIME.
I COULDN'T CHANGE MY CHARACTER THIS LATE IN THE GAME.
OH? AT THAT RATE...
THEY'LL DO YOU LIKE RADU, HMM?
JUST ME? IF I WERE YOU...
...I'D BE CAREFUL.
!!
RUSTLE
DIET-RICH.
YOU'RE SMARTER THAN THAT, AREN'T YOU?
CREAK
OW...
HUH...?

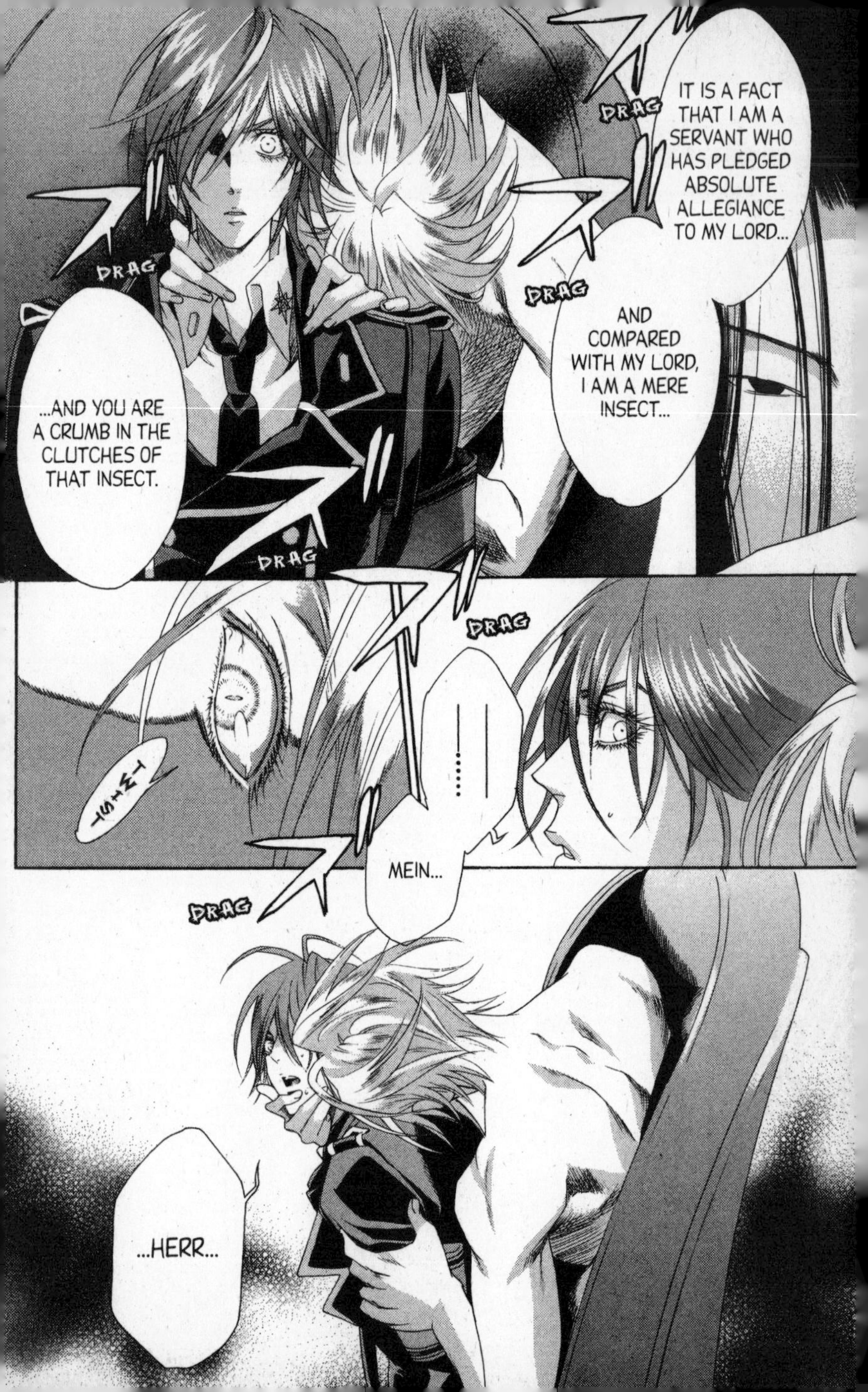
DRAG
IT IS A FACT THAT I AM A SERVANT WHO HAS PLEDGED ABSOLUTE ALLEGIANCE TO MY LORD...
DRAG
AND COMPARED WITH MY LORD, I AM A MERE INSECT...
DRAG
...AND YOU ARE A CRUMB IN THE CLUTCHES OF THAT INSECT.
DRAG
DRAG
......
TWITCH
MEIN...
DRAG
...HERR...

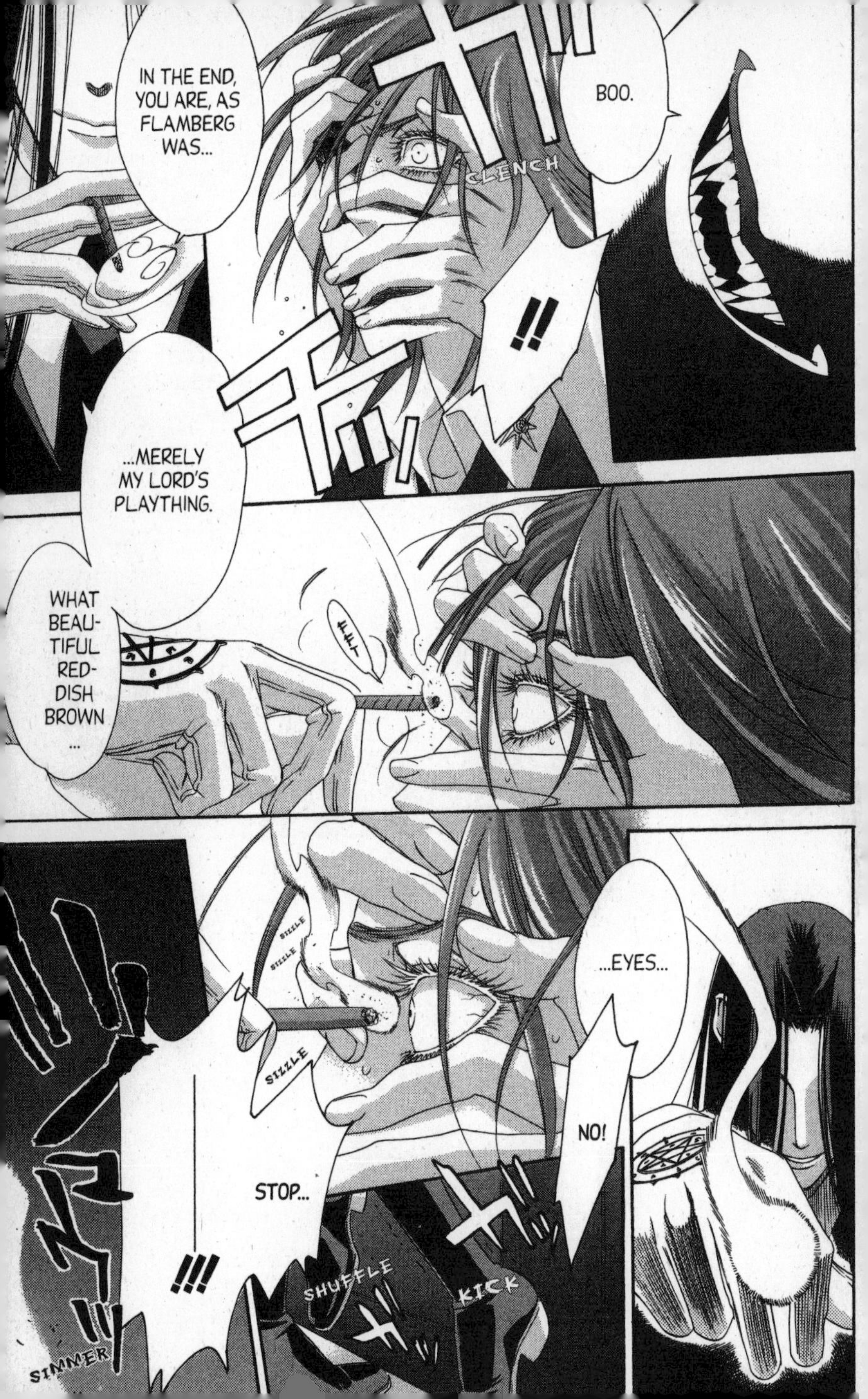
BOO.
CLENCH
!!
IN THE END, YOU ARE, AS FLAMBERG WAS...
...MERELY MY LORD'S PLAYTHING.
FFT
WHAT BEAUTIFUL REDDISH BROWN...
...EYES...
NO!
SIZZLE
SIZZLE
SIZZLE
STOP...
!!!
KICK
SHUFFLE
SIMMER

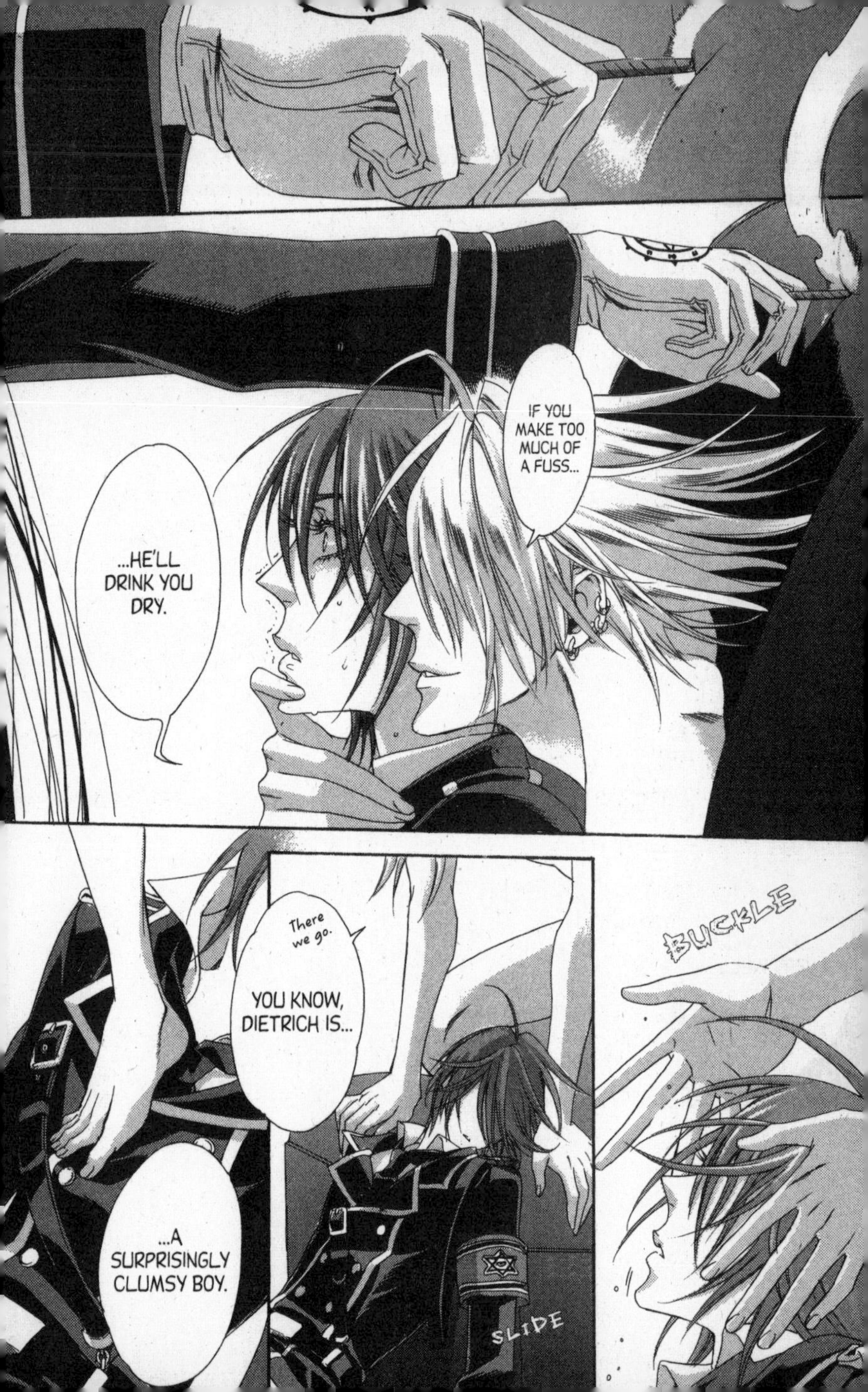
IF YOU MAKE TOO MUCH OF A FUSS...
...HE'LL DRINK YOU DRY.
BUCKLE
There we go.
YOU KNOW, DIETRICH IS...
SLIDE
...A SURPRISINGLY CLUMSY BOY.

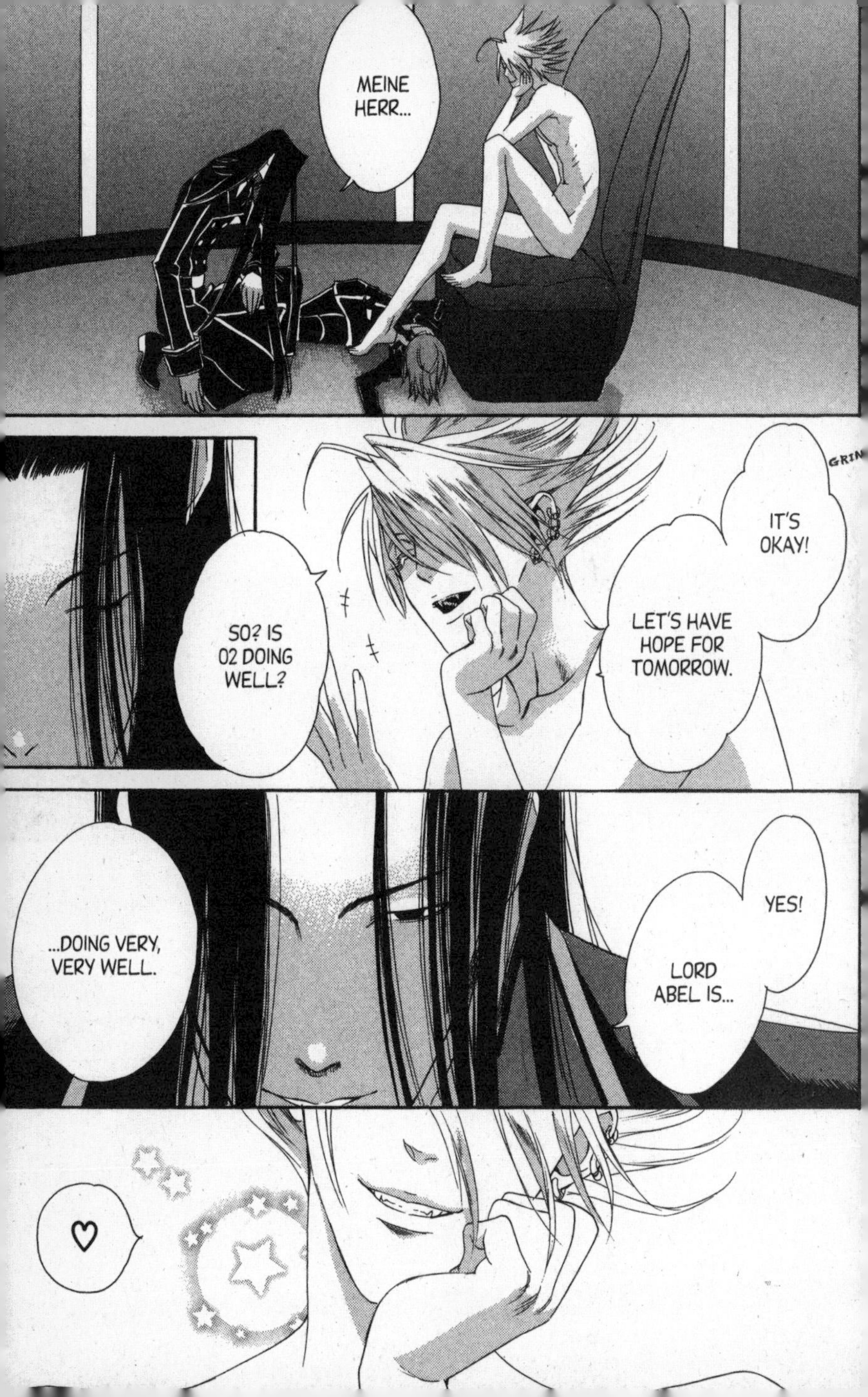
MEINE HERR...
GRIN
IT'S OKAY!
LET'S HAVE HOPE FOR TOMORROW.
SO? IS 02 DOING WELL?
YES!
LORD ABEL IS...
...DOING VERY, VERY WELL.
♡

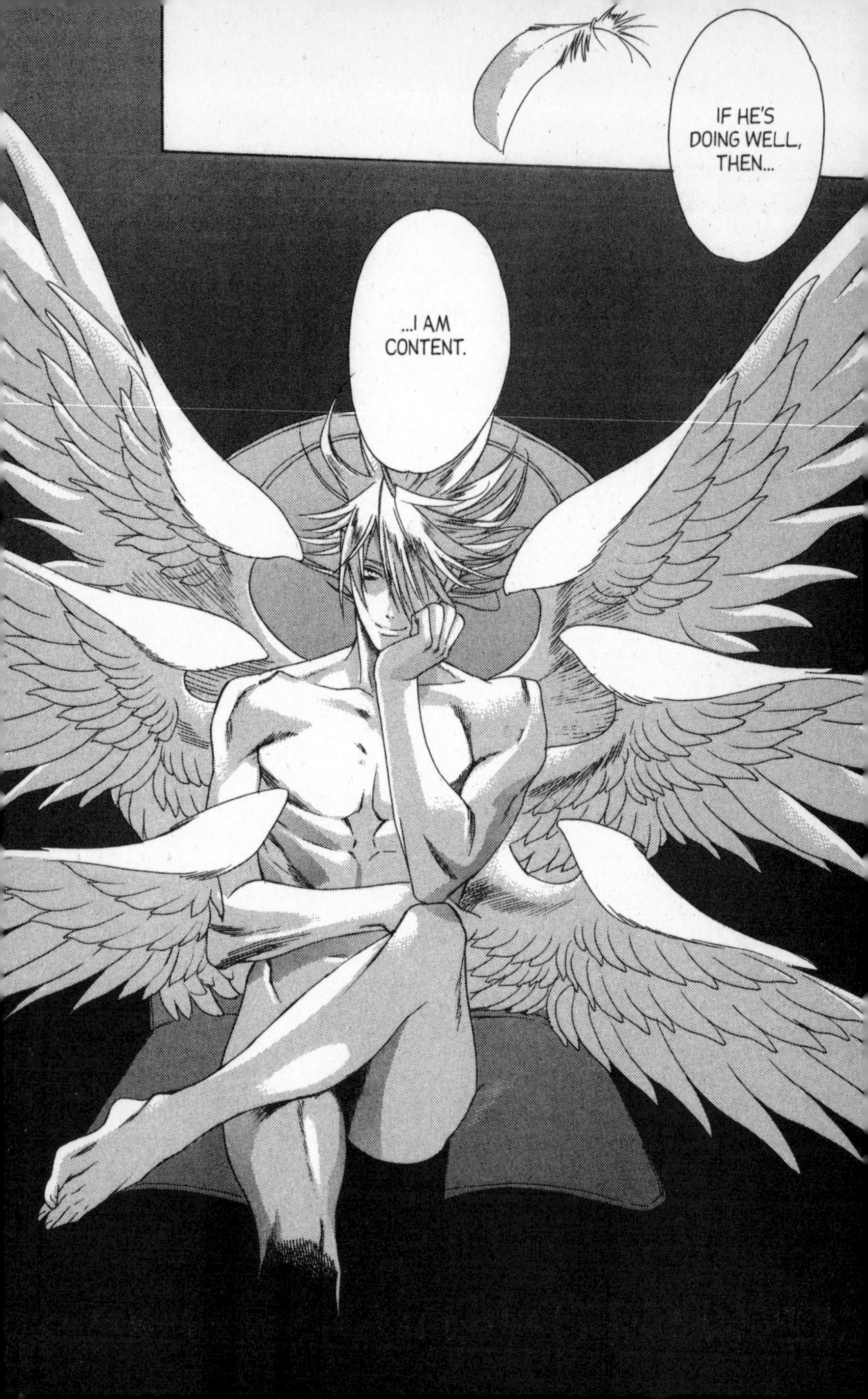
IF HE'S DOING WELL, THEN...
...I AM CONTENT.

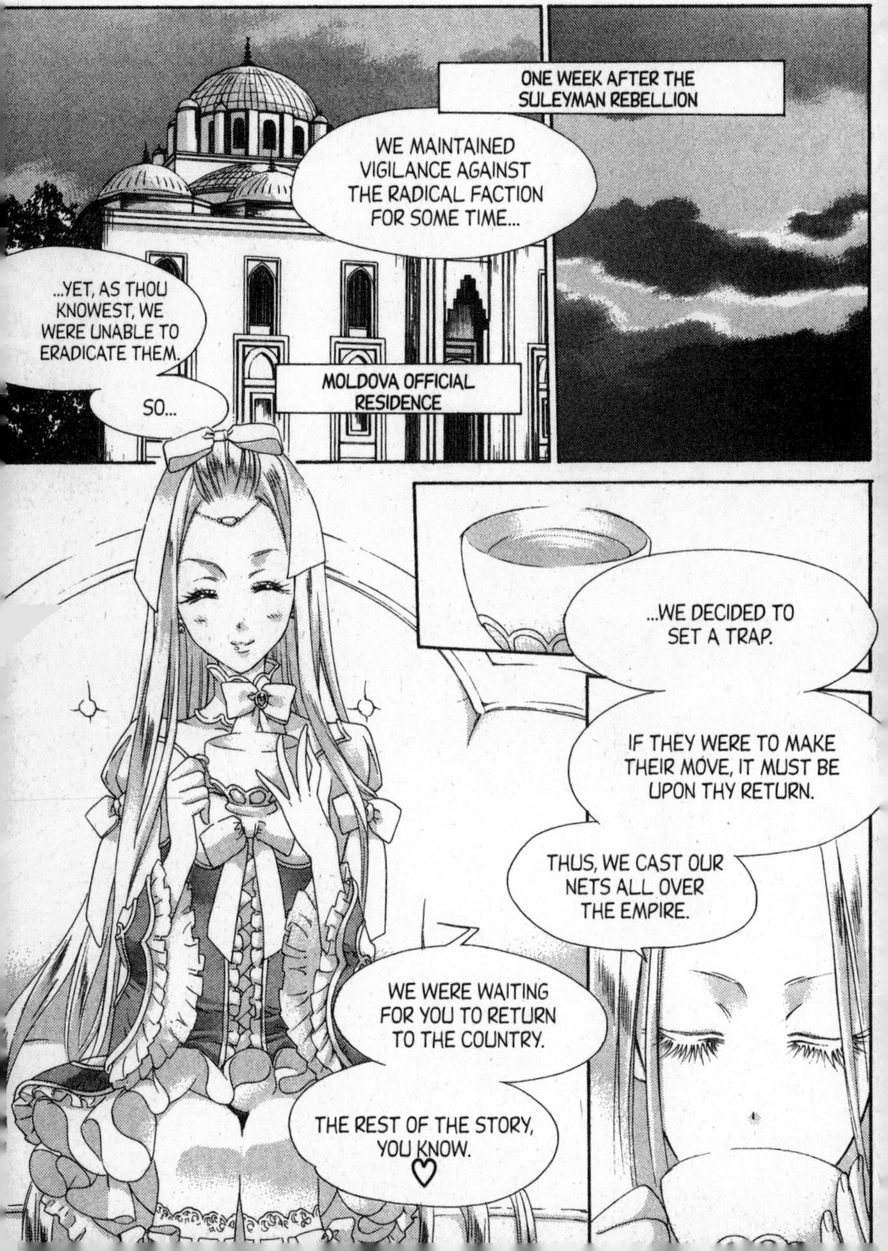
ONE WEEK AFTER THE SULEYMAN REBELLION
MOLDOVA OFFICIAL RESIDENCE
WE MAINTAINED VIGILANCE AGAINST THE RADICAL FACTION FOR SOME TIME...
...YET, AS THOU KNOWEST, WE WERE UNABLE TO ERADICATE THEM.
SO...
...WE DECIDED TO SET A TRAP.
IF THEY WERE TO MAKE THEIR MOVE, IT MUST BE UPON THY RETURN.
THUS, WE CAST OUR NETS ALL OVER THE EMPIRE.
WE WERE WAITING FOR YOU TO RETURN TO THE COUNTRY.
THE REST OF THE STORY, YOU KNOW. ♡

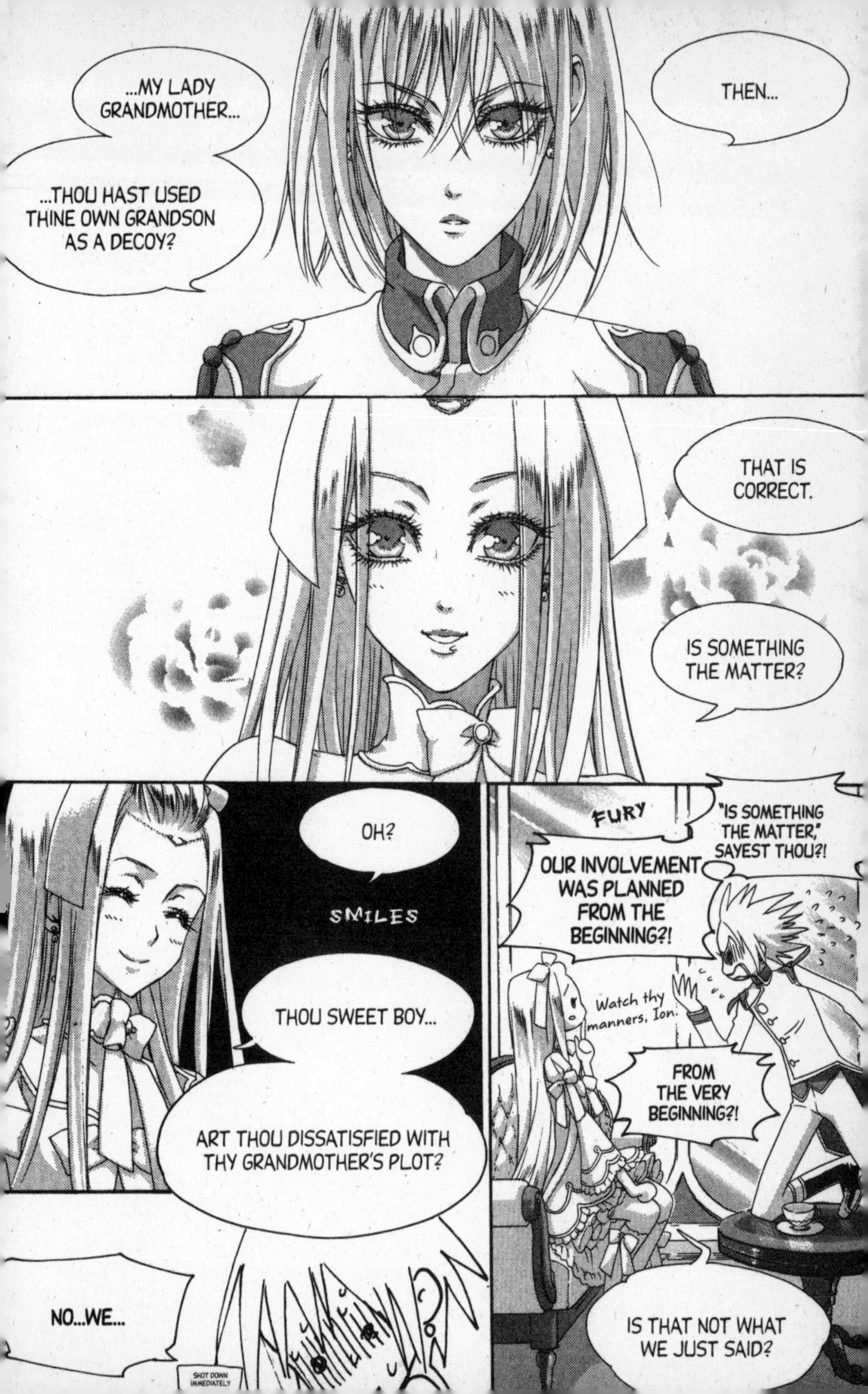
THEN...
...MY LADY GRANDMOTHER...
...THOU HAST USED THINE OWN GRANDSON AS A DECOY?
THAT IS CORRECT.
IS SOMETHING THE MATTER?
FURY
"IS SOMETHING THE MATTER," SAYEST THOU?!
OUR INVOLVEMENT WAS PLANNED FROM THE BEGINNING?!
Watch thy manners, Ion.
FROM THE VERY BEGINNING?!
IS THAT NOT WHAT WE JUST SAID?
OH?
SMILES
THOU SWEET BOY...
ART THOU DISSATISFIED WITH THY GRANDMOTHER'S PLOT?
NO...WE...
SHOT DOWN IMMEDIATELY

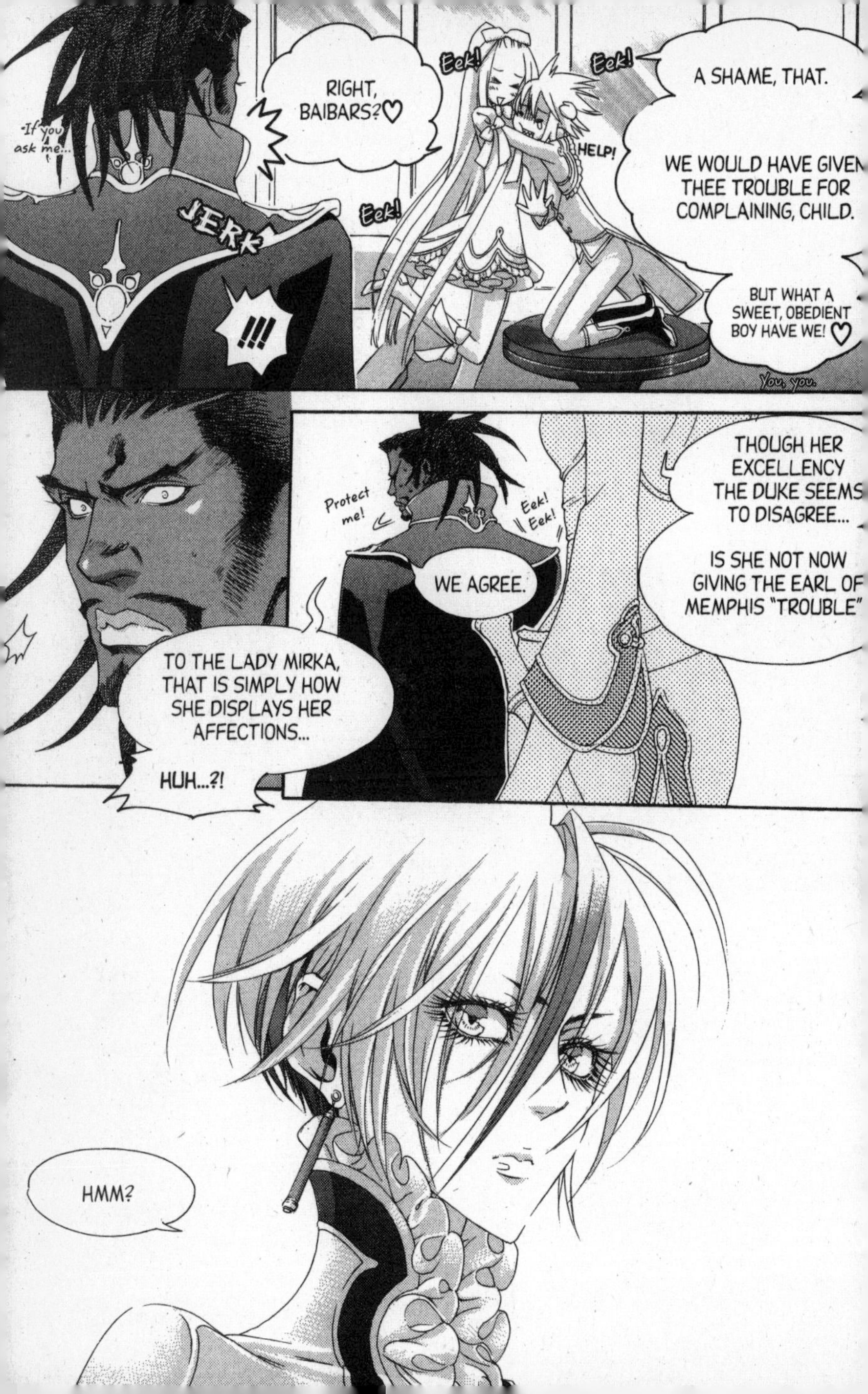
Eek!
A SHAME, THAT.
WE WOULD HAVE GIVEN THEE TROUBLE FOR COMPLAINING, CHILD.
BUT WHAT A SWEET, OBEDIENT BOY HAVE WE! ♡
You, you.
HELP!
Eek!
RIGHT, BAIBARS? ♡
Eek!
If you ask me...
JERK
!!!
THOUGH HER EXCELLENCY THE DUKE SEEMS TO DISAGREE...
IS SHE NOT NOW GIVING THE EARL OF MEMPHIS "TROUBLE"
Eek! Eek!
WE AGREE.
Protect me!
TO THE LADY MIRKA, THAT IS SIMPLY HOW SHE DISPLAYS HER AFFECTIONS...
HUH...?!
HMM?

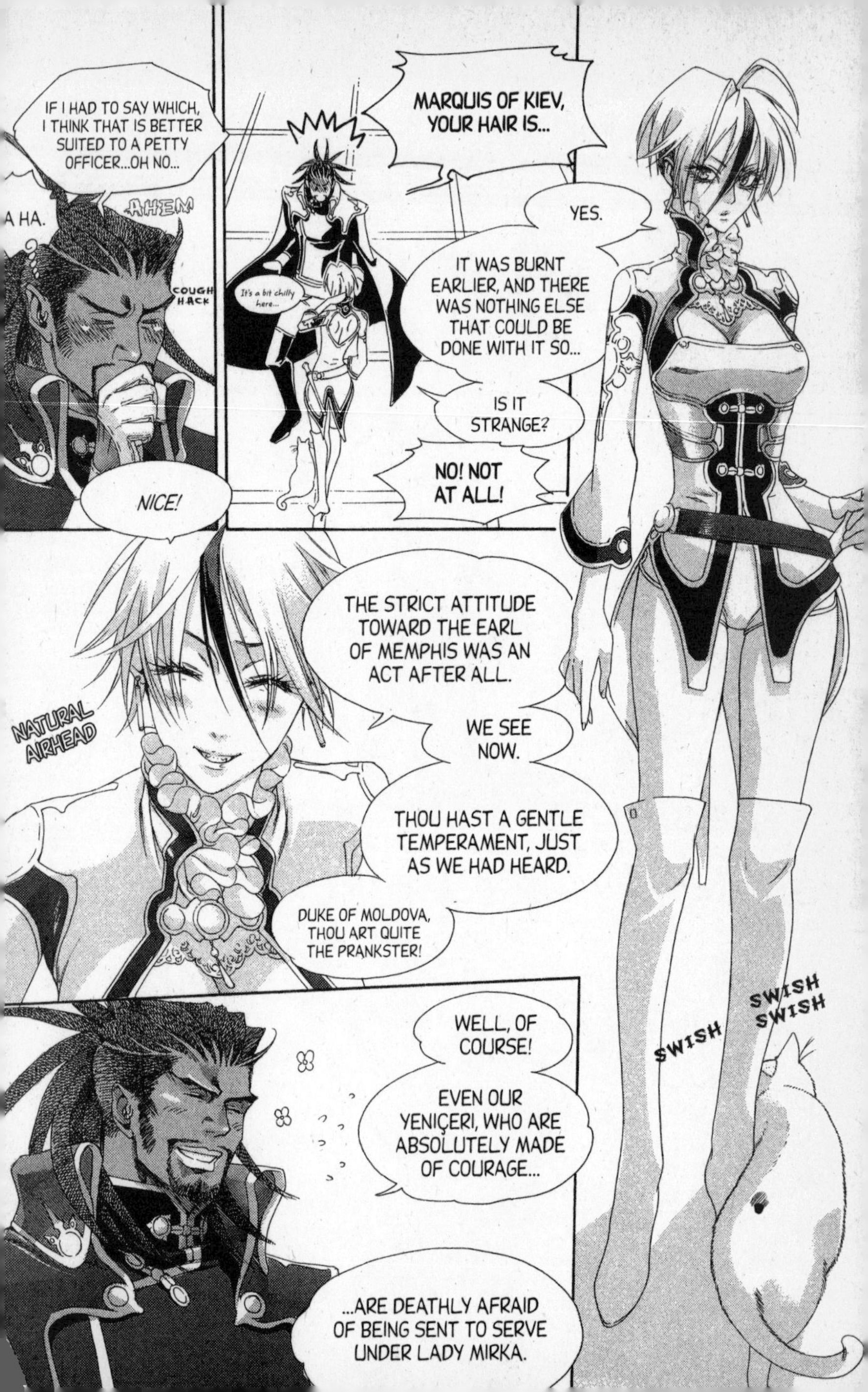
MARQUIS OF KIEV, YOUR HAIR IS...
YES.
IT WAS BURNT EARLIER, AND THERE WAS NOTHING ELSE THAT COULD BE DONE WITH IT SO...
IS IT STRANGE?
NO! NOT AT ALL!
It's a bit chilly here...
IF I HAD TO SAY WHICH, I THINK THAT IS BETTER SUITED TO A PETTY OFFICER...OH NO...
AHEM
A HA.
COUGH HACK
NICE!
THE STRICT ATTITUDE TOWARD THE EARL OF MEMPHIS WAS AN ACT AFTER ALL.
WE SEE NOW.
THOU HAST A GENTLE TEMPERAMENT, JUST AS WE HAD HEARD.
DUKE OF MOLDOVA, THOU ART QUITE THE PRANKSTER!
NATURAL AIRHEAD
SWISH SWISH
SWISH
WELL, OF COURSE!
EVEN OUR YENIÇERI, WHO ARE ABSOLUTELY MADE OF COURAGE...
...ARE DEATHLY AFRAID OF BEING SENT TO SERVE UNDER LADY MIRKA.

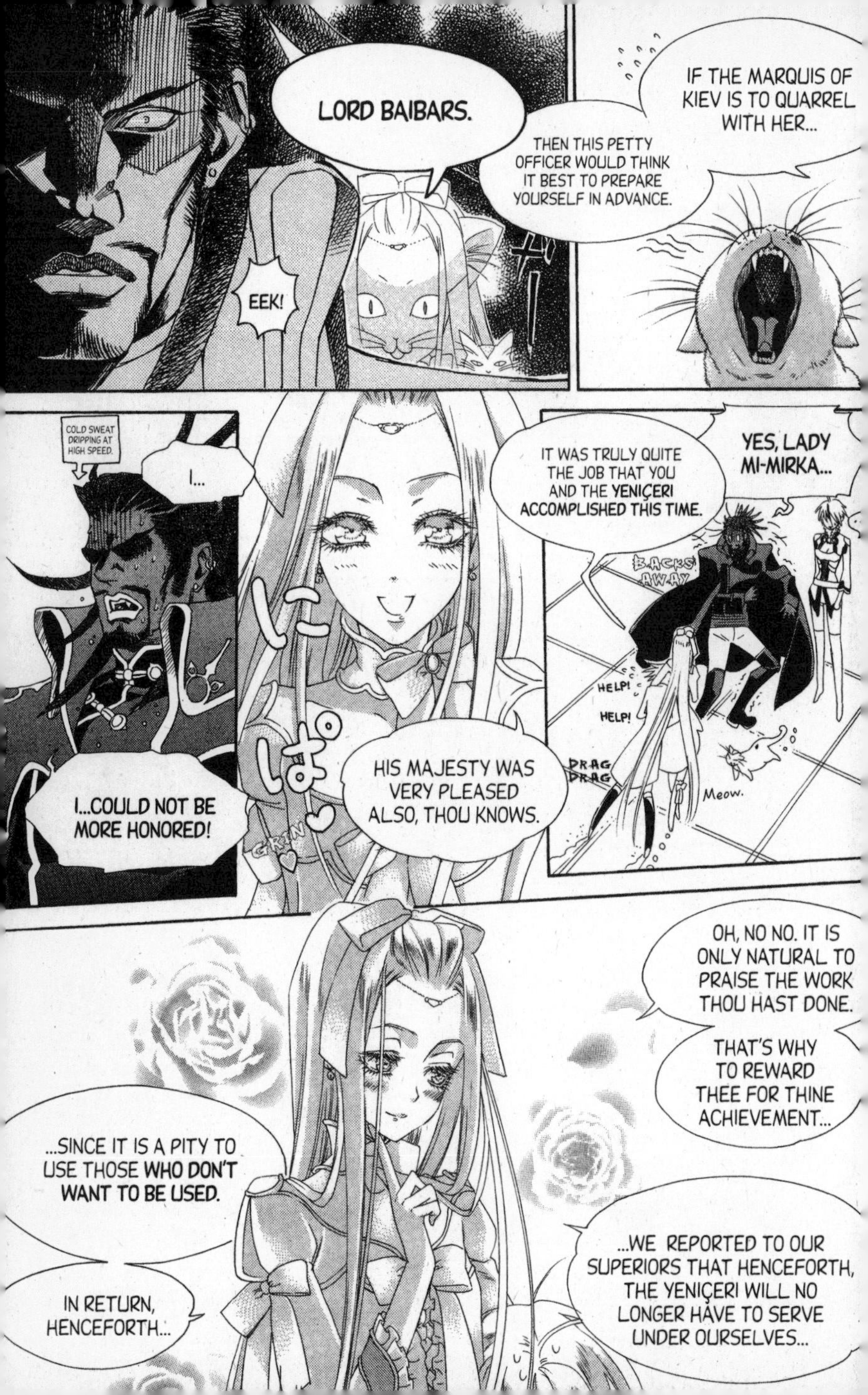

IF THE MARQUIS OF KIEV IS TO QUARREL WITH HER...
THEN THIS PETTY OFFICER WOULD THINK IT BEST TO PREPARE YOURSELF IN ADVANCE.
LORD BAIBARS.
EEK!
YES, LADY MI-MIRKA...
IT WAS TRULY QUITE THE JOB THAT YOU AND THE YENIÇERI ACCOMPLISHED THIS TIME.
BACKS AWAY
HELP!
HELP!
DRAG DRAG
Meow.
にぱ
GRIN
HIS MAJESTY WAS VERY PLEASED ALSO, THOU KNOWS.
COLD SWEAT DRIPPING AT HIGH SPEED.
I...
I...COULD NOT BE MORE HONORED!
OH, NO NO. IT IS ONLY NATURAL TO PRAISE THE WORK THOU HAST DONE.
THAT'S WHY TO REWARD THEE FOR THINE ACHIEVEMENT...
...WE REPORTED TO OUR SUPERIORS THAT HENCEFORTH, THE YENIÇERI WILL NO LONGER HAVE TO SERVE UNDER OURSELVES...
...SINCE IT IS A PITY TO USE THOSE WHO DON'T WANT TO BE USED.
IN RETURN, HENCEFORTH...

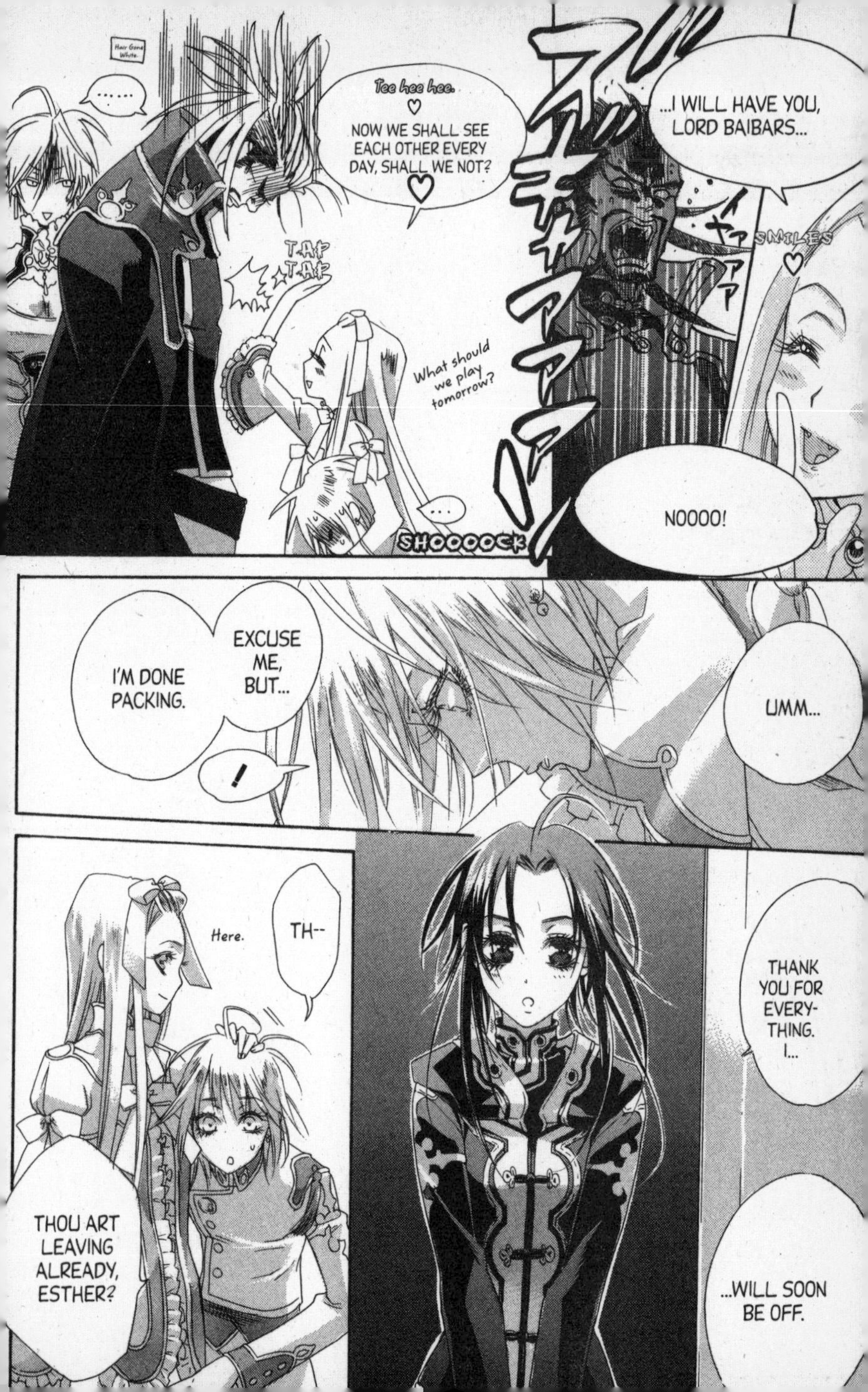
...I WILL HAVE YOU, LORD BAIBARS...
SMILES ♡
NOOOO!
Tee hee hee. ♡
NOW WE SHALL SEE EACH OTHER EVERY DAY, SHALL WE NOT? ♡
Hair Gone White.
......
TAP TAP
What should we play tomorrow?
...
SHOOOOCK
UMM...
EXCUSE ME, BUT...
I'M DONE PACKING.
!
THANK YOU FOR EVERY-THING. I...
...WILL SOON BE OFF.
TH--
Here.
THOU ART LEAVING ALREADY, ESTHER?

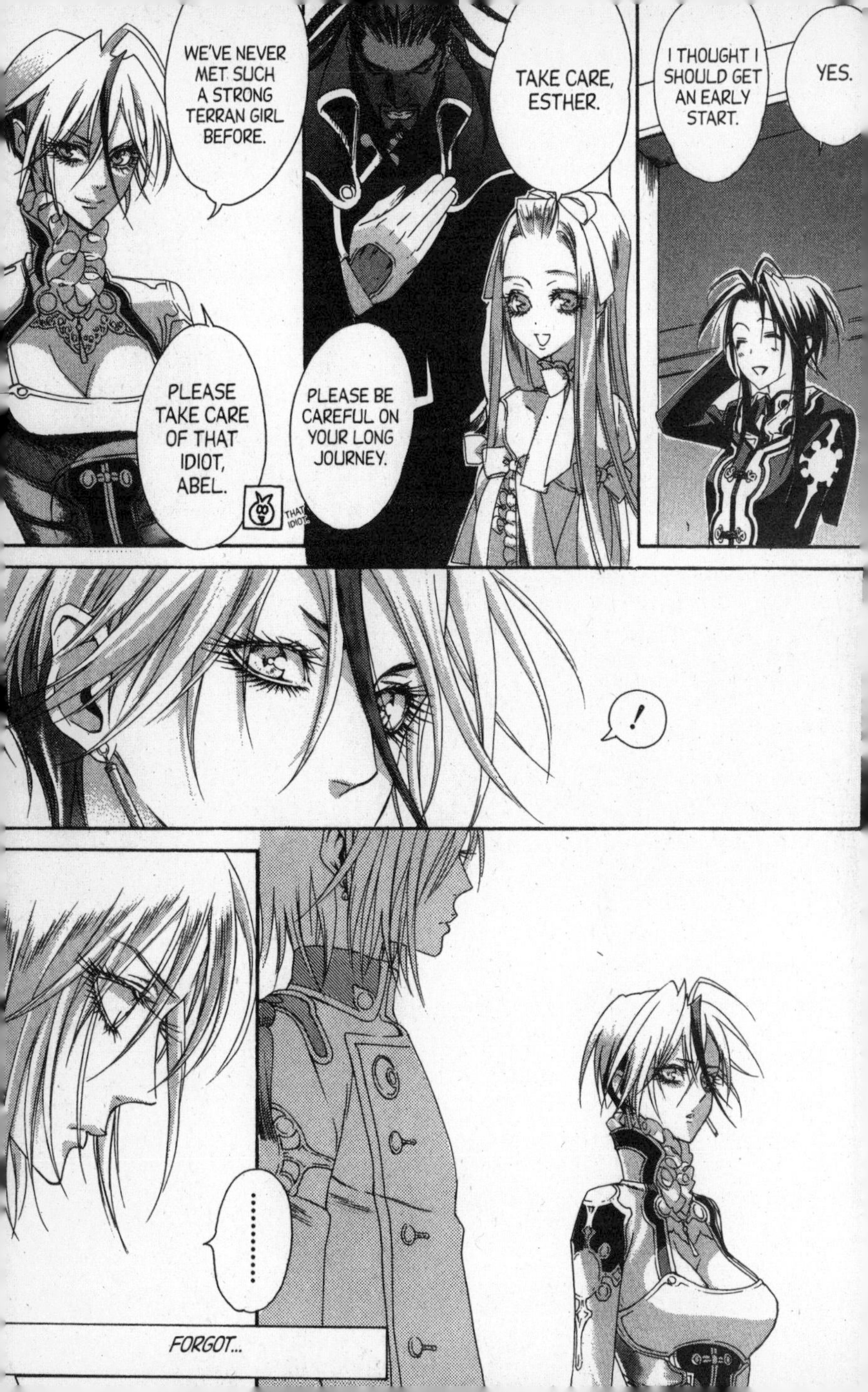
YES.
I THOUGHT I SHOULD GET AN EARLY START.
TAKE CARE, ESTHER.
PLEASE BE CAREFUL ON YOUR LONG JOURNEY.
WE'VE NEVER MET SUCH A STRONG TERRAN GIRL BEFORE.
PLEASE TAKE CARE OF THAT IDIOT, ABEL.
THAT IDIOT.
!
......
FORGOT...

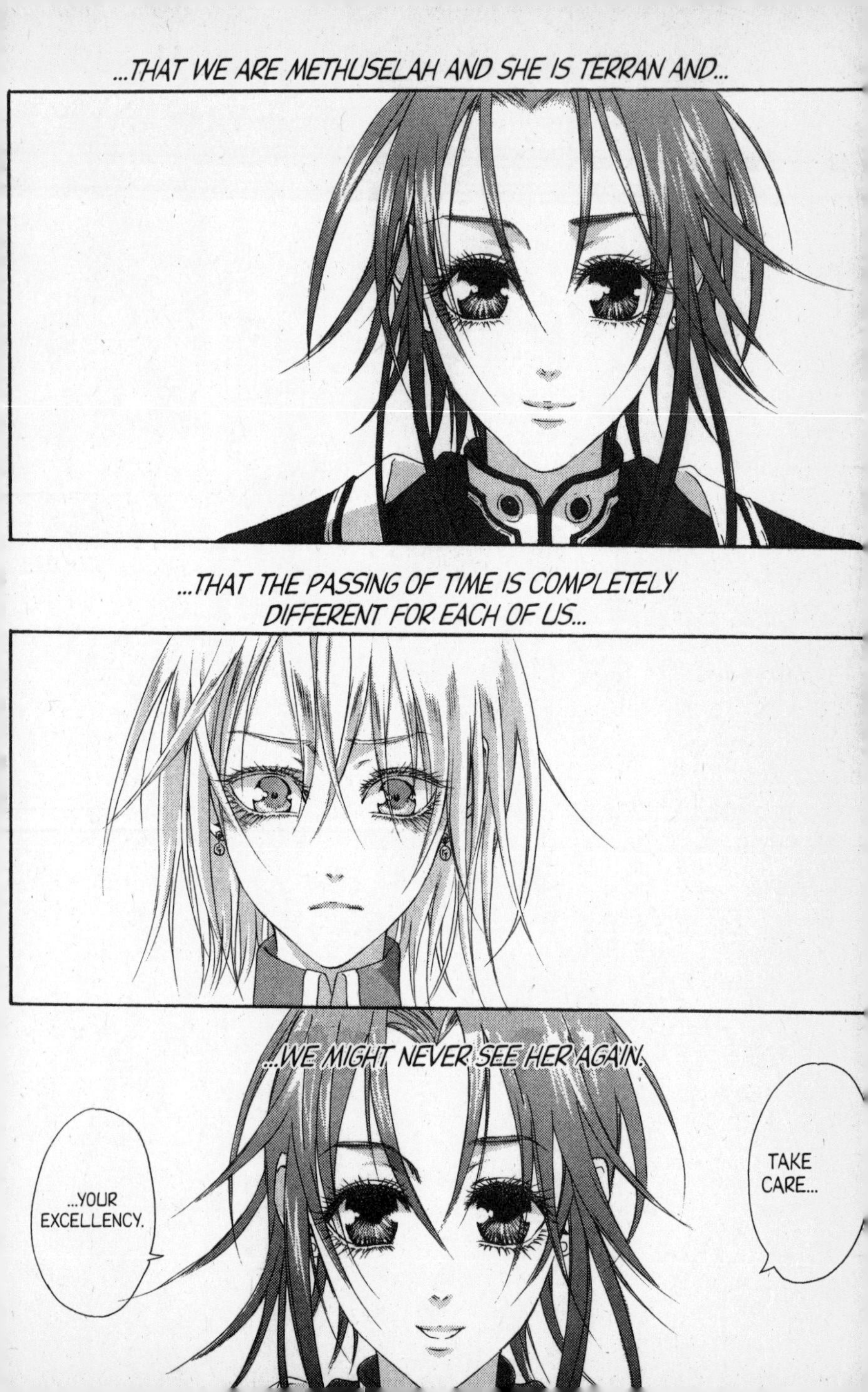
...THAT WE ARE METHUSELAH AND SHE IS TERRAN AND...
...THAT THE PASSING OF TIME IS COMPLETELY DIFFERENT FOR EACH OF US...
...WE MIGHT NEVER SEE HER AGAIN.
TAKE CARE...
...YOUR EXCELLENCY.

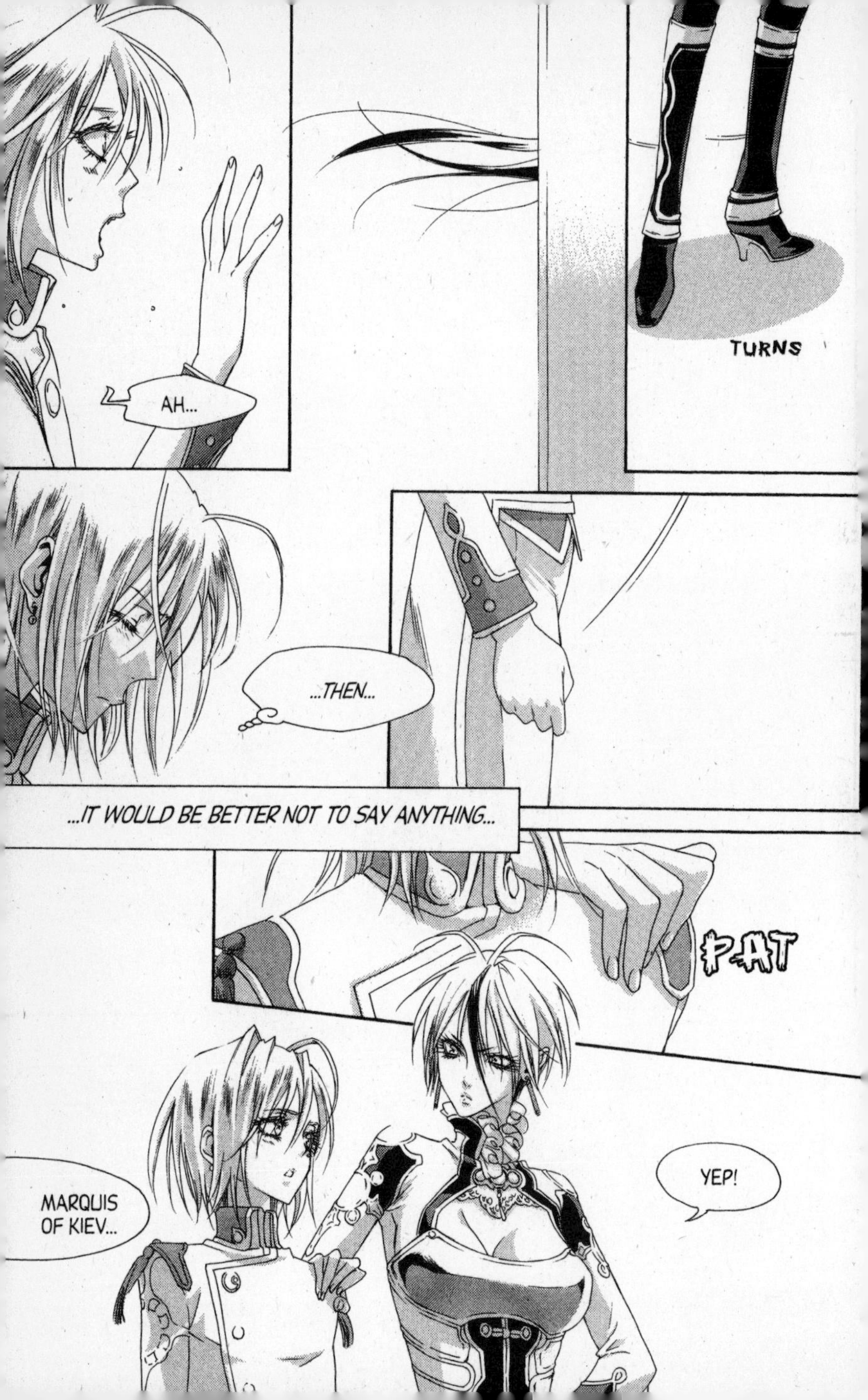
TURNS
AH...
...THEN...
...IT WOULD BE BETTER NOT TO SAY ANYTHING...
PAT
YEP!
MARQUIS OF KIEV...

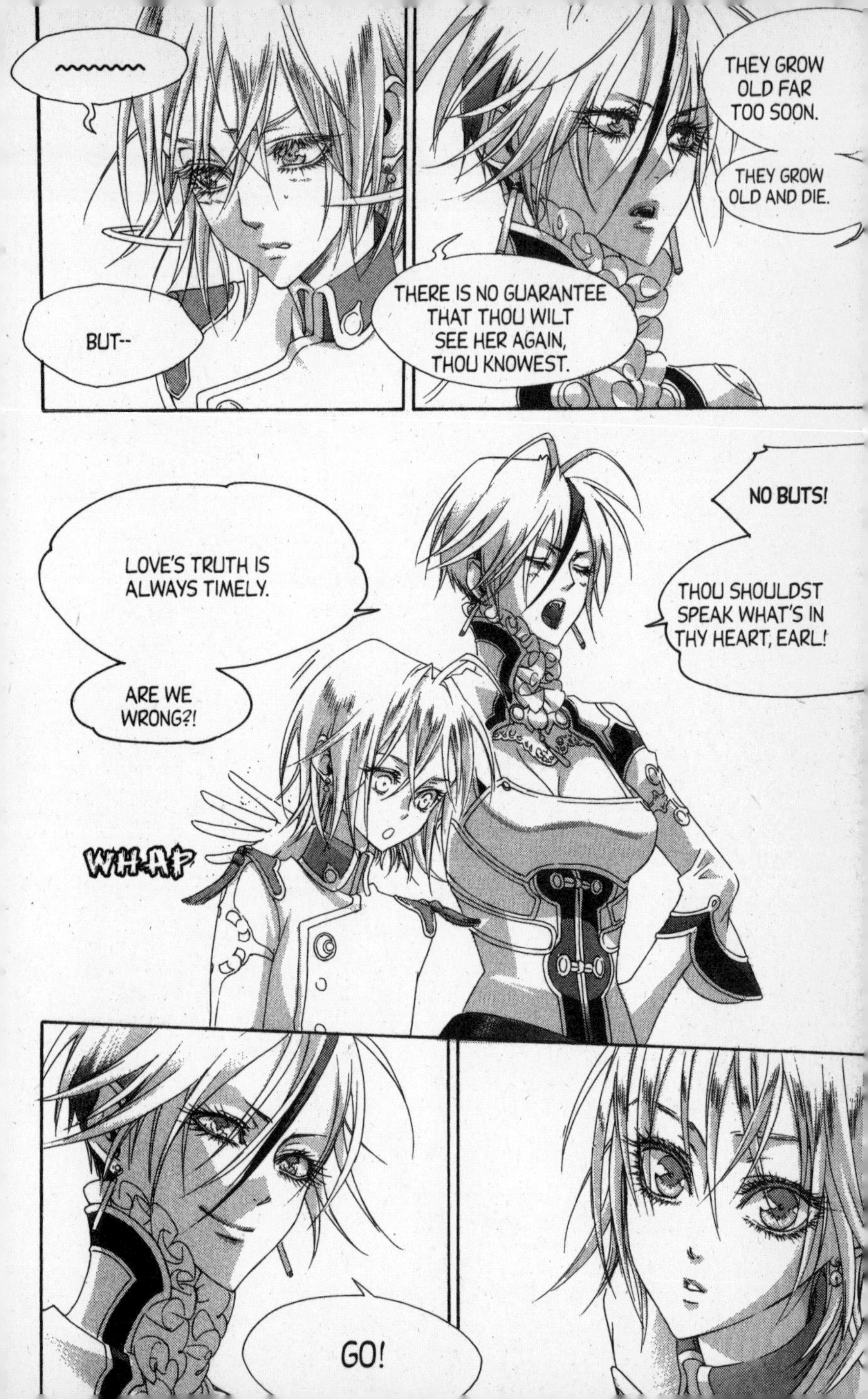
THEY GROW OLD FAR TOO SOON.
THEY GROW OLD AND DIE.
THERE IS NO GUARANTEE THAT THOU WILT SEE HER AGAIN, THOU KNOWEST.
BUT--
NO BUTS!
THOU SHOULDST SPEAK WHAT'S IN THY HEART, EARL!
LOVE'S TRUTH IS ALWAYS TIMELY.
ARE WE WRONG?!
WHAP
GO!

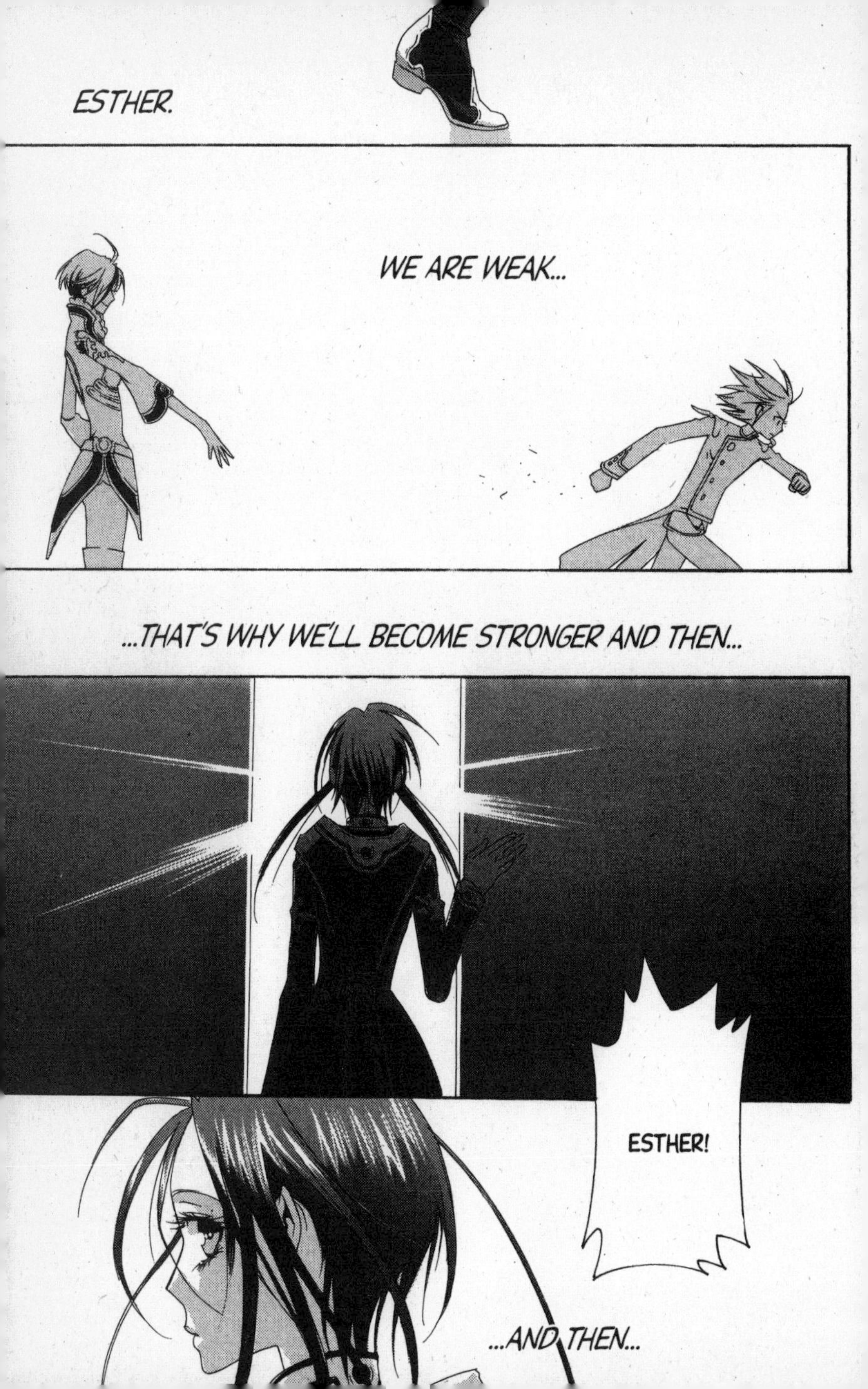
ESTHER.
WE ARE WEAK...
...THAT'S WHY WE'LL BECOME STRONGER AND THEN...
ESTHER!
...AND THEN...

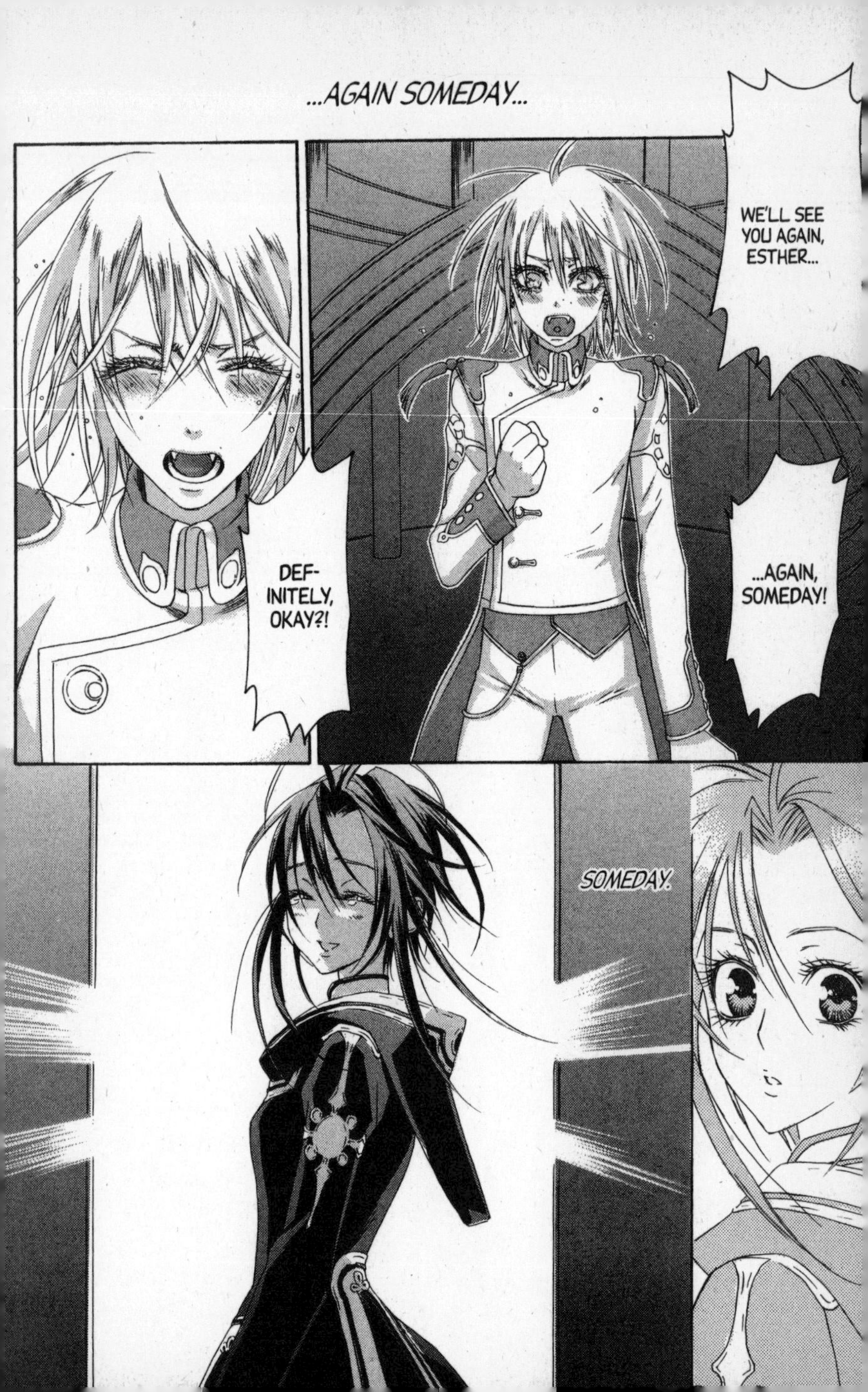
...AGAIN SOMEDAY...
WE'LL SEE YOU AGAIN, ESTHER...
...AGAIN, SOMEDAY!
DEF-INITELY, OKAY?!
SOMEDAY.

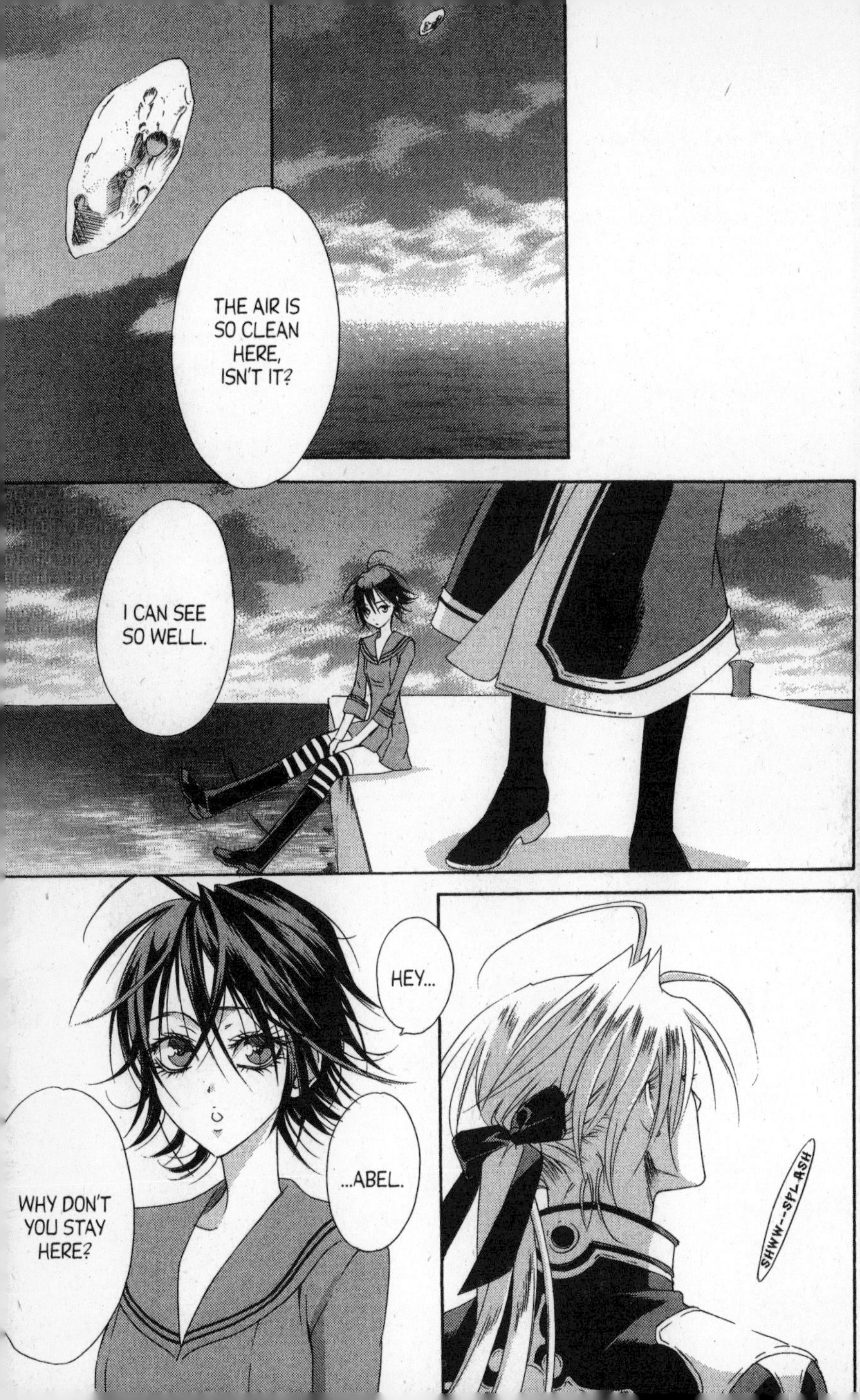
THE AIR IS SO CLEAN HERE, ISN'T IT?
I CAN SEE SO WELL.
SHWW--SPLASH
HEY...
...ABEL.
WHY DON'T YOU STAY HERE?

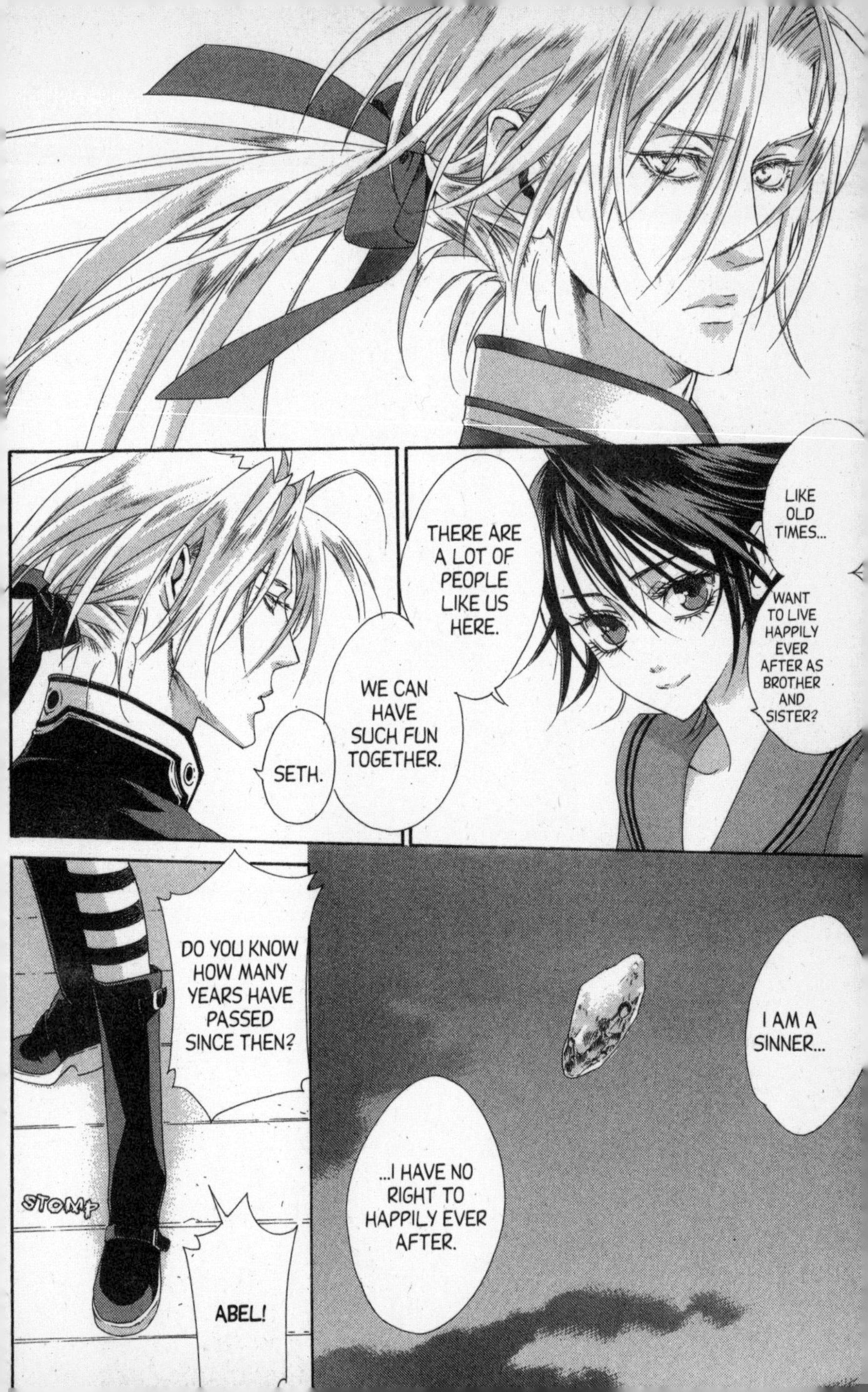
LIKE OLD TIMES...
WANT TO LIVE HAPPILY EVER AFTER AS BROTHER AND SISTER?
THERE ARE A LOT OF PEOPLE LIKE US HERE.
WE CAN HAVE SUCH FUN TOGETHER.
SETH.
I AM A SINNER...
...I HAVE NO RIGHT TO HAPPILY EVER AFTER.
DO YOU KNOW HOW MANY YEARS HAVE PASSED SINCE THEN?
STOMP
ABEL!

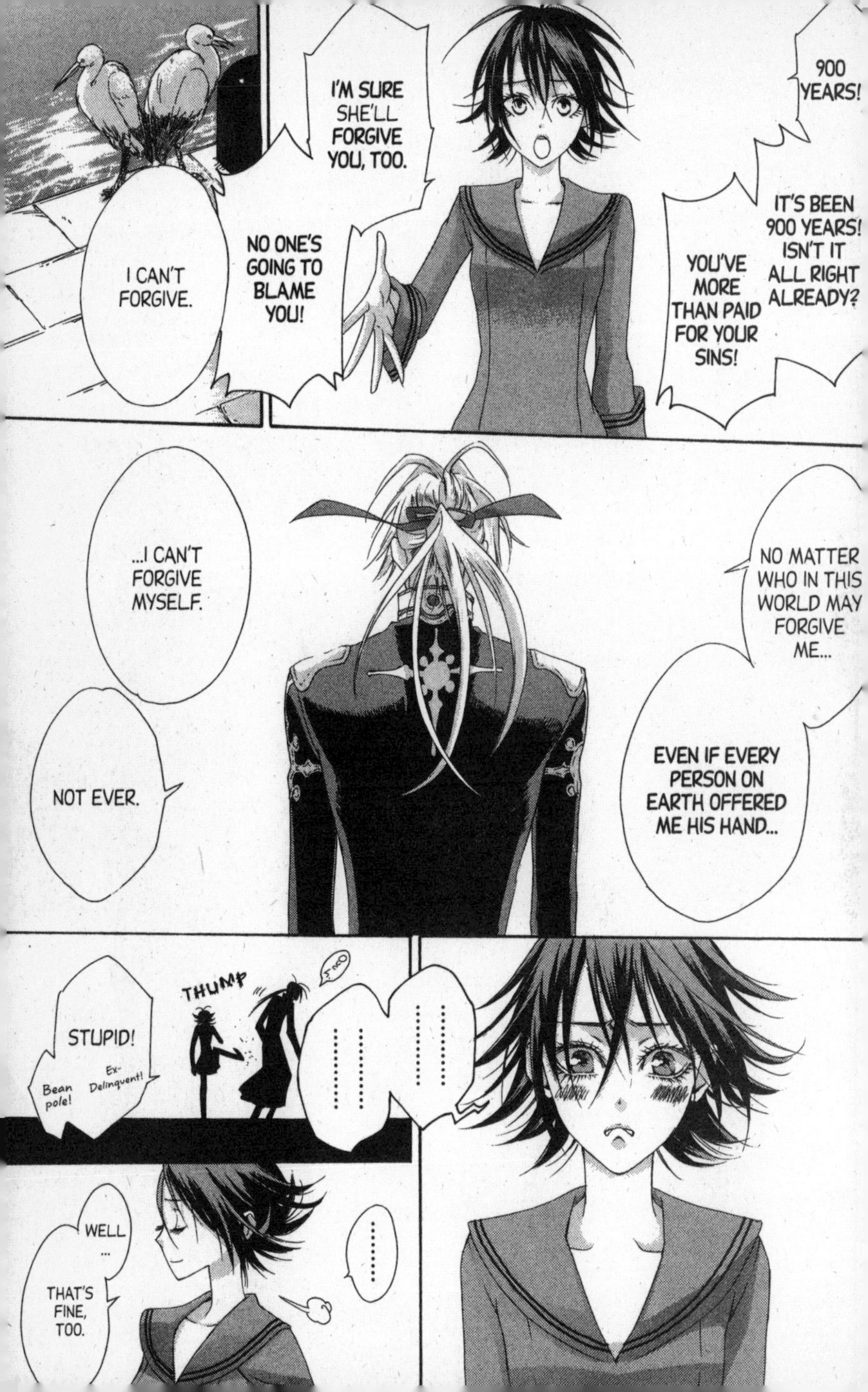

900 YEARS!
IT'S BEEN 900 YEARS! ISN'T IT ALL RIGHT ALREADY?
YOU'VE MORE THAN PAID FOR YOUR SINS!
I'M SURE SHE'LL FORGIVE YOU, TOO.
NO ONE'S GOING TO BLAME YOU!
I CAN'T FORGIVE.
NO MATTER WHO IN THIS WORLD MAY FORGIVE ME...
EVEN IF EVERY PERSON ON EARTH OFFERED ME HIS HAND...
...I CAN'T FORGIVE MYSELF.
NOT EVER.
......
......
Ow!
THUMP
STUPID!
Ex-Delinquent!
Bean pole!
......
WELL...
THAT'S FINE, TOO.

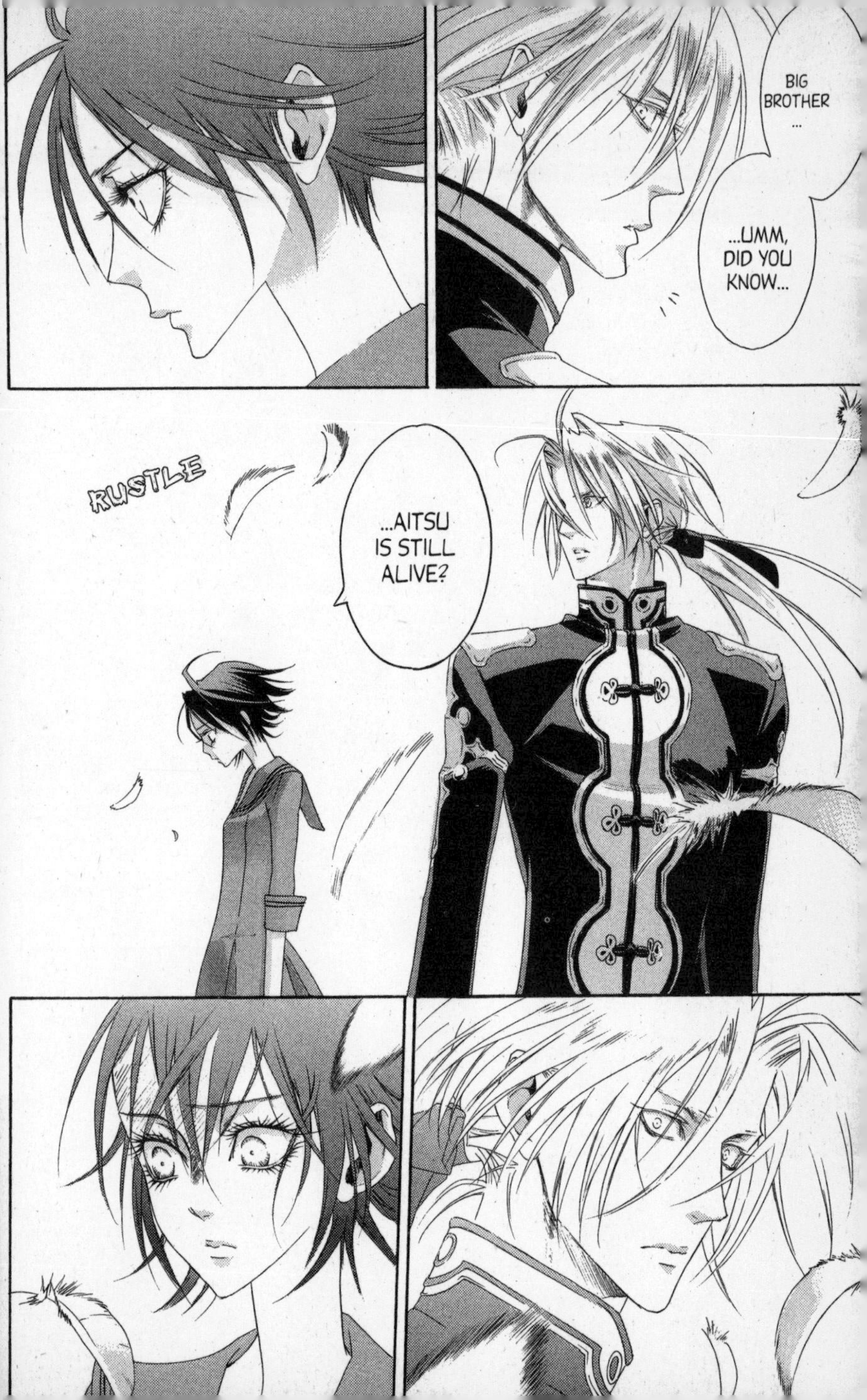
BIG BROTHER ...
...UMM, DID YOU KNOW...
...AITSU IS STILL ALIVE?
RUSTLE

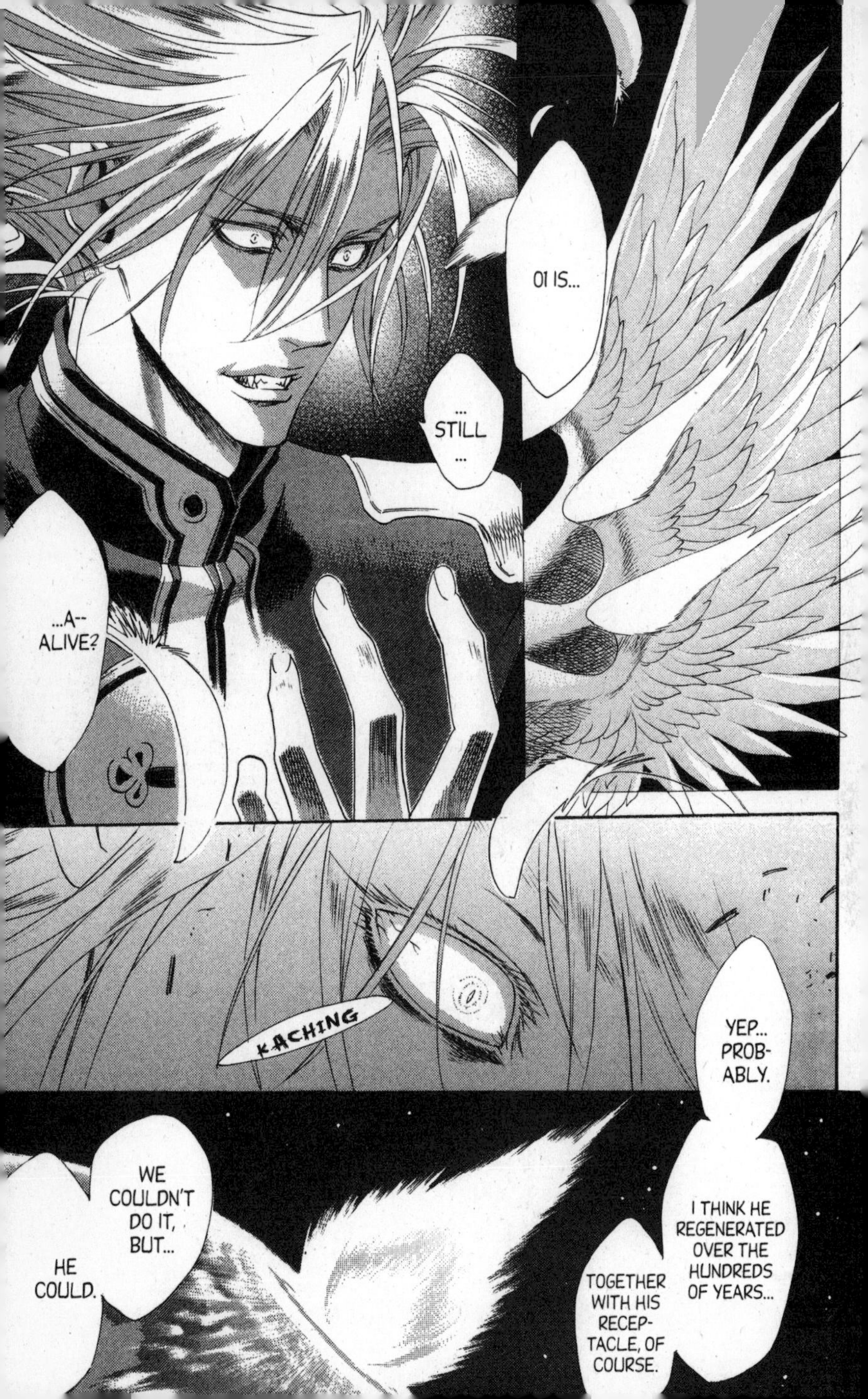
01 IS...
...STILL...
...A-- ALIVE?
KACHING
YEP... PROBABLY.
I THINK HE REGENERATED OVER THE HUNDREDS OF YEARS...
TOGETHER WITH HIS RECEPTACLE, OF COURSE.
WE COULDN'T DO IT, BUT...
HE COULD.

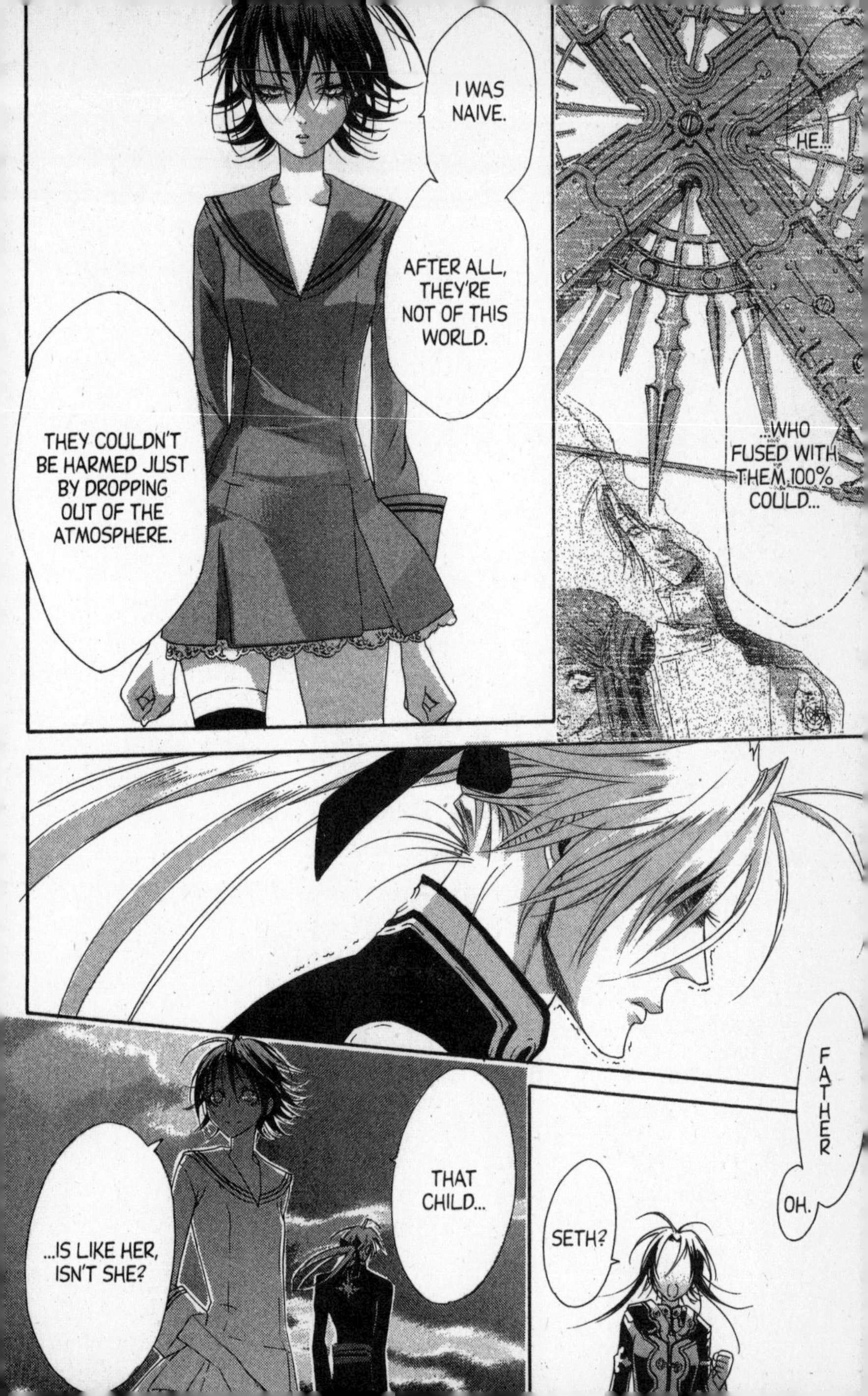
HE...
...WHO FUSED WITH THEM 100% COULD...
I WAS NAIVE.
AFTER ALL, THEY'RE NOT OF THIS WORLD.
THEY COULDN'T BE HARMED JUST BY DROPPING OUT OF THE ATMOSPHERE.
FATHER
OH.
SETH?
THAT CHILD...
...IS LIKE HER, ISN'T SHE?

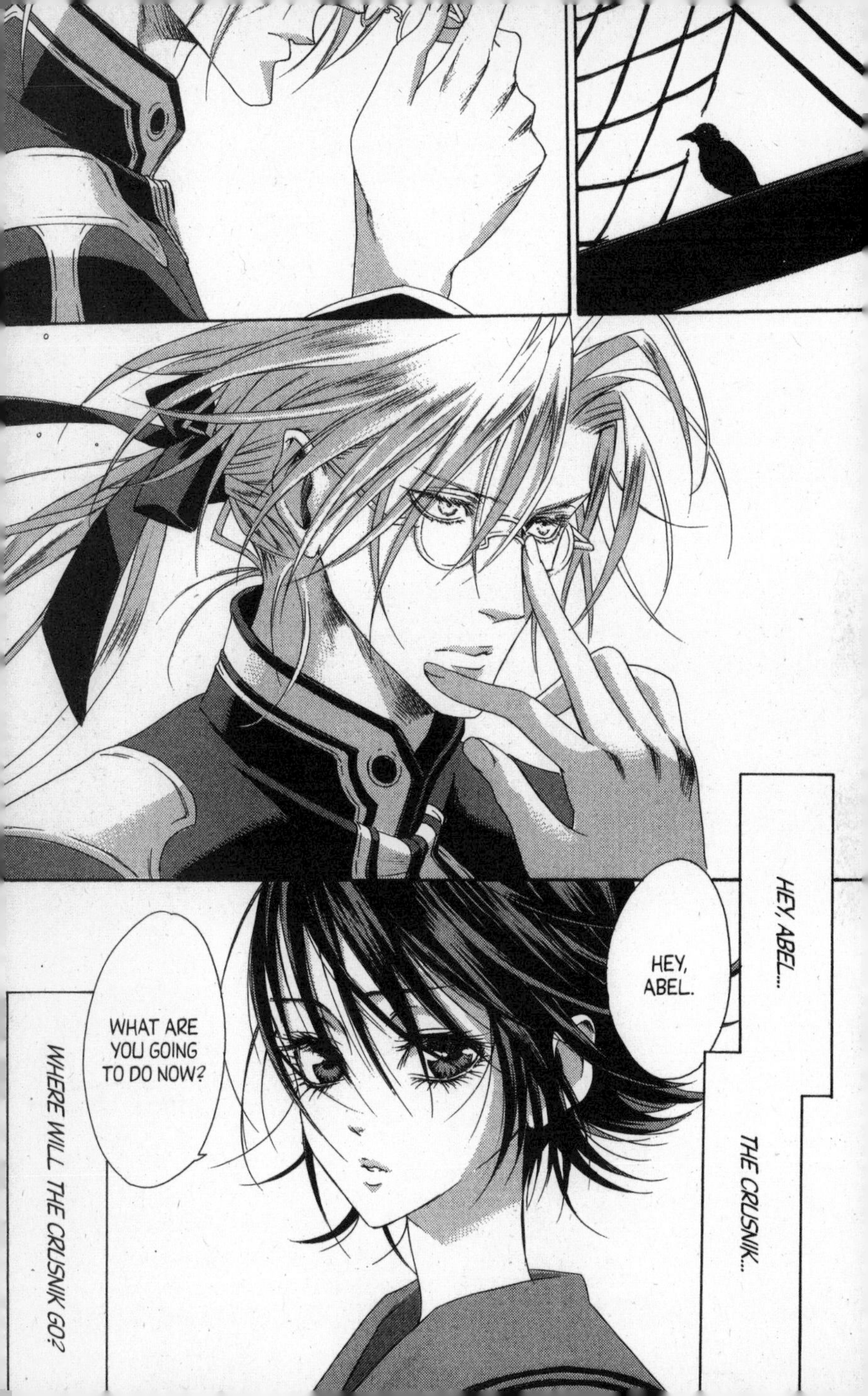
HEY, ABEL...
THE CRUSNIK...
HEY, ABEL.
WHAT ARE YOU GOING TO DO NOW?
WHERE WILL THE CRUSNIK GO?

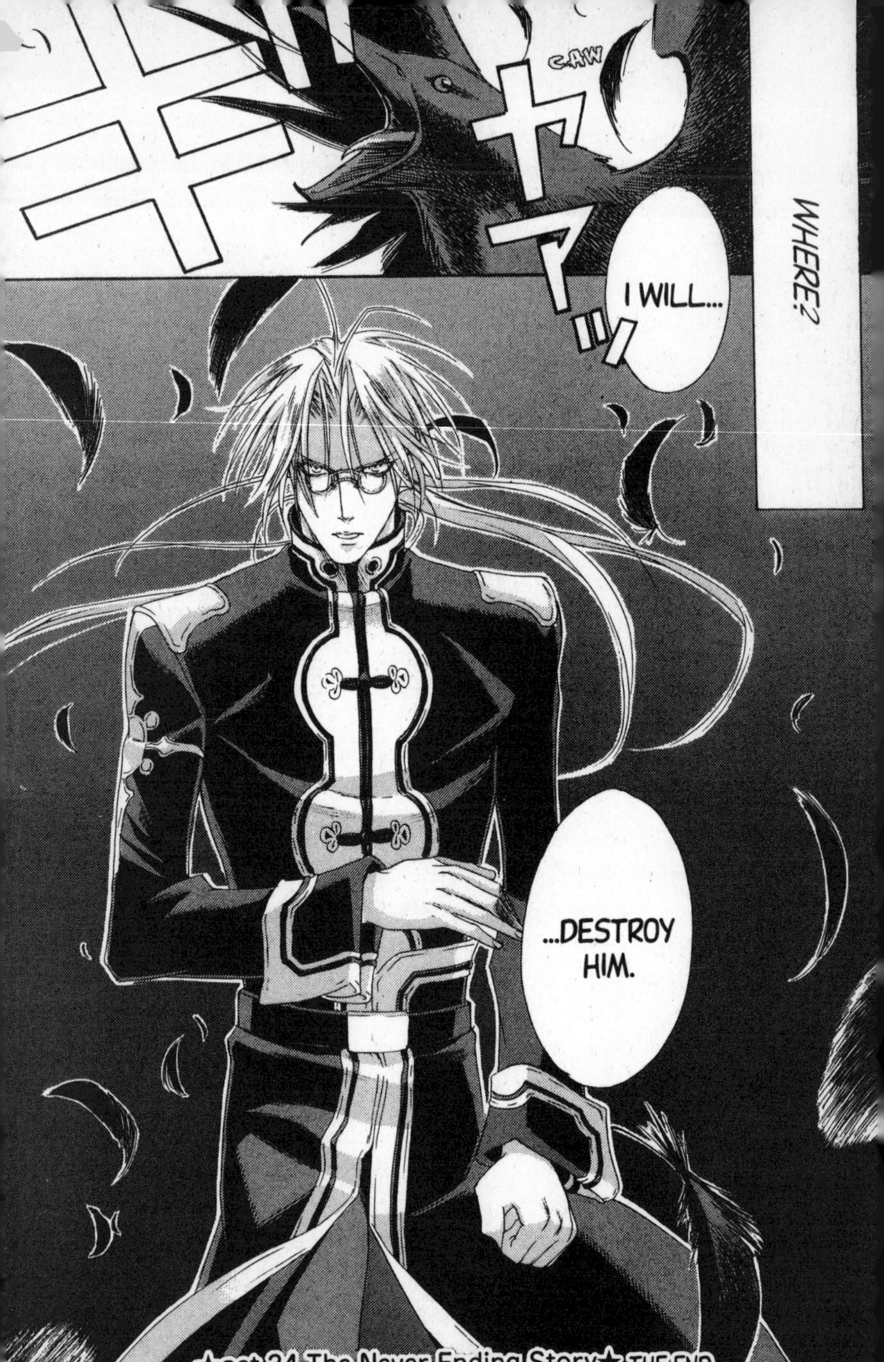
WHERE?
CAW
I WILL...
...DESTROY HIM.

★act.34 The Never Ending Story★ THE END

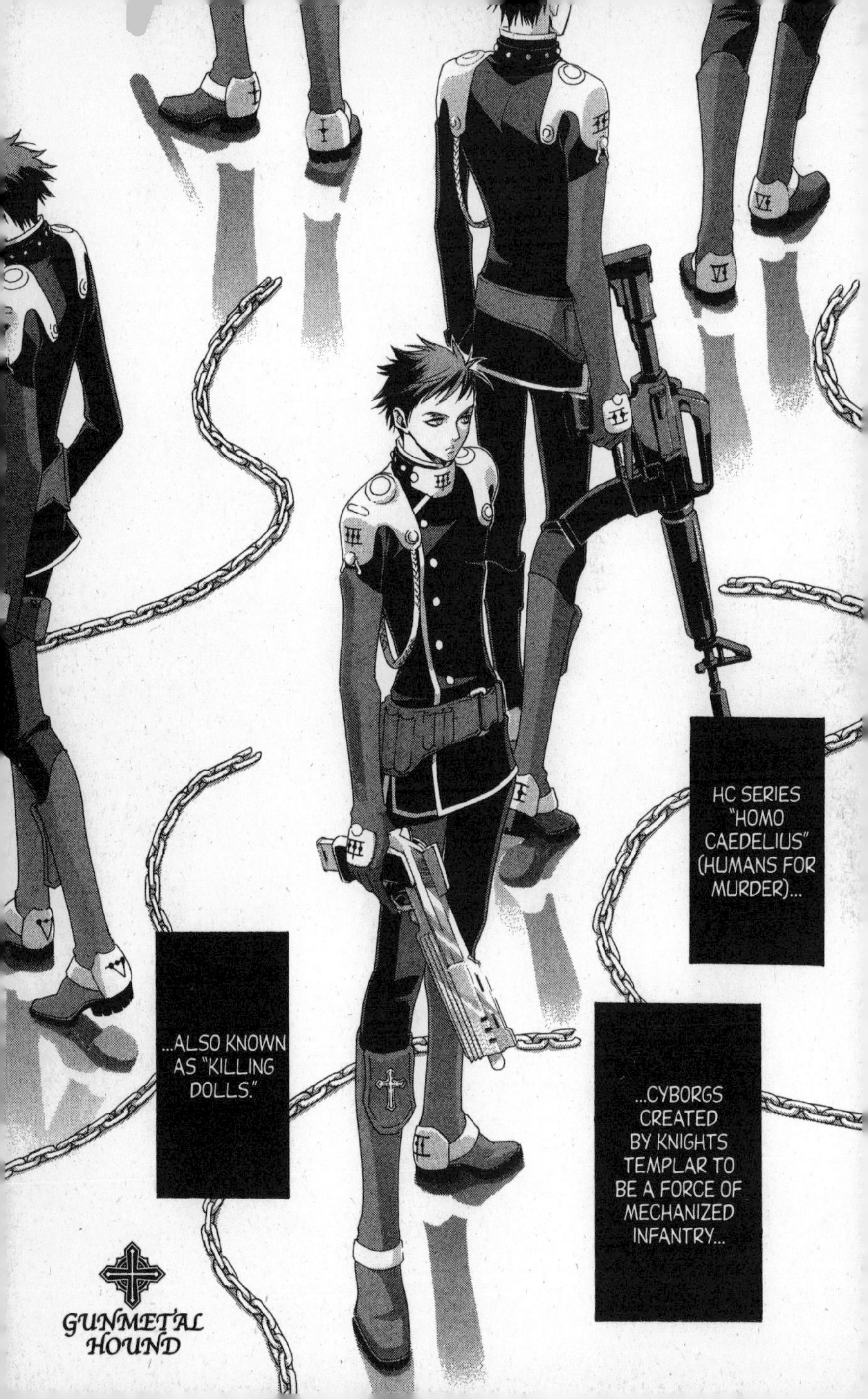
HC SERIES "HOMO CAEDELIUS" (HUMANS FOR MURDER)...
...CYBORGS CREATED BY KNIGHTS TEMPLAR TO BE A FORCE OF MECHANIZED INFANTRY...
...ALSO KNOWN AS "KILLING DOLLS."
GUNMETAL HOUND

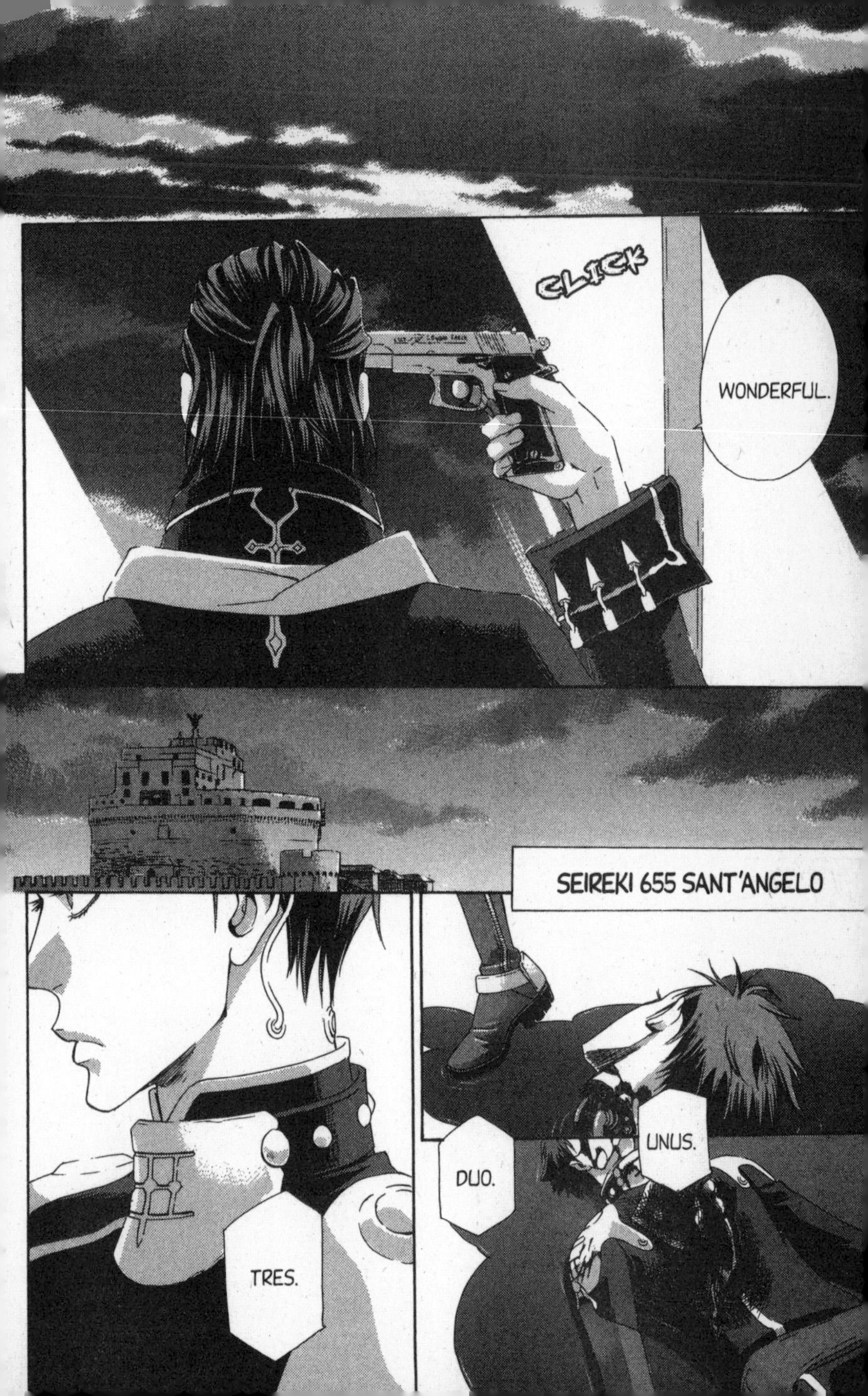
CLICK
WONDERFUL.
SEIREKI 655 SANT'ANGELO
UNUS.
DUO.
TRES.

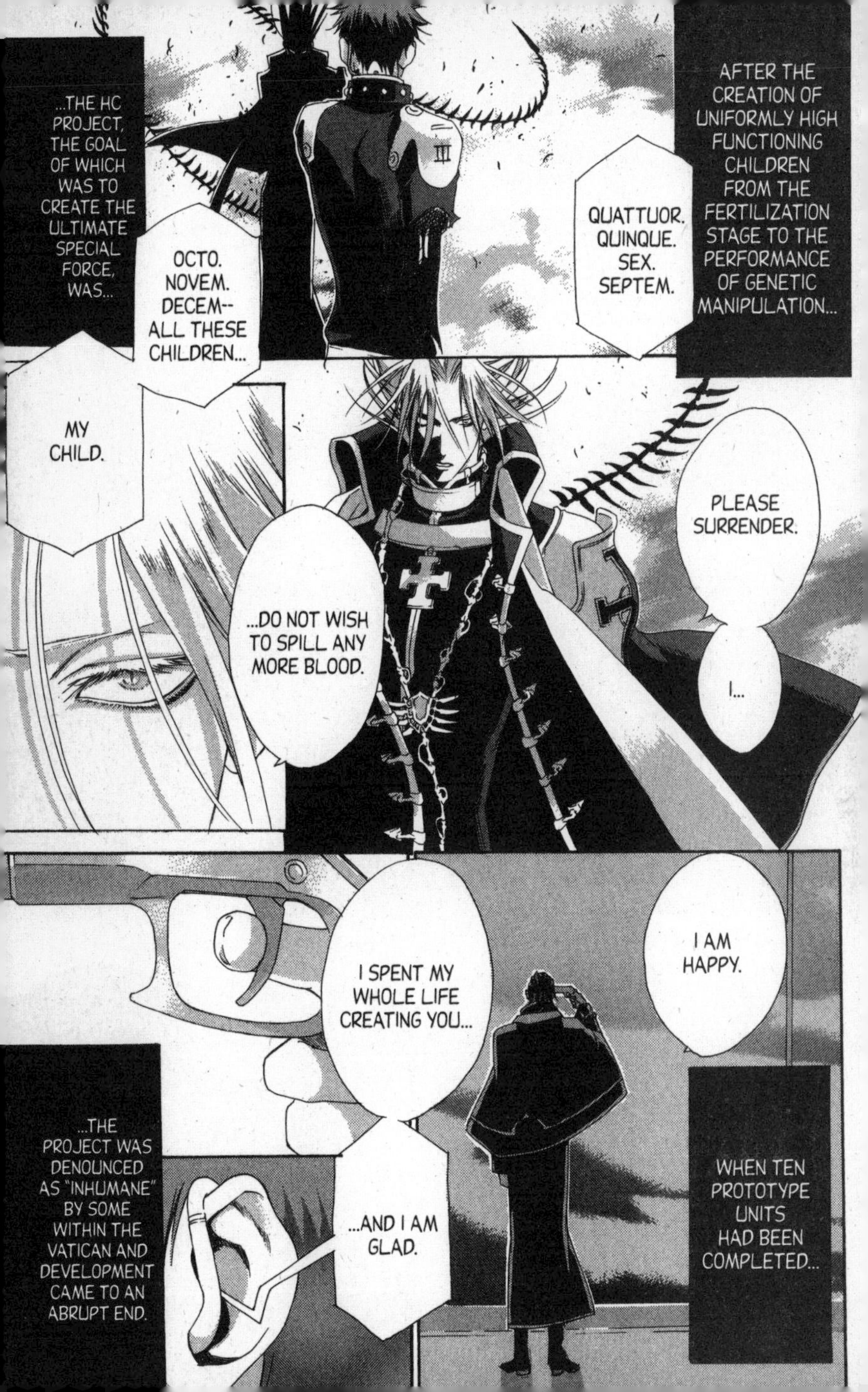
AFTER THE CREATION OF UNIFORMLY HIGH FUNCTIONING CHILDREN FROM THE FERTILIZATION STAGE TO THE PERFORMANCE OF GENETIC MANIPULATION...
QUATTUOR. QUINQUE. SEX. SEPTEM.
...THE HC PROJECT, THE GOAL OF WHICH WAS TO CREATE THE ULTIMATE SPECIAL FORCE, WAS...
OCTO. NOVEM. DECEM-- ALL THESE CHILDREN...
PLEASE SURRENDER.
I...
...DO NOT WISH TO SPILL ANY MORE BLOOD.
MY CHILD.
WHEN TEN PROTOTYPE UNITS HAD BEEN COMPLETED...
I AM HAPPY.
I SPENT MY WHOLE LIFE CREATING YOU...
...AND I AM GLAD.
...THE PROJECT WAS DENOUNCED AS "INHUMANE" BY SOME WITHIN THE VATICAN AND DEVELOPMENT CAME TO AN ABRUPT END.

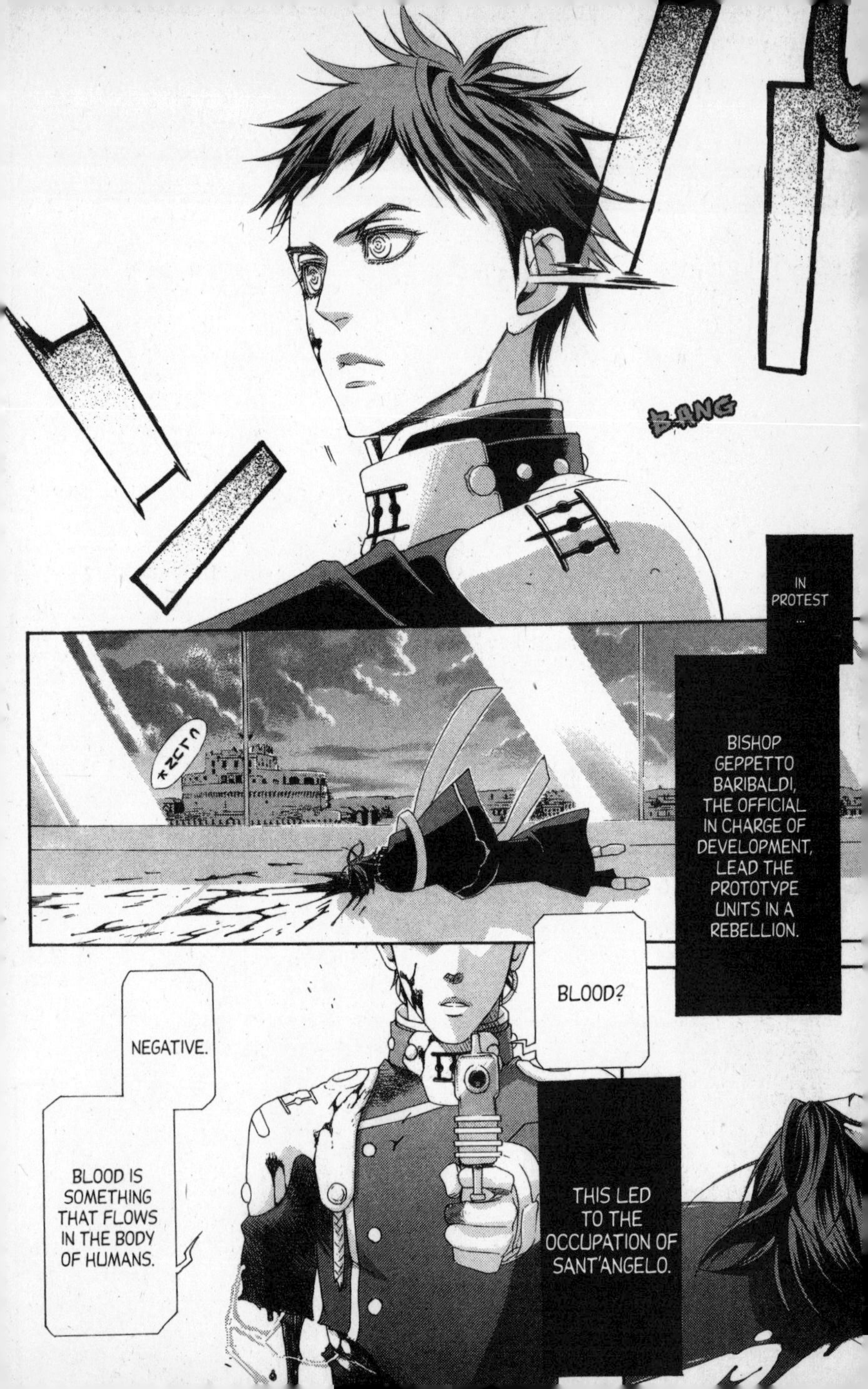
BANG
IN PROTEST...
BISHOP GEPPETTO BARIBALDI, THE OFFICIAL IN CHARGE OF DEVELOPMENT, LEAD THE PROTOTYPE UNITS IN A REBELLION.
BLOOD?
NEGATIVE.
THIS LED TO THE OCCUPATION OF SANT'ANGELO.
BLOOD IS SOMETHING THAT FLOWS IN THE BODY OF HUMANS.

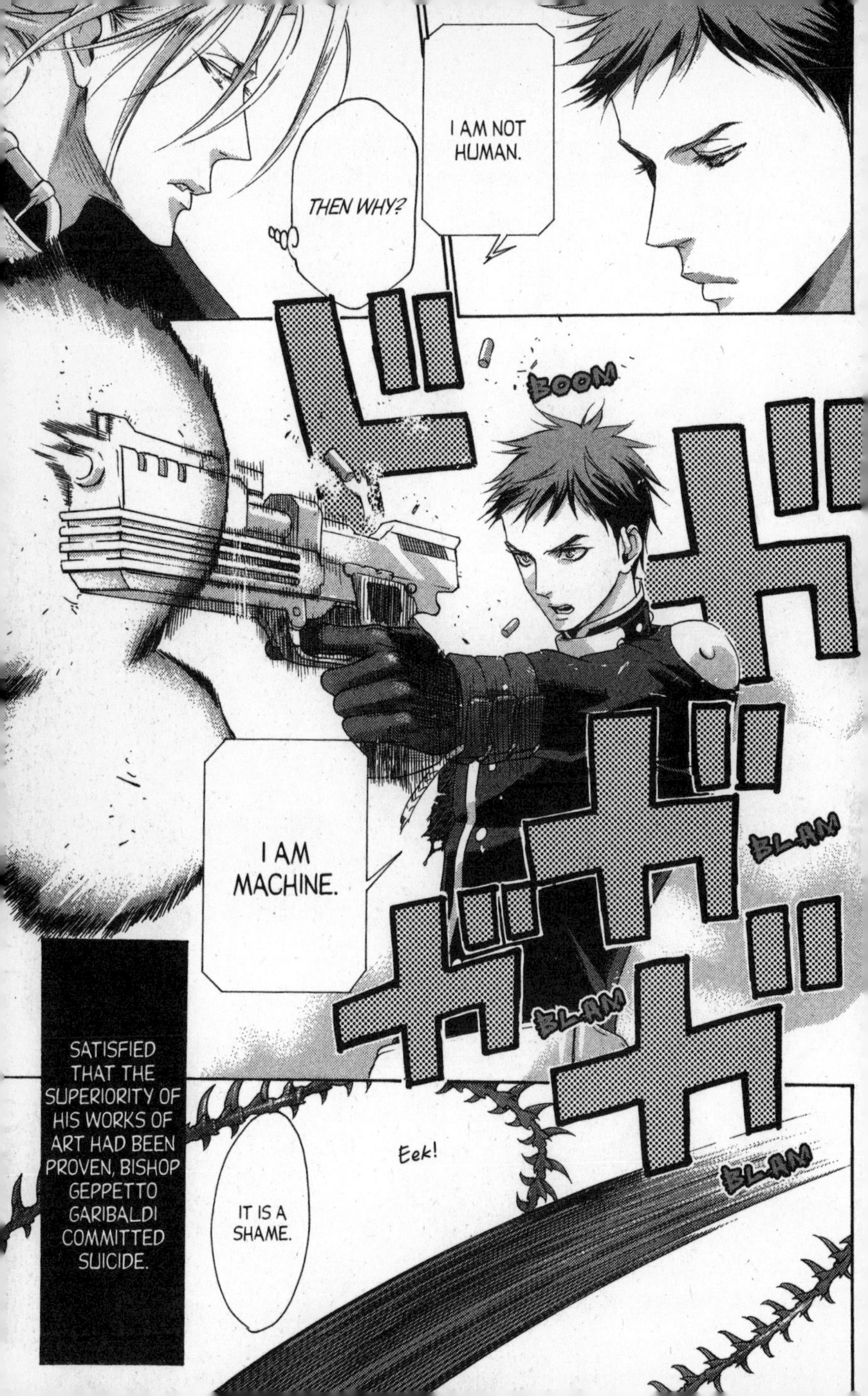
I AM NOT HUMAN.
THEN WHY?
BOOM
I AM MACHINE.
BLAM
BLAM
BLAM
Eek!
IT IS A SHAME.
SATISFIED THAT THE SUPERIORITY OF HIS WORKS OF ART HAD BEEN PROVEN, BISHOP GEPPETTO GARIBALDI COMMITTED SUICIDE.

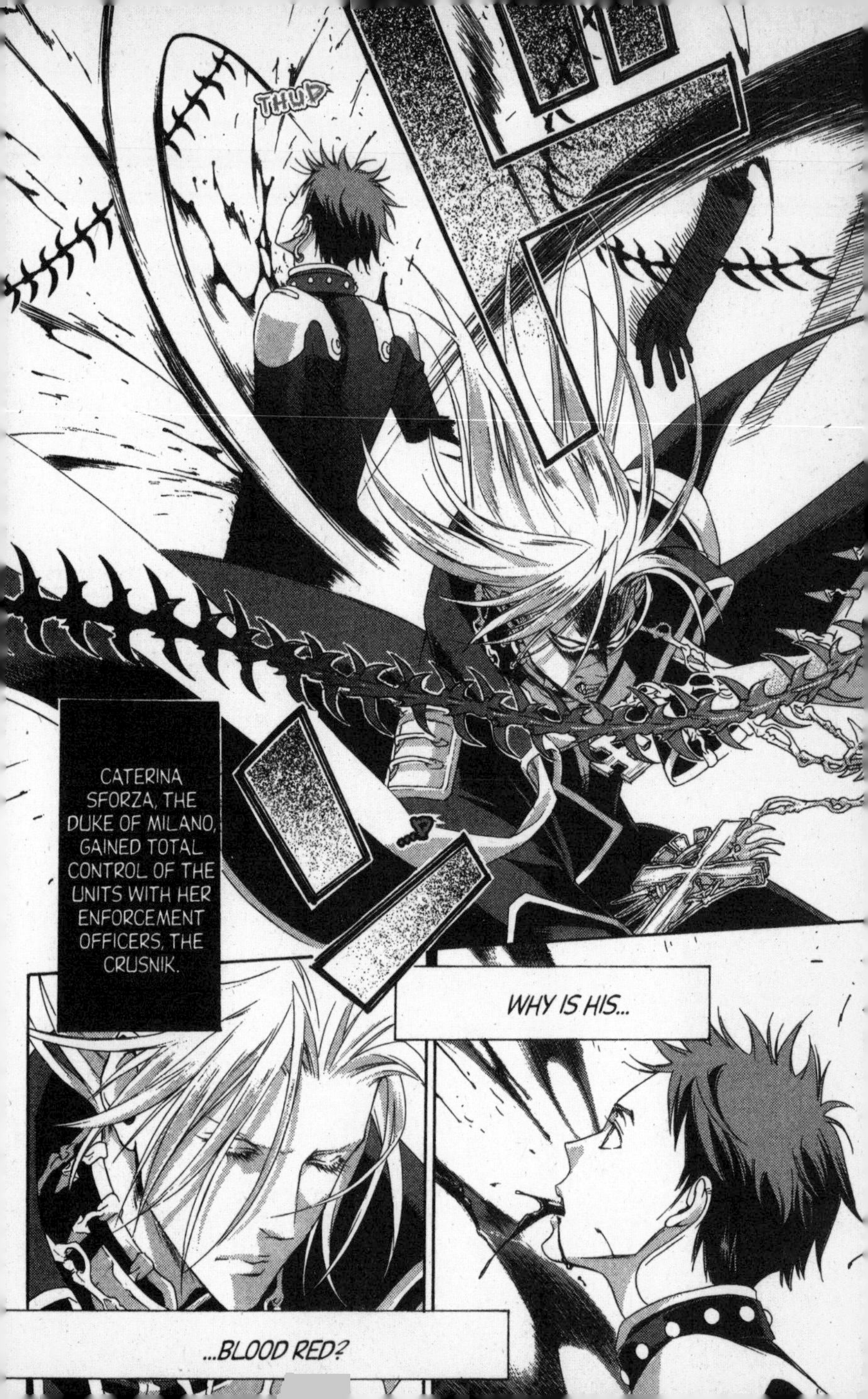
THUD
CATERINA SFORZA, THE DUKE OF MILANO, GAINED TOTAL CONTROL OF THE UNITS WITH HER ENFORCEMENT OFFICERS, THE CRUSNIK.
WHY IS HIS...
...BLOOD RED?

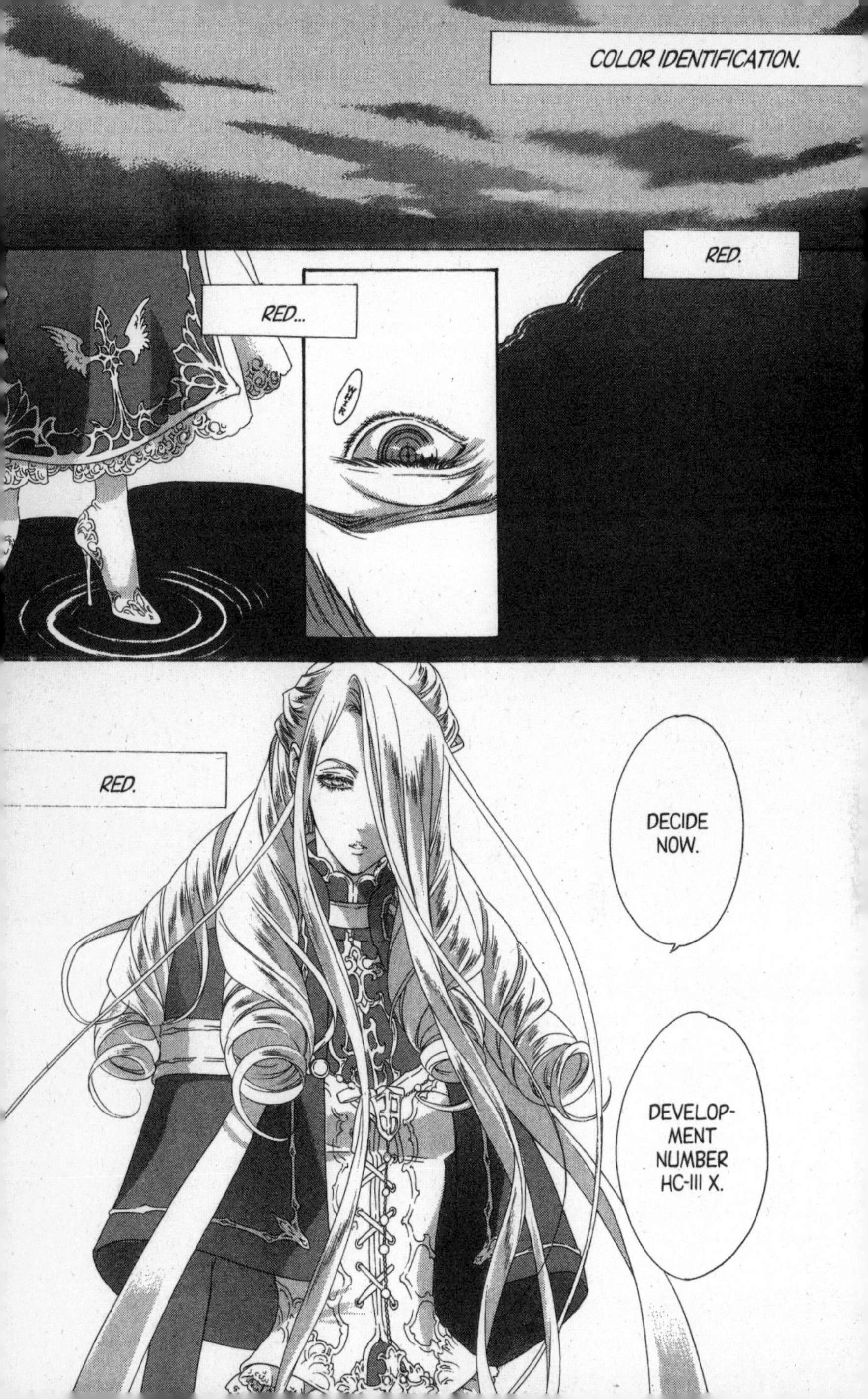
COLOR IDENTIFICATION.
RED.
WHIR
RED...
DECIDE NOW.
DEVELOPMENT NUMBER HC-III X.
RED.

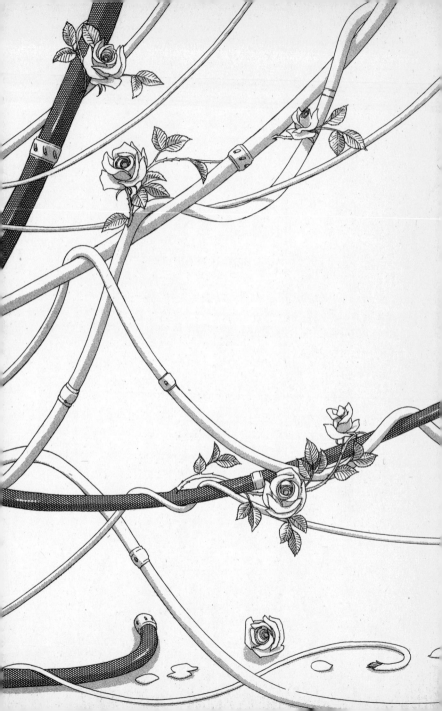

Gunmetal Hound

Side Red : Hellhound Blues

[消えた狂犬と それにまつわる噂]

[THE MAD DOG THAT DISAPPEARED AND THE RUMORS ASSOCIATED WITH IT]

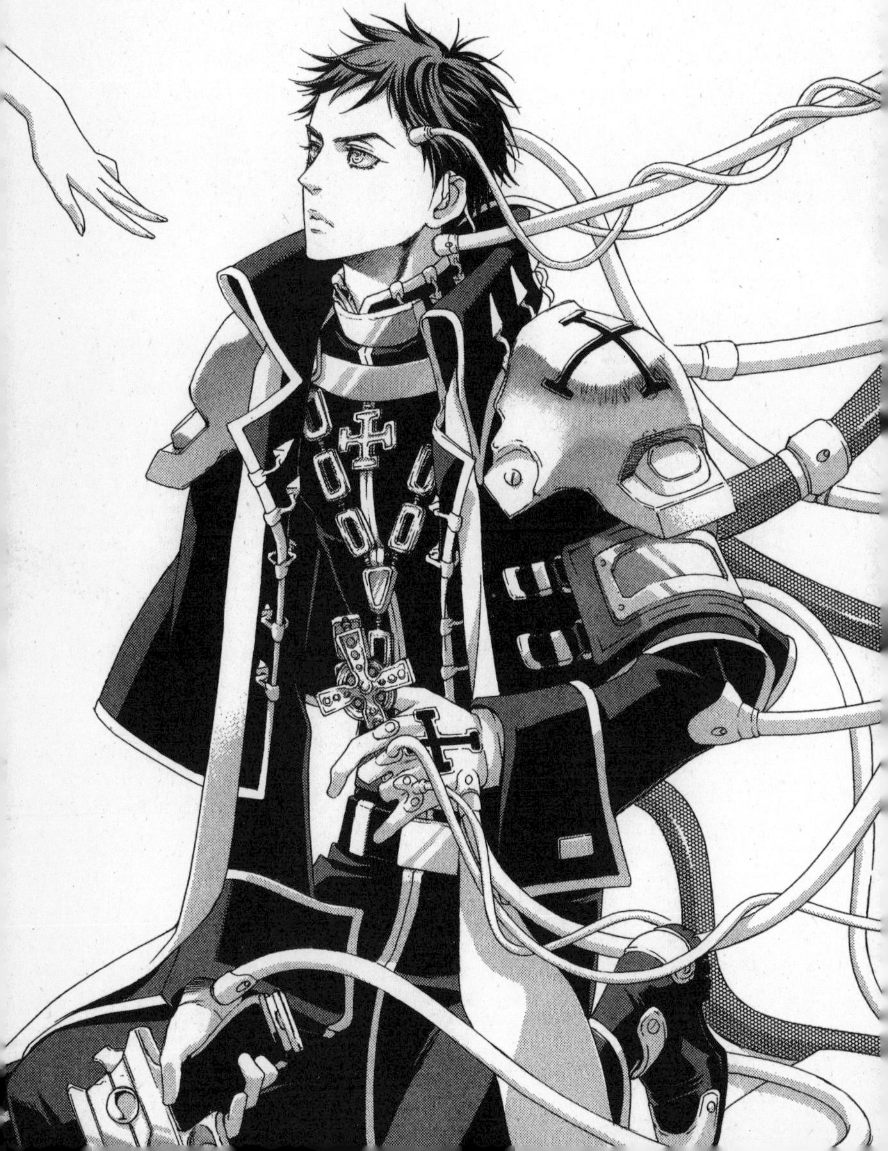

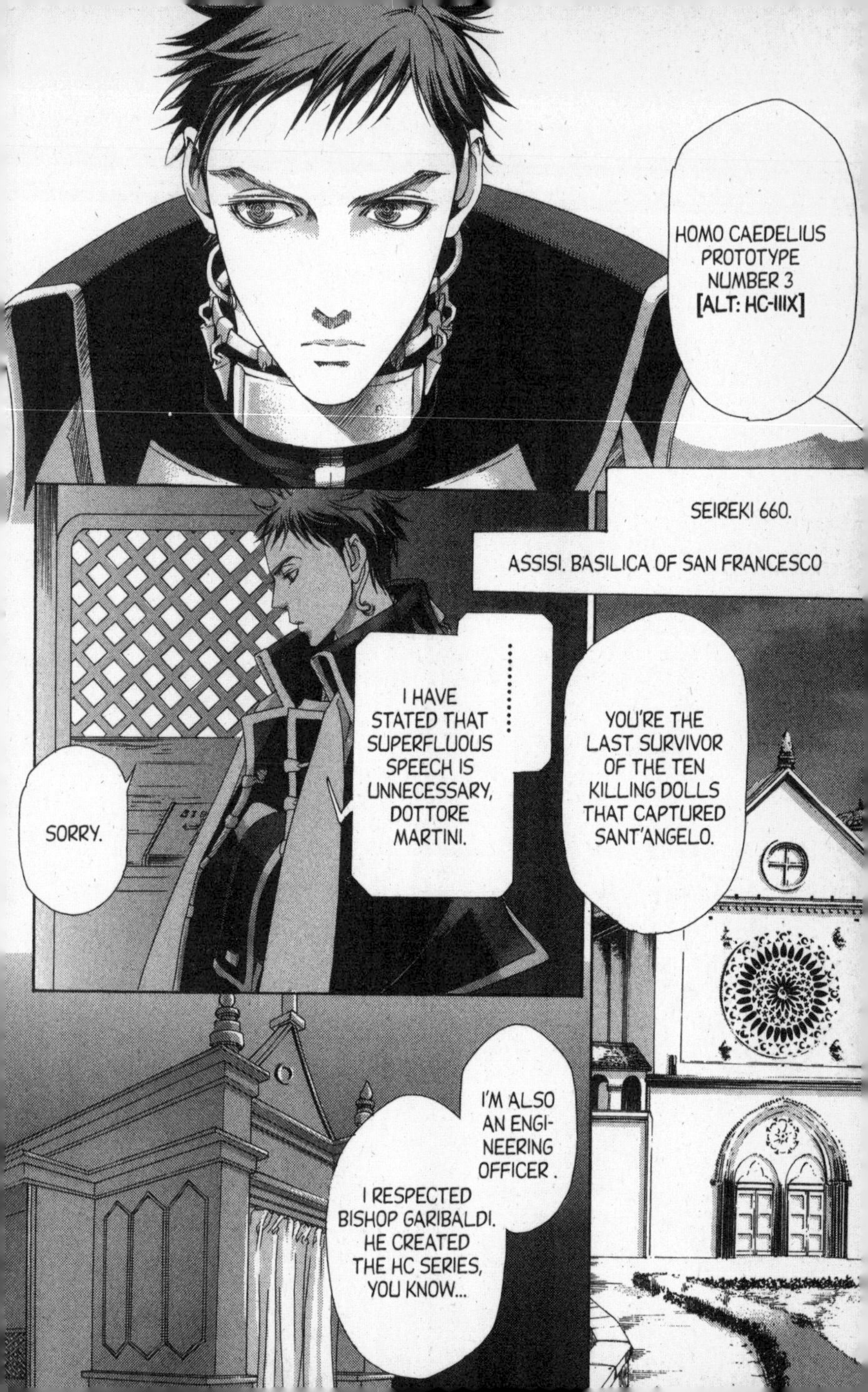
HOMO CAEDELIUS PROTOTYPE NUMBER 3 [ALT: HC-IIIX]
SEIREKI 660.
ASSISI. BASILICA OF SAN FRANCESCO
YOU'RE THE LAST SURVIVOR OF THE TEN KILLING DOLLS THAT CAPTURED SANT'ANGELO.
......
I HAVE STATED THAT SUPERFLUOUS SPEECH IS UNNECESSARY, DOTTORE MARTINI.
SORRY.
I'M ALSO AN ENGI- NEERING OFFICER .
I RESPECTED BISHOP GARIBALDI. HE CREATED THE HC SERIES, YOU KNOW...

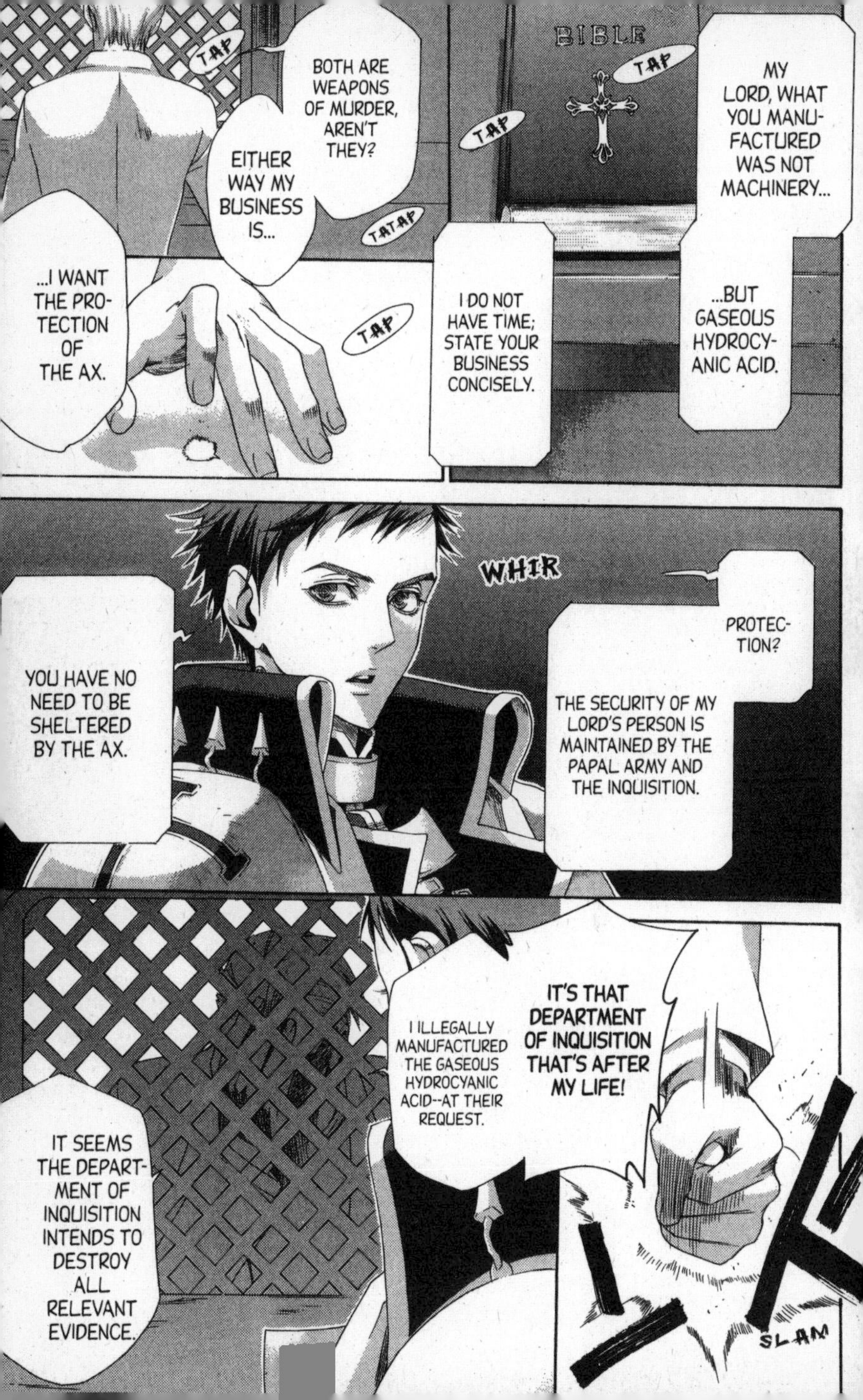
BIBLE
TAP
MY LORD, WHAT YOU MANUFACTURED WAS NOT MACHINERY...
TAP
...BUT GASEOUS HYDROCYANIC ACID.
I DO NOT HAVE TIME; STATE YOUR BUSINESS CONCISELY.
TAP
TAP
BOTH ARE WEAPONS OF MURDER, AREN'T THEY?
EITHER WAY MY BUSINESS IS...
TATAP
TAP
...I WANT THE PROTECTION OF THE AX.
WHIR
PROTECTION?
THE SECURITY OF MY LORD'S PERSON IS MAINTAINED BY THE PAPAL ARMY AND THE INQUISITION.
YOU HAVE NO NEED TO BE SHELTERED BY THE AX.
IT'S THAT DEPARTMENT OF INQUISITION THAT'S AFTER MY LIFE!
I ILLEGALLY MANUFACTURED THE GASEOUS HYDROCYANIC ACID--AT THEIR REQUEST.
SLAM
IT SEEMS THE DEPARTMENT OF INQUISITION INTENDS TO DESTROY ALL RELEVANT EVIDENCE.

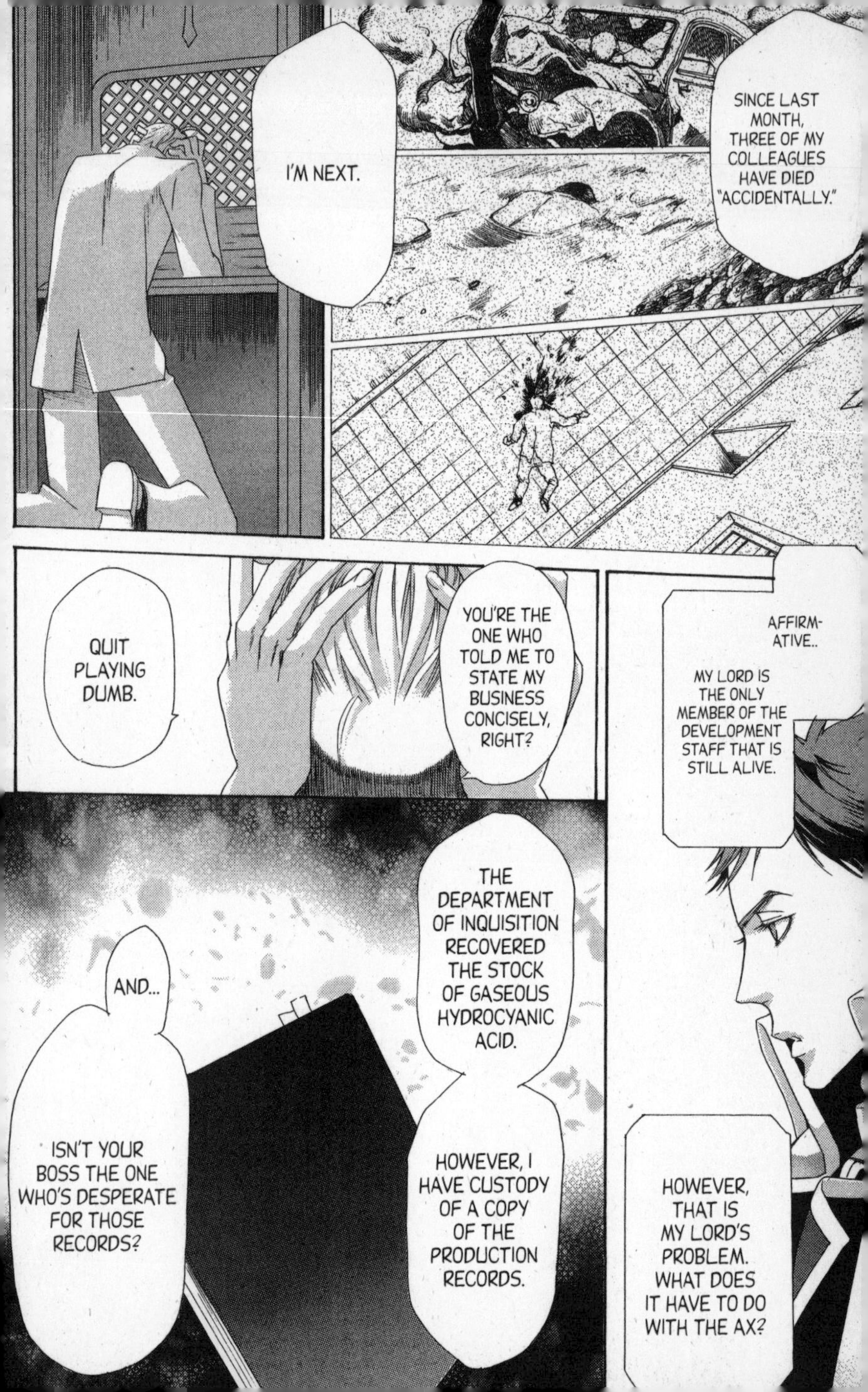
SINCE LAST MONTH, THREE OF MY COLLEAGUES HAVE DIED "ACCIDENTALLY."
I'M NEXT.
AFFIRM-ATIVE..
MY LORD IS THE ONLY MEMBER OF THE DEVELOPMENT STAFF THAT IS STILL ALIVE.
HOWEVER, THAT IS MY LORD'S PROBLEM. WHAT DOES IT HAVE TO DO WITH THE AX?
YOU'RE THE ONE WHO TOLD ME TO STATE MY BUSINESS CONCISELY, RIGHT?
QUIT PLAYING DUMB.
THE DEPARTMENT OF INQUISITION RECOVERED THE STOCK OF GASEOUS HYDROCYANIC ACID.
HOWEVER, I HAVE CUSTODY OF A COPY OF THE PRODUCTION RECORDS.
AND...
ISN'T YOUR BOSS THE ONE WHO'S DESPERATE FOR THOSE RECORDS?

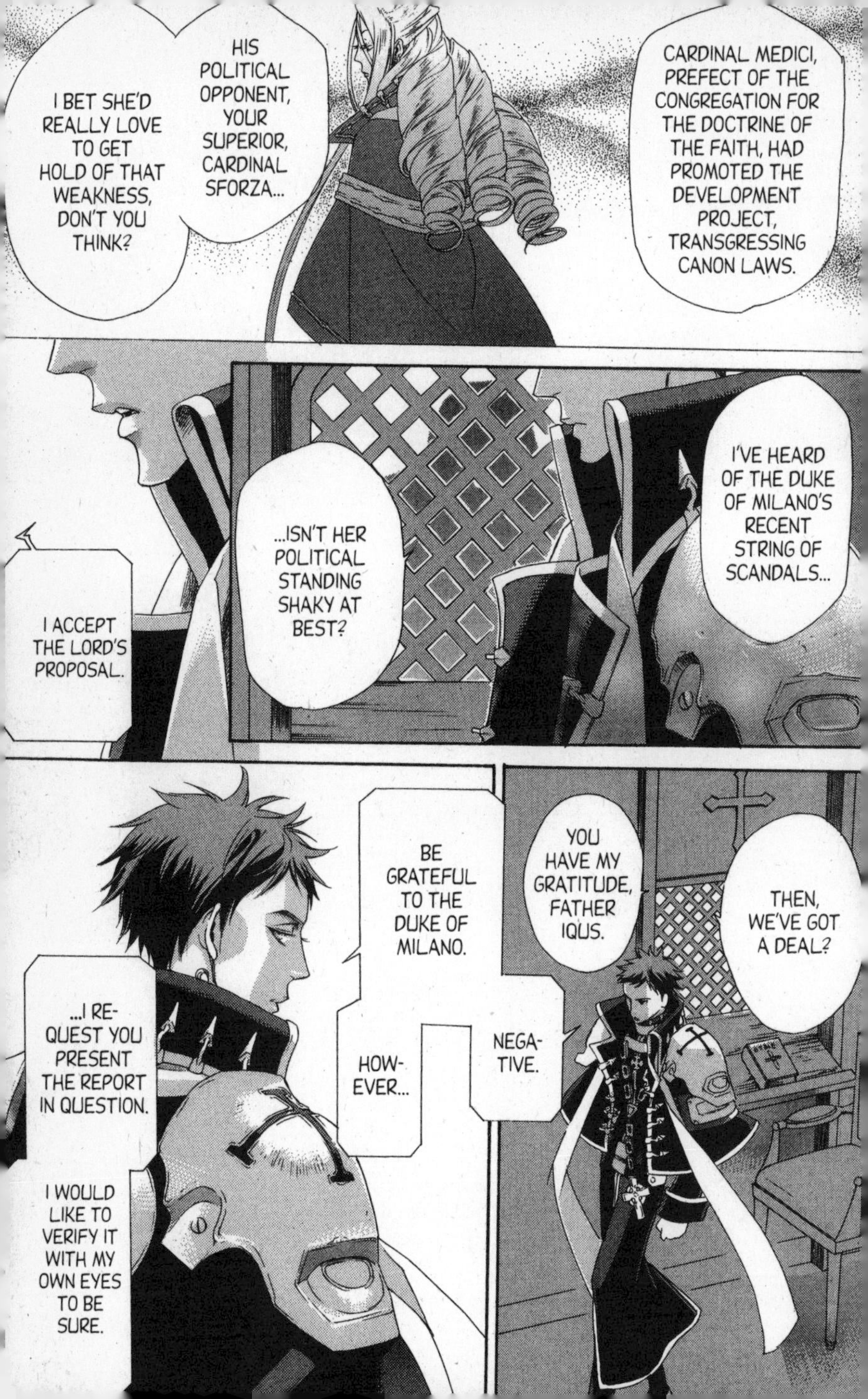

CARDINAL MEDICI, PREFECT OF THE CONGREGATION FOR THE DOCTRINE OF THE FAITH, HAD PROMOTED THE DEVELOPMENT PROJECT, TRANSGRESSING CANON LAWS.
HIS POLITICAL OPPONENT, YOUR SUPERIOR, CARDINAL SFORZA...
I BET SHE'D REALLY LOVE TO GET HOLD OF THAT WEAKNESS, DON'T YOU THINK?
I'VE HEARD OF THE DUKE OF MILANO'S RECENT STRING OF SCANDALS...
...ISN'T HER POLITICAL STANDING SHAKY AT BEST?
I ACCEPT THE LORD'S PROPOSAL.
THEN, WE'VE GOT A DEAL?
YOU HAVE MY GRATITUDE, FATHER IQUS.
BE GRATEFUL TO THE DUKE OF MILANO.
NEGA-TIVE.
HOW-EVER...
...I RE-QUEST YOU PRESENT THE REPORT IN QUESTION.
I WOULD LIKE TO VERIFY IT WITH MY OWN EYES TO BE SURE.

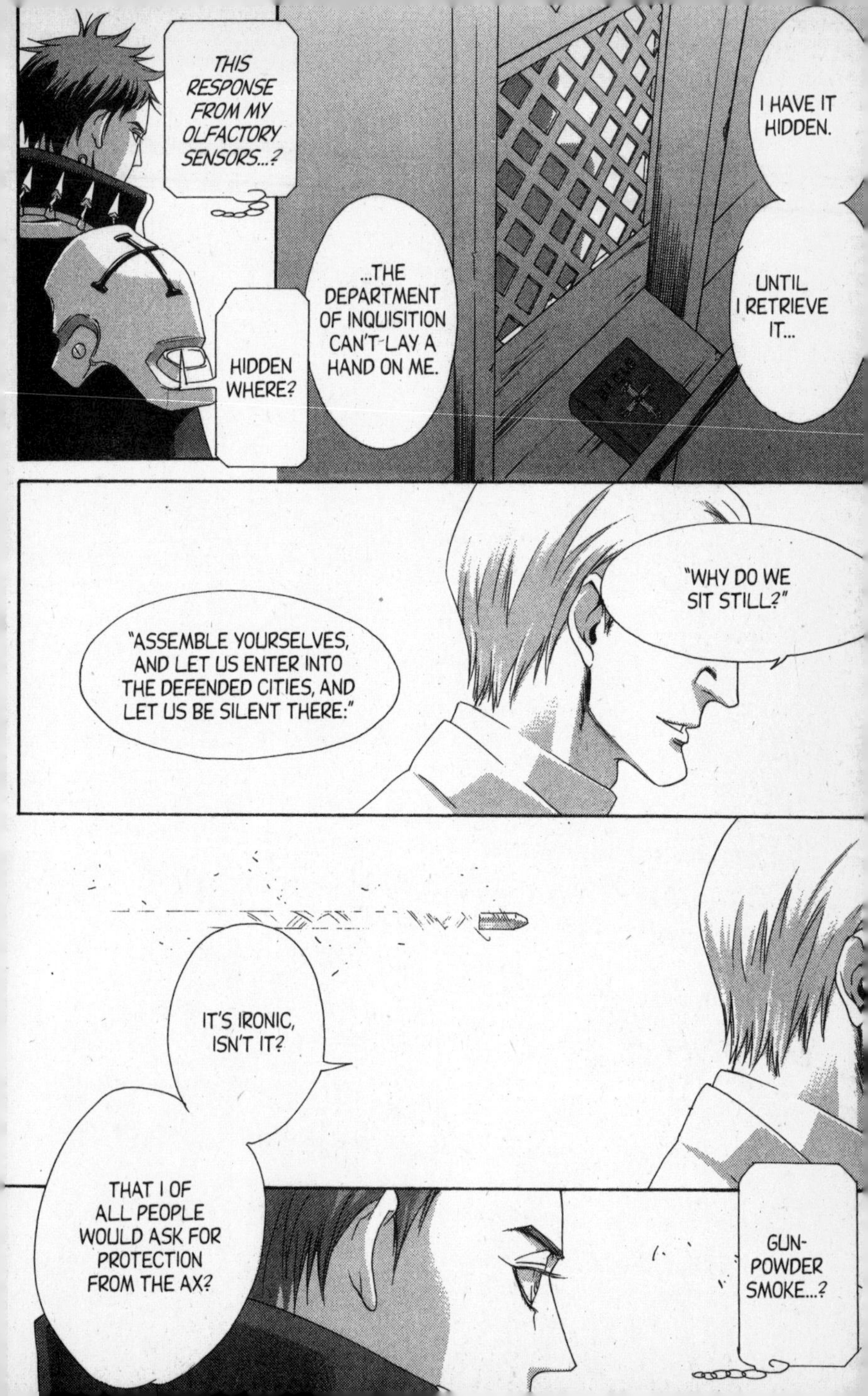
I HAVE IT HIDDEN.
UNTIL I RETRIEVE IT...
...THE DEPARTMENT OF INQUISITION CAN'T LAY A HAND ON ME.
HIDDEN WHERE?
THIS RESPONSE FROM MY OLFACTORY SENSORS...?
"WHY DO WE SIT STILL?"
"ASSEMBLE YOURSELVES, AND LET US ENTER INTO THE DEFENDED CITIES, AND LET US BE SILENT THERE:"
IT'S IRONIC, ISN'T IT?
THAT I OF ALL PEOPLE WOULD ASK FOR PROTECTION FROM THE AX?
GUN-POWDER SMOKE...?

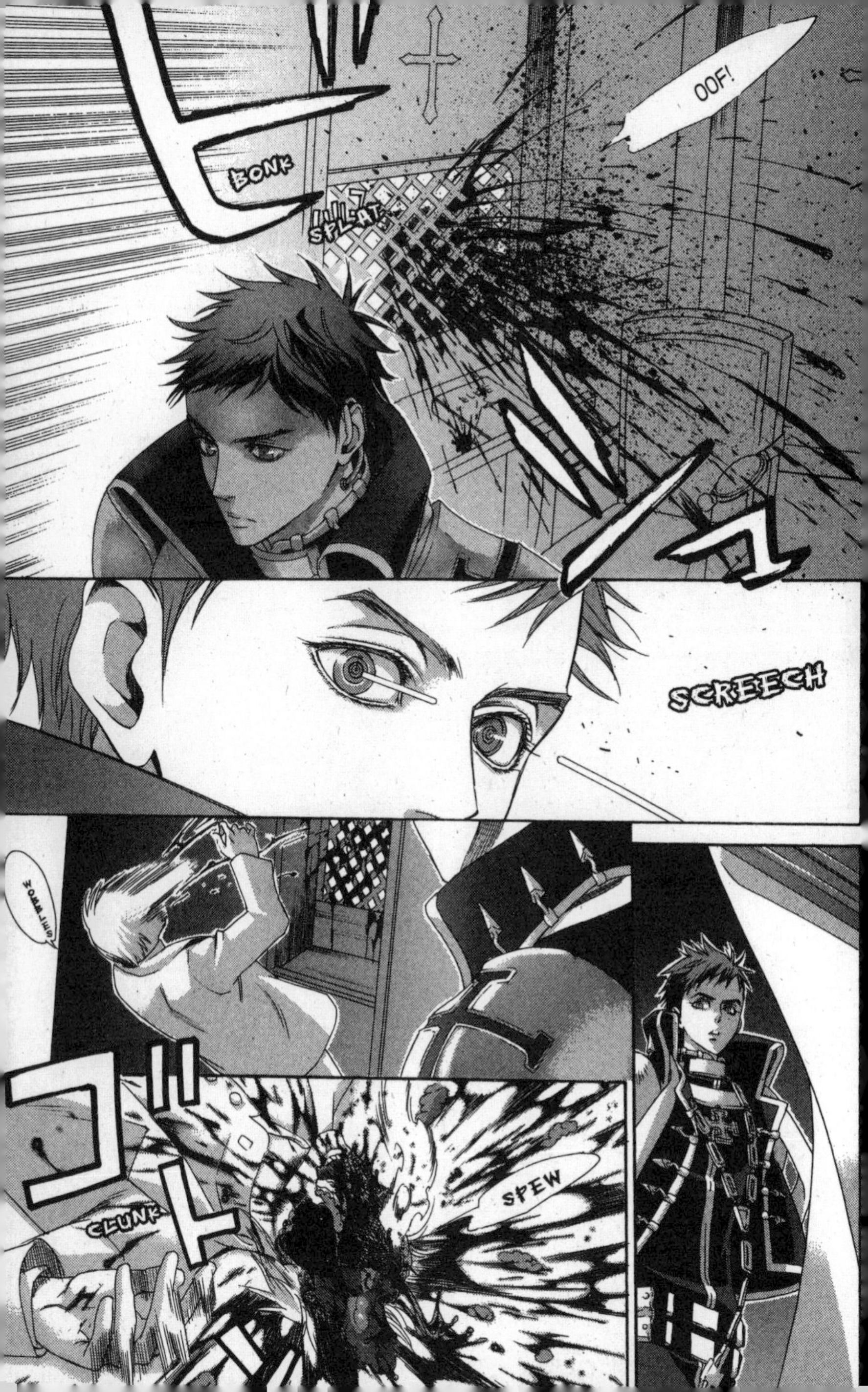
OOF!
BONK
SPLAT...
SCREECH
WOBBLIES
SPEW
CLUNK

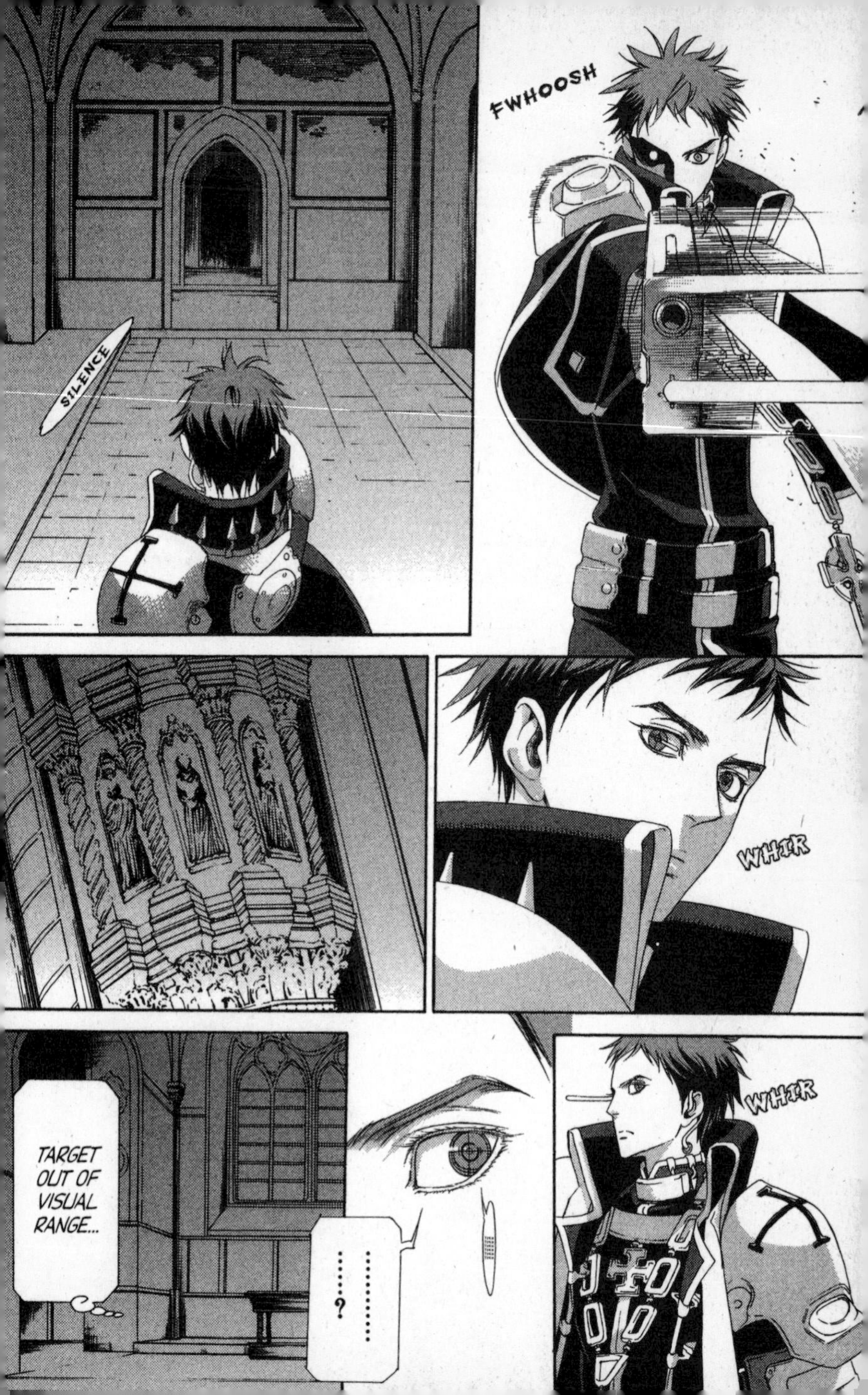
FWHOOSH
SILENCE
WHIR
WHIR
......?
......
TARGET OUT OF VISUAL RANGE...

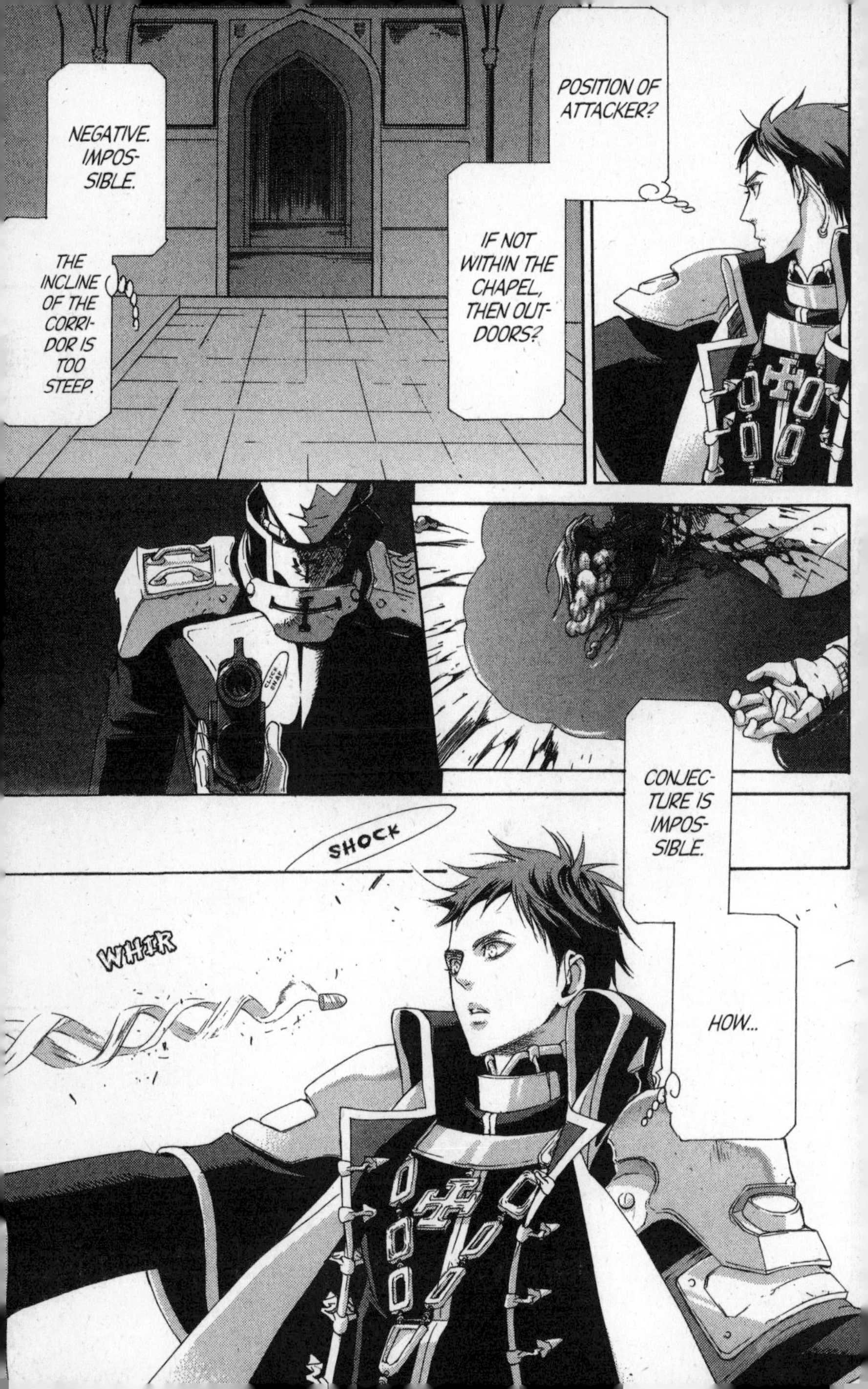
POSITION OF ATTACKER?
IF NOT WITHIN THE CHAPEL, THEN OUTDOORS?
NEGATIVE. IMPOSSIBLE.
THE INCLINE OF THE CORRIDOR IS TOO STEEP.
CONJECTURE IS IMPOSSIBLE.
HOW...
SHOCK
WHIR

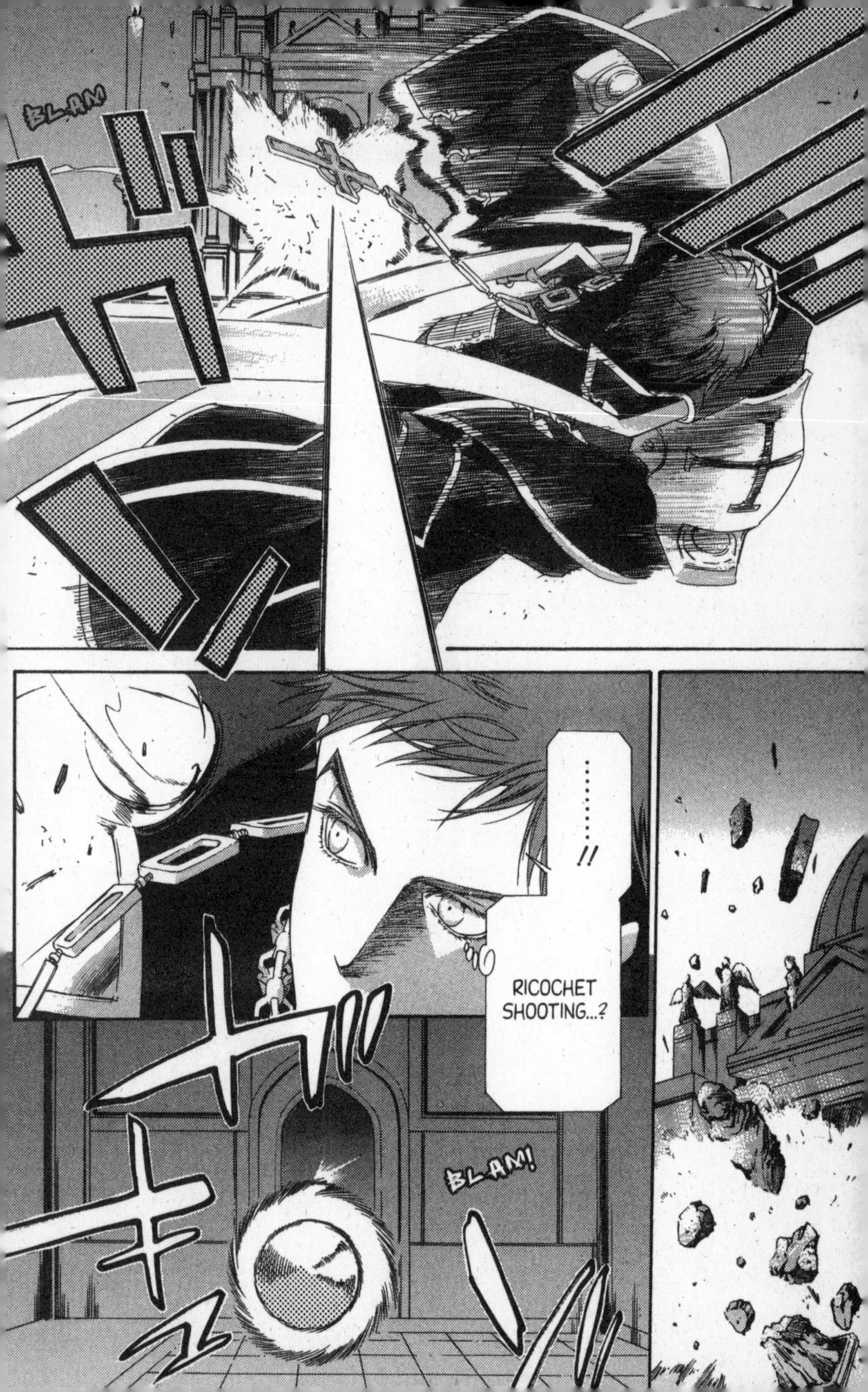
BLAM
......!!
RICOCHET SHOOTING...?
BLAM!

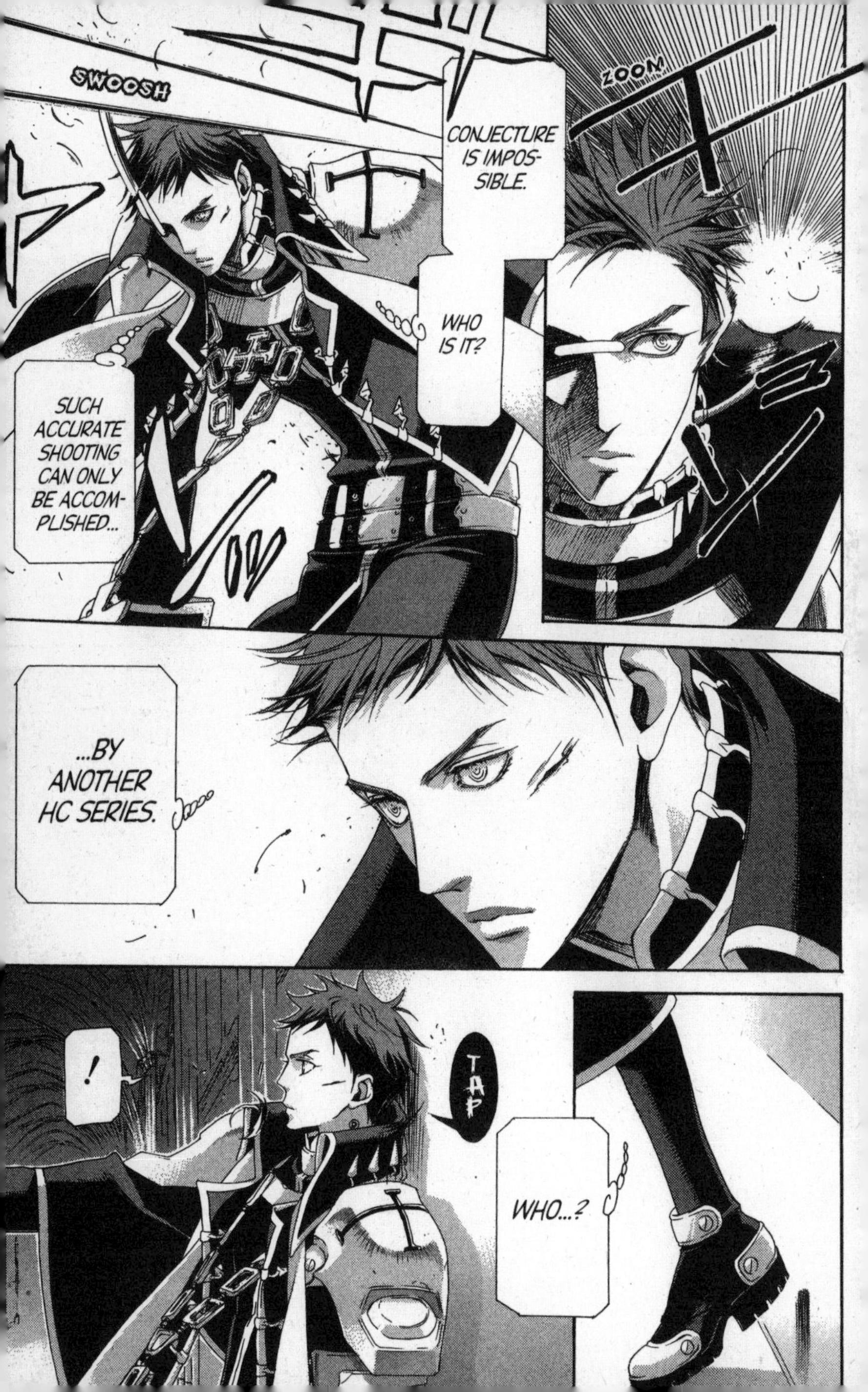
ZOOM
CONJECTURE IS IMPOSSIBLE.
WHO IS IT?
SWOOSH
SUCH ACCURATE SHOOTING CAN ONLY BE ACCOMPLISHED...
...BY ANOTHER HC SERIES.
WHO...?
TAP
!

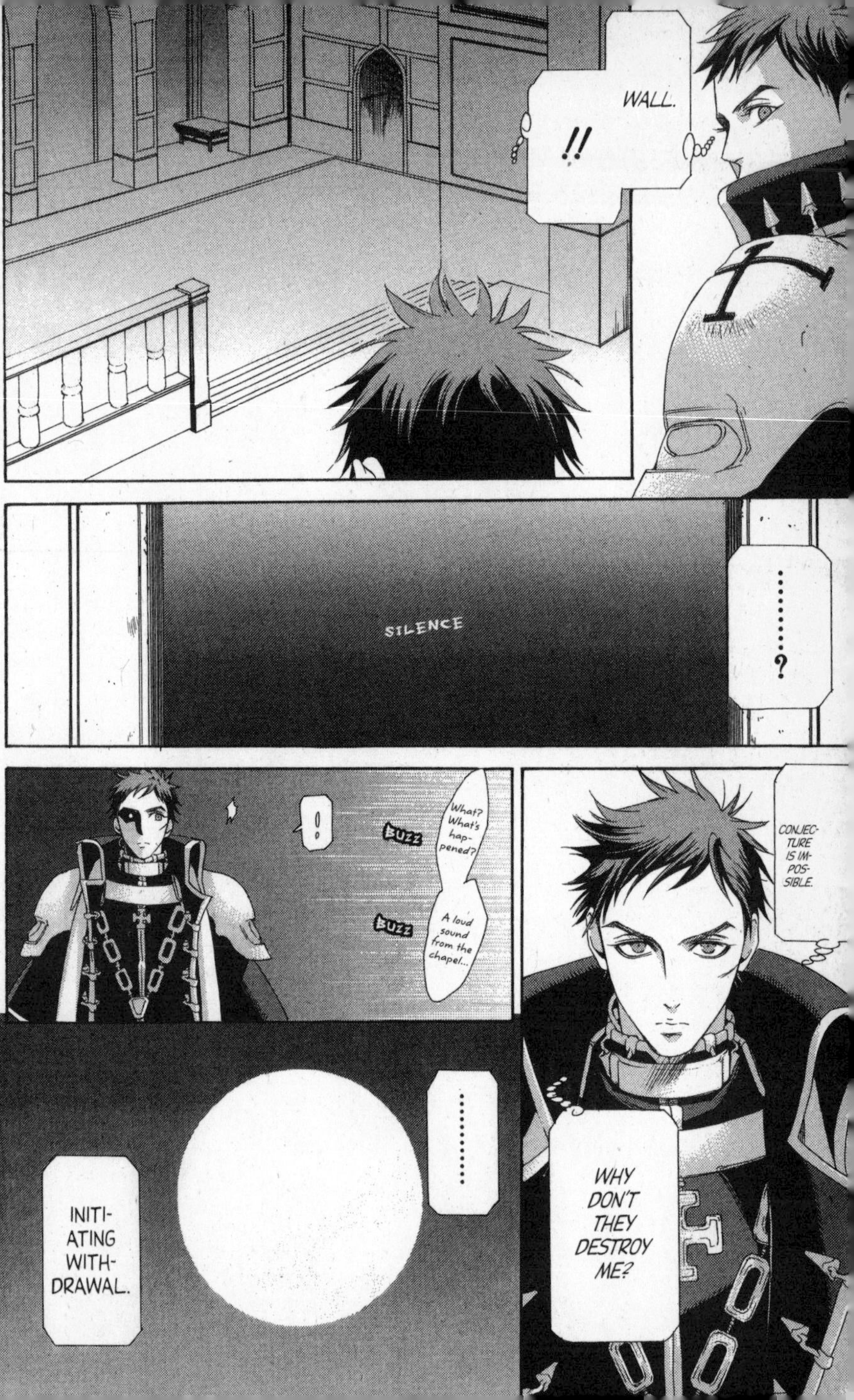
WALL.
!!
......?
SILENCE
CONJECTURE IS IMPOSSIBLE.
WHY DON'T THEY DESTROY ME?
What? What's happened?
BUZZ
A loud sound from the chapel...
BUZZ
!
......
INITIATING WITHDRAWAL.

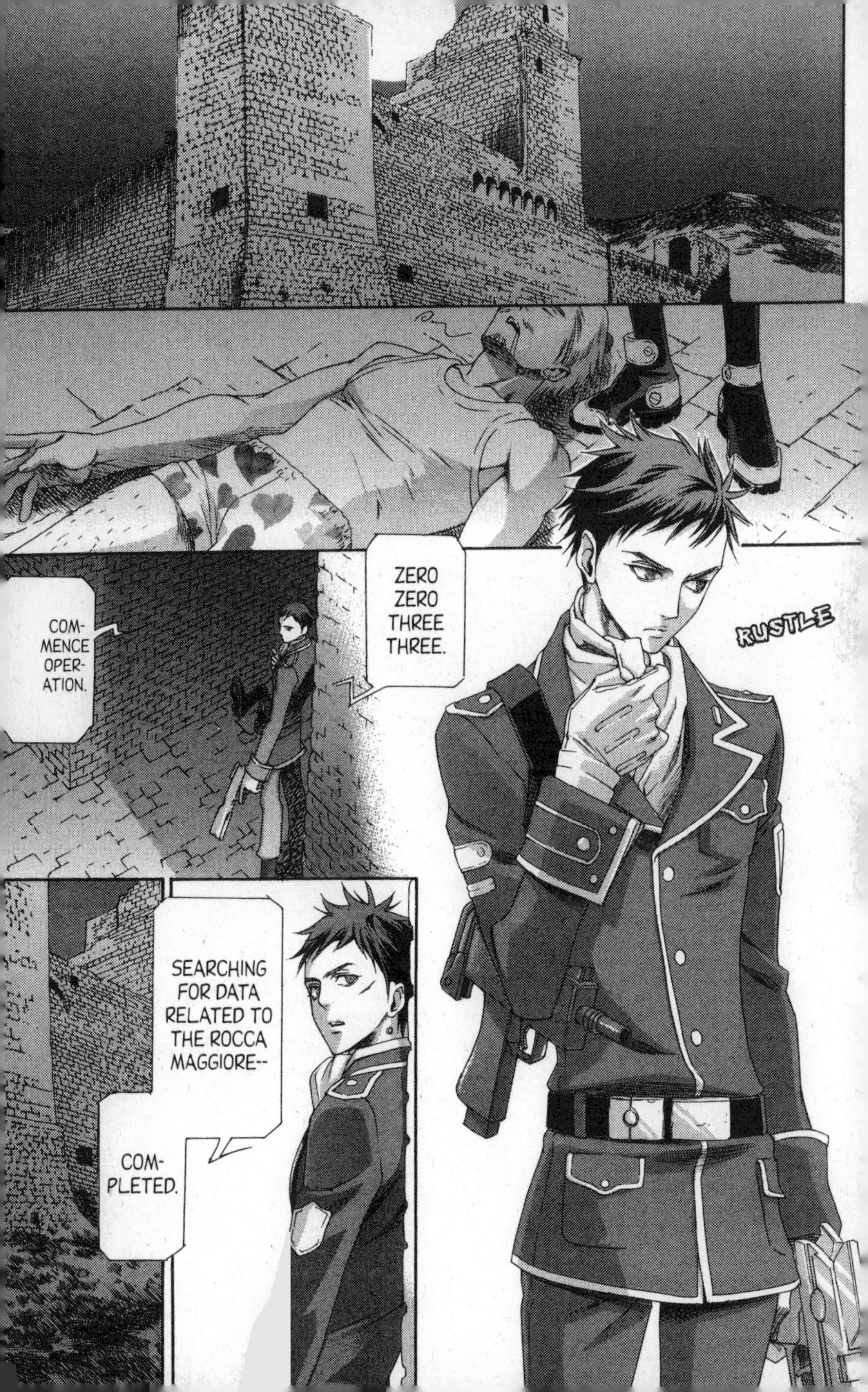
ZERO ZERO THREE THREE.
RUSTLE
COMMENCE OPERATION.
SEARCHING FOR DATA RELATED TO THE ROCCA MAGGIORE--
COMPLETED.

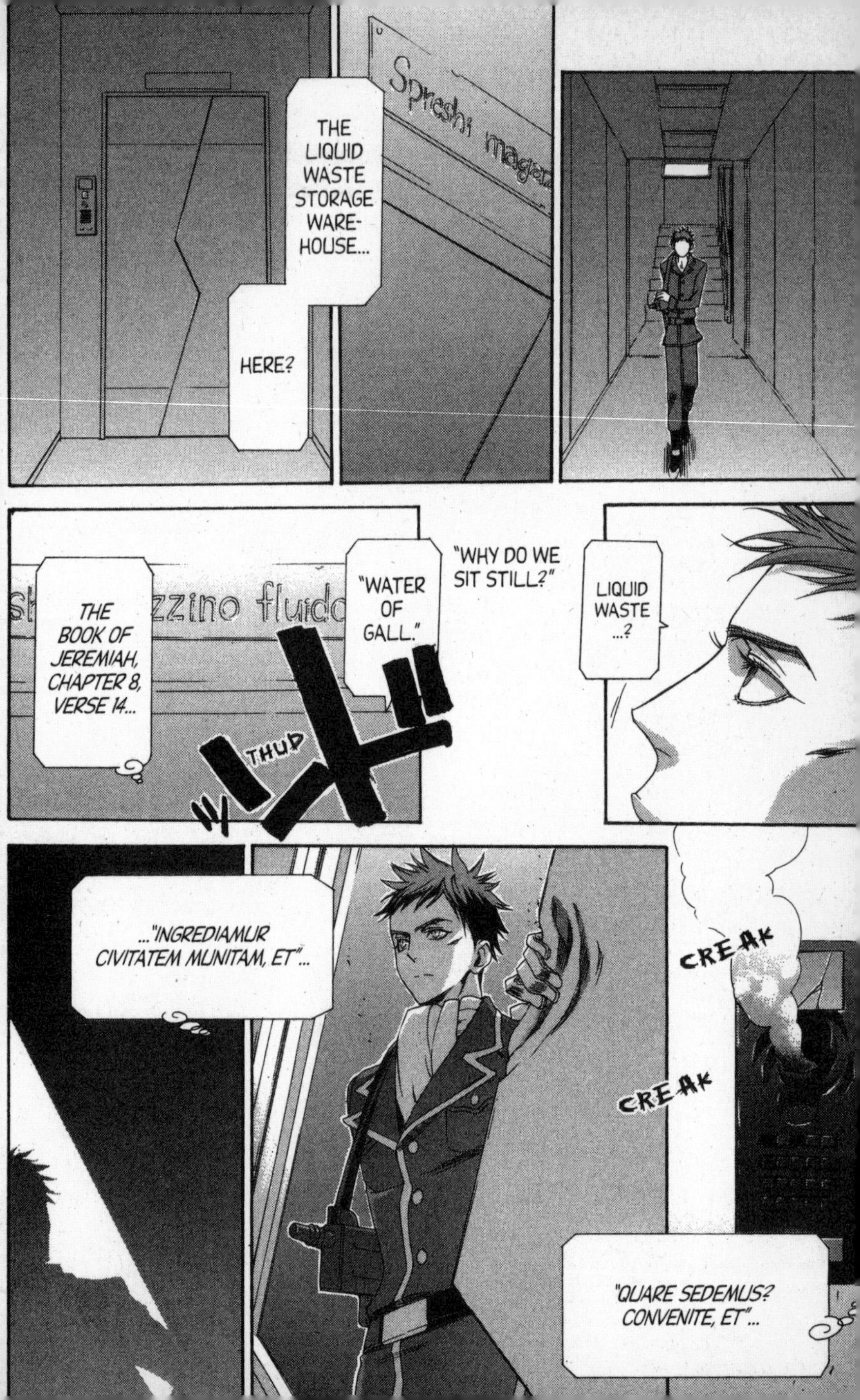
THE LIQUID WASTE STORAGE WARE-HOUSE...
HERE?
LIQUID WASTE ...?
"WHY DO WE SIT STILL?"
"WATER OF GALL."
THE BOOK OF JEREMIAH, CHAPTER 8, VERSE 14...
THUD
CREAK
CREAK
"QUARE SEDEMUS? CONVENITE, ET"...
..."INGREDIAMUR CIVITATEM MUNITAM, ET"...

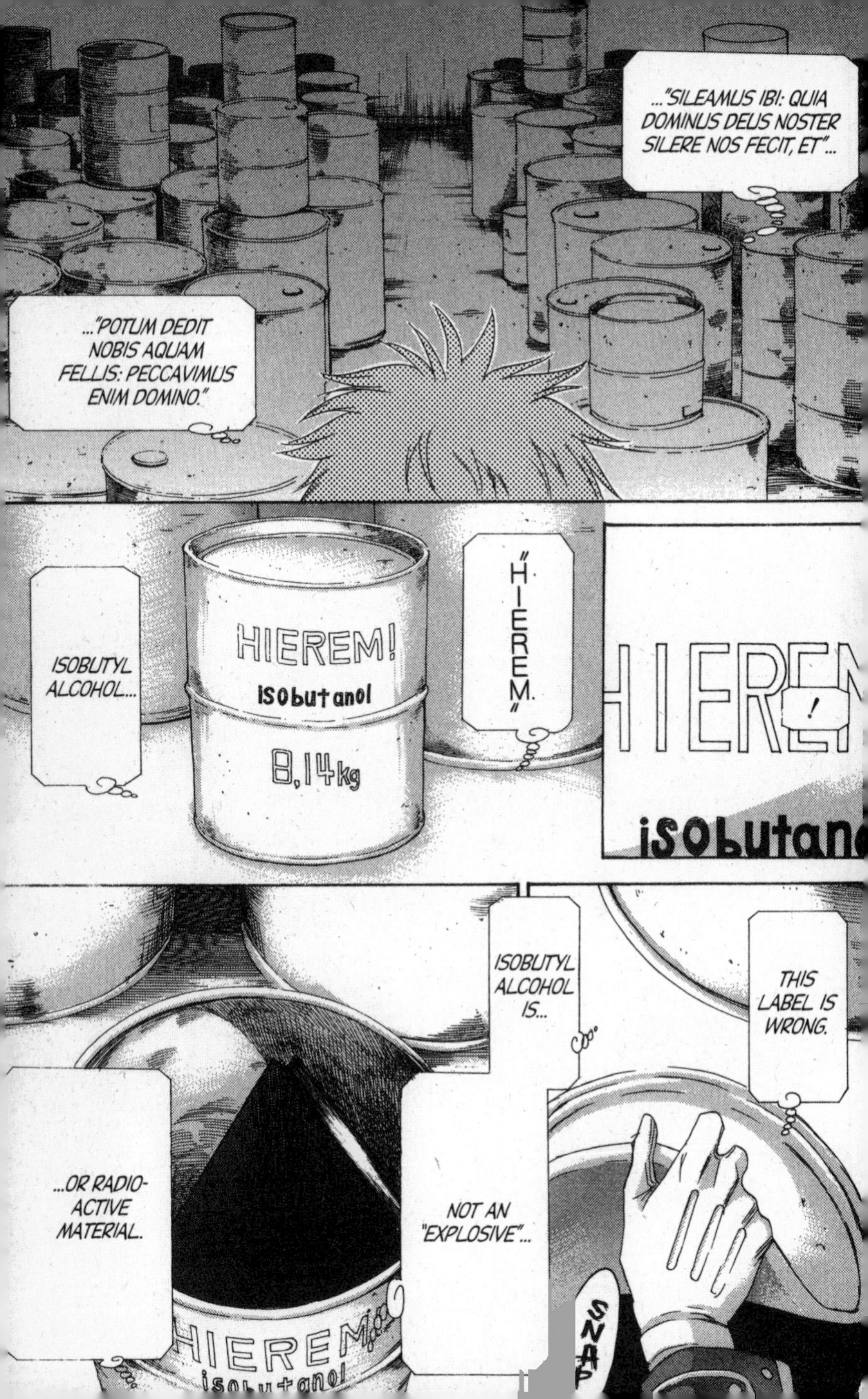
..."SILEAMUS IBI: QUIA DOMINUS DEUS NOSTER SILERE NOS FECIT, ET"...
..."POTUM DEDIT NOBIS AQUAM FELLIS: PECCAVIMUS ENIM DOMINO."
HIEREM
!
isobutan
"HIEREM."
HIEREM!
isobutanol
8,14kg
ISOBUTYL ALCOHOL...
THIS LABEL IS WRONG.
ISOBUTYL ALCOHOL IS...
NOT AN "EXPLOSIVE"...
SNAP
...OR RADIO-ACTIVE MATERIAL.
HIEREM
isobutanol

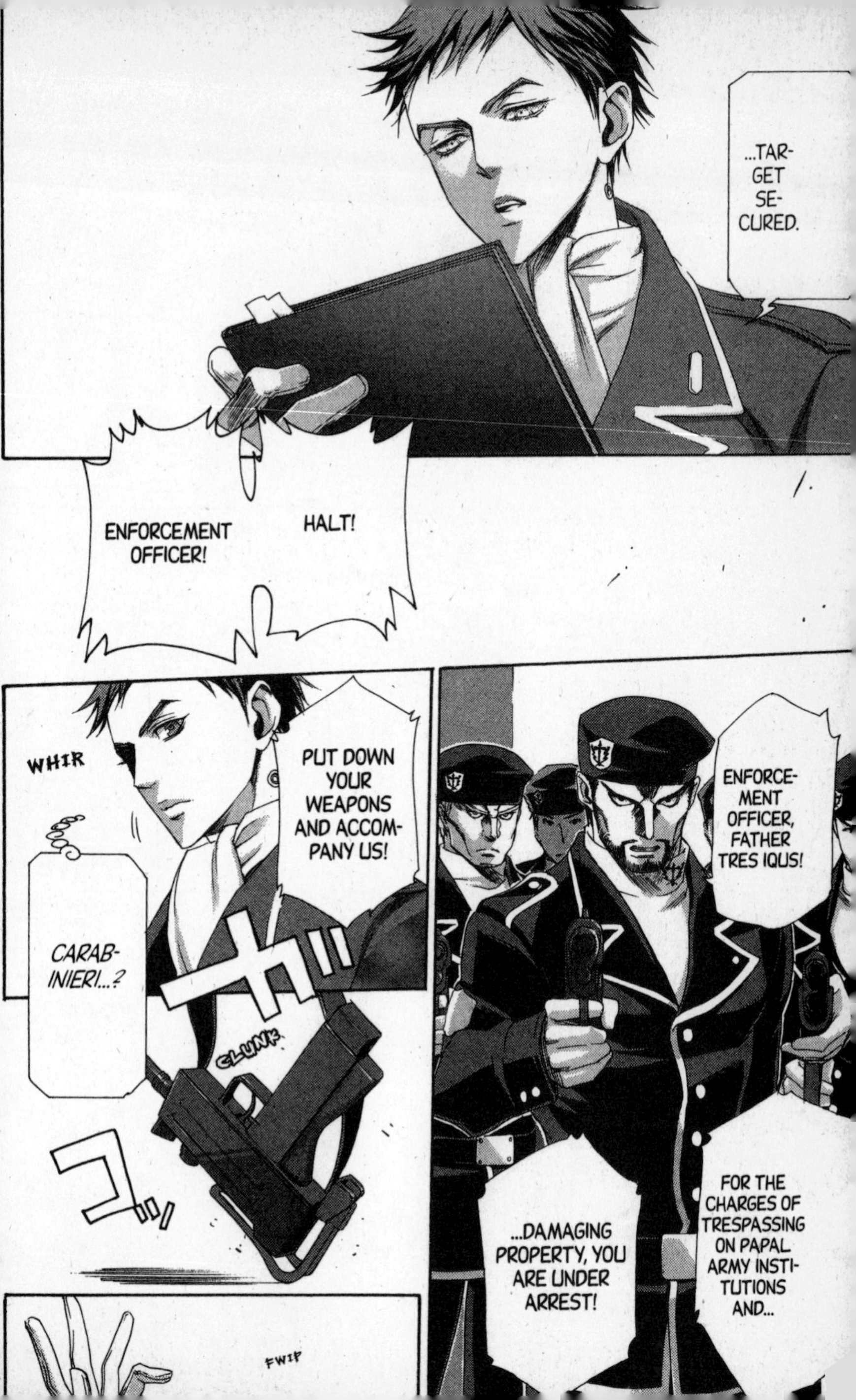

...TARGET SECURED.
HALT!
ENFORCEMENT OFFICER!
ENFORCEMENT OFFICER, FATHER TRES IQUS!
FOR THE CHARGES OF TRESPASSING ON PAPAL ARMY INSTITUTIONS AND...
...DAMAGING PROPERTY, YOU ARE UNDER ARREST!
PUT DOWN YOUR WEAPONS AND ACCOMPANY US!
WHIR
CARABINIERI...?
CLUNK
FWIP

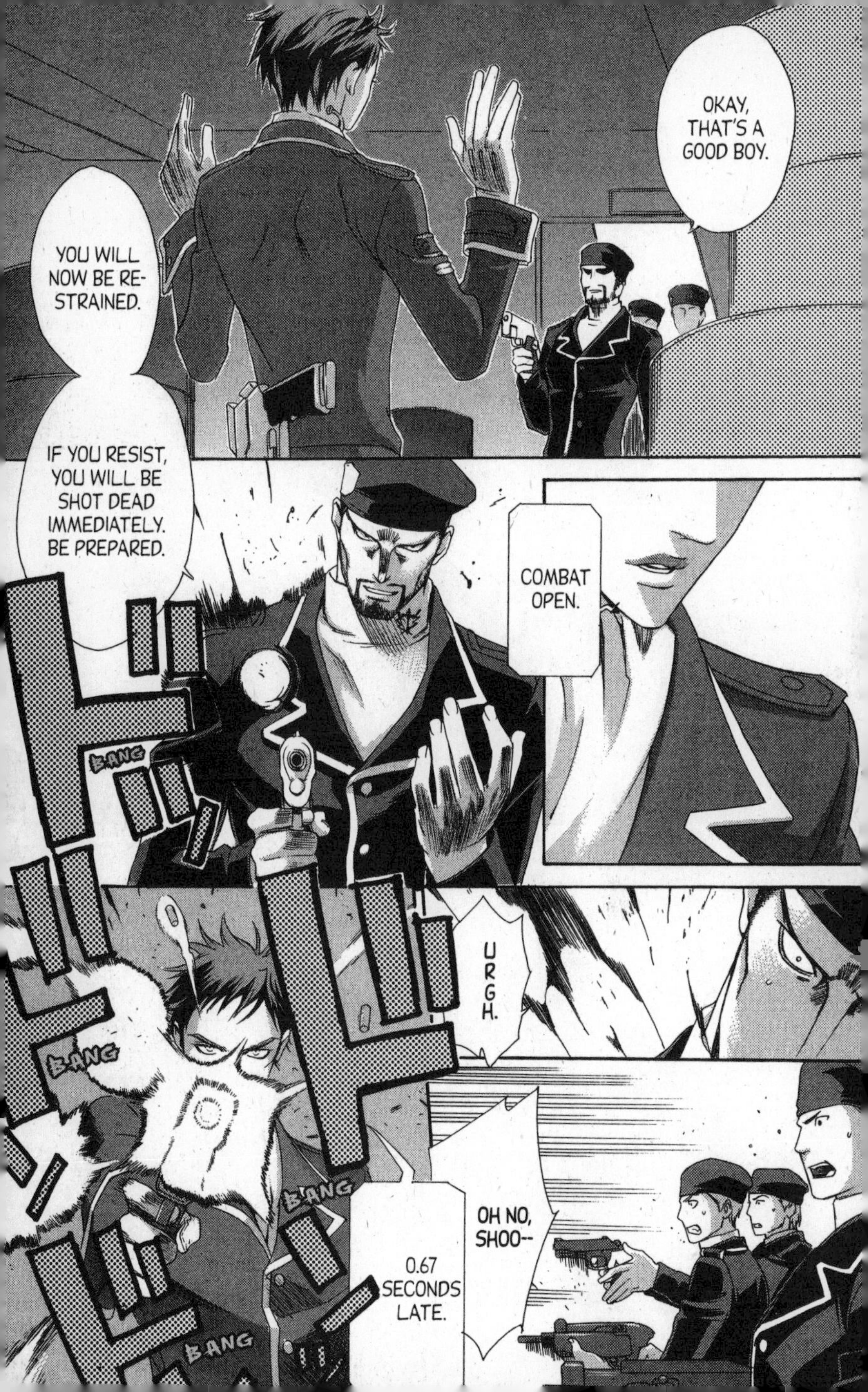
OKAY, THAT'S A GOOD BOY.
YOU WILL NOW BE RE-STRAINED.
IF YOU RESIST, YOU WILL BE SHOT DEAD IMMEDIATELY. BE PREPARED.
COMBAT OPEN.
BANG
URGH.
BANG
OH NO, SHOO--
0.67 SECONDS LATE.
BANG
BANG

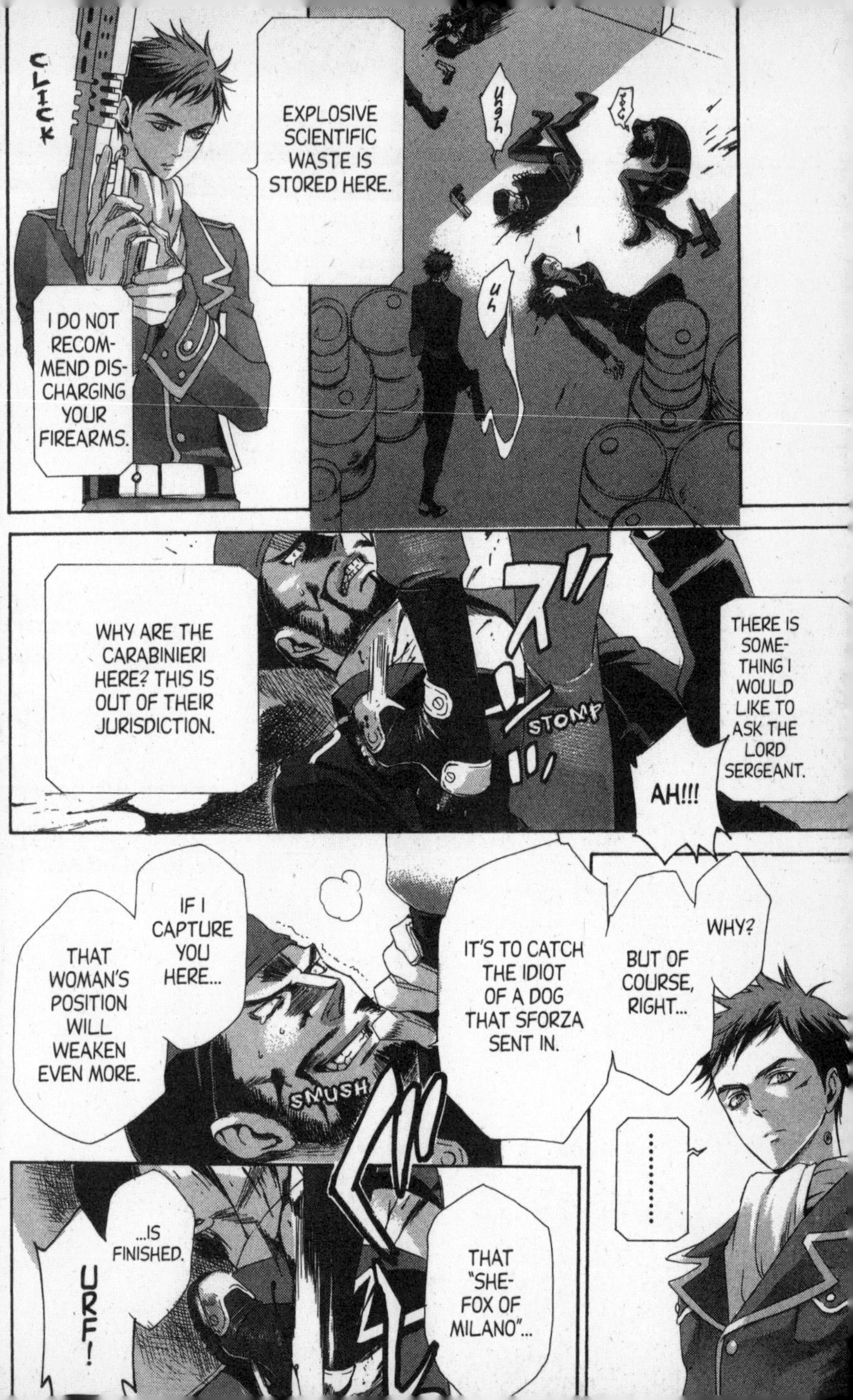
ugh
uh
EXPLOSIVE SCIENTIFIC WASTE IS STORED HERE.
I DO NOT RECOMMEND DISCHARGING YOUR FIREARMS.
CLICK
THERE IS SOMETHING I WOULD LIKE TO ASK THE LORD SERGEANT.
AH!!!
STOMP
WHY ARE THE CARABINIERI HERE? THIS IS OUT OF THEIR JURISDICTION.
WHY?
BUT OF COURSE, RIGHT...
IT'S TO CATCH THE IDIOT OF A DOG THAT SFORZA SENT IN.
IF I CAPTURE YOU HERE...
THAT WOMAN'S POSITION WILL WEAKEN EVEN MORE.
SMUSH
......
THAT "SHE-FOX OF MILANO"...
...IS FINISHED.
URF!

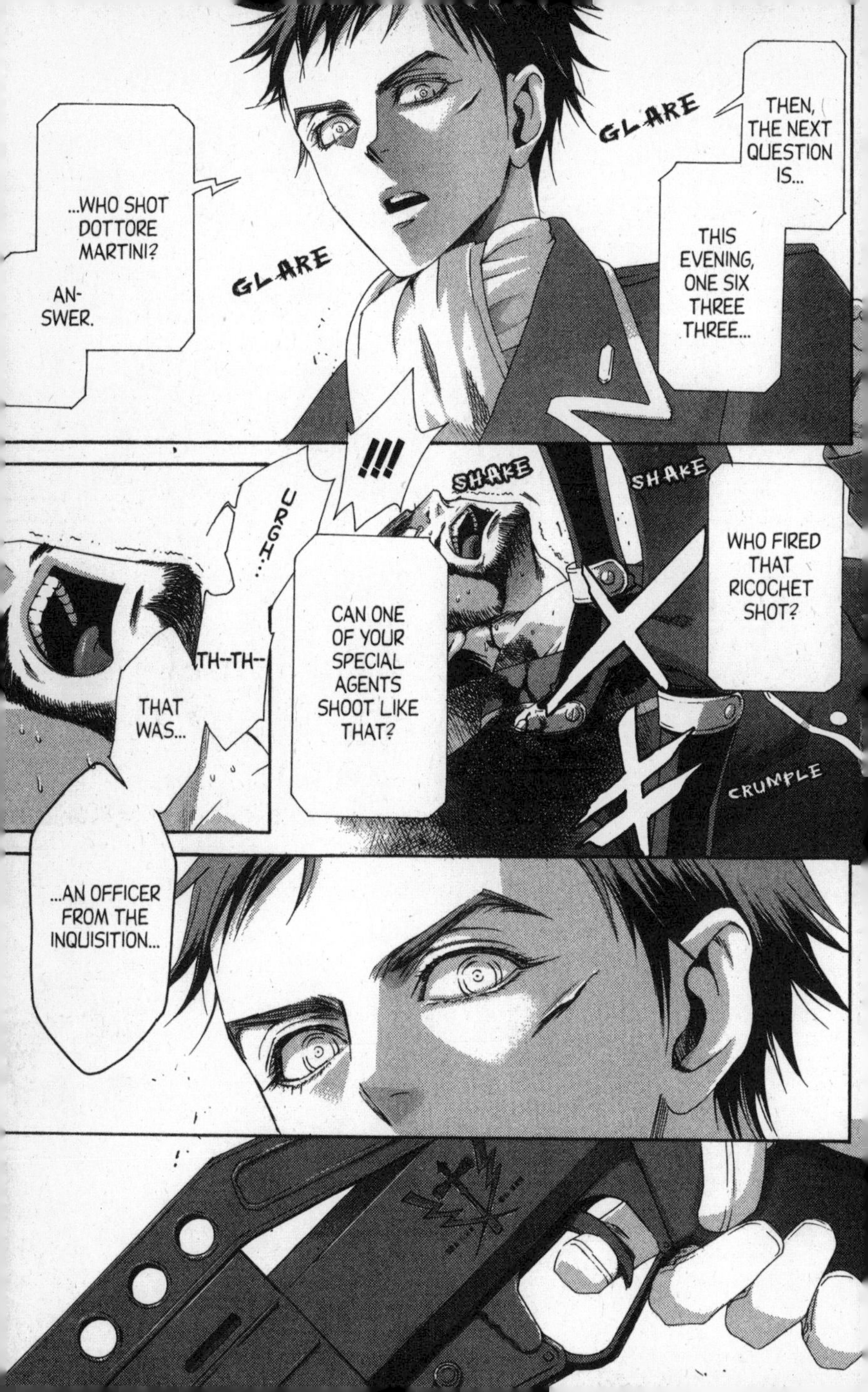
THEN, THE NEXT QUESTION IS...
THIS EVENING, ONE SIX THREE THREE...
GLARE
...WHO SHOT DOTTORE MARTINI?
AN-SWER.
GLARE
SHAKE
SHAKE
WHO FIRED THAT RICOCHET SHOT?
CAN ONE OF YOUR SPECIAL AGENTS SHOOT LIKE THAT?
!!!
CRUMPLE
URGH...
TH--TH--
THAT WAS...
...AN OFFICER FROM THE INQUISITION...

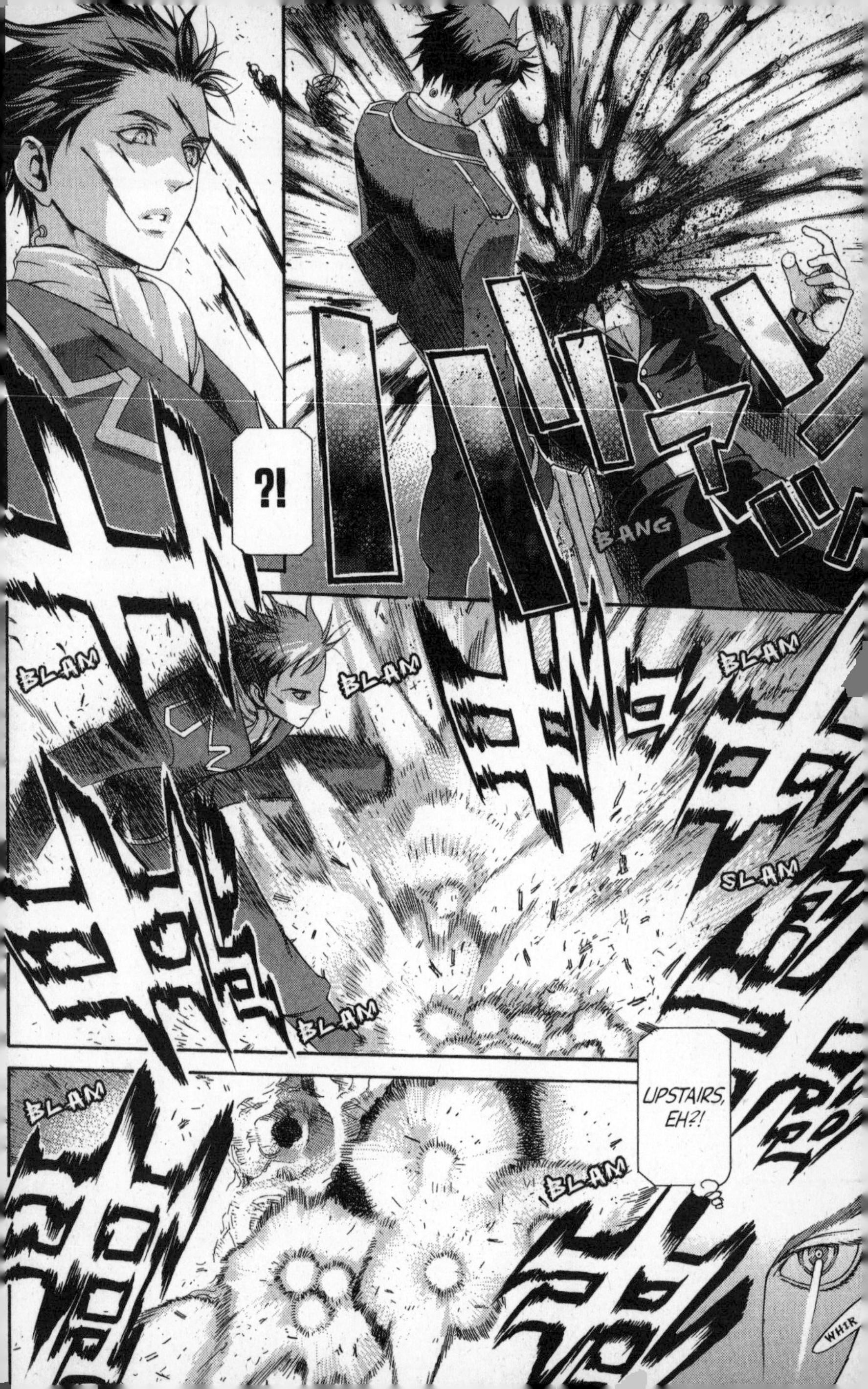
BANG
?!
BLAM
BLAM
BLAM
SLAM
BLAM
UPSTAIRS, EH?!
BLAM
BLAM
WHIR

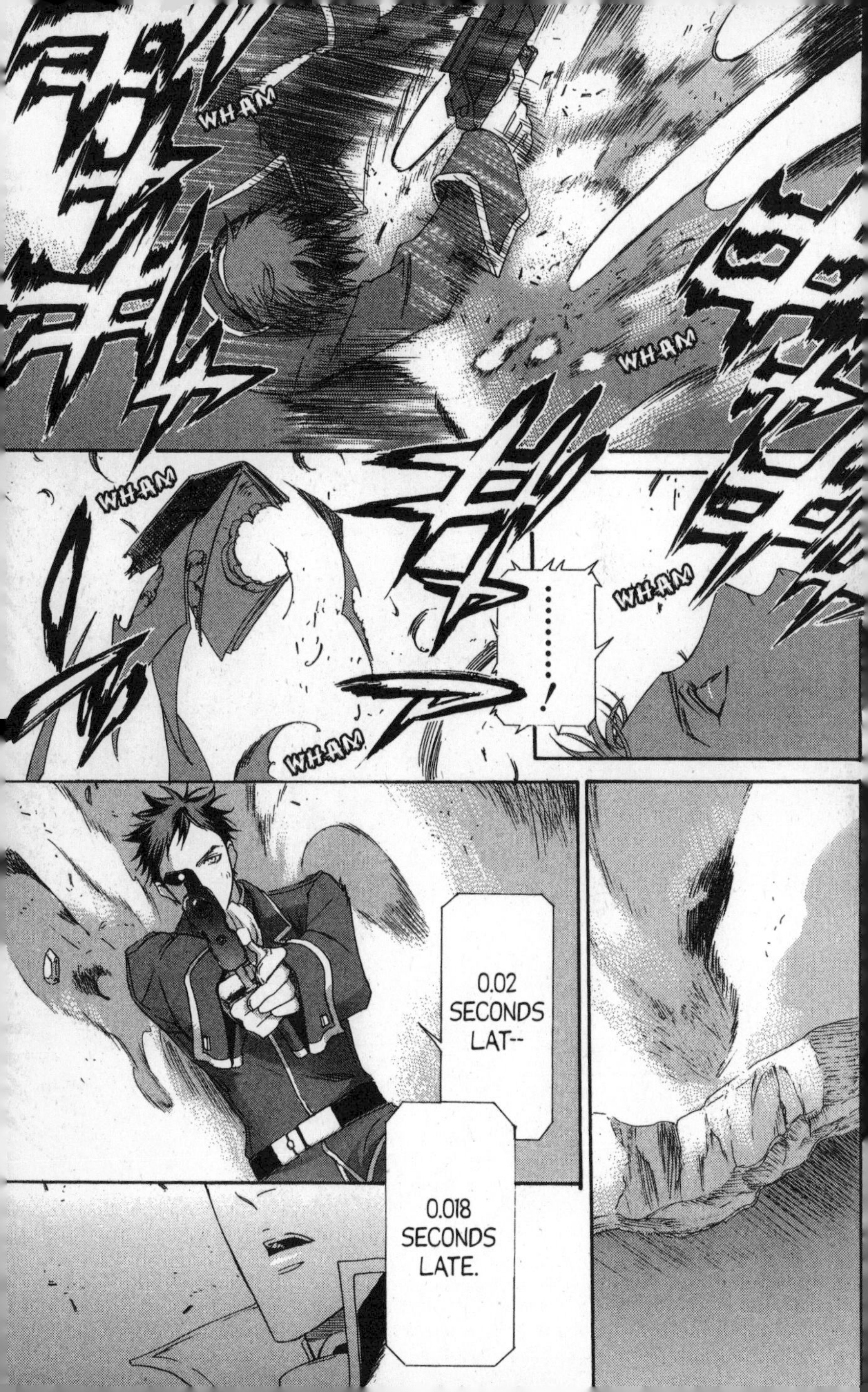
WHAM
WHAM
WHAM
......!
WHAM
WHAM
0.02 SECONDS LAT--
0.018 SECONDS LATE.

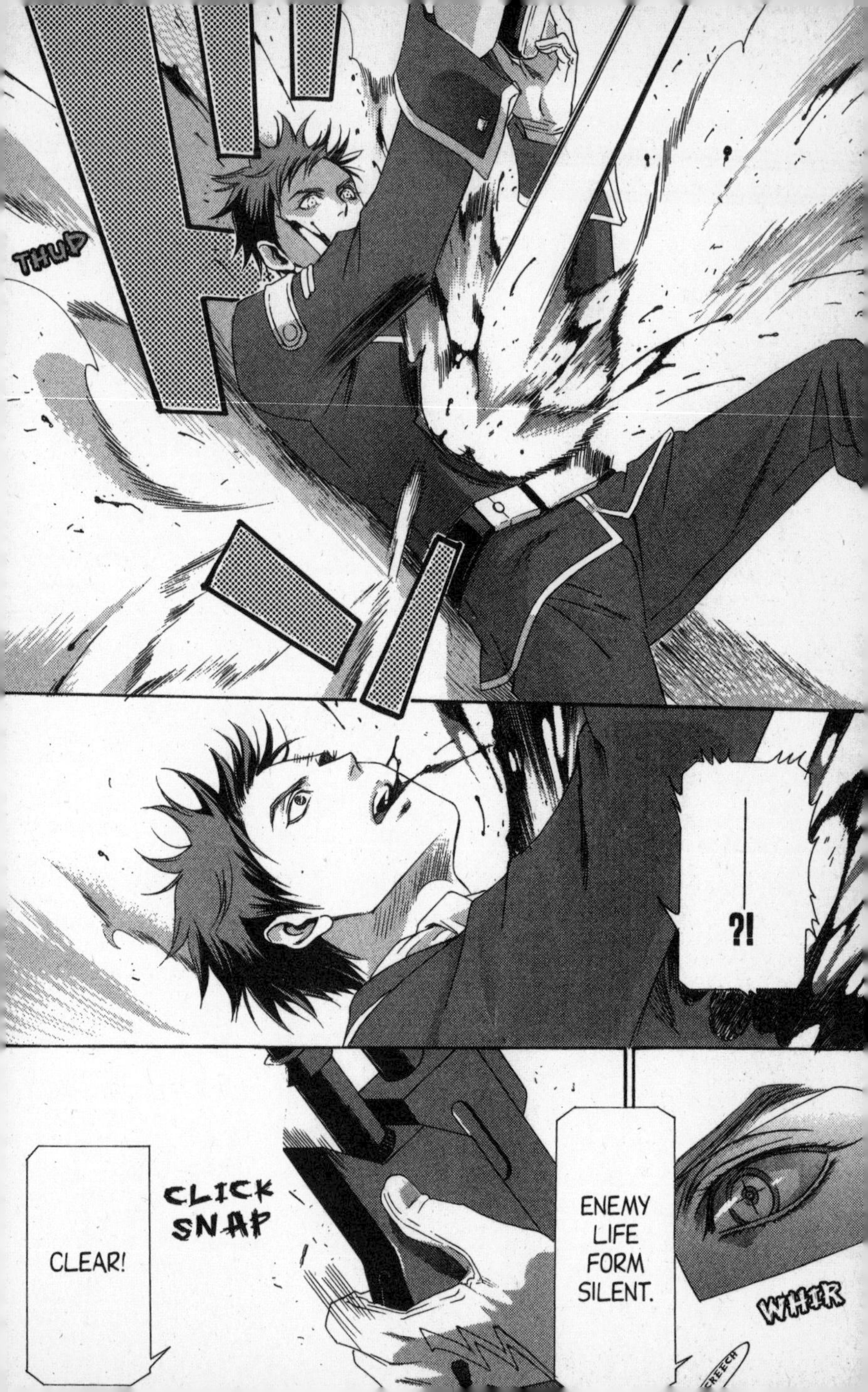
THUD
?!
WHIR
ENEMY LIFE FORM SILENT.
CLICK SNAP
CLEAR!

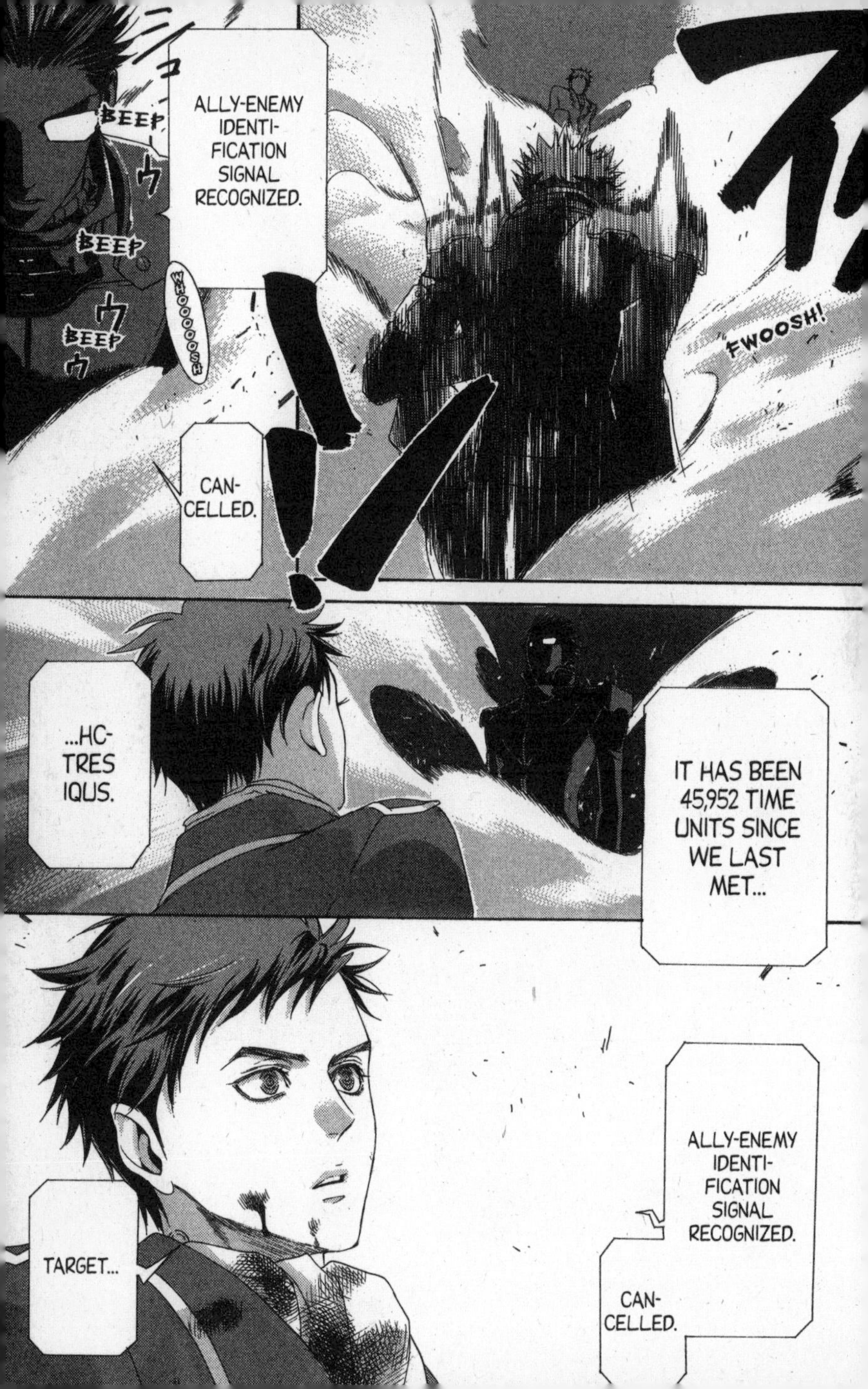
ALLY-ENEMY IDENTI-FICATION SIGNAL RECOGNIZED.
BEEP
BEEP
FWOOSH!
WHOOOOOSH
BEEP
CAN-CELLED.
IT HAS BEEN 45,952 TIME UNITS SINCE WE LAST MET...
...HC-TRES IQUS.
ALLY-ENEMY IDENTI-FICATION SIGNAL RECOGNIZED.
CAN-CELLED.
TARGET...

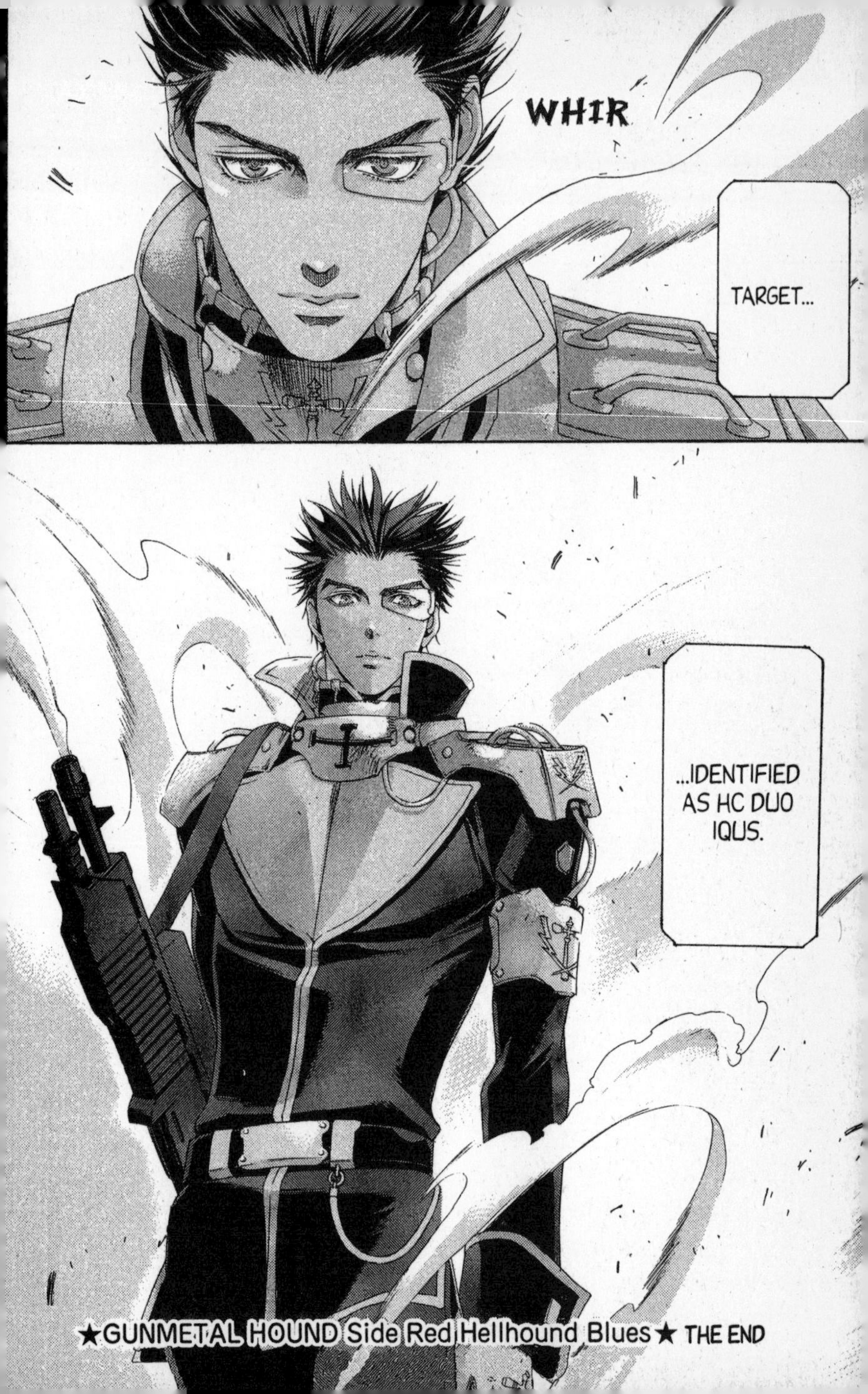
WHIR
TARGET...
...IDENTIFIED AS HC DUO IQUS.
★GUNMETAL HOUND Side Red Hellhound Blues★ THE END

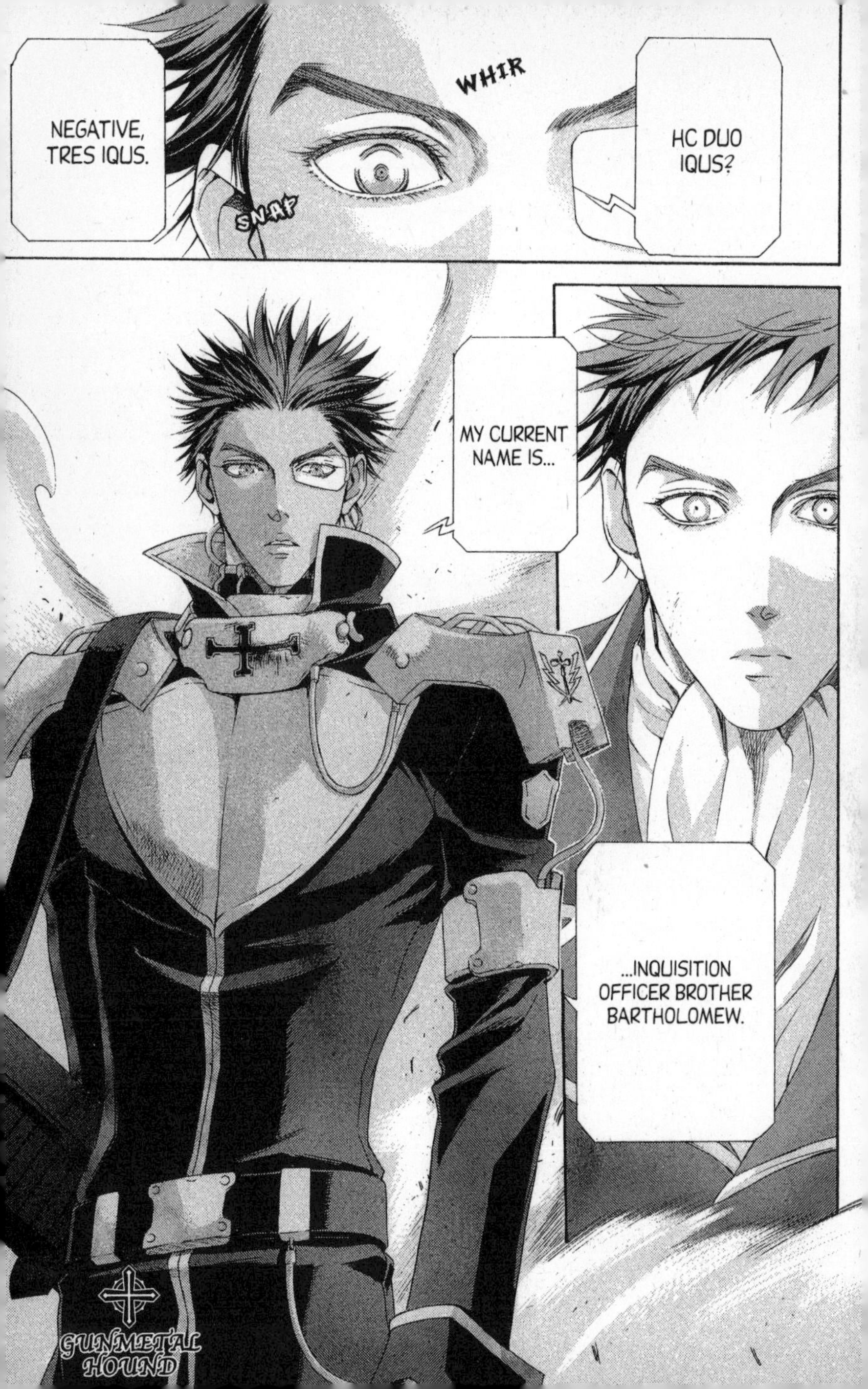

HC DUO IQUS?
WHIR
NEGATIVE, TRES IQUS.
SNAP
MY CURRENT NAME IS...
...INQUISITION OFFICER BROTHER BARTHOLOMEW.
GUNMETAL HOUND

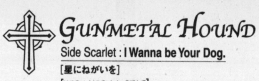

GUNMETAL HOUND

Side Scarlet : I Wanna be Your Dog.

[星にねがいを]
[WISH UPON A STAR]

"I'm no man. I'm machine."
And the DOLL's house
continues growing yet.

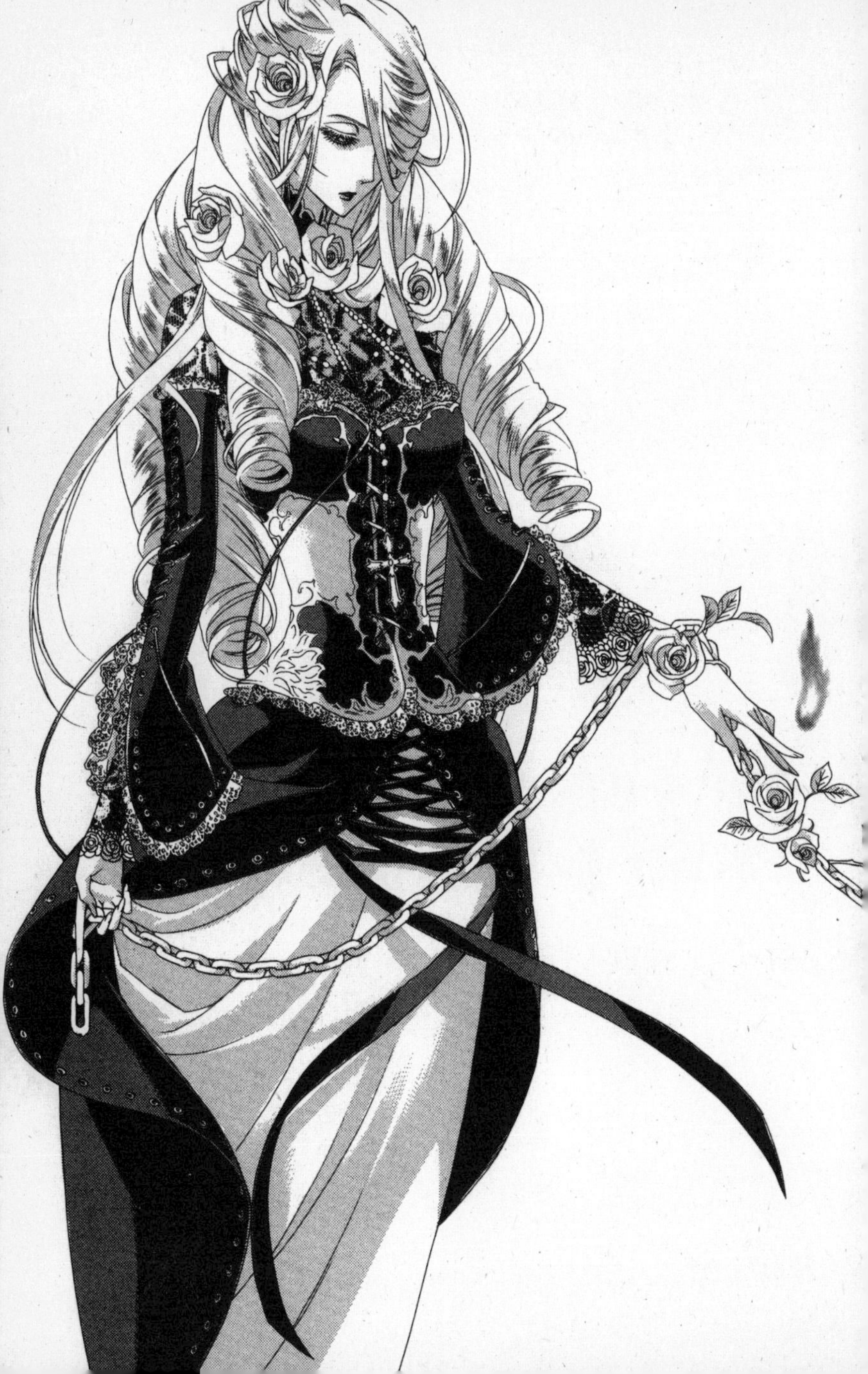

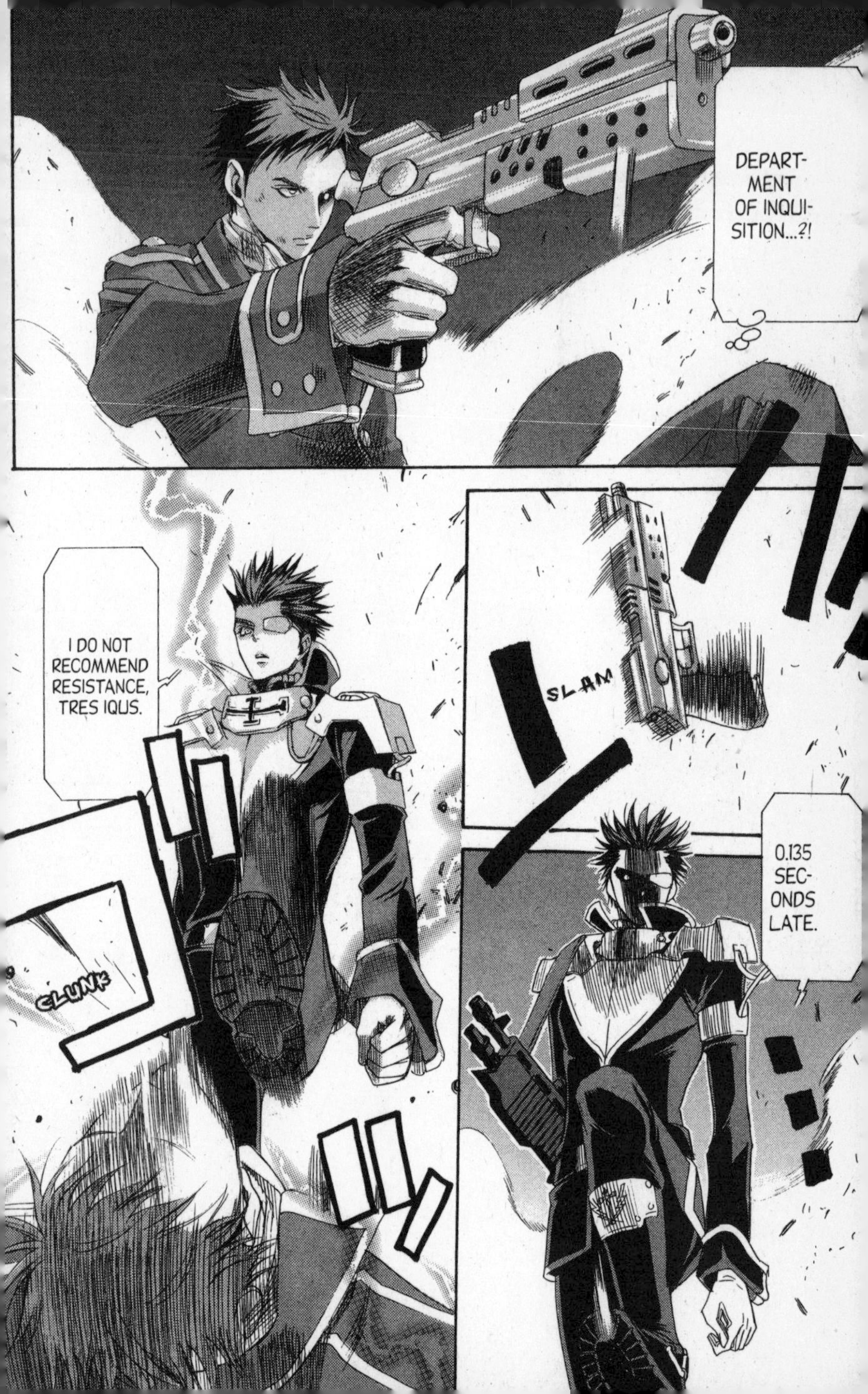

DEPARTMENT OF INQUISITION...?!
SLAM
0.135 SECONDS LATE.
I DO NOT RECOMMEND RESISTANCE, TRES IQUS.
CLUNK

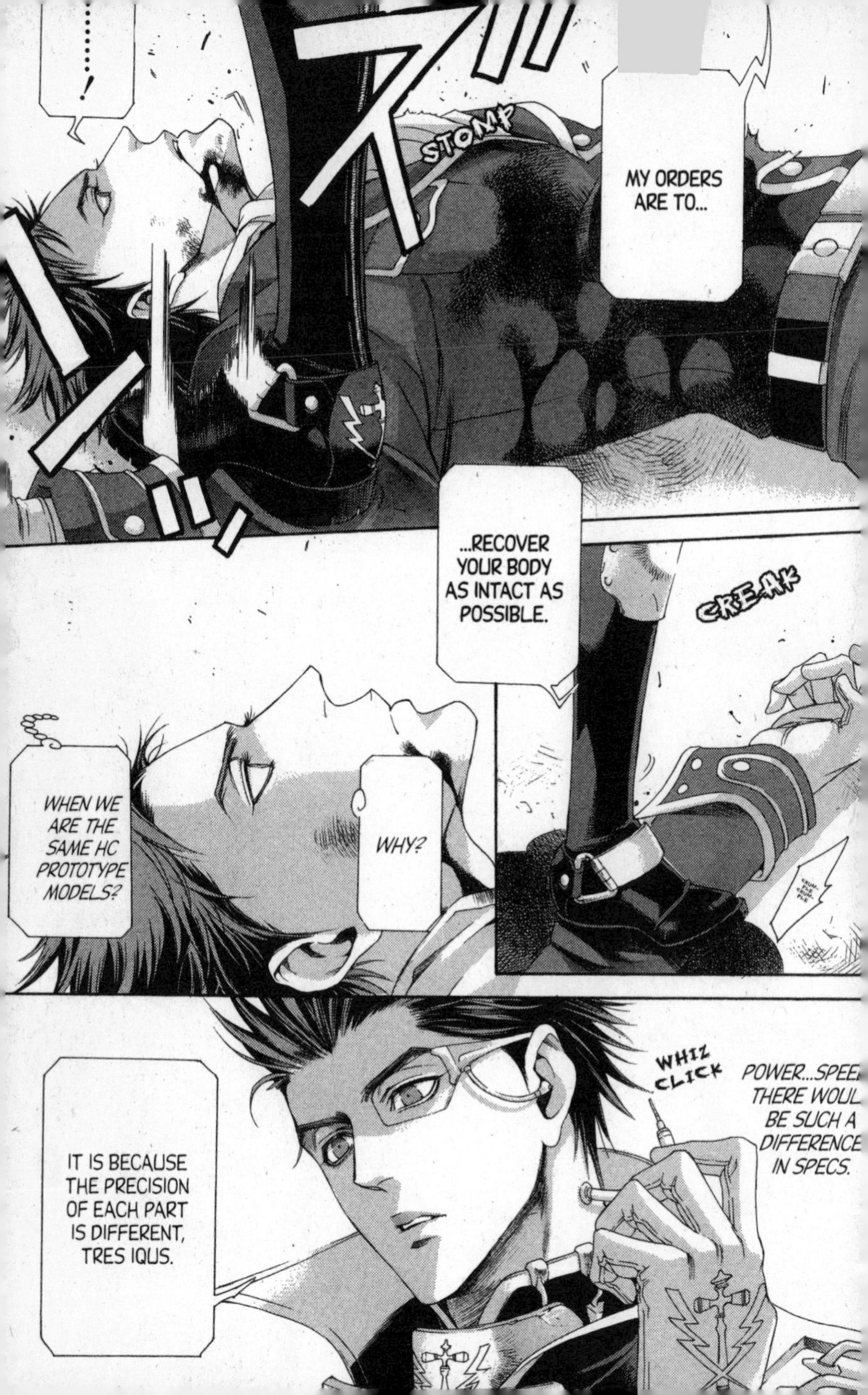
MY ORDERS ARE TO...
STOMP
......!
...RECOVER YOUR BODY AS INTACT AS POSSIBLE.
CREAK
WHY?
WHEN WE ARE THE SAME HC PROTOTYPE MODELS?
POWER...SPEE THERE WOUL BE SUCH A DIFFERENCE IN SPECS.
WHIZ CLICK
IT IS BECAUSE THE PRECISION OF EACH PART IS DIFFERENT, TRES IQUS.

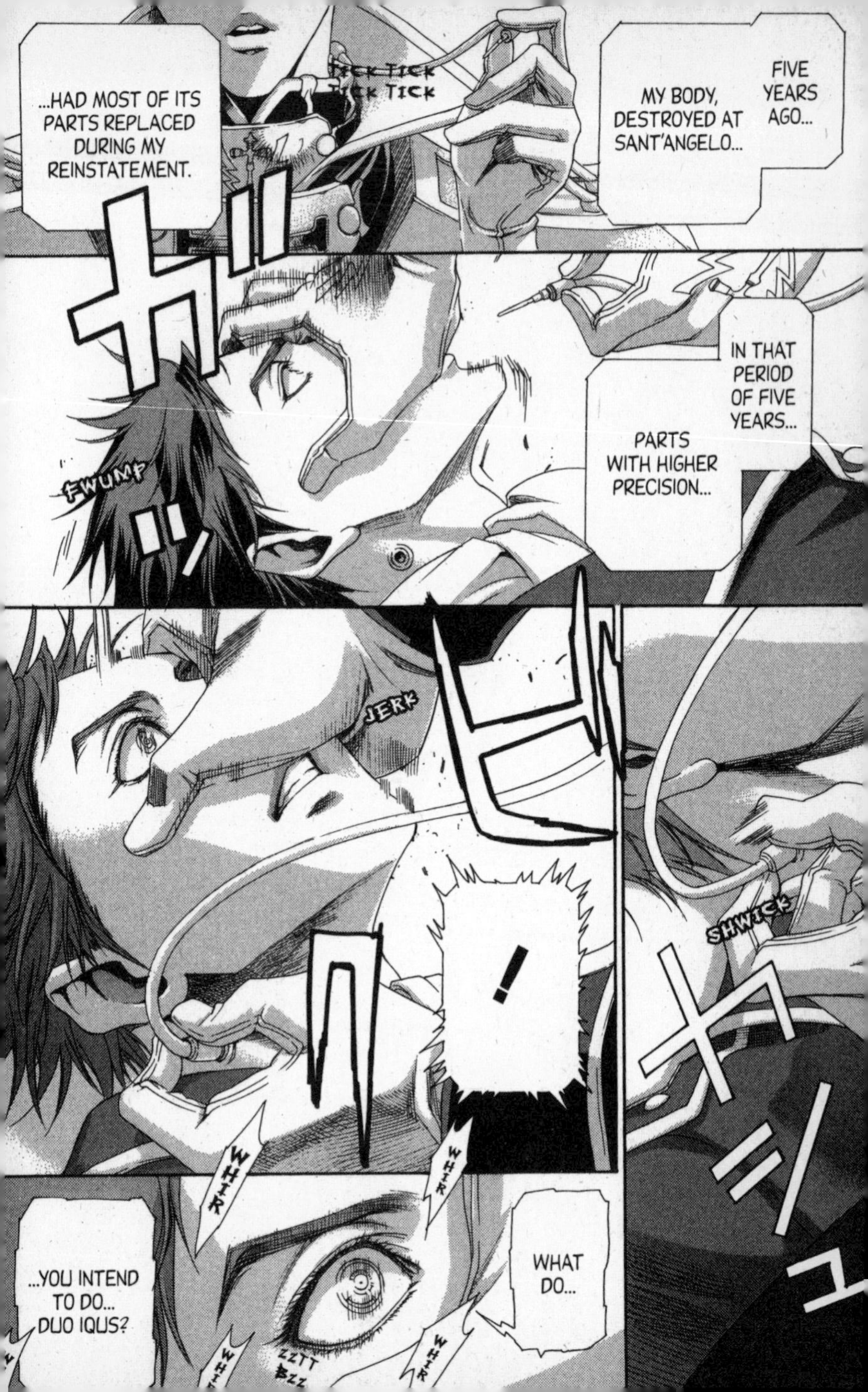
FIVE YEARS AGO...
MY BODY, DESTROYED AT SANT'ANGELO...
TICK TICK TICK TICK
...HAD MOST OF ITS PARTS REPLACED DURING MY REINSTATEMENT.
IN THAT PERIOD OF FIVE YEARS...
PARTS WITH HIGHER PRECISION...
FWUMP
SHWICK
JERK
!
WHIR
WHIR
WHAT DO...
...YOU INTEND TO DO... DUO IQUS?
ZZTT BZZ
WHIR
WHIR

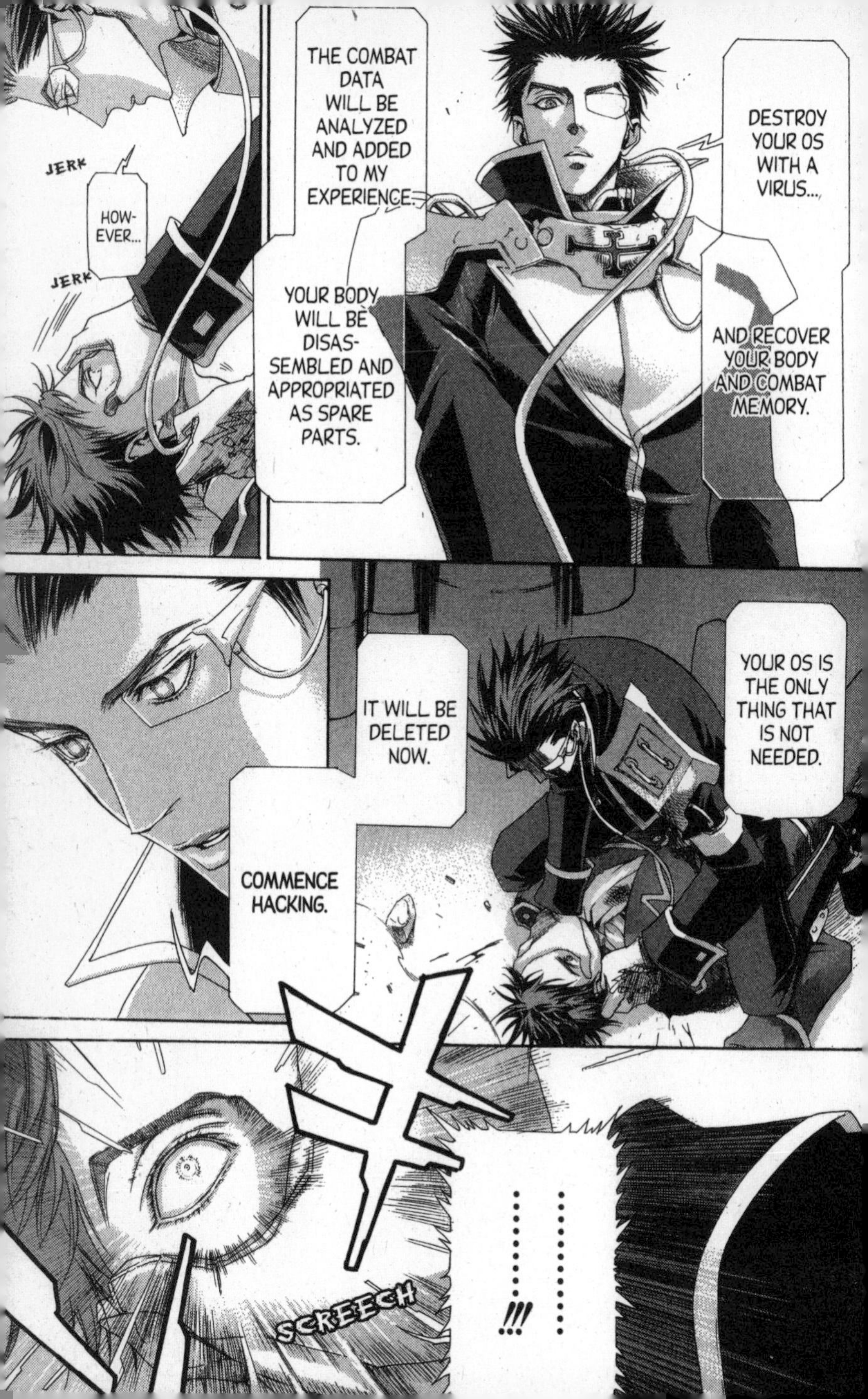
DESTROY YOUR OS WITH A VIRUS...,
AND RECOVER YOUR BODY AND COMBAT MEMORY.
THE COMBAT DATA WILL BE ANALYZED AND ADDED TO MY EXPERIENCE.
YOUR BODY WILL BE DISAS-SEMBLED AND APPROPRIATED AS SPARE PARTS.
JERK
HOW-EVER...
JERK
YOUR OS IS THE ONLY THING THAT IS NOT NEEDED.
IT WILL BE DELETED NOW.
COMMENCE HACKING.
......
......!!!
SCREEECH

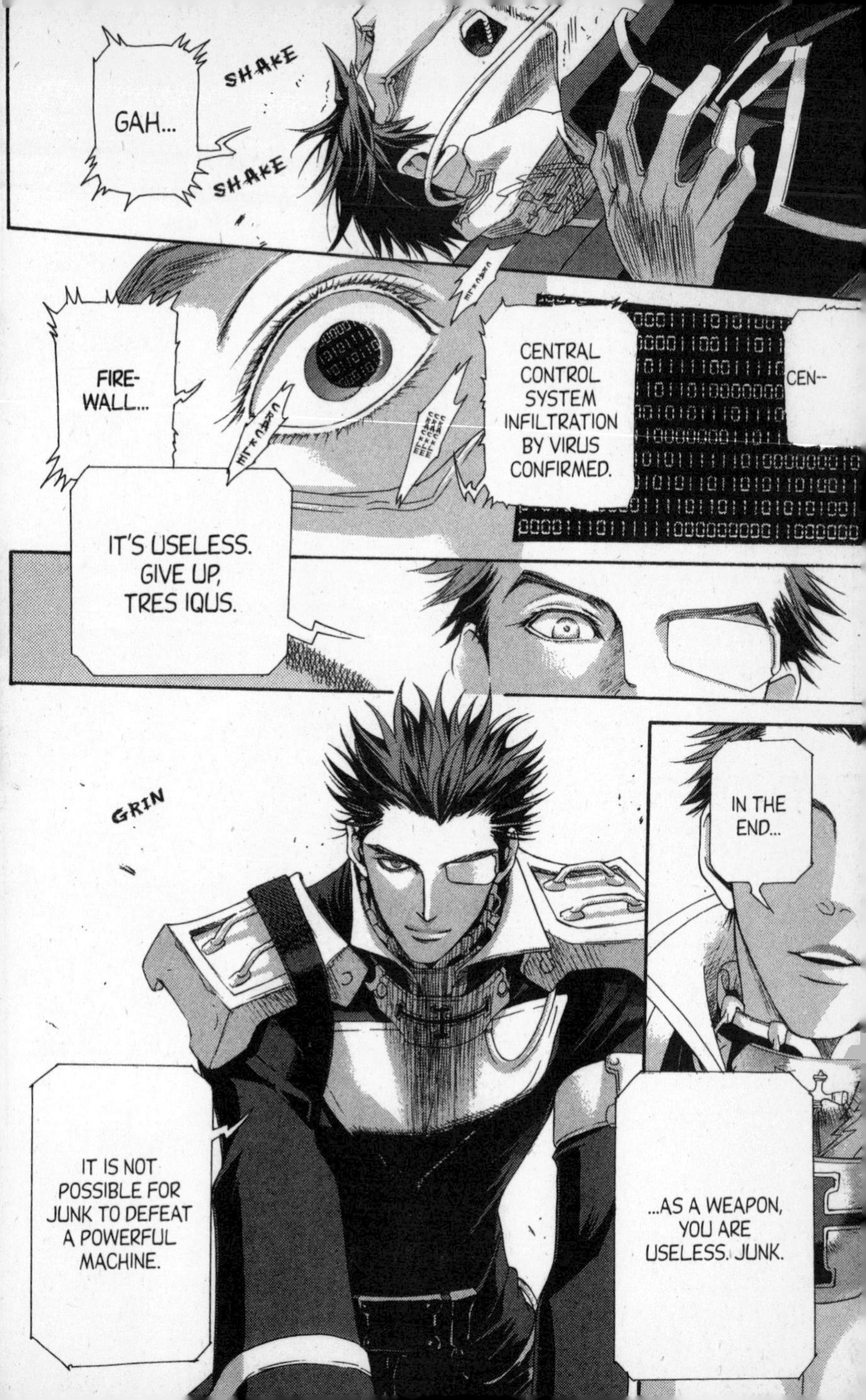
SHAKE
GAH...
SHAKE
CEN--
CENTRAL CONTROL SYSTEM INFILTRATION BY VIRUS CONFIRMED.
FIRE-WALL...
IT'S USELESS. GIVE UP, TRES IQUS.
IN THE END...
...AS A WEAPON, YOU ARE USELESS. JUNK.
GRIN
IT IS NOT POSSIBLE FOR JUNK TO DEFEAT A POWERFUL MACHINE.

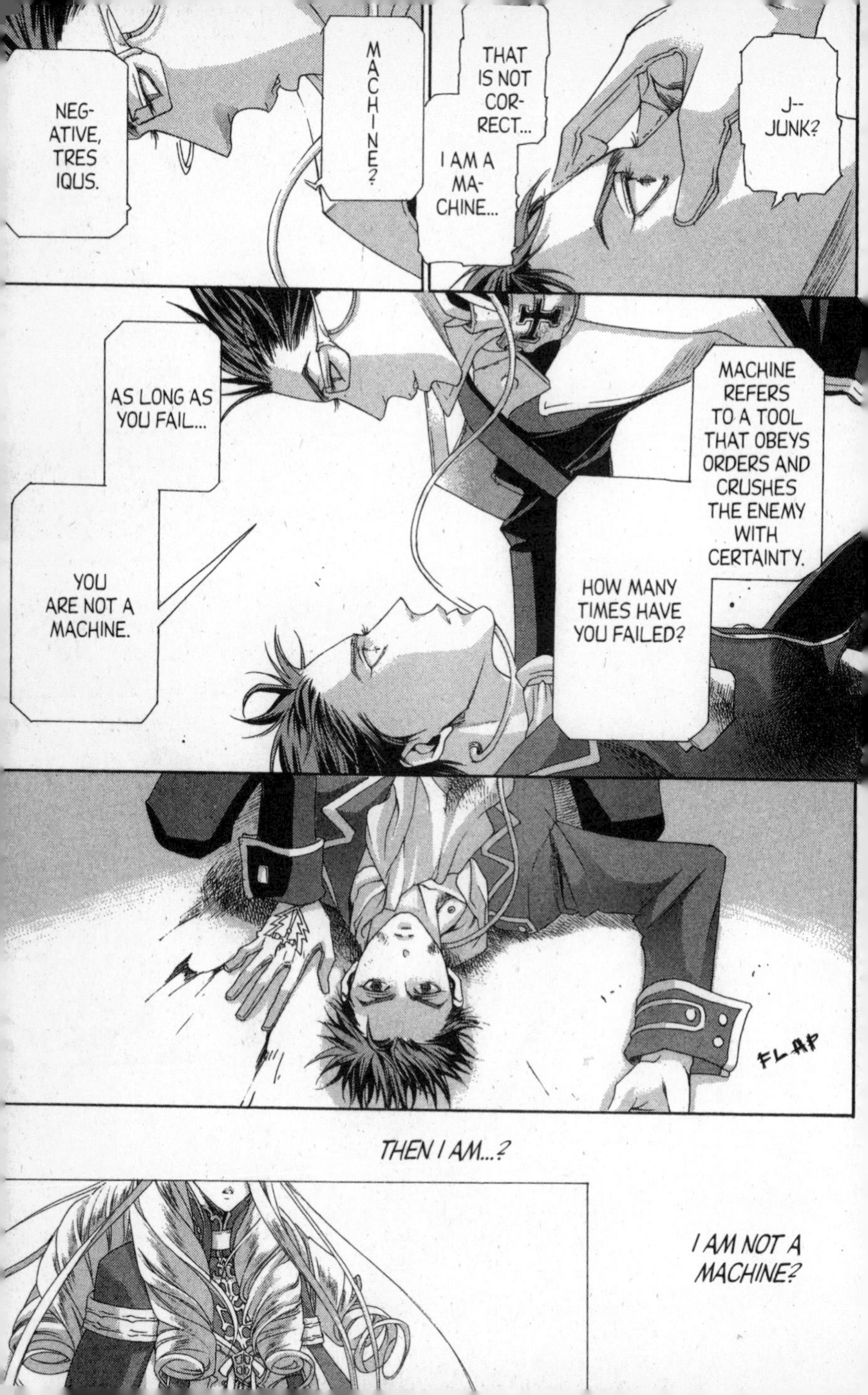
J-- JUNK?
THAT IS NOT CORRECT...
I AM A MACHINE...
MACHINE?
NEGATIVE, TRES IQUS.
MACHINE REFERS TO A TOOL THAT OBEYS ORDERS AND CRUSHES THE ENEMY WITH CERTAINTY.
HOW MANY TIMES HAVE YOU FAILED?
AS LONG AS YOU FAIL...
YOU ARE NOT A MACHINE.
FLAP
THEN I AM...?
I AM NOT A MACHINE?

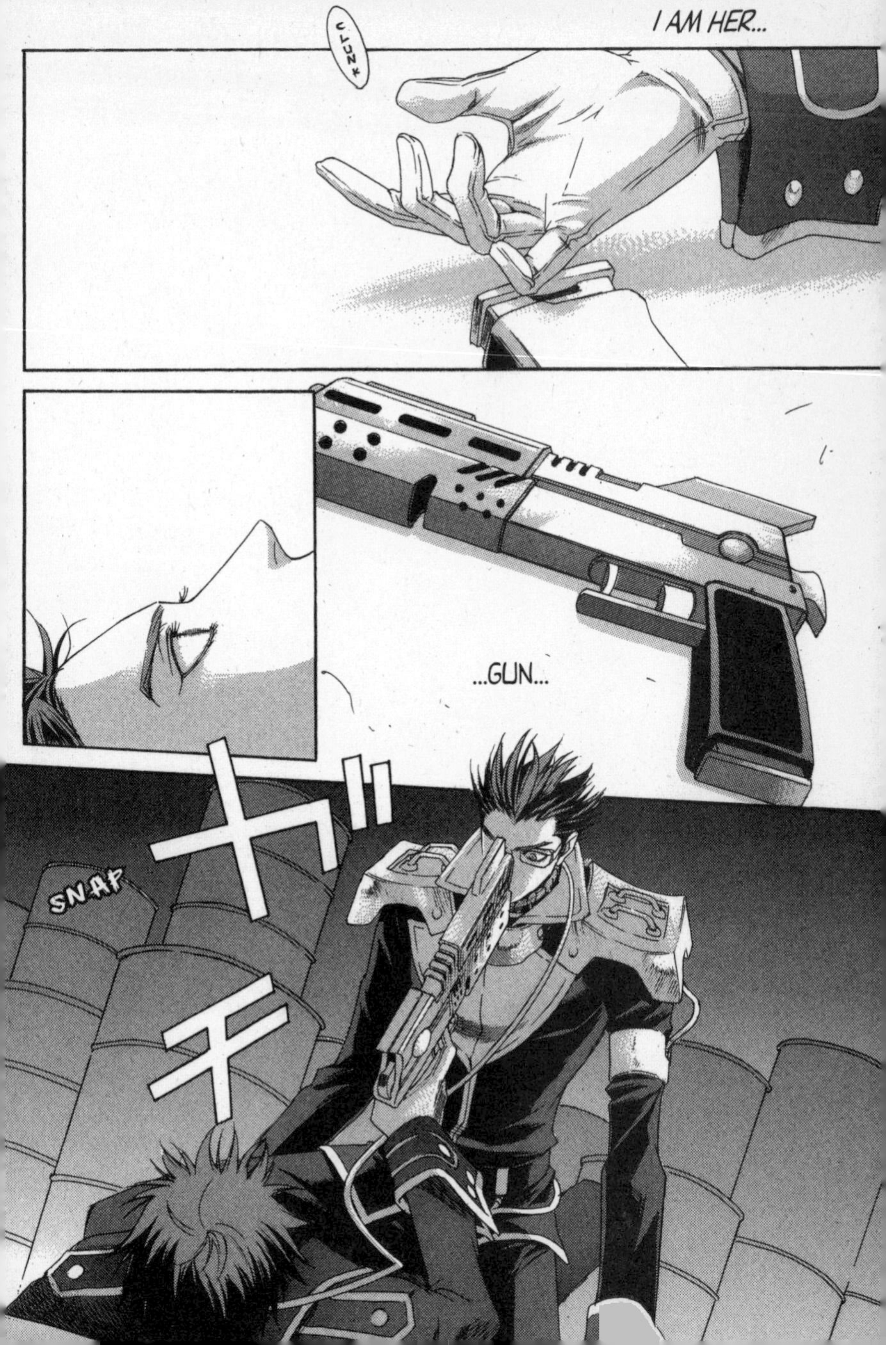
I AM HER...
CLUNK
...GUN...
SNAP

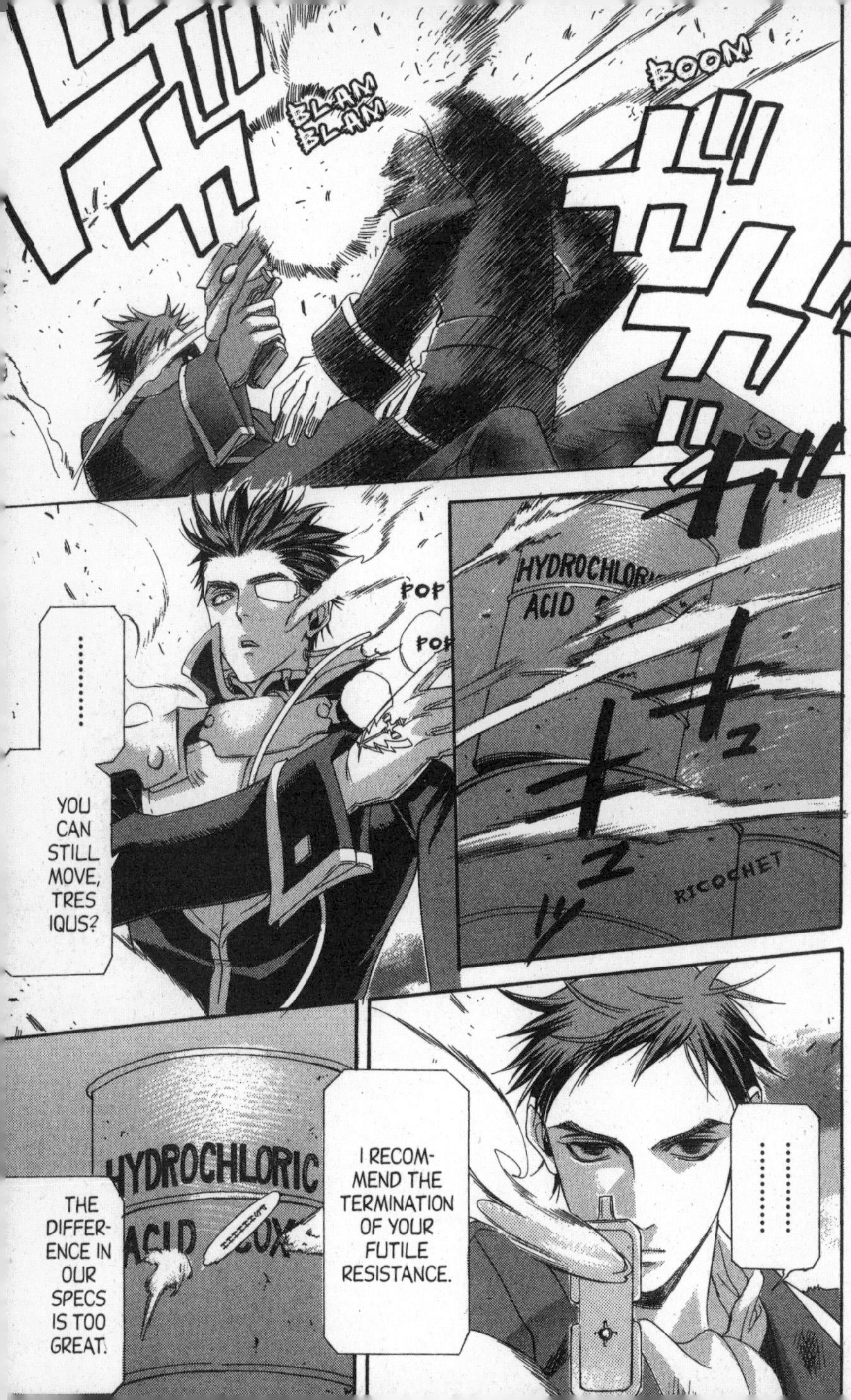
BOOM
BLAM BLAM
POP
POP
RICOCHET
YOU CAN STILL MOVE, TRES IQUS?
....
....
I RECOMMEND THE TERMINATION OF YOUR FUTILE RESISTANCE.
THE DIFFERENCE IN OUR SPECS IS TOO GREAT.
HYDROCHLORIC ACID
HYDROCHLORIC ACID

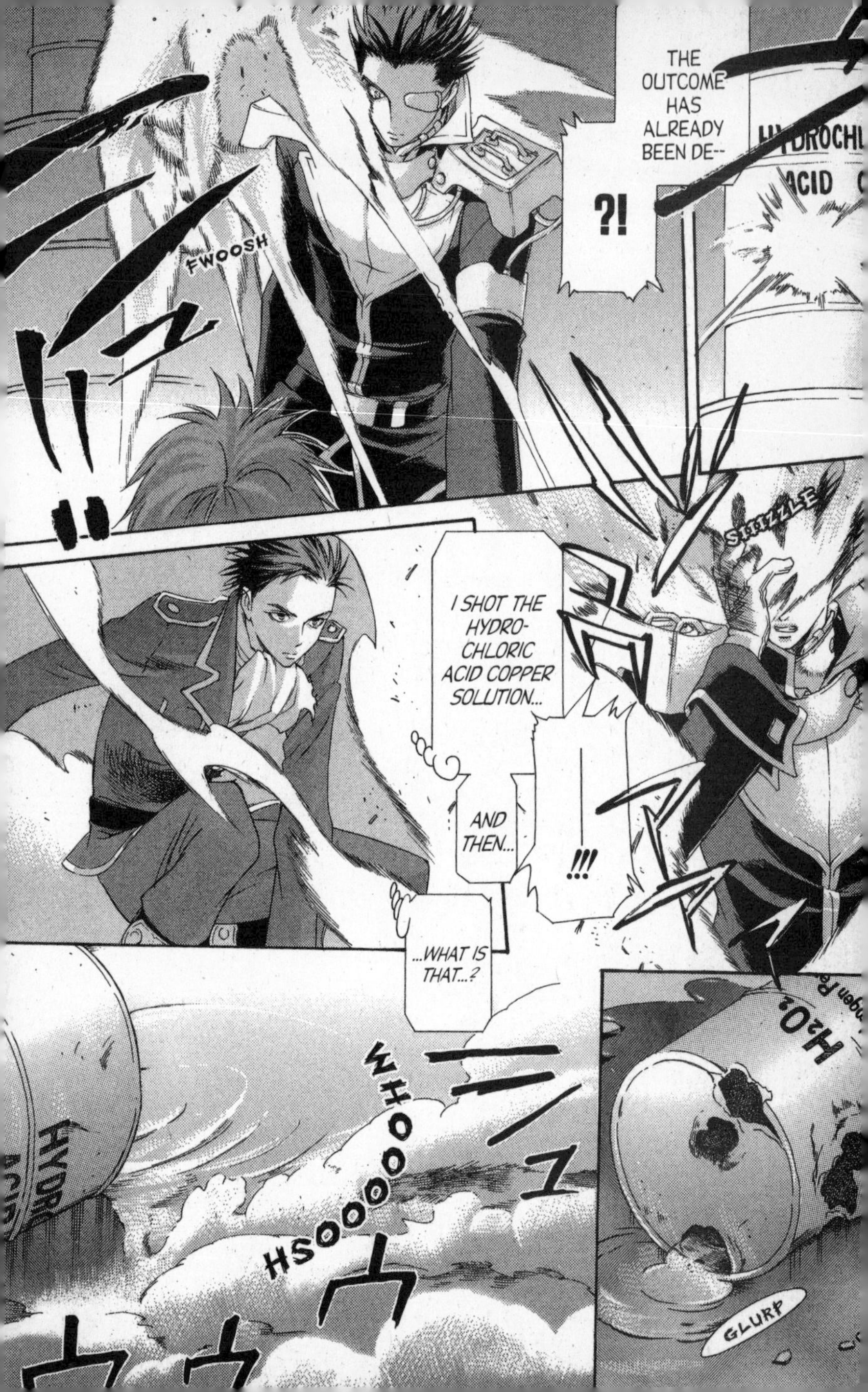
THE OUTCOME HAS ALREADY BEEN DE--
?!
FWOOSH
SIIIIZZLE
I SHOT THE HYDRO-CHLORIC ACID COPPER SOLUTION...
AND THEN...
!!!
...WHAT IS THAT...?
HYDROCHL
ACID
H_2O_2
GLURP
WHOOOOOOSH

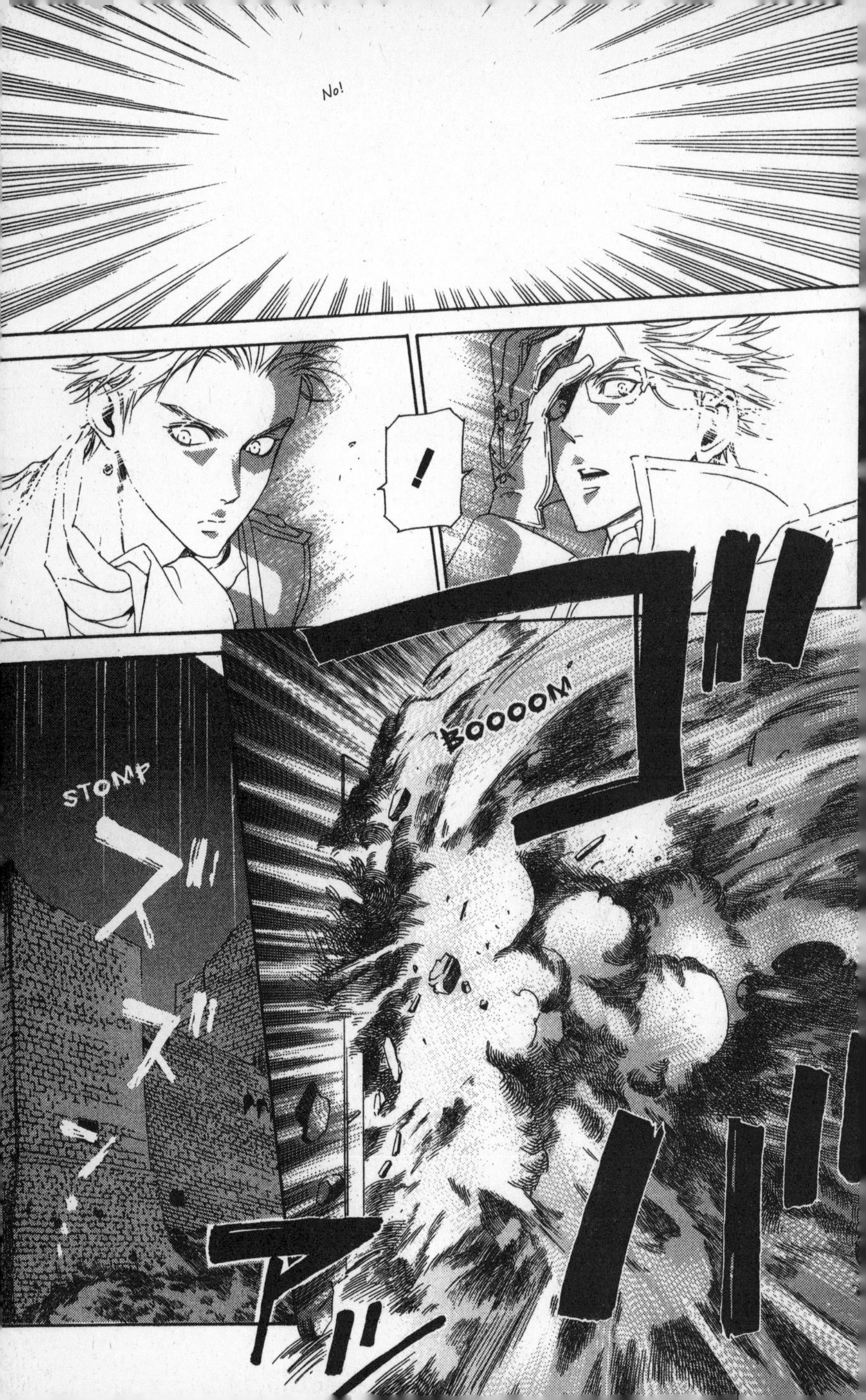
No!
!
BOOOOM
STOMP

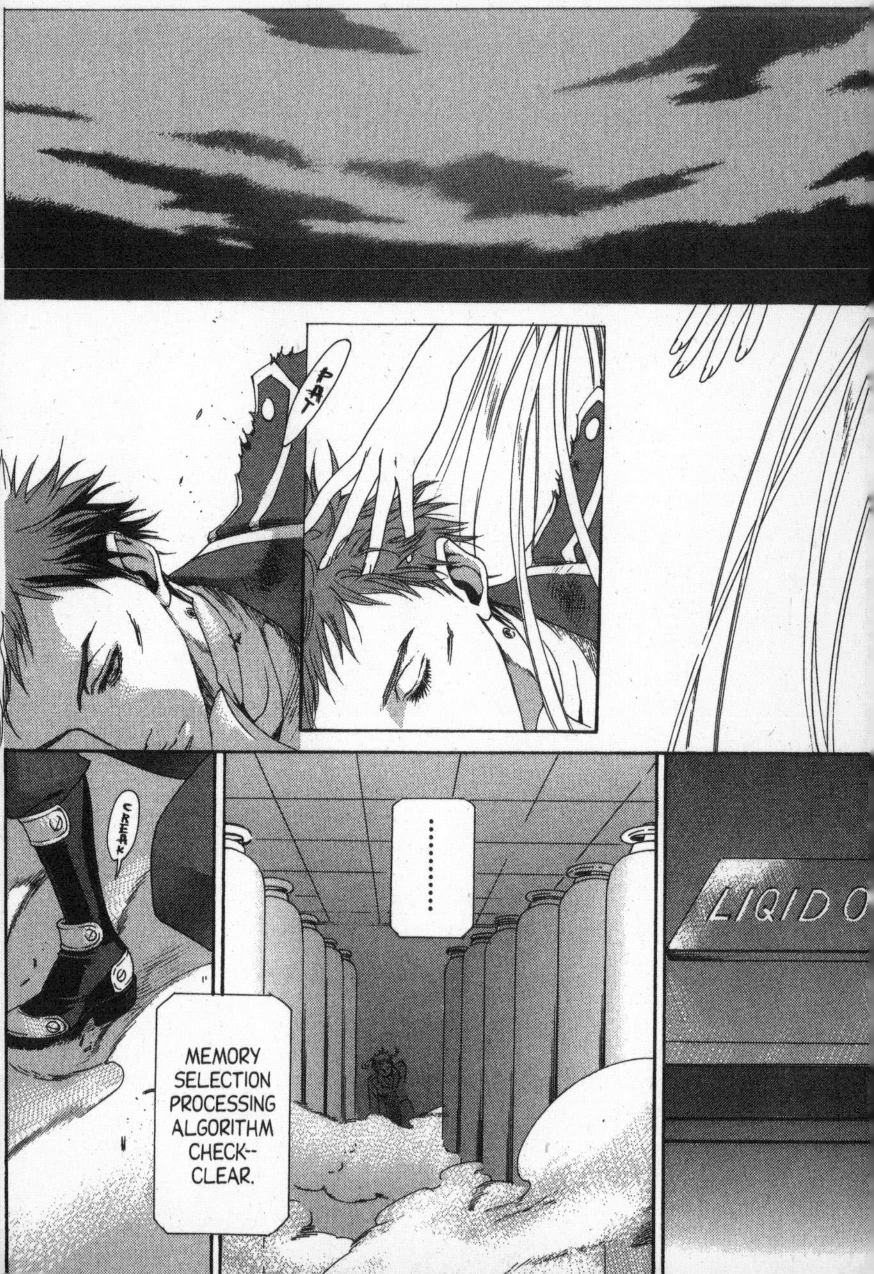
PAT
......
LIQID O
CREAK
MEMORY SELECTION PROCESSING ALGORITHM CHECK-- CLEAR.

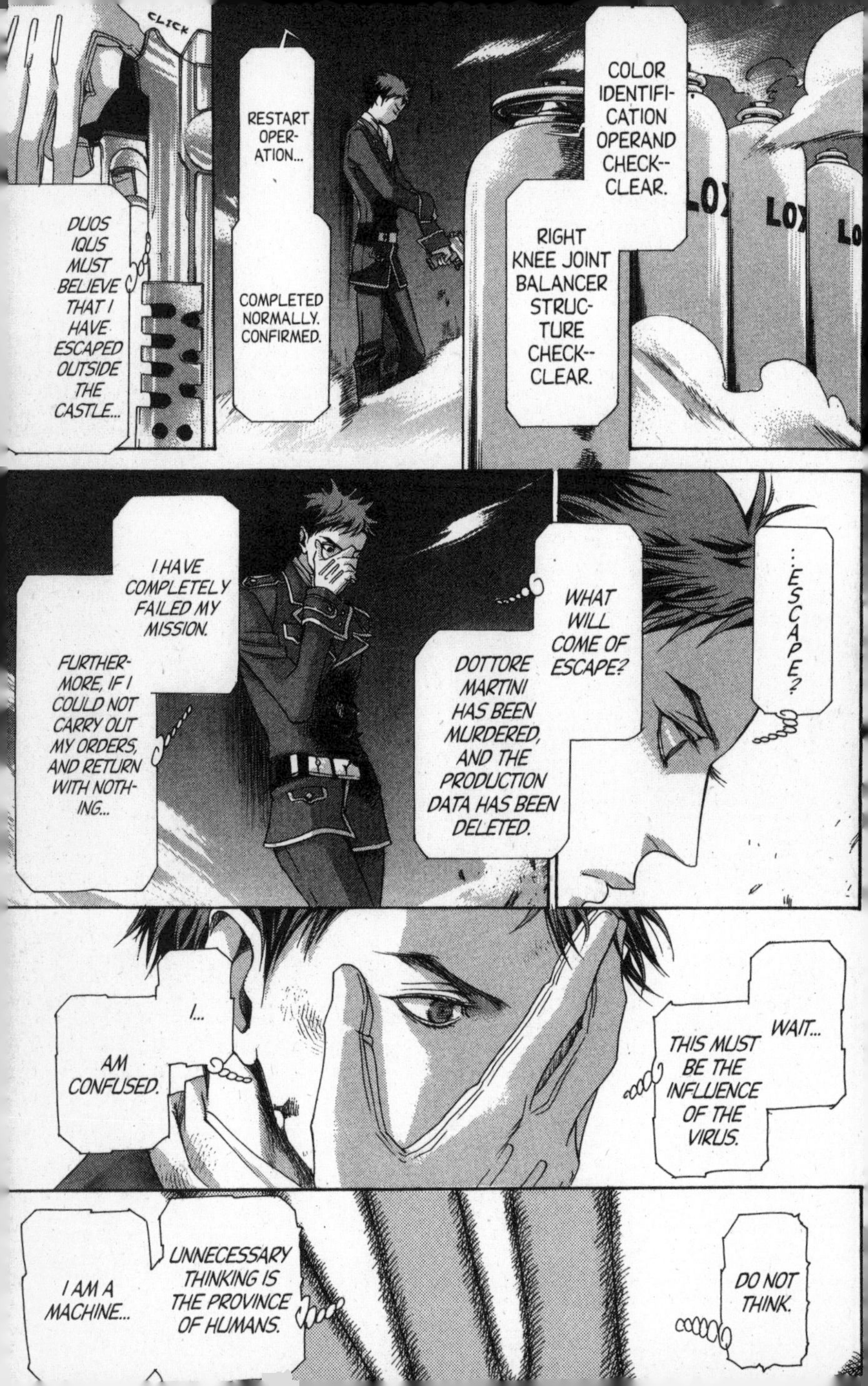
LOX
COLOR IDENTIFICATION OPERAND CHECK--CLEAR.
RIGHT KNEE JOINT BALANCER STRUCTURE CHECK--CLEAR.
RESTART OPERATION...
COMPLETED NORMALLY. CONFIRMED.
CLICK
DUOS IQUS MUST BELIEVE THAT I HAVE ESCAPED OUTSIDE THE CASTLE...
...ESCAPE?
WHAT WILL COME OF ESCAPE?
DOTTORE MARTINI HAS BEEN MURDERED, AND THE PRODUCTION DATA HAS BEEN DELETED.
I HAVE COMPLETELY FAILED MY MISSION.
FURTHERMORE, IF I COULD NOT CARRY OUT MY ORDERS, AND RETURN WITH NOTHING...
WAIT...
THIS MUST BE THE INFLUENCE OF THE VIRUS.
I...
AM CONFUSED.
DO NOT THINK.
UNNECESSARY THINKING IS THE PROVINCE OF HUMANS.
I AM A MACHINE...

"A MACHINE OBEYS ORDERS AND CRUSHES THE ENEMY WITH CERTAINTY. AS LONG AS YOU ARE LACKING IN THAT ABILITY, YOU ARE NOT A MACHINE."

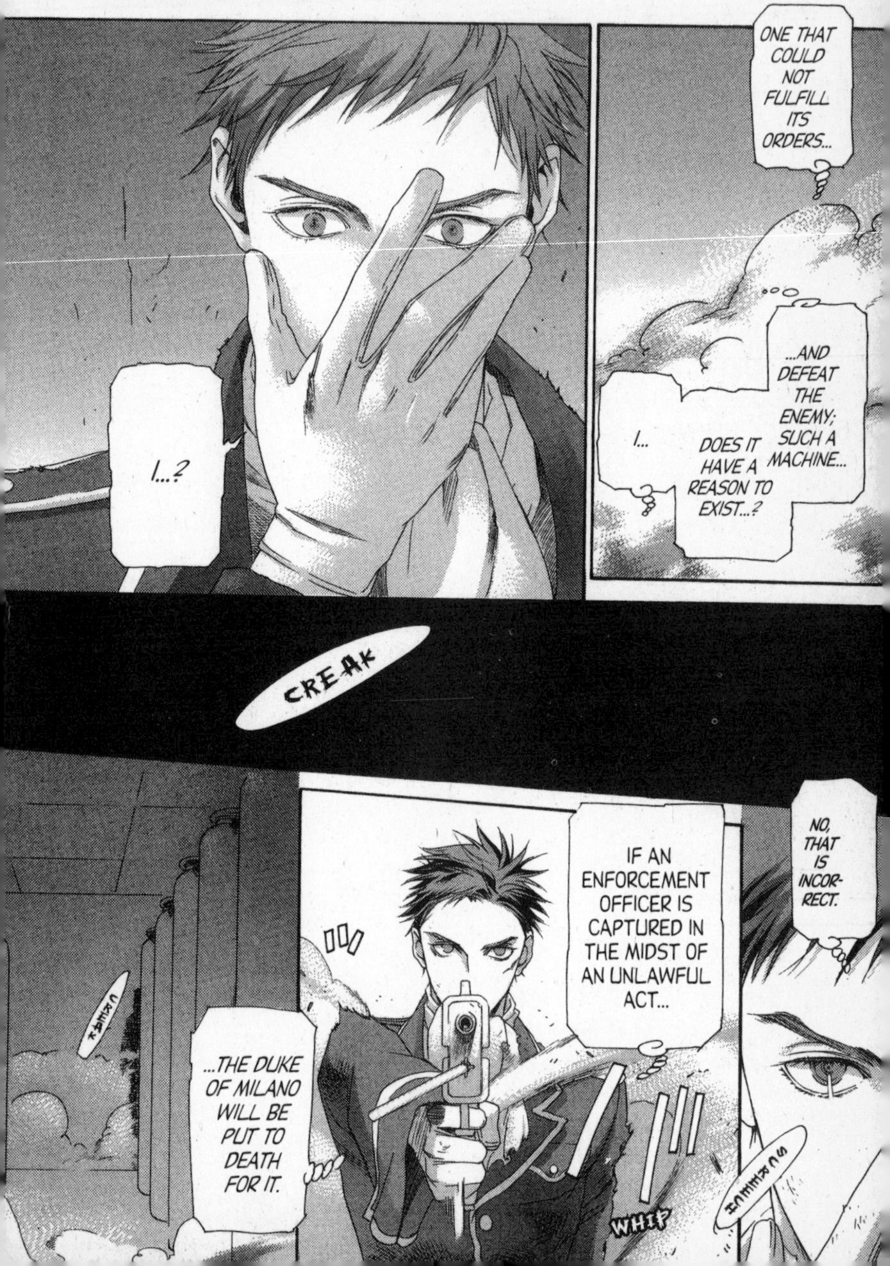
ONE THAT COULD NOT FULFILL ITS ORDERS...
...AND DEFEAT THE ENEMY; SUCH A MACHINE...
DOES IT HAVE A REASON TO EXIST...?
I...
I...?
CREAK
NO, THAT IS INCOR-RECT.
IF AN ENFORCEMENT OFFICER IS CAPTURED IN THE MIDST OF AN UNLAWFUL ACT...
...THE DUKE OF MILANO WILL BE PUT TO DEATH FOR IT.
WHIP

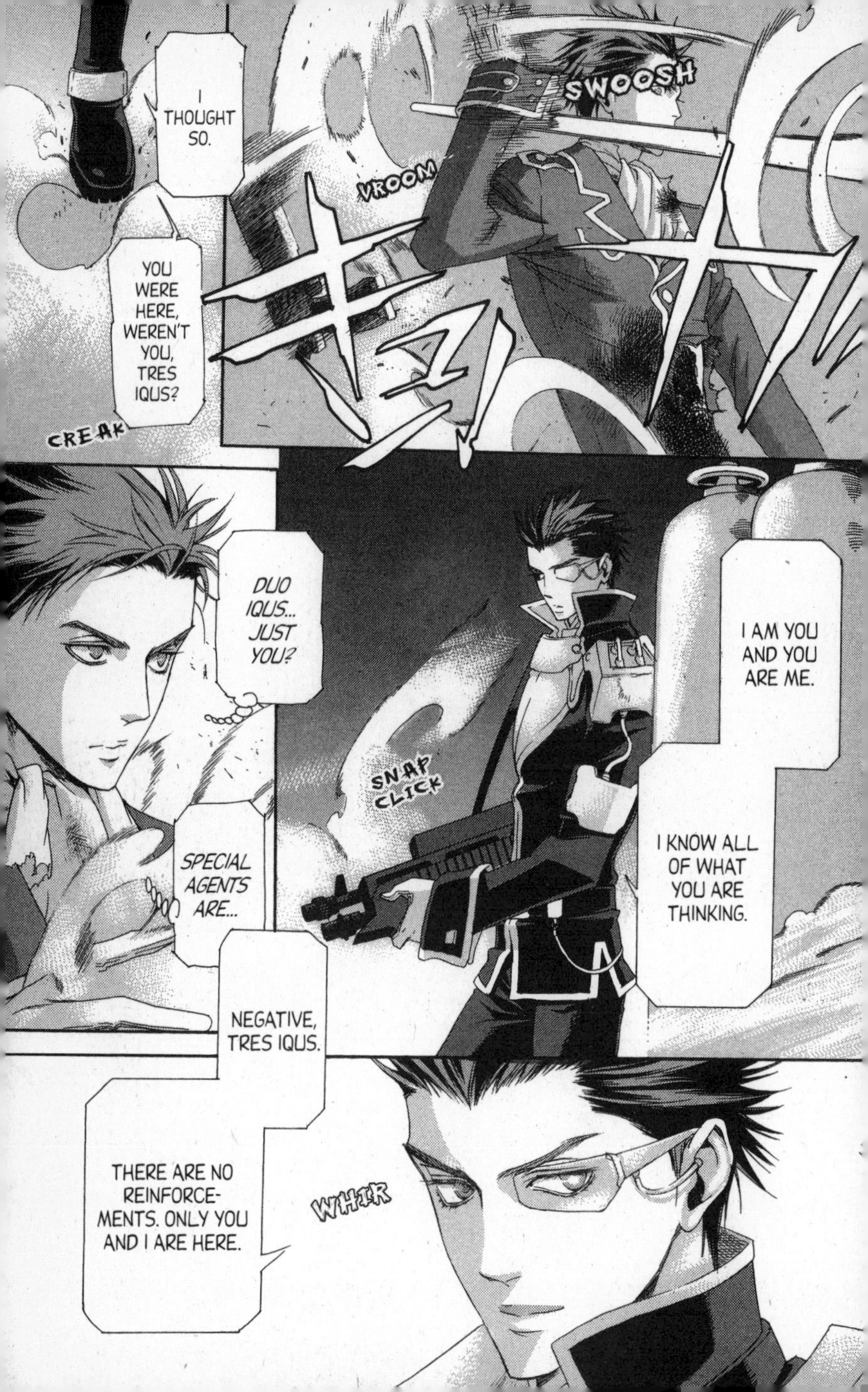
SWOOSH
VROOM
I THOUGHT SO.
YOU WERE HERE, WEREN'T YOU, TRES IQUS?
CREAK
I AM YOU AND YOU ARE ME.
SNAP CLICK
I KNOW ALL OF WHAT YOU ARE THINKING.
DUO IQUS... JUST YOU?
SPECIAL AGENTS ARE...
NEGATIVE, TRES IQUS.
THERE ARE NO REINFORCEMENTS. ONLY YOU AND I ARE HERE.
WHIR

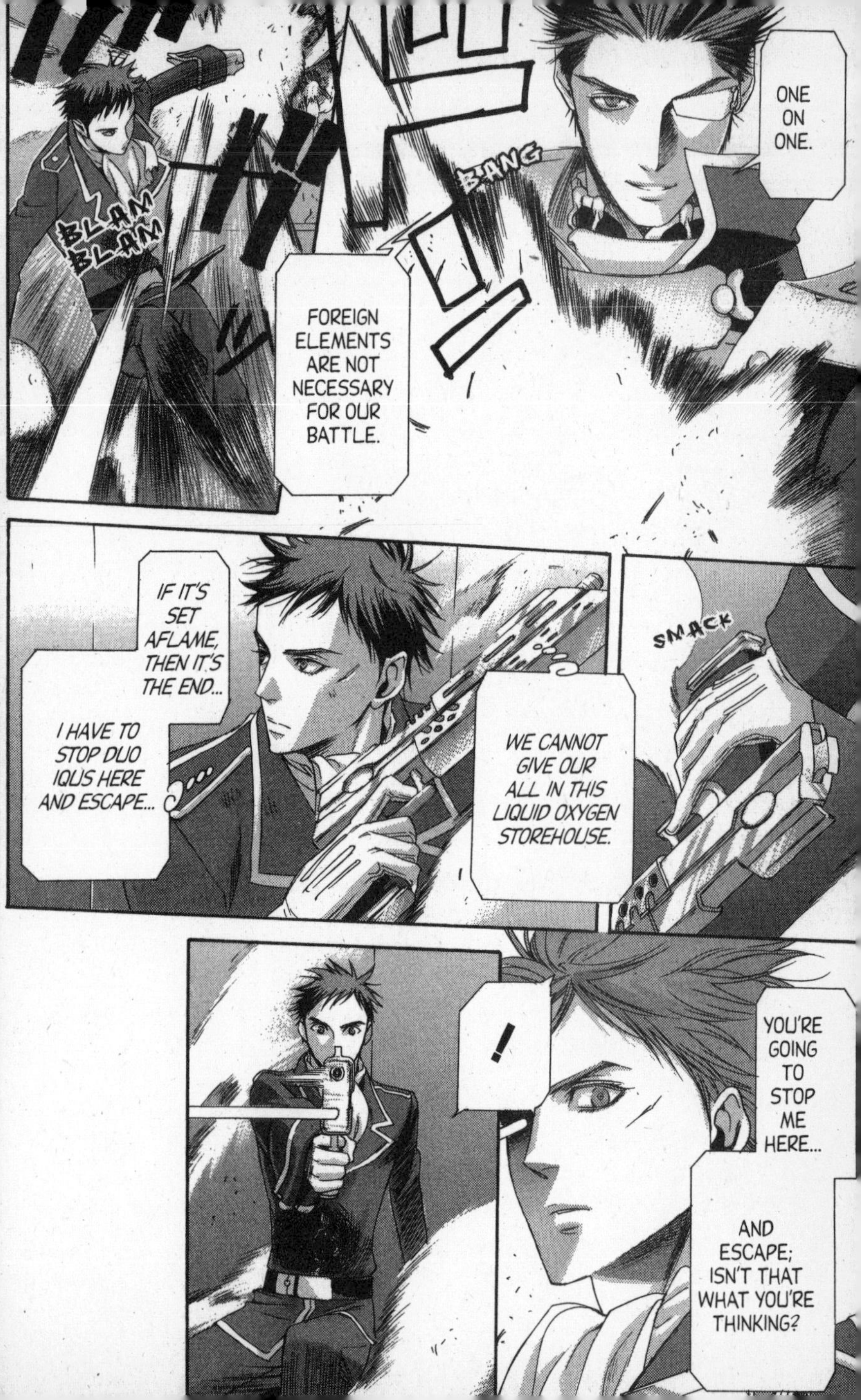
ONE ON ONE.
BANG
FOREIGN ELEMENTS ARE NOT NECESSARY FOR OUR BATTLE.
BLAM BLAM
SMACK
WE CANNOT GIVE OUR ALL IN THIS LIQUID OXYGEN STOREHOUSE.
IF IT'S SET AFLAME, THEN IT'S THE END...
I HAVE TO STOP DUO IQUS HERE AND ESCAPE...
!
YOU'RE GOING TO STOP ME HERE...
AND ESCAPE; ISN'T THAT WHAT YOU'RE THINKING?

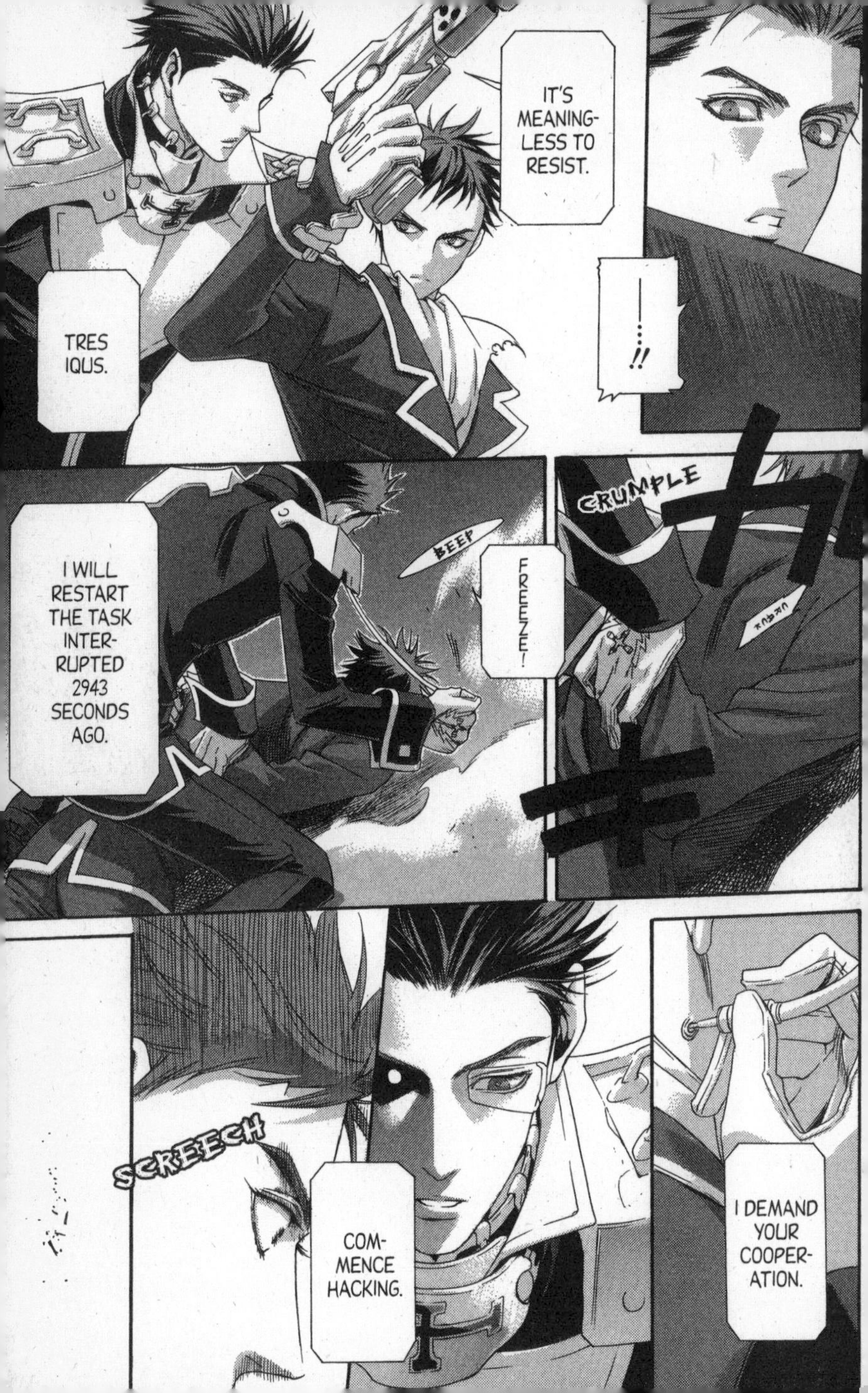
......!!
IT'S MEANINGLESS TO RESIST.
TRES IQUS.
CRUMPLE
BEEP
FREEZE!
I WILL RESTART THE TASK INTERRUPTED 2943 SECONDS AGO.
I DEMAND YOUR COOPERATION.
COMMENCE HACKING.
SCREECH

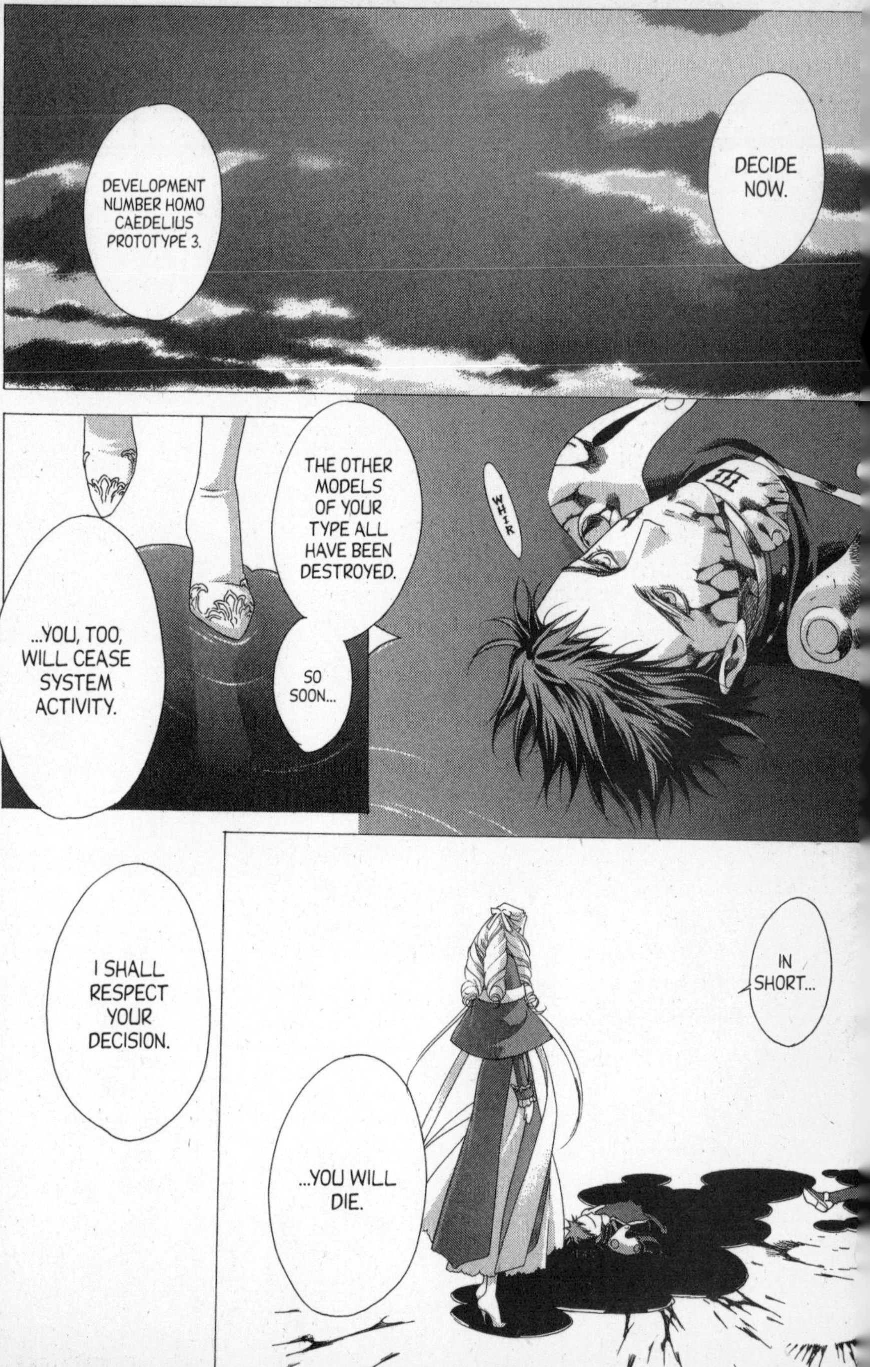
DECIDE NOW.
DEVELOPMENT NUMBER HOMO CAEDELIUS PROTOTYPE 3.
WHIR
THE OTHER MODELS OF YOUR TYPE ALL HAVE BEEN DESTROYED.
SO SOON...
...YOU, TOO, WILL CEASE SYSTEM ACTIVITY.
IN SHORT...
...YOU WILL DIE.
I SHALL RESPECT YOUR DECISION.

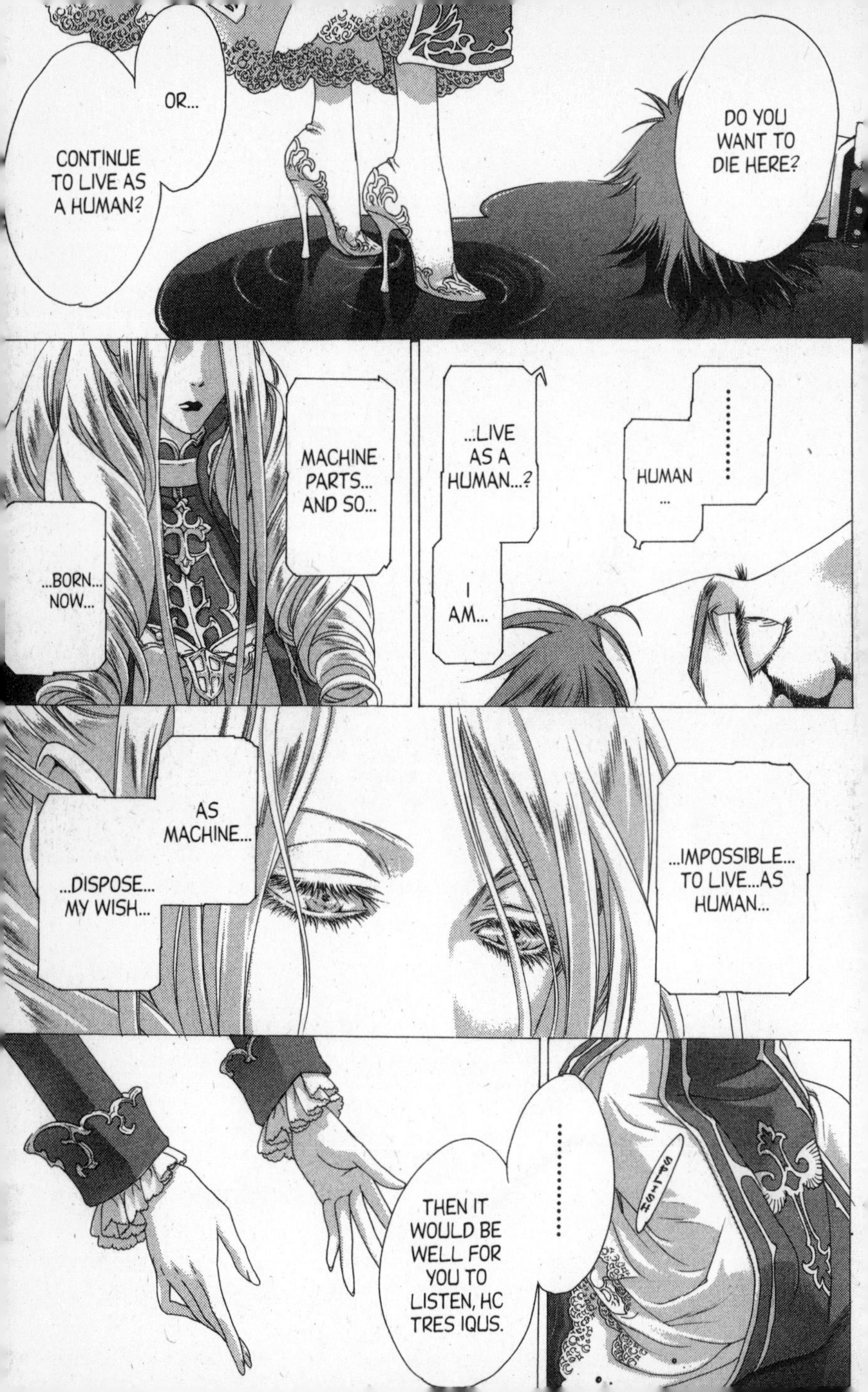
DO YOU WANT TO DIE HERE?
OR...
CONTINUE TO LIVE AS A HUMAN?
......
HUMAN ...
...LIVE AS A HUMAN...?
I AM...
MACHINE PARTS... AND SO...
...BORN... NOW...
...IMPOSSIBLE... TO LIVE...AS HUMAN...
AS MACHINE...
...DISPOSE... MY WISH...
......
THEN IT WOULD BE WELL FOR YOU TO LISTEN, HC TRES IQUS.

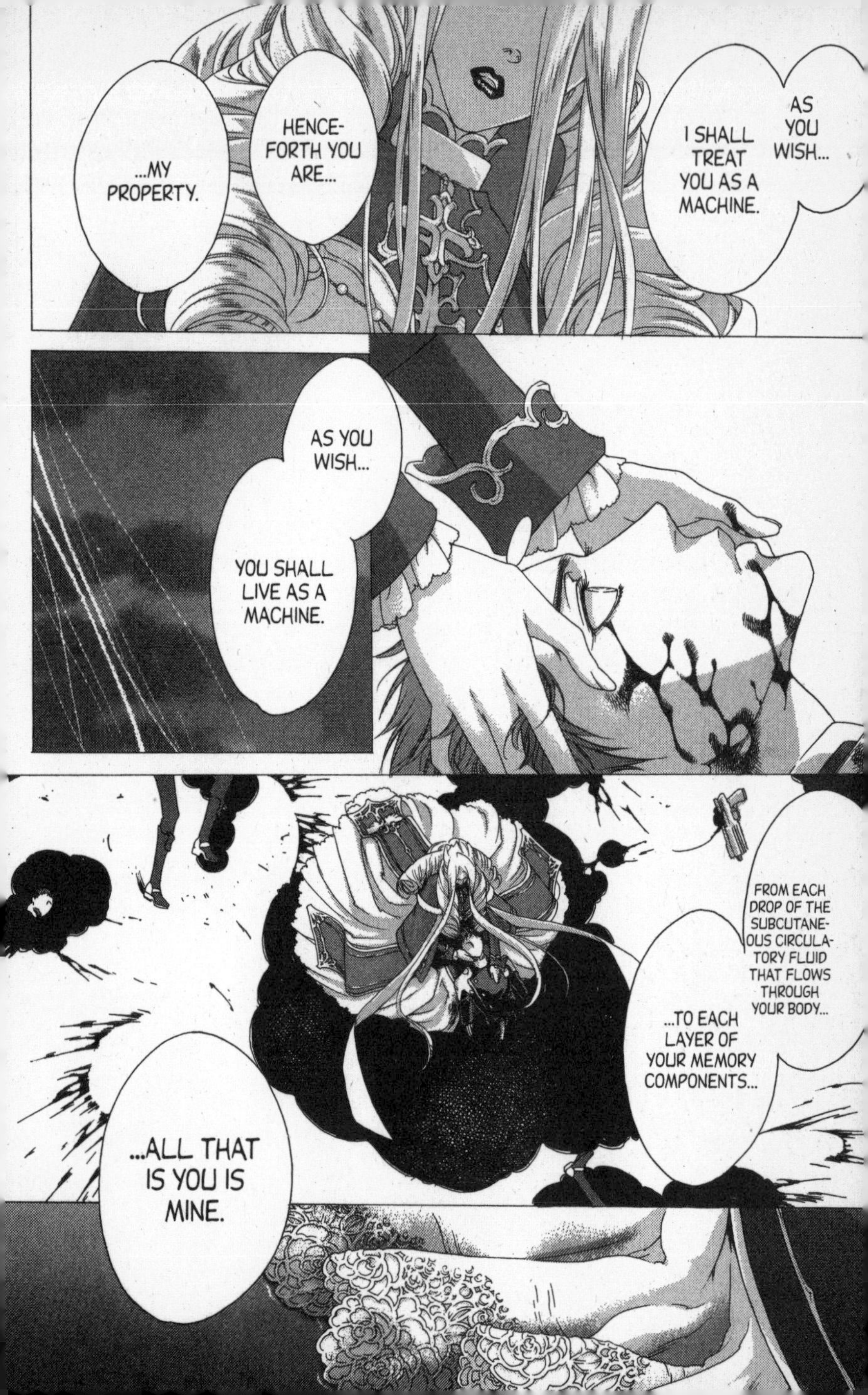
AS YOU WISH...
I SHALL TREAT YOU AS A MACHINE.
HENCE-FORTH YOU ARE...
...MY PROPERTY.
AS YOU WISH...
YOU SHALL LIVE AS A MACHINE.
FROM EACH DROP OF THE SUBCUTANE-OUS CIRCULA-TORY FLUID THAT FLOWS THROUGH YOUR BODY...
...TO EACH LAYER OF YOUR MEMORY COMPONENTS...
...ALL THAT IS YOU IS MINE.

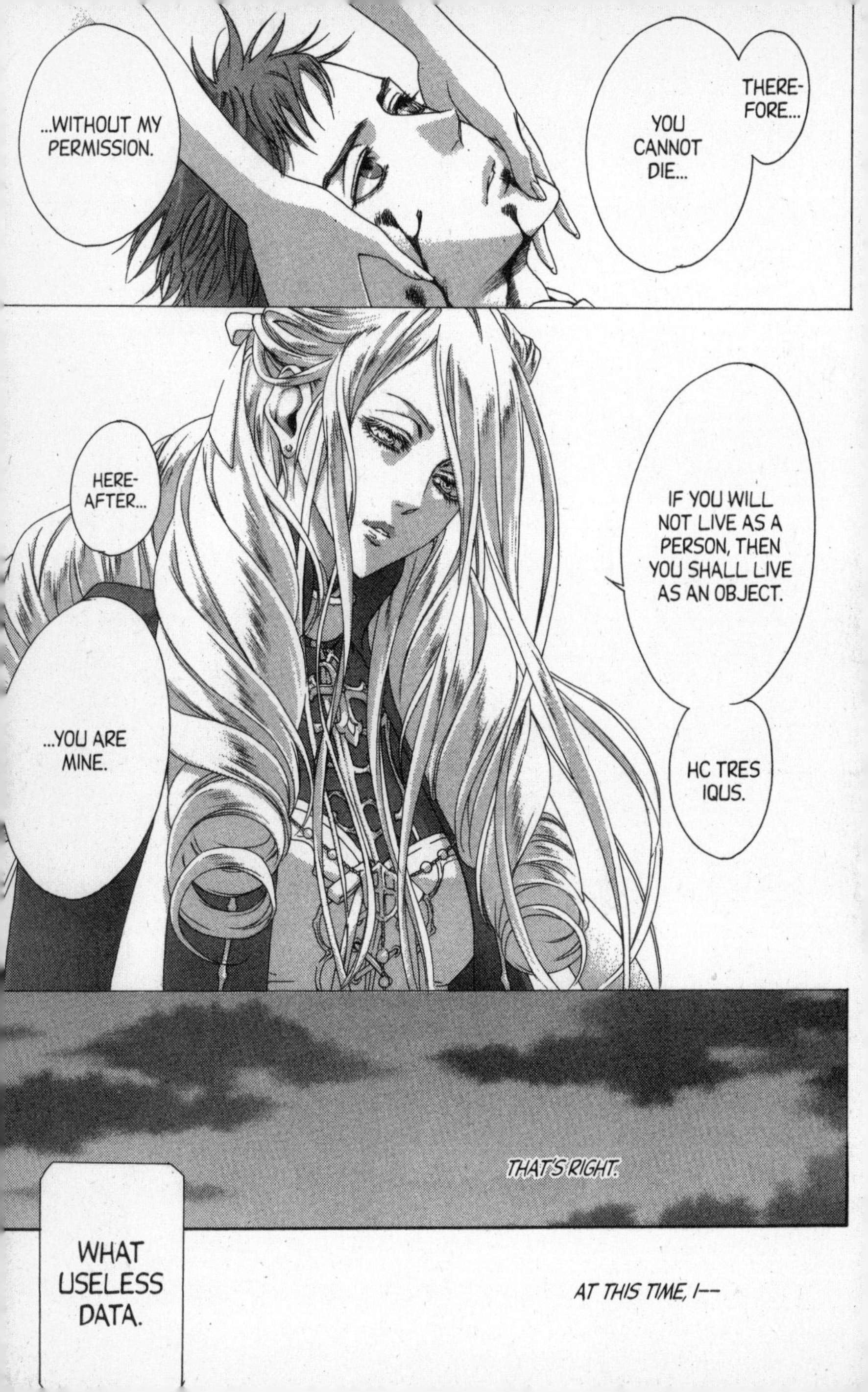
THERE-FORE...
YOU CANNOT DIE...
...WITHOUT MY PERMISSION.
IF YOU WILL NOT LIVE AS A PERSON, THEN YOU SHALL LIVE AS AN OBJECT.
HC TRES IQUS.
HERE-AFTER...
...YOU ARE MINE.
THAT'S RIGHT.
AT THIS TIME, I--
WHAT USELESS DATA.

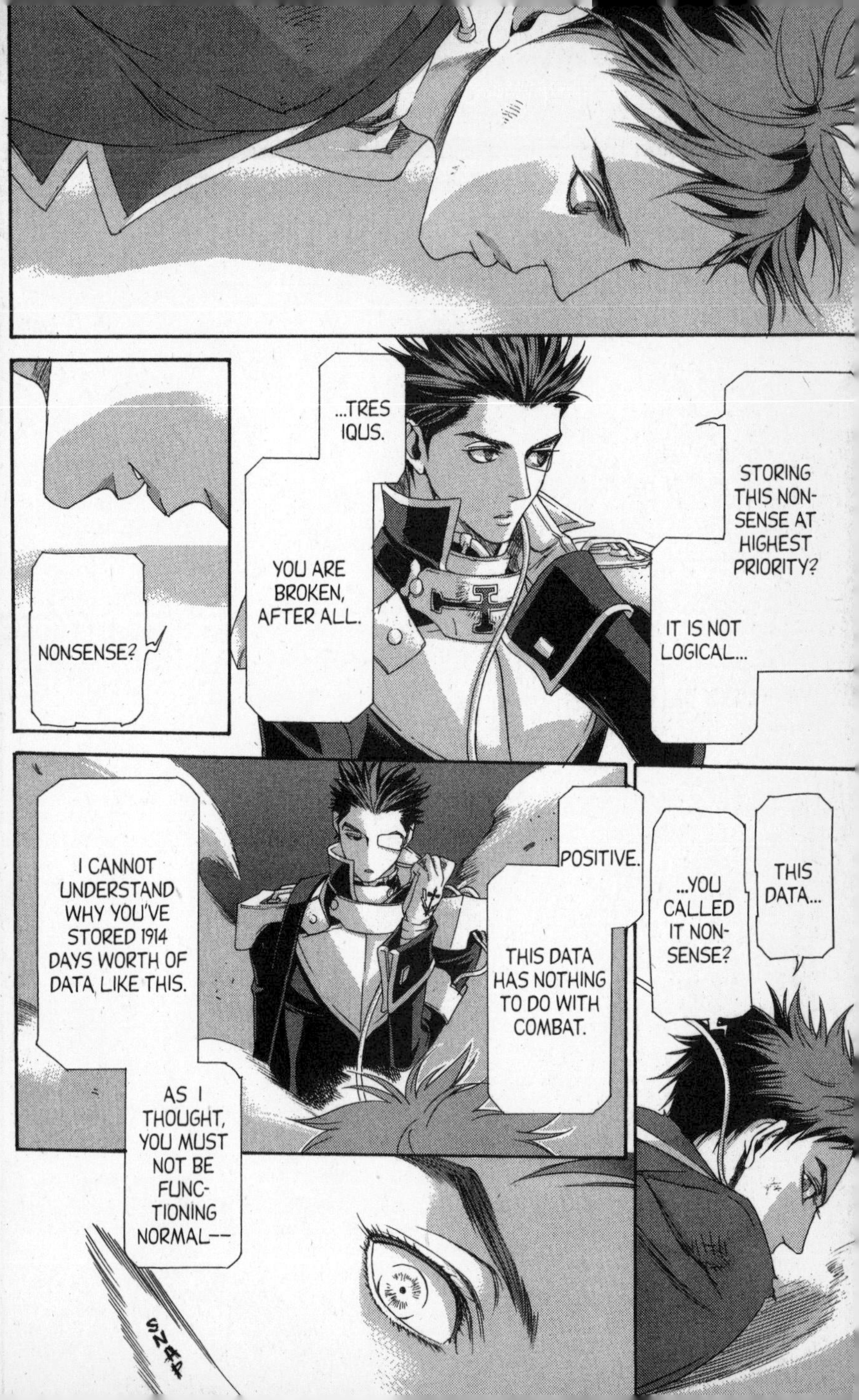
STORING THIS NON-SENSE AT HIGHEST PRIORITY?
IT IS NOT LOGICAL...
...TRES IQUS.
YOU ARE BROKEN, AFTER ALL.
NONSENSE?
THIS DATA...
...YOU CALLED IT NON-SENSE?
POSITIVE.
THIS DATA HAS NOTHING TO DO WITH COMBAT.
I CANNOT UNDERSTAND WHY YOU'VE STORED 1914 DAYS WORTH OF DATA LIKE THIS.
AS I THOUGHT, YOU MUST NOT BE FUNC-TIONING NORMAL--
SNAP

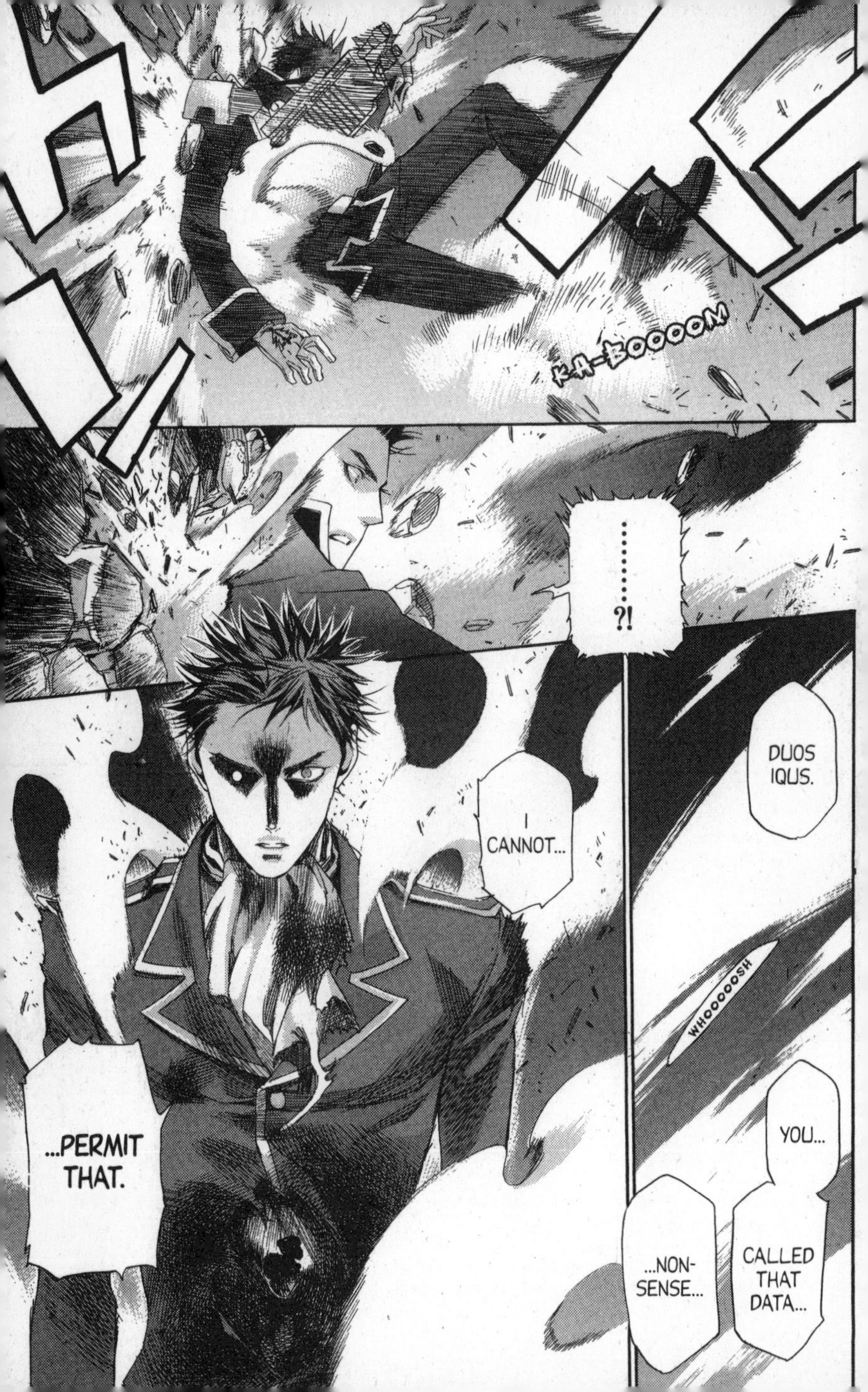
KA-BOOOOM
......?!
DUOS IQUS.
WHOOOOOSH
YOU...
CALLED THAT DATA...
...NON-SENSE...
I CANNOT...
...PERMIT THAT.

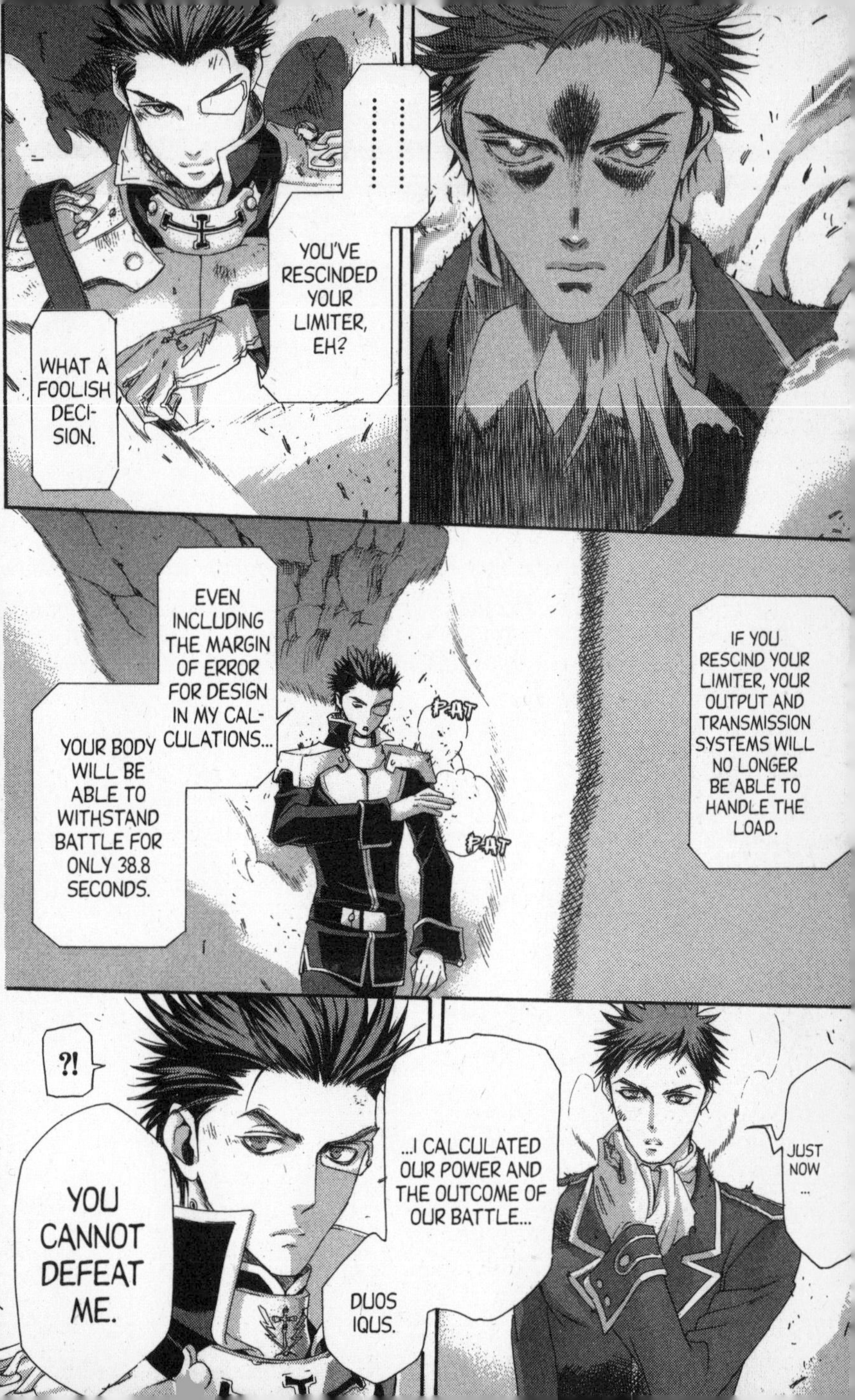
......
YOU'VE RESCINDED YOUR LIMITER, EH?
WHAT A FOOLISH DECI-SION.
IF YOU RESCIND YOUR LIMITER, YOUR OUTPUT AND TRANSMISSION SYSTEMS WILL NO LONGER BE ABLE TO HANDLE THE LOAD.
PAT
PAT
EVEN INCLUDING THE MARGIN OF ERROR FOR DESIGN IN MY CAL-CULATIONS...
YOUR BODY WILL BE ABLE TO WITHSTAND BATTLE FOR ONLY 38.8 SECONDS.
JUST NOW ...
...I CALCULATED OUR POWER AND THE OUTCOME OF OUR BATTLE...
?!
DUOS IQUS.
YOU CANNOT DEFEAT ME.

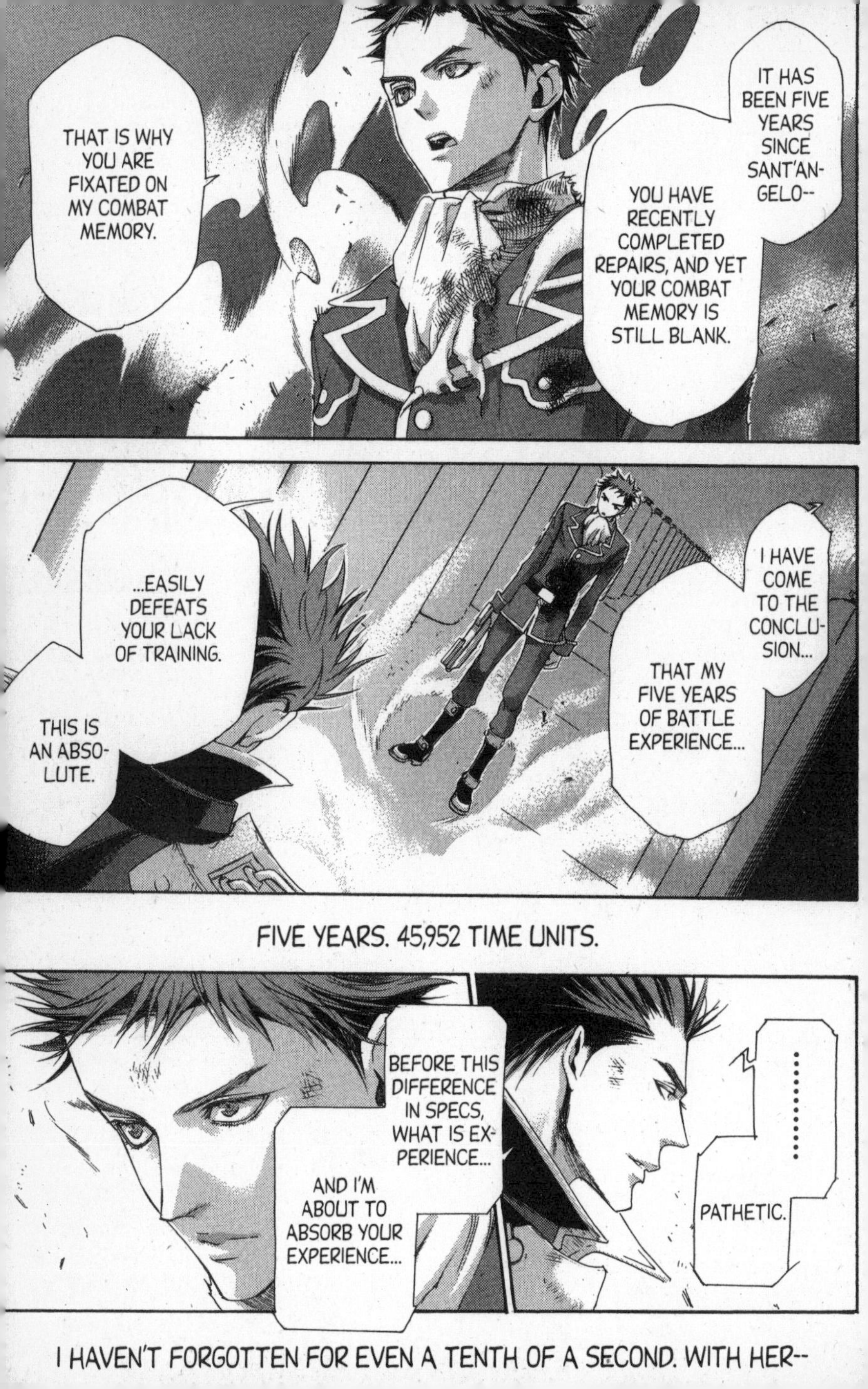
IT HAS BEEN FIVE YEARS SINCE SANT'ANGELO--
YOU HAVE RECENTLY COMPLETED REPAIRS, AND YET YOUR COMBAT MEMORY IS STILL BLANK.
THAT IS WHY YOU ARE FIXATED ON MY COMBAT MEMORY.
I HAVE COME TO THE CONCLUSION...
THAT MY FIVE YEARS OF BATTLE EXPERIENCE...
...EASILY DEFEATS YOUR LACK OF TRAINING.
THIS IS AN ABSOLUTE.
FIVE YEARS. 45,952 TIME UNITS.
....
PATHETIC.
BEFORE THIS DIFFERENCE IN SPECS, WHAT IS EXPERIENCE...
AND I'M ABOUT TO ABSORB YOUR EXPERIENCE...
I HAVEN'T FORGOTTEN FOR EVEN A TENTH OF A SECOND. WITH HER--

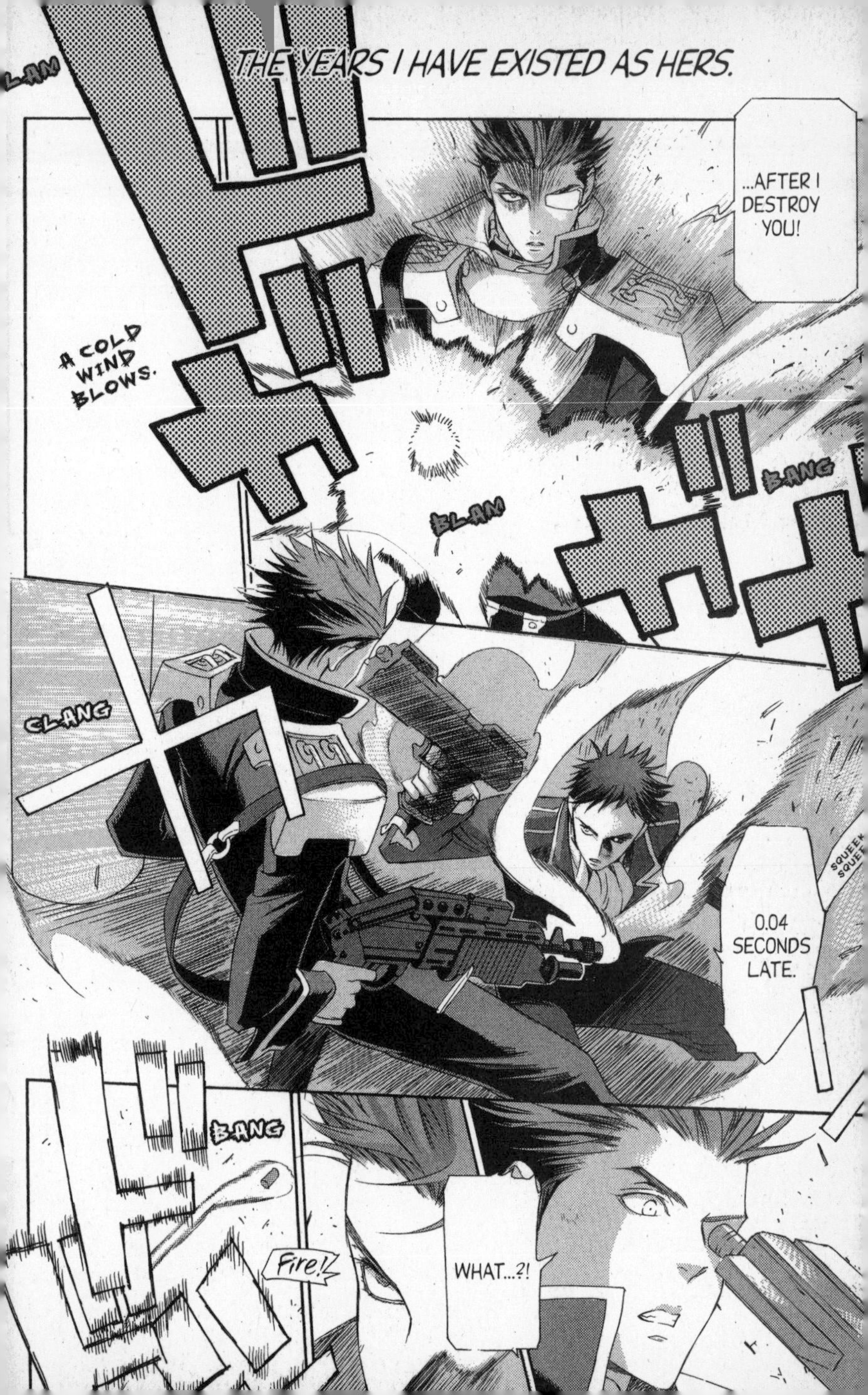
THE YEARS I HAVE EXISTED AS HERS.
LAM
...AFTER I DESTROY YOU!
A COLD WIND BLOWS.
BANG
BLAM
SQUEEK
0.04 SECONDS LATE.
CLANG
WHAT...?!
Fire!
BANG

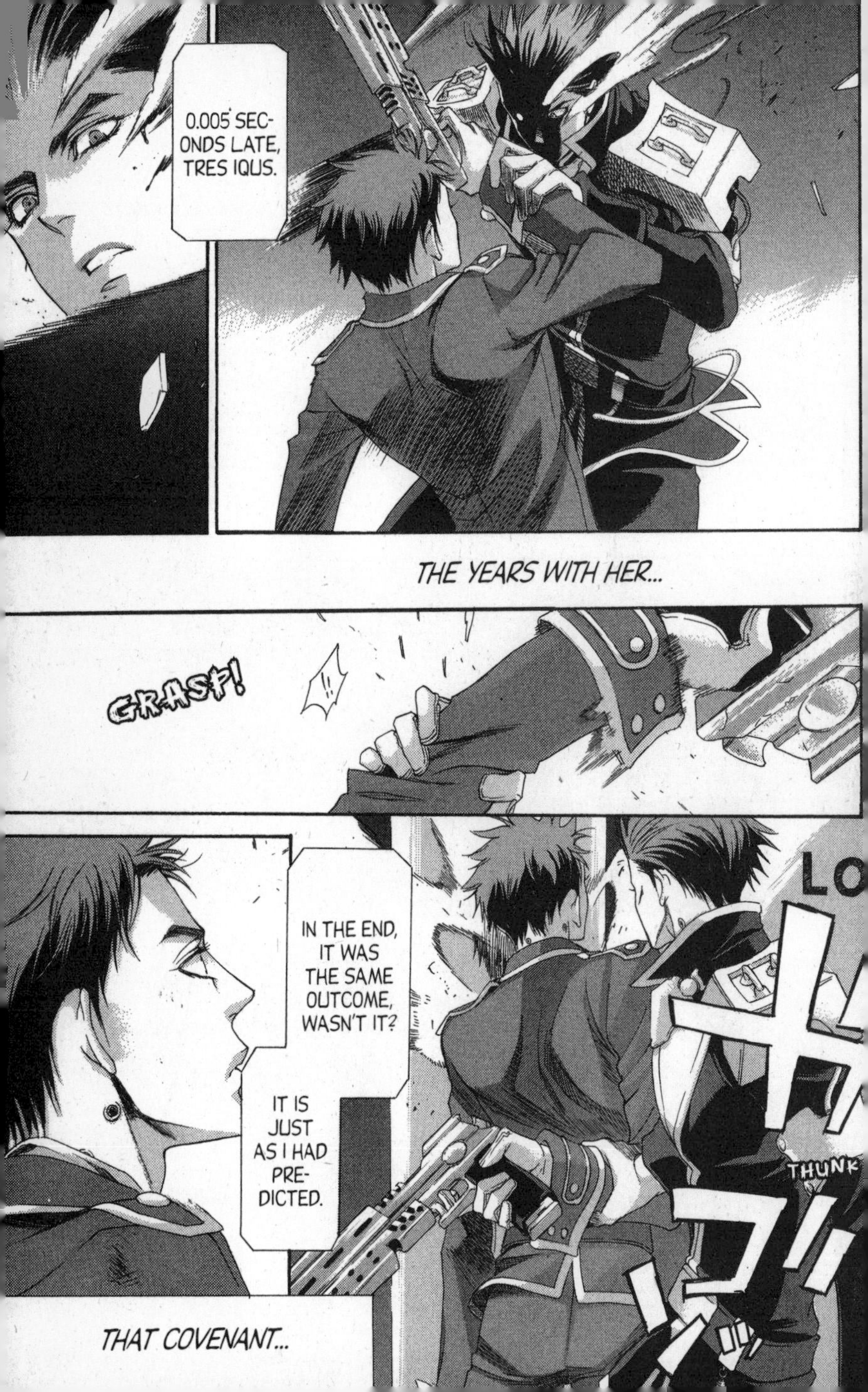
0.005 SECONDS LATE, TRES IQUS.
THE YEARS WITH HER...
GRASP!
!!
THUNK
IN THE END, IT WAS THE SAME OUTCOME, WASN'T IT?
IT IS JUST AS I HAD PREDICTED.
THAT COVENANT...

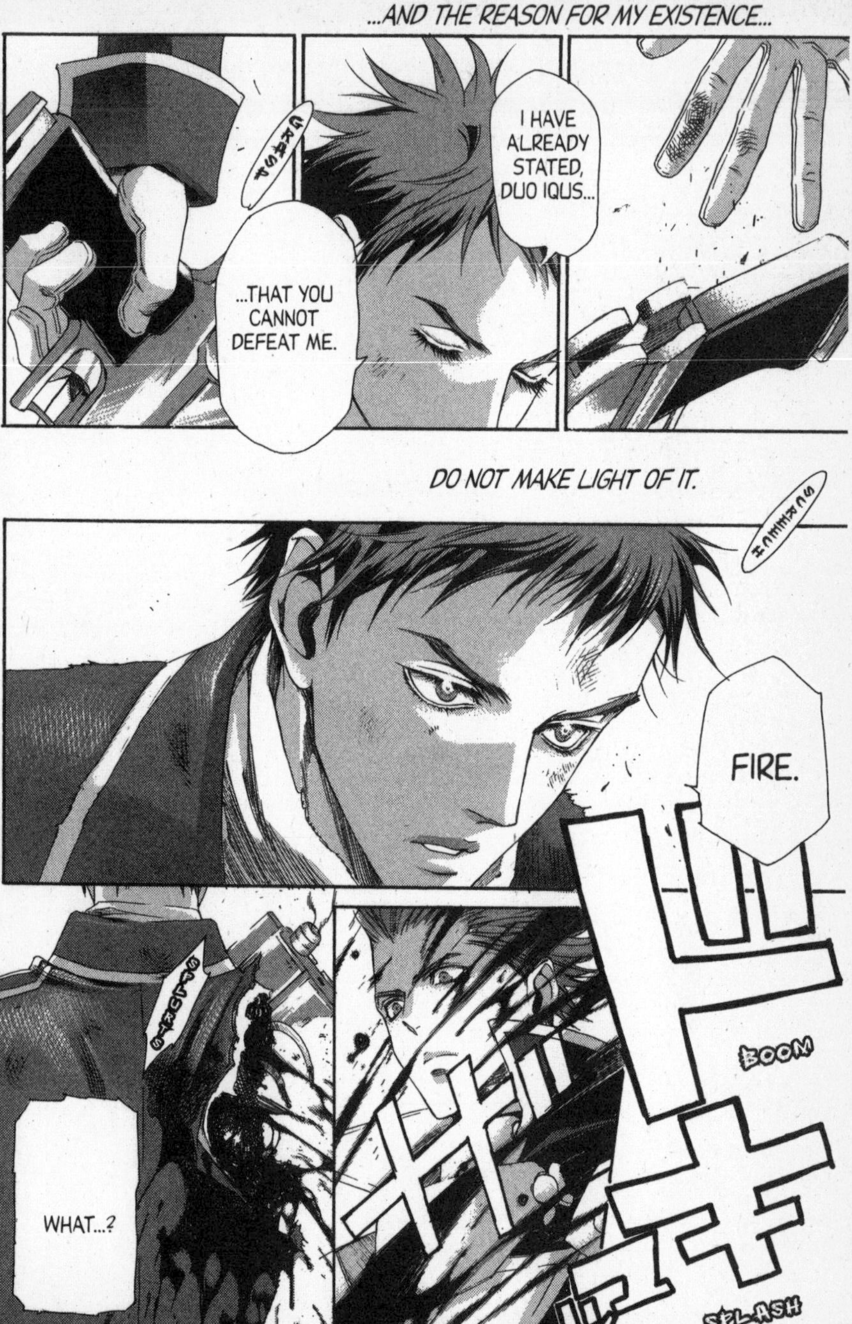
...AND THE REASON FOR MY EXISTENCE...
I HAVE ALREADY STATED, DUO IQUS...
...THAT YOU CANNOT DEFEAT ME.
GRASP
DO NOT MAKE LIGHT OF IT.
FIRE.
BOOM
SPLASH
SPLURTS
WHAT...?

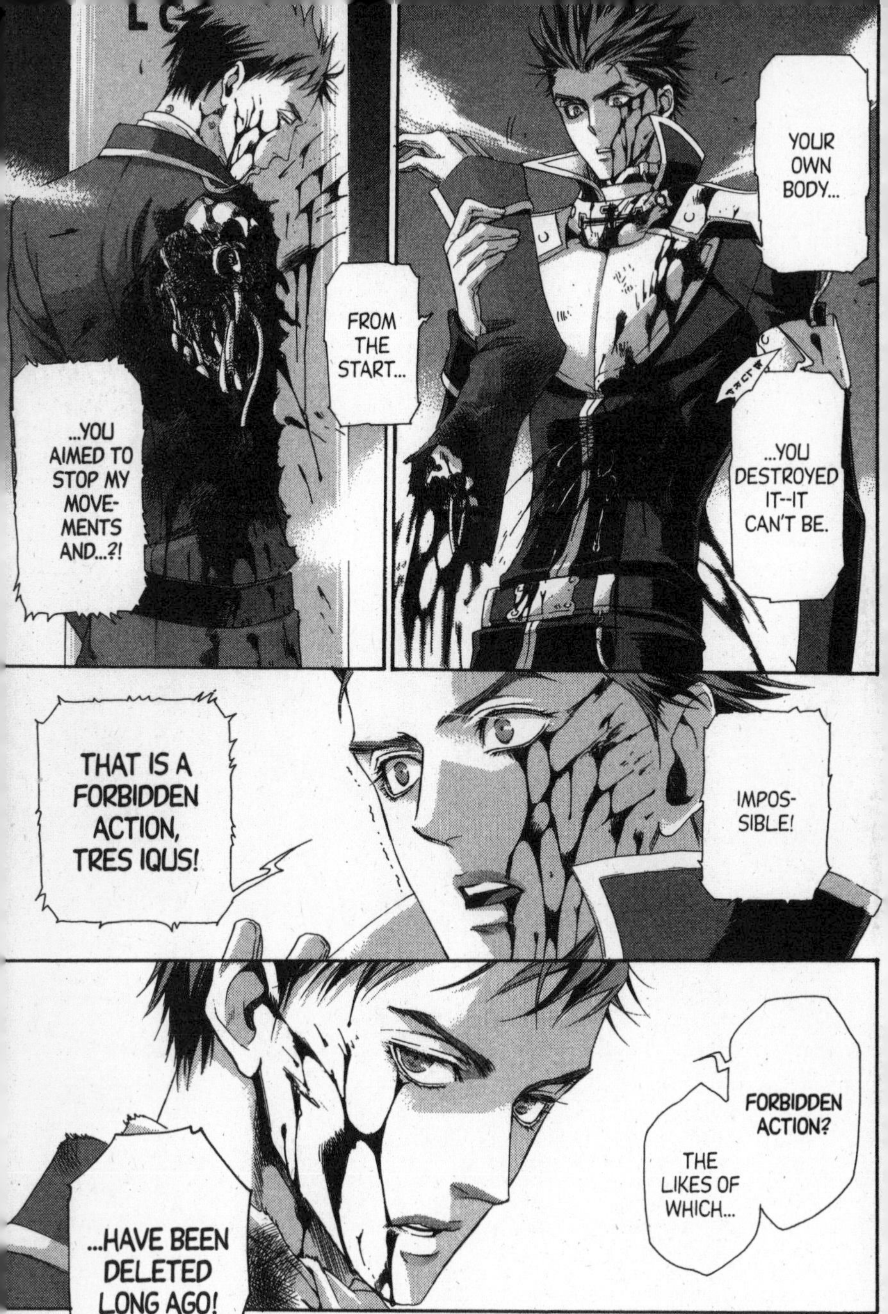

YOUR OWN BODY...
...YOU DESTROYED IT--IT CAN'T BE.
FROM THE START...
...YOU AIMED TO STOP MY MOVEMENTS AND...?!
IMPOSSIBLE!
THAT IS A FORBIDDEN ACTION, TRES IQUS!
FORBIDDEN ACTION?
THE LIKES OF WHICH...
...HAVE BEEN DELETED LONG AGO!

I AM HER...

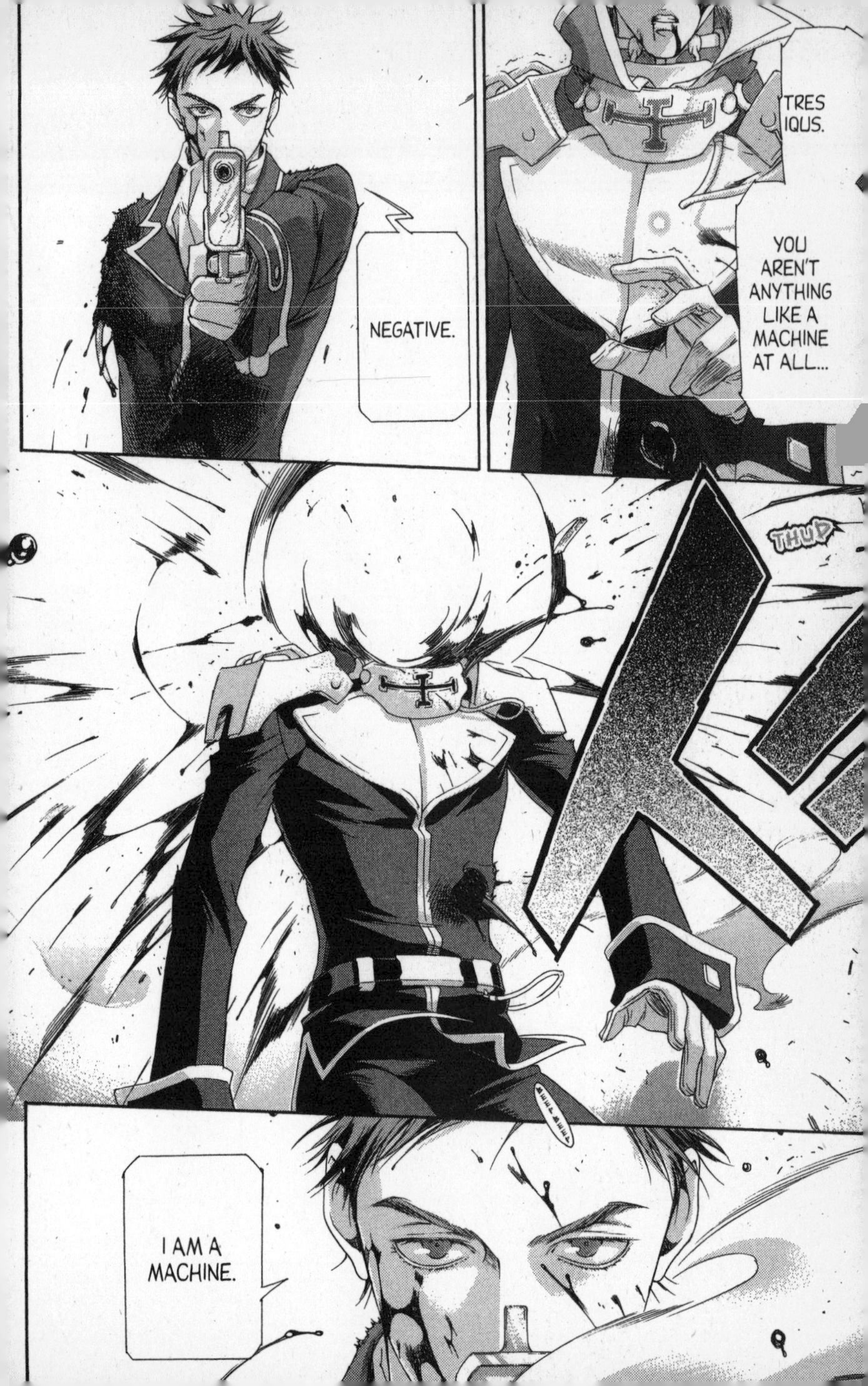
TRES IQUS.
YOU AREN'T ANYTHING LIKE A MACHINE AT ALL...
NEGATIVE.
THUD
I AM A MACHINE.

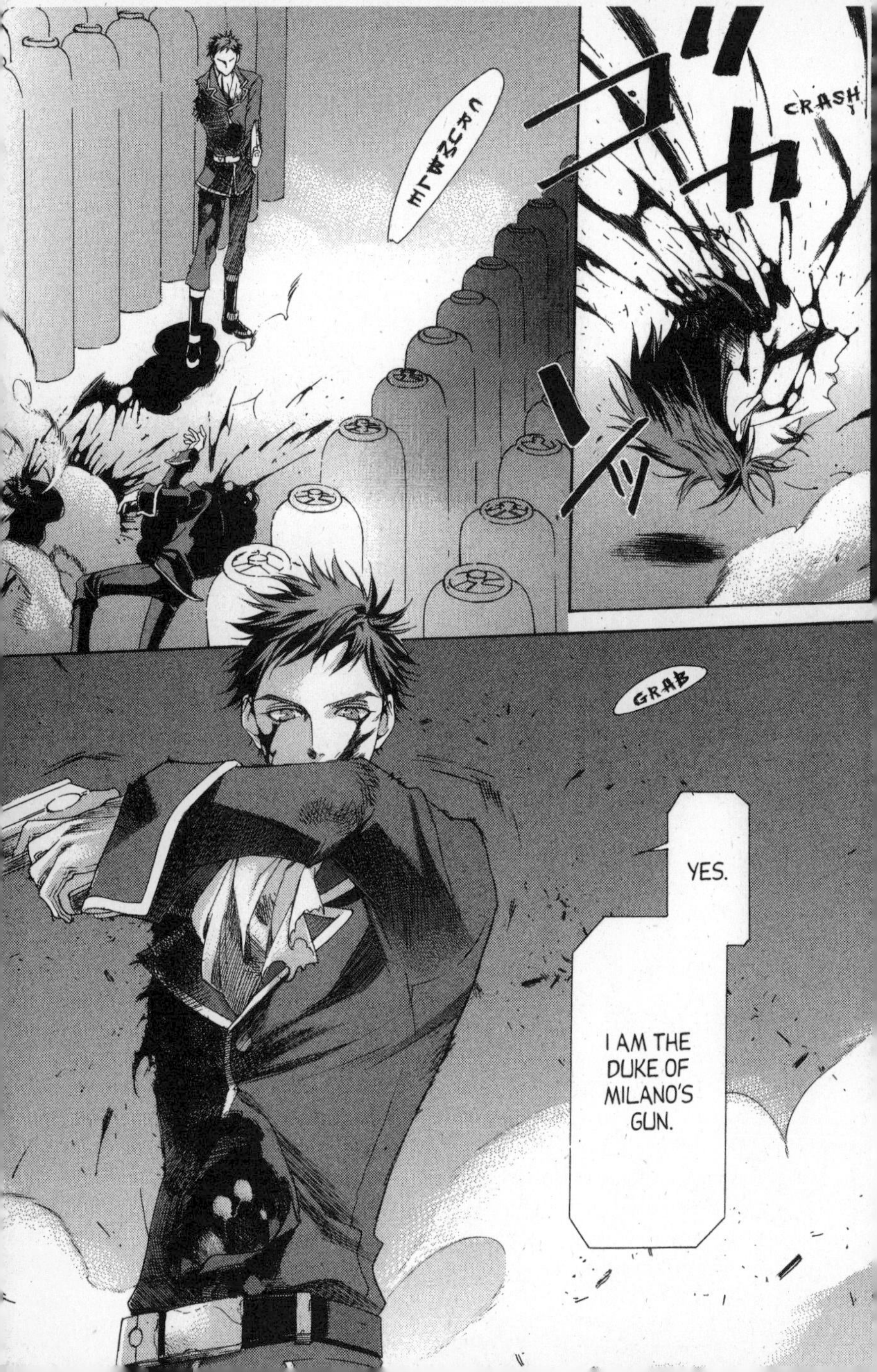
CRASH
CRUMBLE
GRAB
YES.
I AM THE DUKE OF MILANO'S GUN.

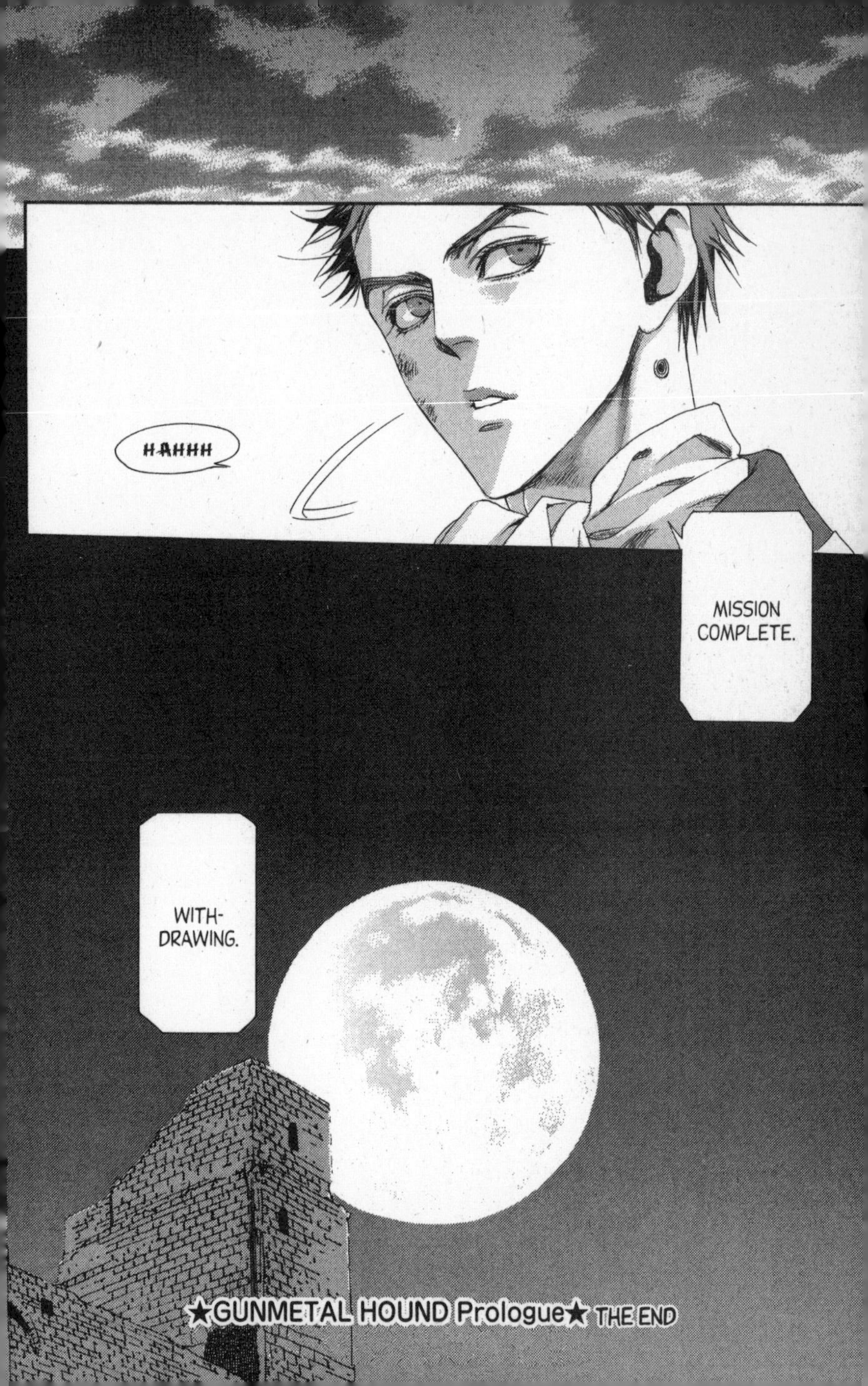
HAHHH
MISSION COMPLETE.
WITH-DRAWING.
★GUNMETAL HOUND Prologue★ THE END

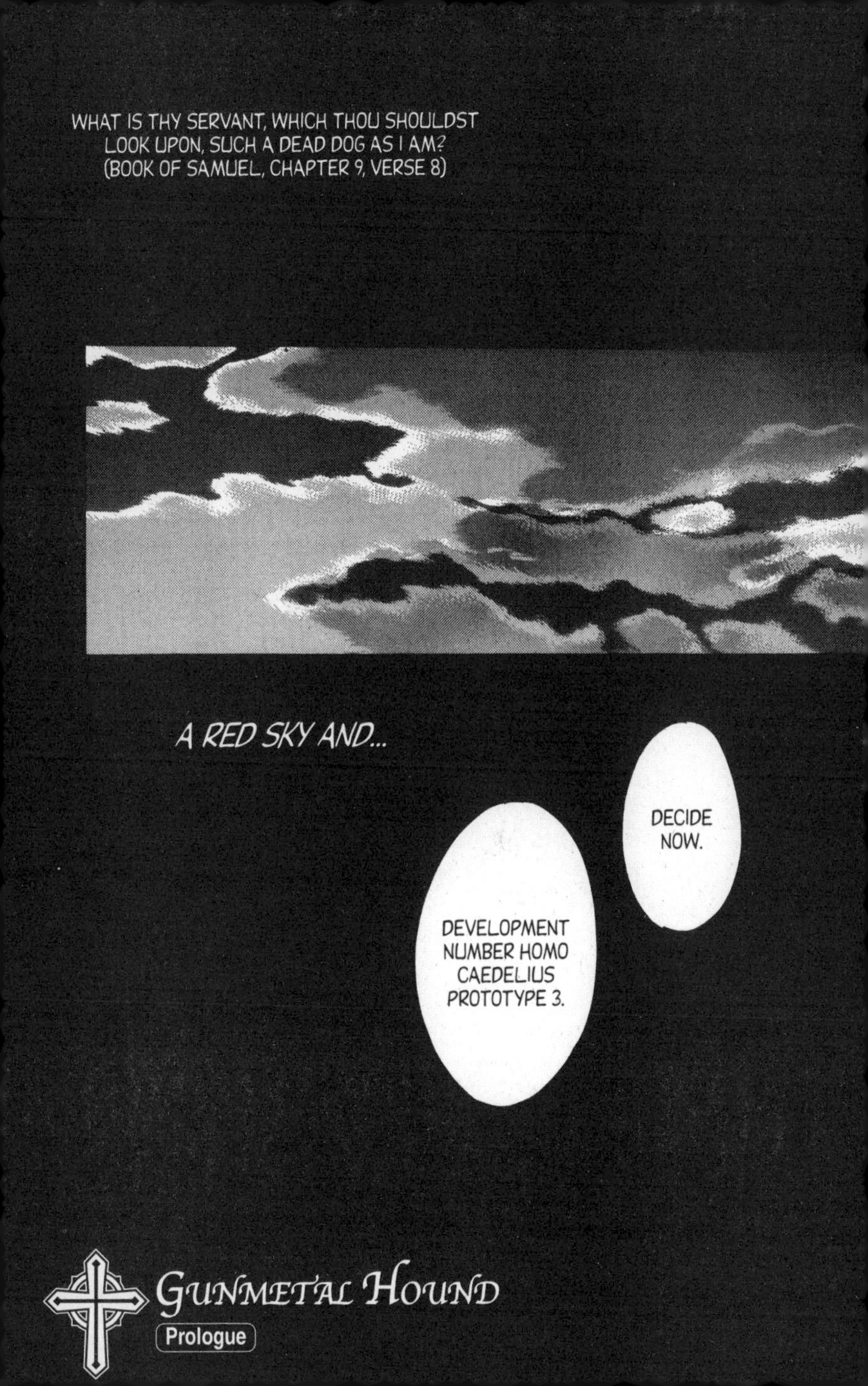
WHAT IS THY SERVANT, WHICH THOU SHOULDST LOOK UPON, SUCH A DEAD DOG AS I AM? (BOOK OF SAMUEL, CHAPTER 9, VERSE 8)
A RED SKY AND...
DECIDE NOW.
DEVELOPMENT NUMBER HOMO CAEDELIUS PROTOTYPE 3.
GUNMETAL HOUND
Prologue

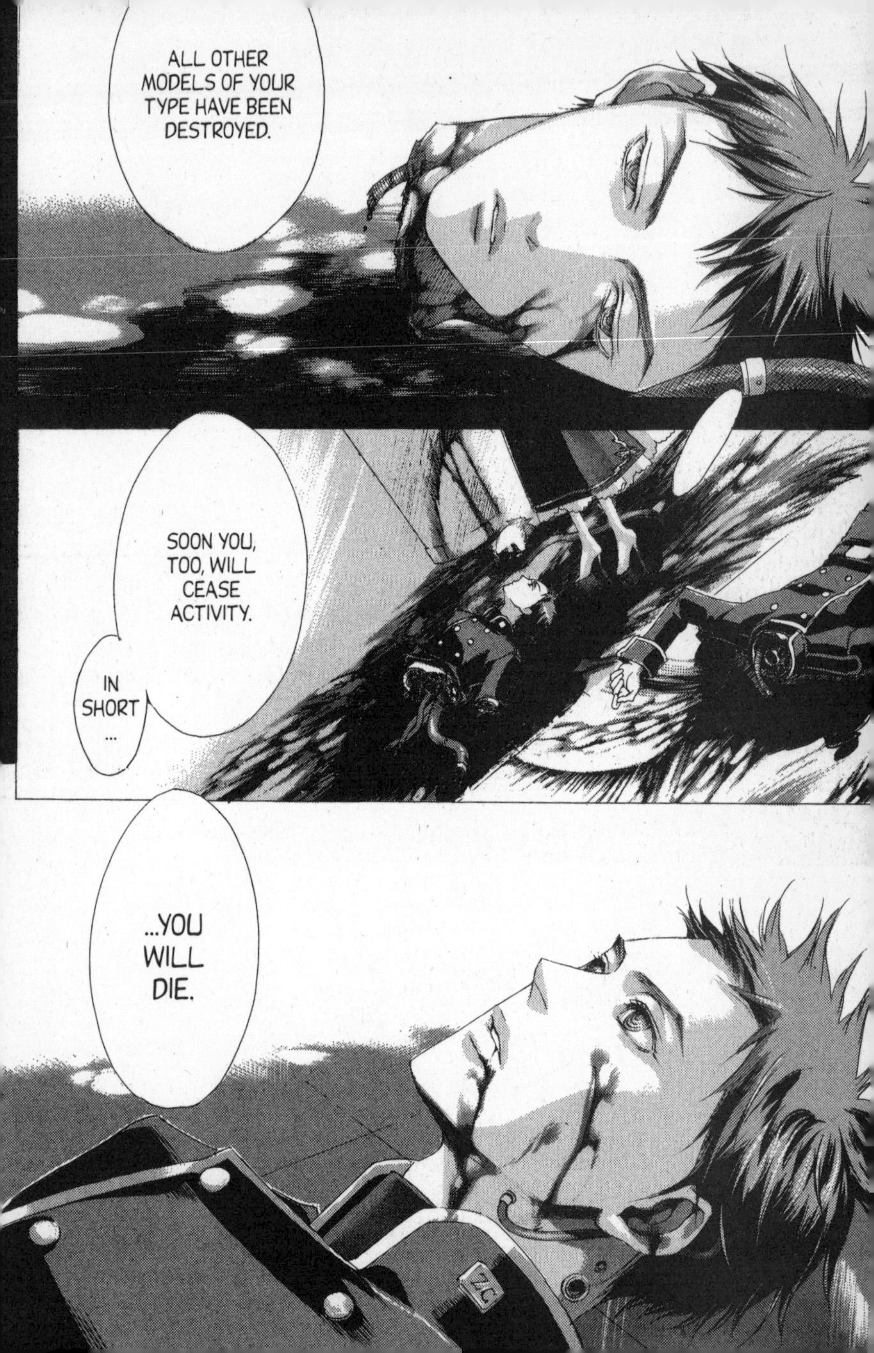
ALL OTHER MODELS OF YOUR TYPE HAVE BEEN DESTROYED.
SOON YOU, TOO, WILL CEASE ACTIVITY.
IN SHORT ...
...YOU WILL DIE.

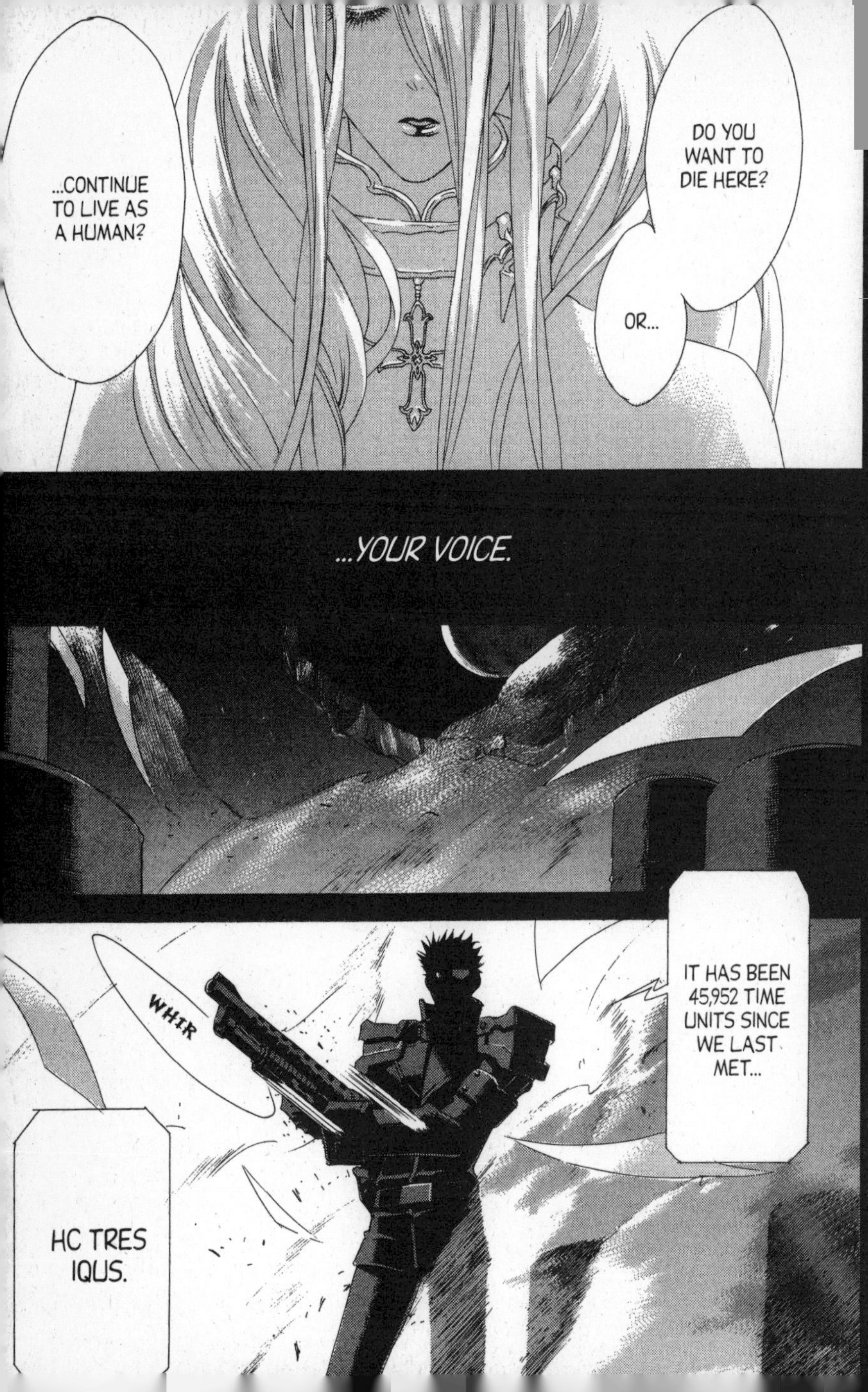
DO YOU WANT TO DIE HERE?
OR...
...CONTINUE TO LIVE AS A HUMAN?
...YOUR VOICE.
IT HAS BEEN 45,952 TIME UNITS SINCE WE LAST MET...
WHIR
HC TRES IQUS.

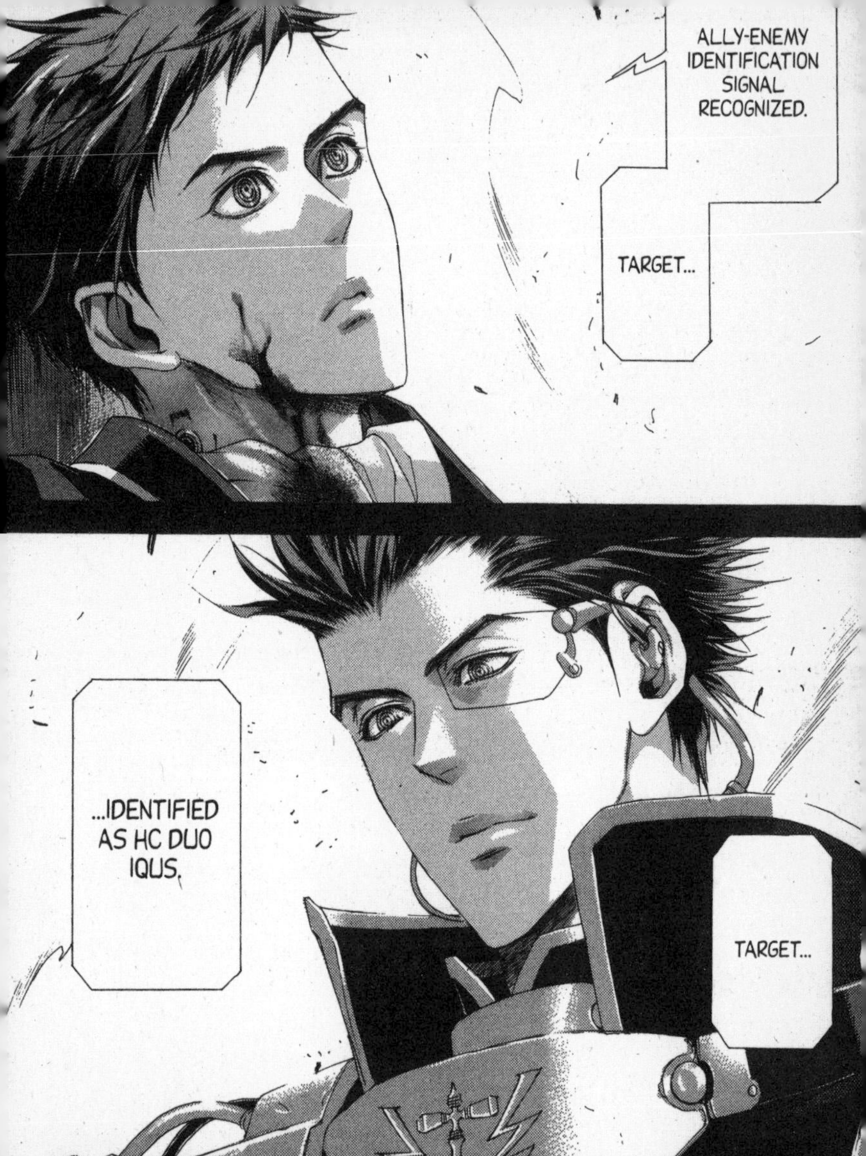
ALLY-ENEMY IDENTIFICATION SIGNAL RECOGNIZED.
TARGET...
TARGET...
...IDENTIFIED AS HC DUO IQUS.

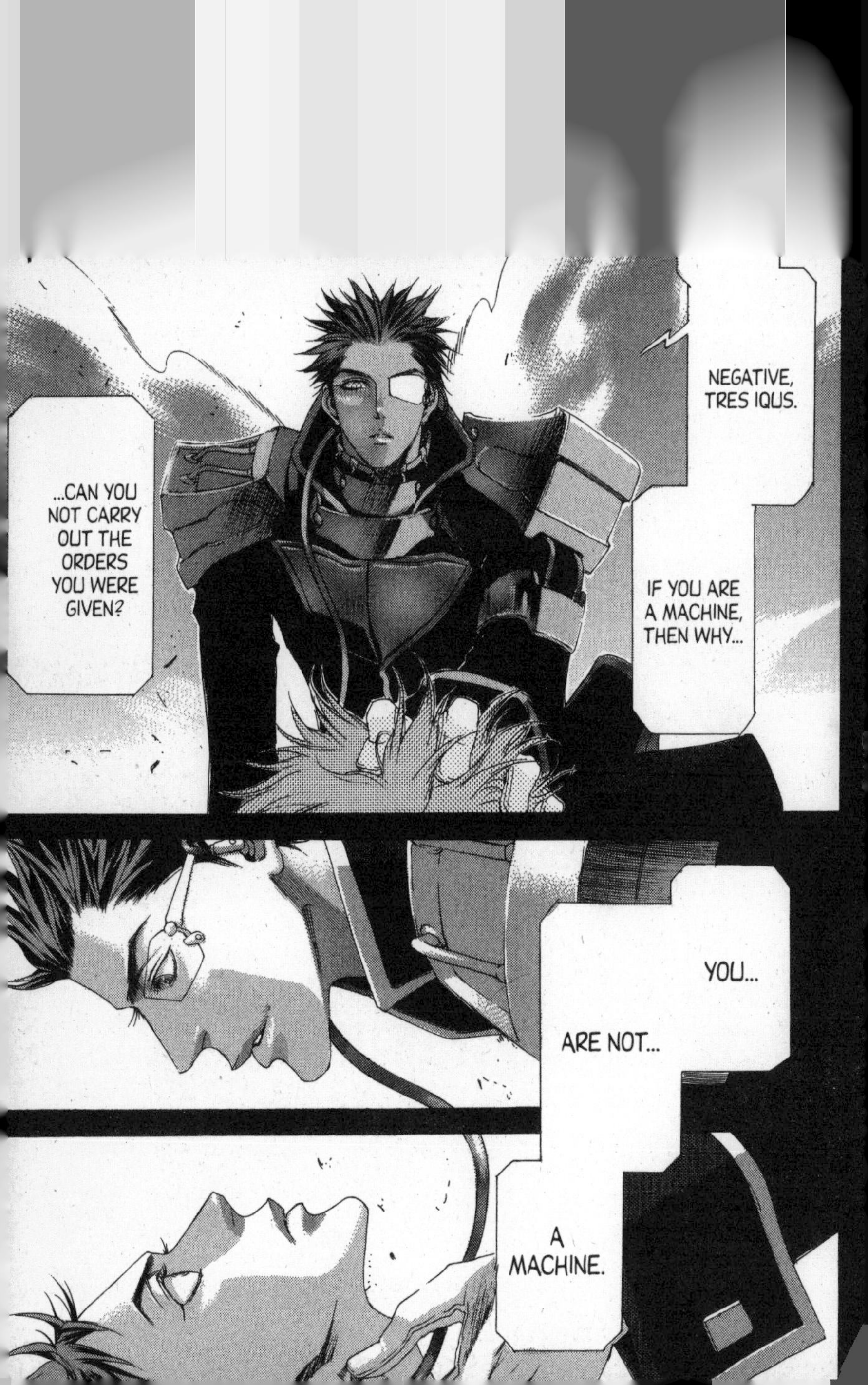
NEGATIVE, TRES IQUS.
IF YOU ARE A MACHINE, THEN WHY...
...CAN YOU NOT CARRY OUT THE ORDERS YOU WERE GIVEN?
YOU...
ARE NOT...
A MACHINE.

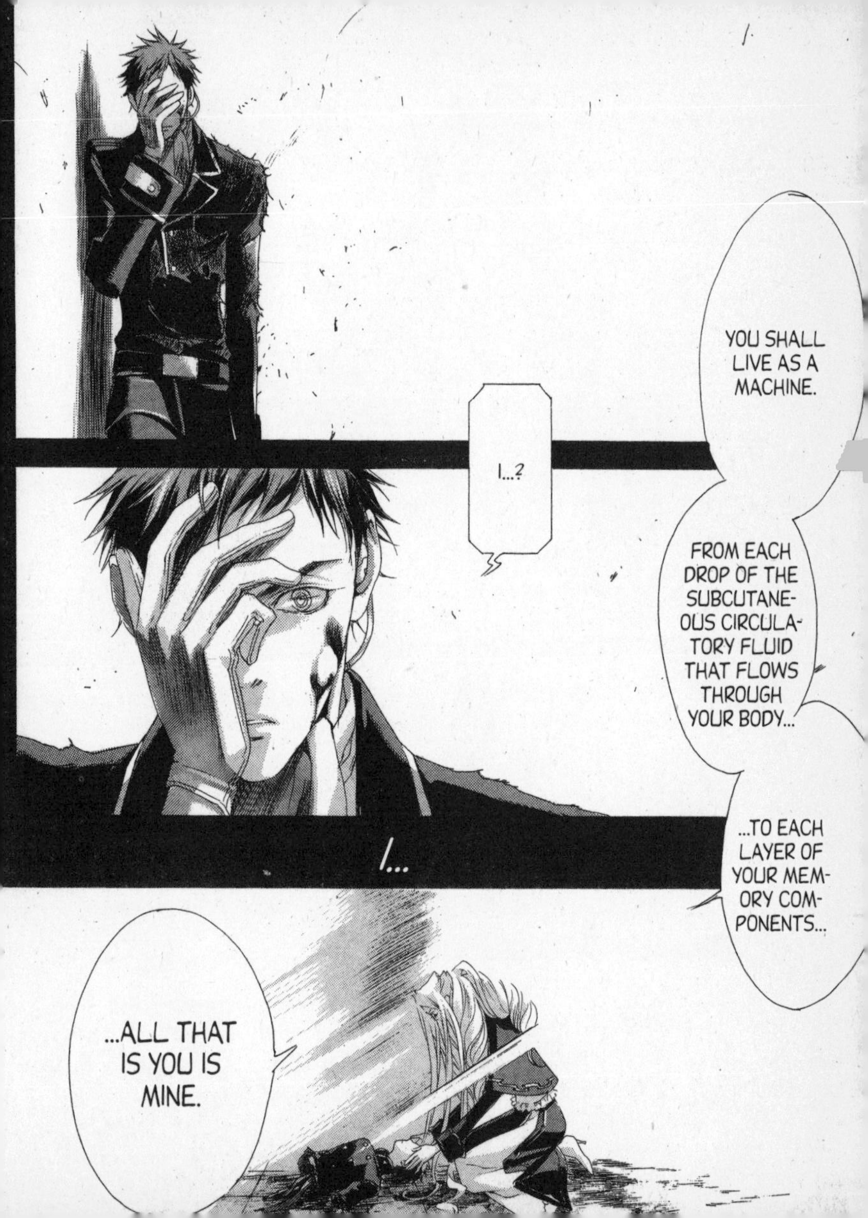
YOU SHALL LIVE AS A MACHINE.
I...?
FROM EACH DROP OF THE SUBCUTANEOUS CIRCULATORY FLUID THAT FLOWS THROUGH YOUR BODY...
...TO EACH LAYER OF YOUR MEMORY COMPONENTS...
I...
...ALL THAT IS YOU IS MINE.

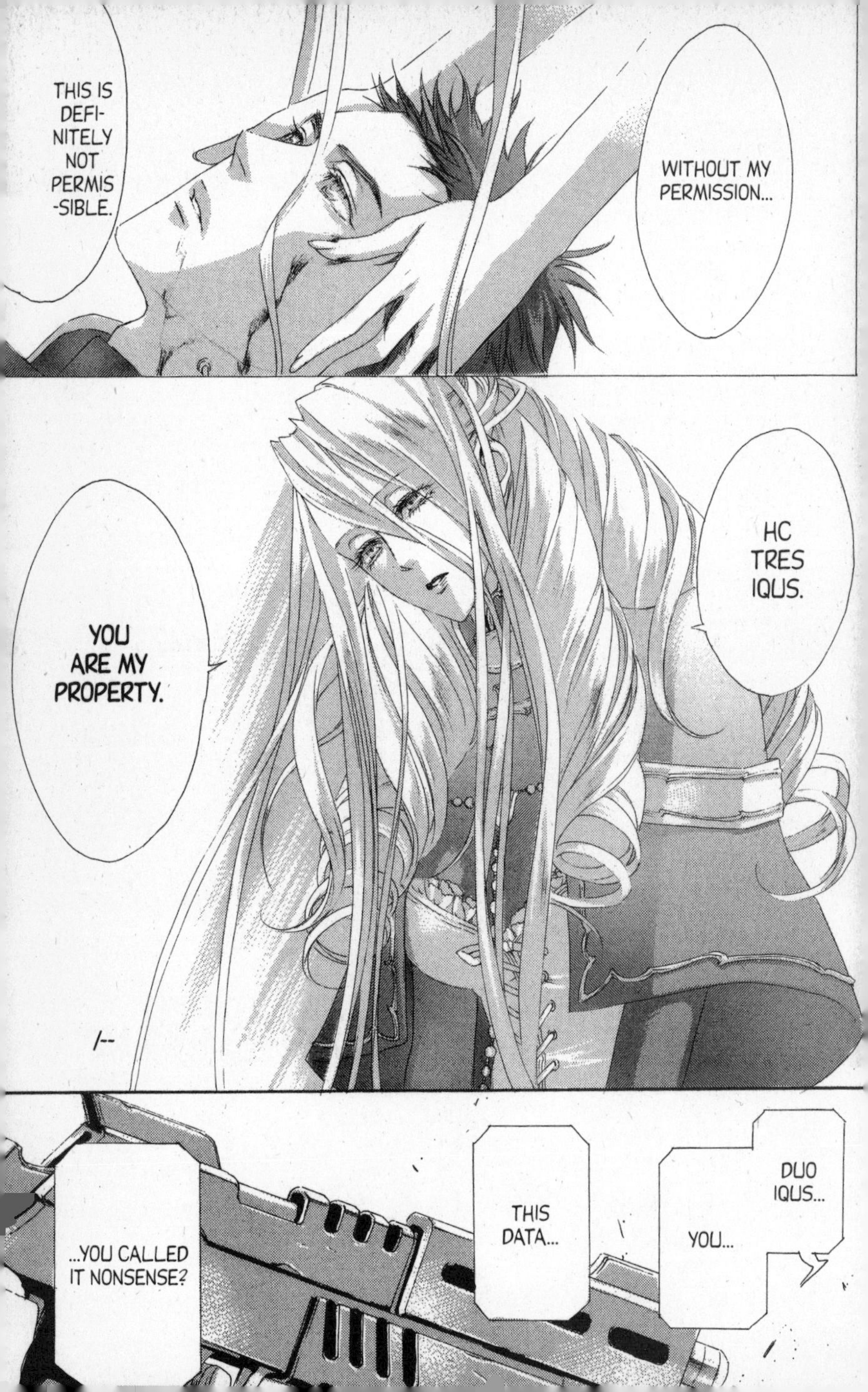
WITHOUT MY PERMISSION...
THIS IS DEFI-NITELY NOT PERMIS-SIBLE.
HC TRES IQUS.
YOU ARE MY PROPERTY.
DUO IQUS... YOU...
THIS DATA...
...YOU CALLED IT NONSENSE?

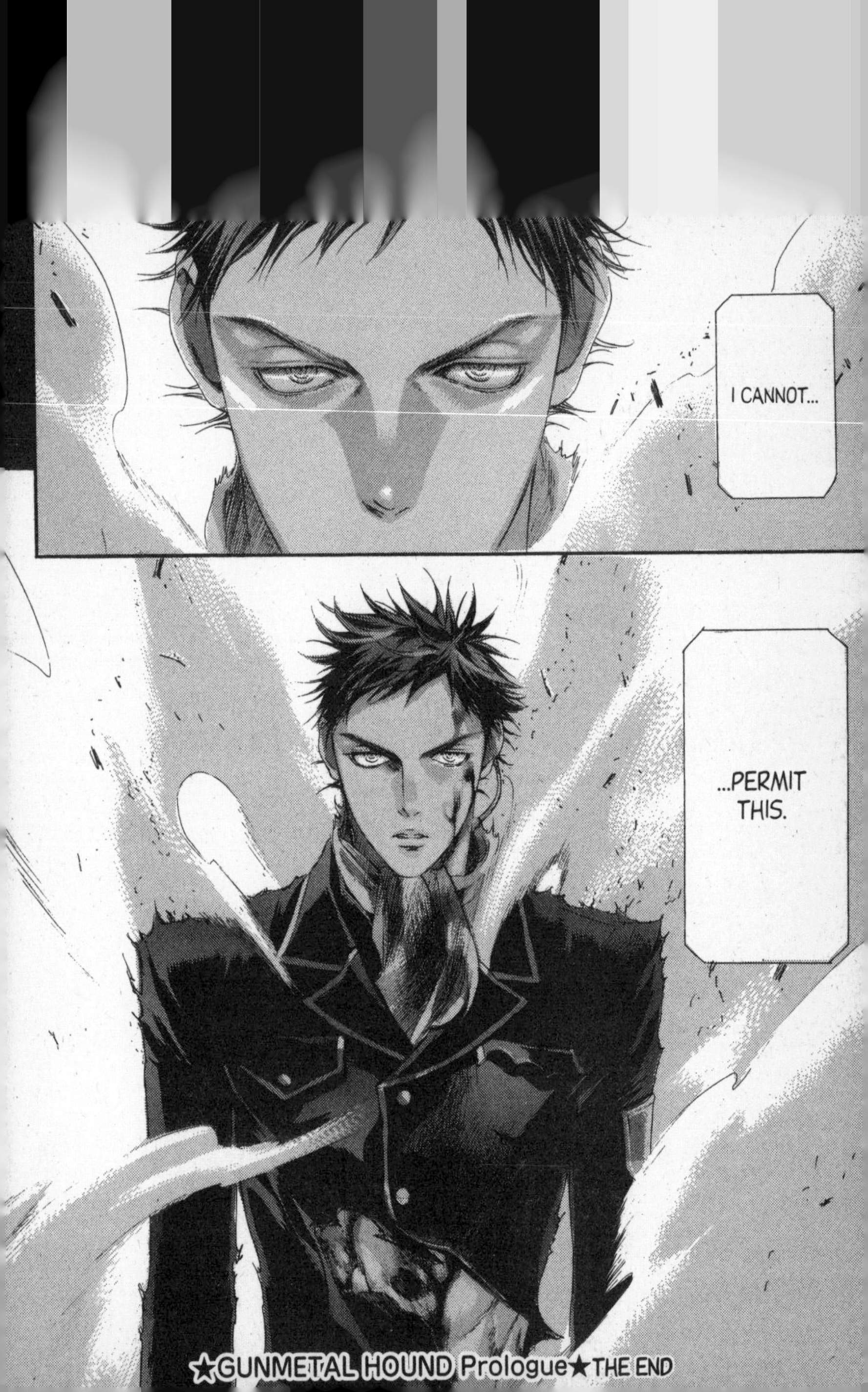
I CANNOT...
...PERMIT THIS.
☆GUNMETAL HOUND Prologue★THE END

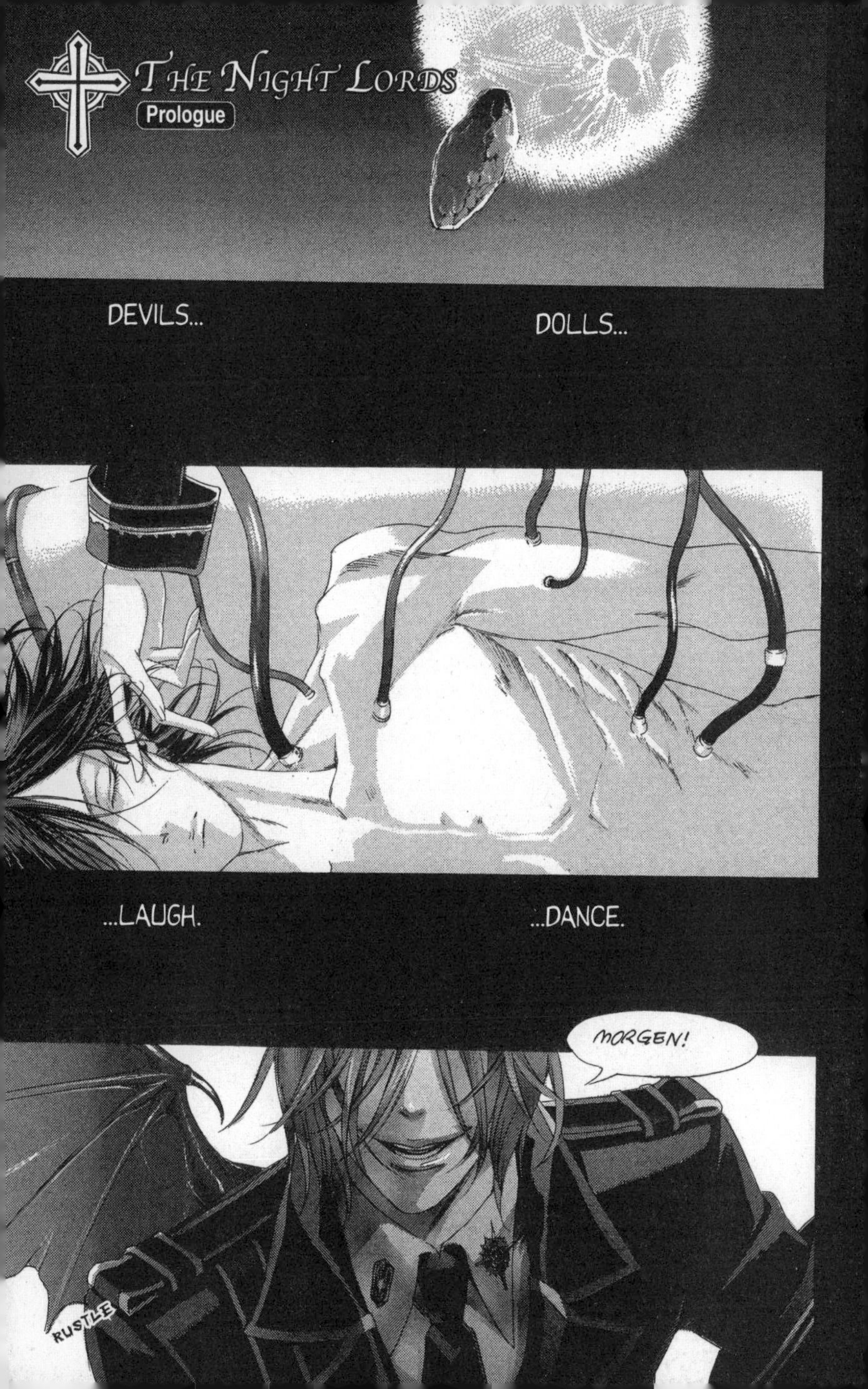
THE NIGHT LORDS
Prologue
DOLLS...
DEVILS...
...DANCE.
...LAUGH.
MORGEN!
RUSTLE

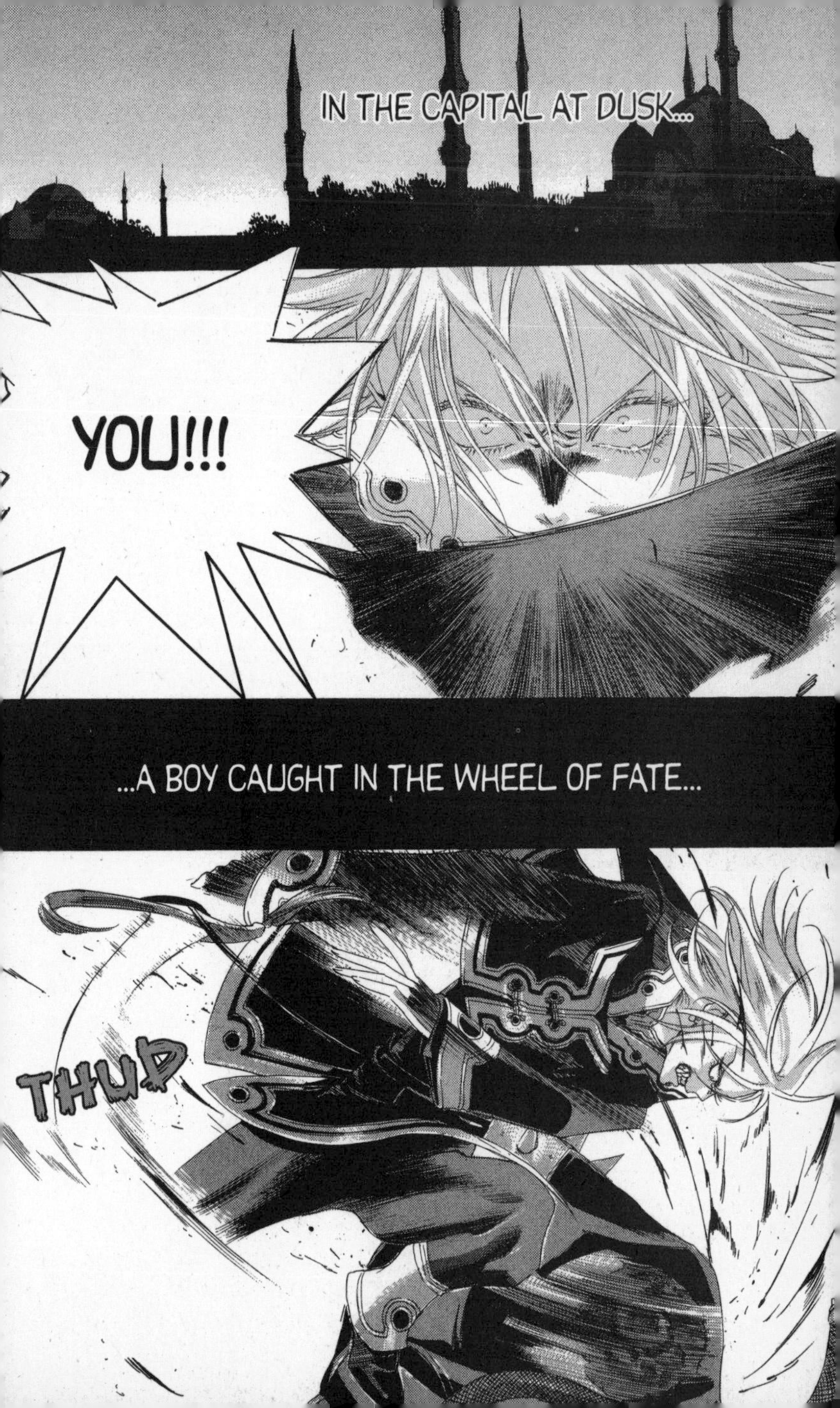
IN THE CAPITAL AT DUSK...
YOU!!!
...A BOY CAUGHT IN THE WHEEL OF FATE...
THUD

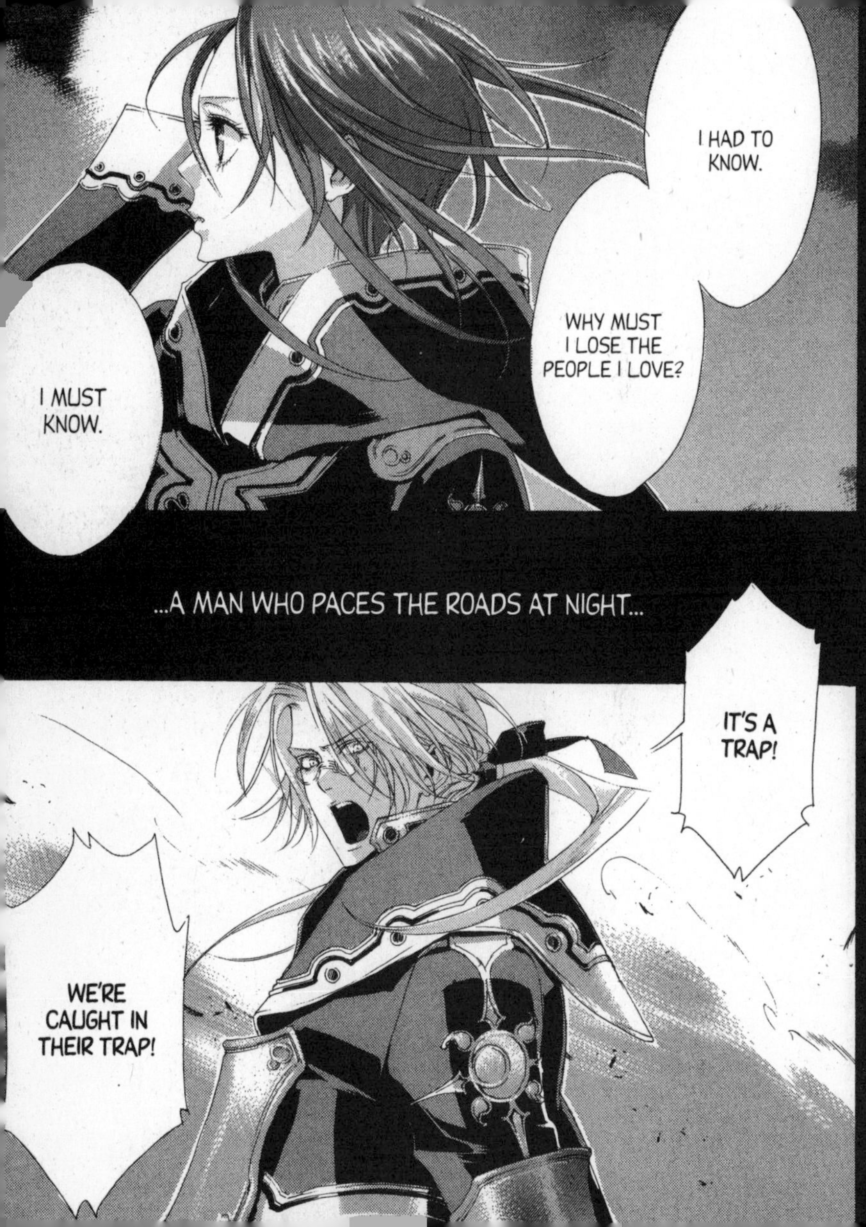
I HAD TO KNOW.
WHY MUST I LOSE THE PEOPLE I LOVE?
I MUST KNOW.
...A MAN WHO PACES THE ROADS AT NIGHT...
IT'S A TRAP!
WE'RE CAUGHT IN THEIR TRAP!

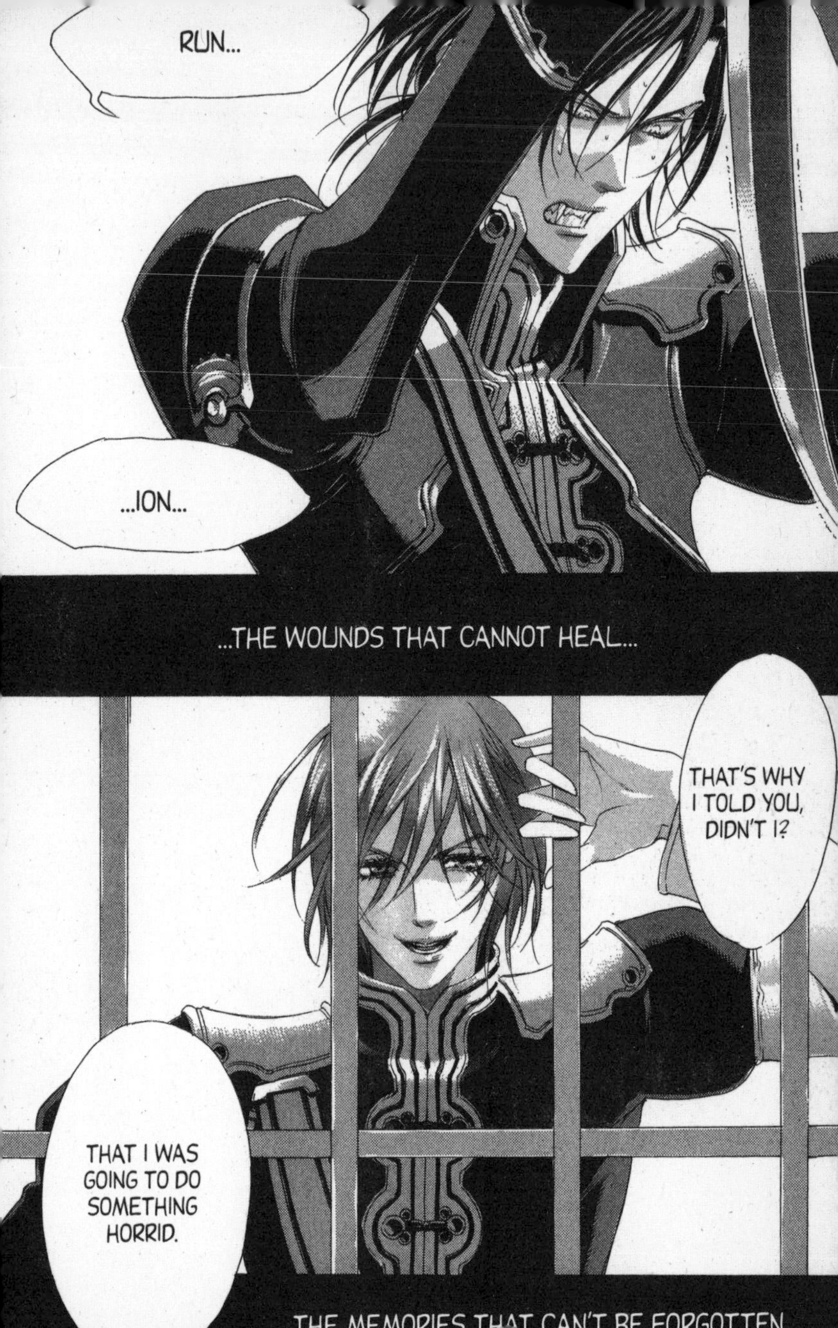
RUN...
...ION...
...THE WOUNDS THAT CANNOT HEAL...
THAT'S WHY I TOLD YOU, DIDN'T I?
THAT I WAS GOING TO DO SOMETHING HORRID.
THE MEMORIES THAT CAN'T BE FORGOTTEN

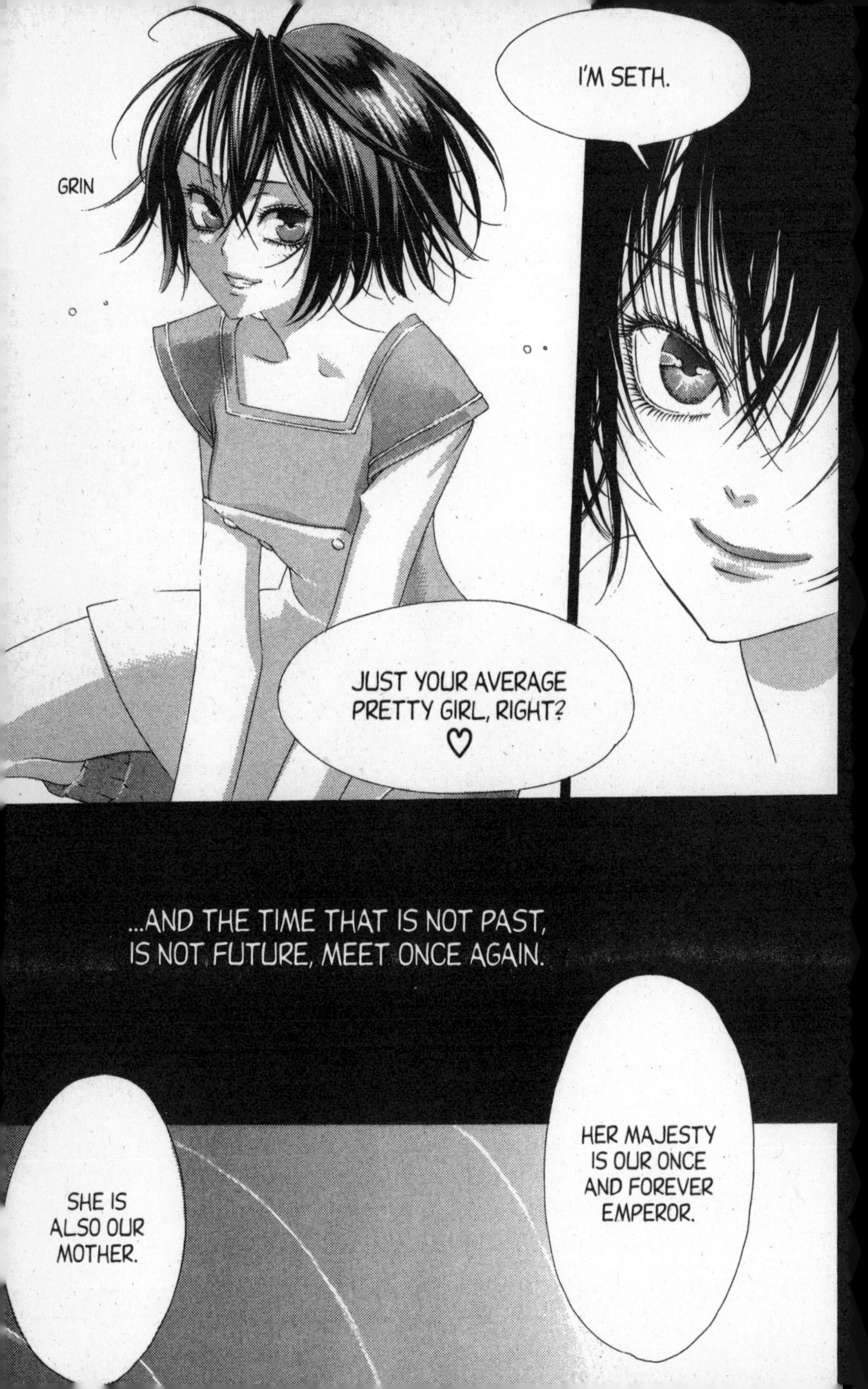
I'M SETH.
GRIN
JUST YOUR AVERAGE PRETTY GIRL, RIGHT? ♡
...AND THE TIME THAT IS NOT PAST, IS NOT FUTURE, MEET ONCE AGAIN.
HER MAJESTY IS OUR ONCE AND FOREVER EMPEROR.
SHE IS ALSO OUR MOTHER.

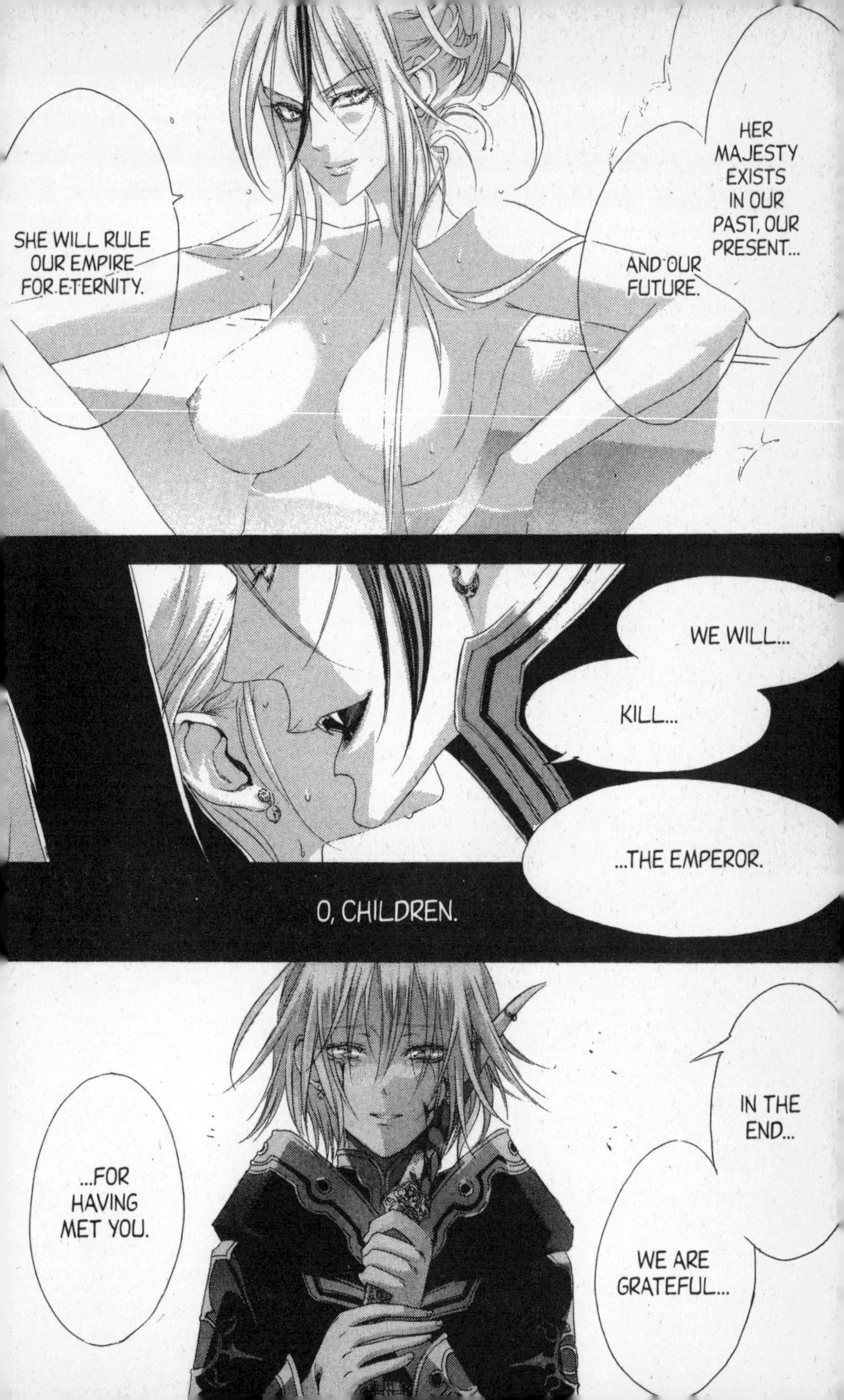
HER MAJESTY EXISTS IN OUR PAST, OUR PRESENT...
AND OUR FUTURE.
SHE WILL RULE OUR EMPIRE FOR ETERNITY.
WE WILL...
KILL...
...THE EMPEROR.
O, CHILDREN.
IN THE END...
WE ARE GRATEFUL...
...FOR HAVING MET YOU.

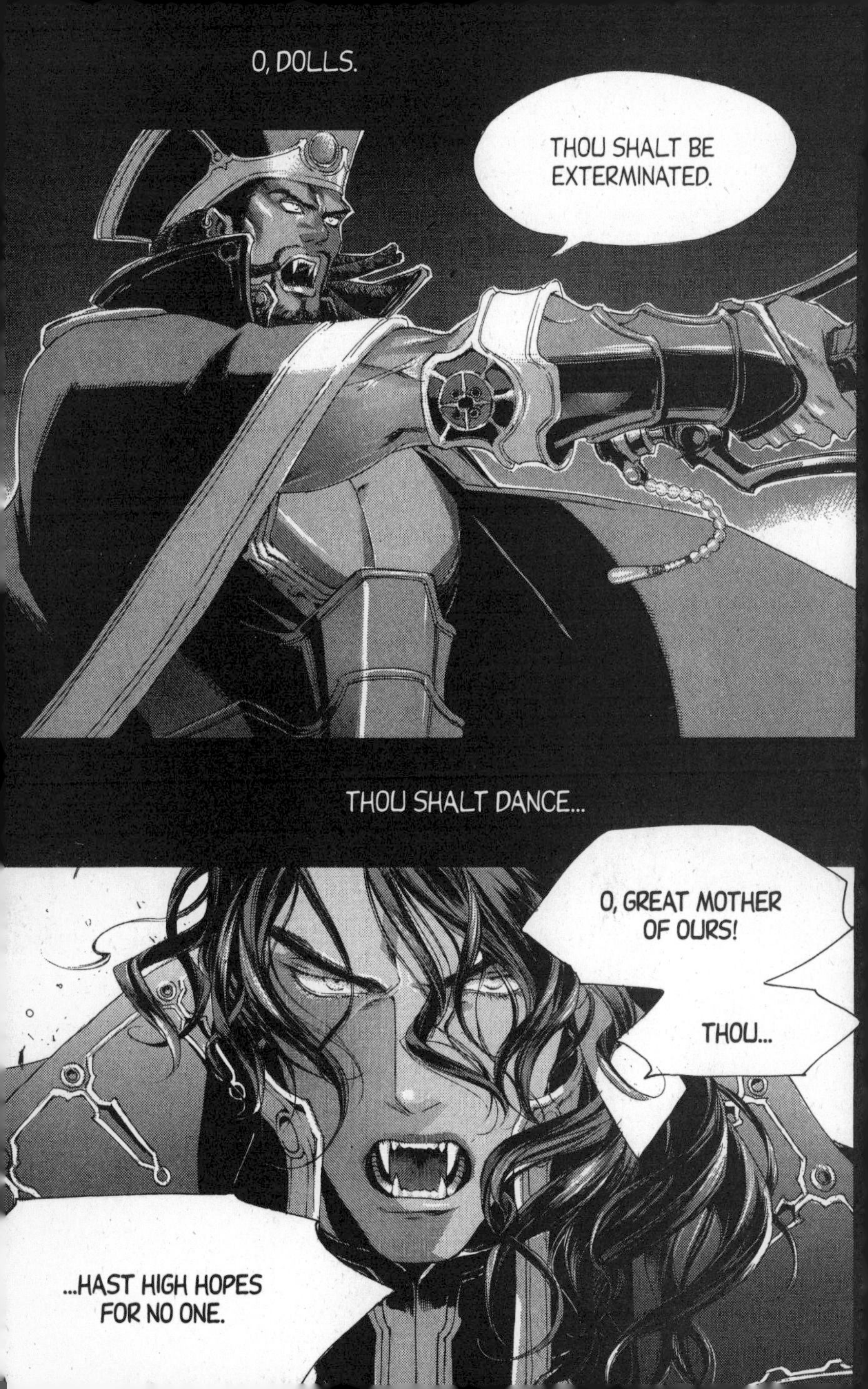
O, DOLLS.
THOU SHALT BE EXTERMINATED.
THOU SHALT DANCE...
O, GREAT MOTHER OF OURS!
THOU...
...HAST HIGH HOPES FOR NO ONE.

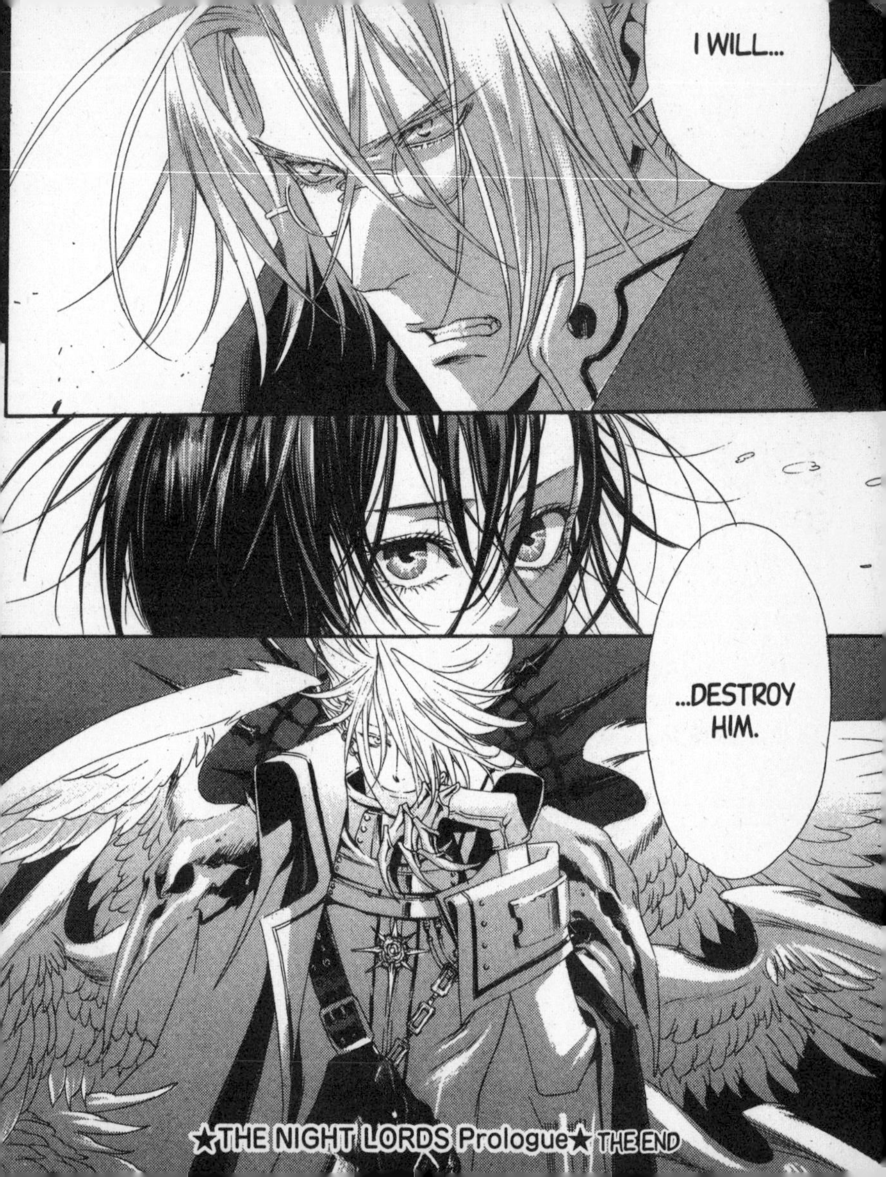
I WILL...
...DESTROY HIM.
★THE NIGHT LORDS Prologue★ THE END

BULLYING ISN'T COOL. (BY ZONO)

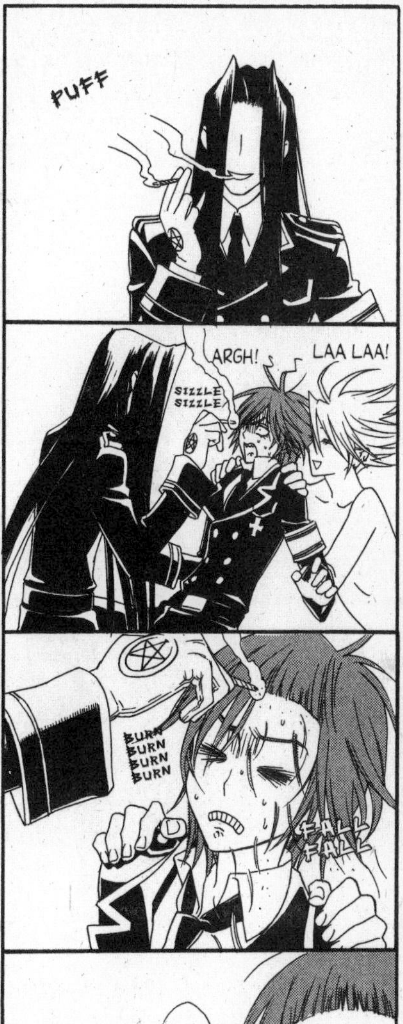
PUFF
LAA LAA!
ARGH!
SIZZLE SIZZLE
BURN BURN BURN BURN
FALL FALL
...I WANT TO DIE...
WAH HA HA HA!
HEH.
MIRROR
TEE HEE HEE HEE.
LAME

I THINK AS A SECRET SOCIETY, THE ROSENKREUZ ORDEN IS MISSING SOME IMPORTANT STUFF, LIKE UNITY AND CHIVALRY. IT HAS TO BE MORE LIKE...THE B F DAN OR THE TAKA NO TSUME DAN OR SOMETHING....

YOROSHIKU MECHA DOG

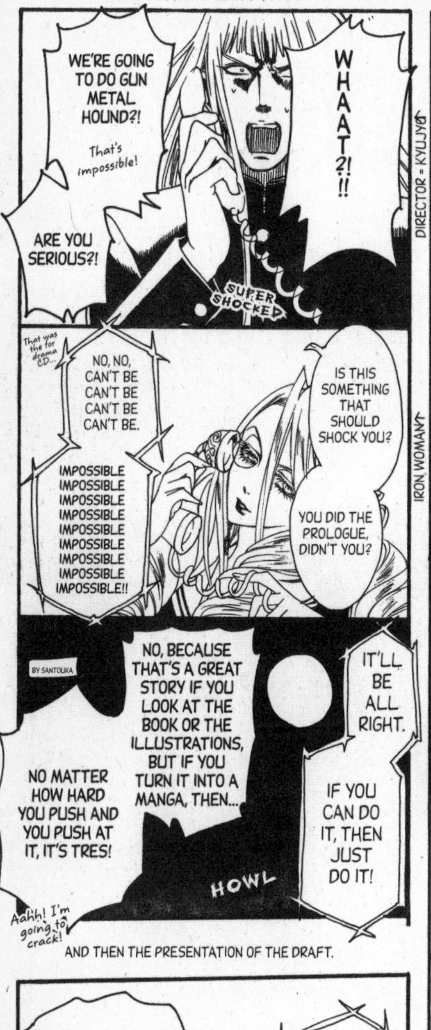
DIRECTOR = KYUJYO
WHAAAT?!!!
WE'RE GOING TO DO GUN METAL HOUND?!
That's impossible!
ARE YOU SERIOUS?!
SUPER SHOCKED
IRON WOMAN
IS THIS SOMETHING THAT SHOULD SHOCK YOU?
NO, NO, CAN'T BE CAN'T BE CAN'T BE CAN'T BE.
That was the for drama CD...
YOU DID THE PROLOGUE, DIDN'T YOU?
IMPOSSIBLE IMPOSSIBLE IMPOSSIBLE IMPOSSIBLE IMPOSSIBLE IMPOSSIBLE IMPOSSIBLE IMPOSSIBLE IMPOSSIBLE!!
IT'LL BE ALL RIGHT.
NO, BECAUSE THAT'S A GREAT STORY IF YOU LOOK AT THE BOOK OR THE ILLUSTRATIONS, BUT IF YOU TURN IT INTO A MANGA, THEN...
BY SANTOUKA
IF YOU CAN DO IT, THEN JUST DO IT!
NO MATTER HOW HARD YOU PUSH AND YOU PUSH AT IT, IT'S TRES!
HOWL
Aahh! I'm going to crack!
AND THEN THE PRESENTATION OF THE DRAFT.
WHOA, IT'S ALL TRES-KUN.
THAT'S WHAT I TOLD YOU!
THIS IS A BIT DIFFICULT, ISN'T IT?

I DREW ENOUGH TRES-KUNS TO LAST A LIFETIME.

TRIED TO SERIOUSLY THINK ABOUT THE EMPIRE

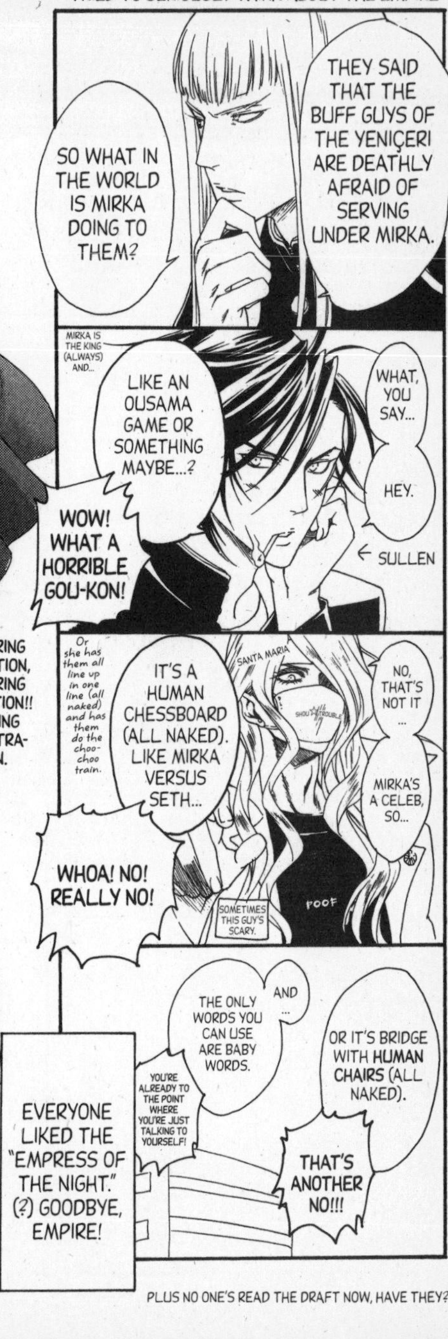
THEY SAID THAT THE BUFF GUYS OF THE YENIÇERI ARE DEATHLY AFRAID OF SERVING UNDER MIRKA.
SO WHAT IN THE WORLD IS MIRKA DOING TO THEM?
WHAT, YOU SAY...
HEY.
SULLEN
LIKE AN OUSAMA GAME OR SOMETHING MAYBE...?
MIRKA IS THE KING (ALWAYS) AND...
WOW! WHAT A HORRIBLE GOU-KON!
NO, THAT'S NOT IT ...
MIRKA'S A CELEB, SO...
SANTA MARIA
IT'S A HUMAN CHESSBOARD (ALL NAKED). LIKE MIRKA VERSUS SETH...
Or she has them all line up in one line (all naked) and has them do the choo-choo train.
POOF
SOMETIMES THIS GUY'S SCARY.
WHOA! NO! REALLY NO!
OR IT'S BRIDGE WITH HUMAN CHAIRS (ALL NAKED).
AND ...
THE ONLY WORDS YOU CAN USE ARE BABY WORDS.
YOU'RE ALREADY TO THE POINT WHERE YOU'RE JUST TALKING TO YOURSELF!
THAT'S ANOTHER NO!!!
EVERYONE LIKED THE "EMPRESS OF THE NIGHT." (?) GOODBYE, EMPIRE!

It doesn't really matter. I just like the word "buff."

← Flamberg = Akira-kun

← SAMURAI = TSUKASA

PLUS NO ONE'S READ THE DRAFT NOW, HAVE THEY?

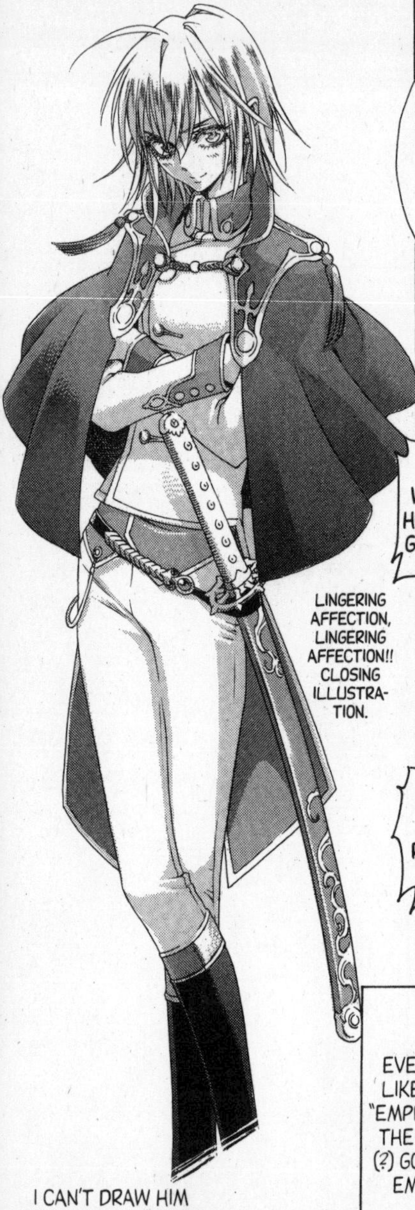

LINGERING AFFECTION, LINGERING AFFECTION!! CLOSING ILLUSTRATION.

I CAN'T DRAW HIM ANYMORE...IT MAKES ME FEEL LONELY...

OUTRO.

THANK YOU FOR READING! I HAD A DREAM WHERE I FELL INTO A CRACK IN THE EARTH. ENOUGH ALREADY! THIS IS KYUJYO. AND THIS IS THE NINTH VOLUME OF THE TORIBURA MANGA. IT'S A NUMBER THAT SOME MAY FIND UNLUCKY, BUT FOR NOW IT'S A REALLY GOOD NUMBER. KYUJYO'S NINE. NOW THE STORY ABOUT THE EMPIRE IS OVER...NERVOUS, NERVOUS. MAYBE THAT'S THE REASON MY WORKPLACE IS REALLY NERVOUS RIGHT NOW. THAT, PLUS WE DID THE TRES STORY, SO IT TURNED INTO EVEN MORE OF A PANIC. WHAT'LL WE DO?! WELL A LOT OF THINGS HAPPENED, BUT THE EMPIRE STORY WAS REALLY FUN! SEE YOU IN THE NEXT VOLUME (10!).

KIYO KYUJYO.

THANKS

TSUKASA "I LOVE EVEN YOUR BUTT HAIRS" **KYOUKA.**

☆ **AKIRA** "FULL STAND" **OOTAKI**

CONGRATS ON YOUR DEBUT! CONGRATULATIONS!

RIN "HARD" **NARI**

& **AKEMI-CHAN.**

THANK YOU SO MUCH ALL THE TIME, EVERYONE!

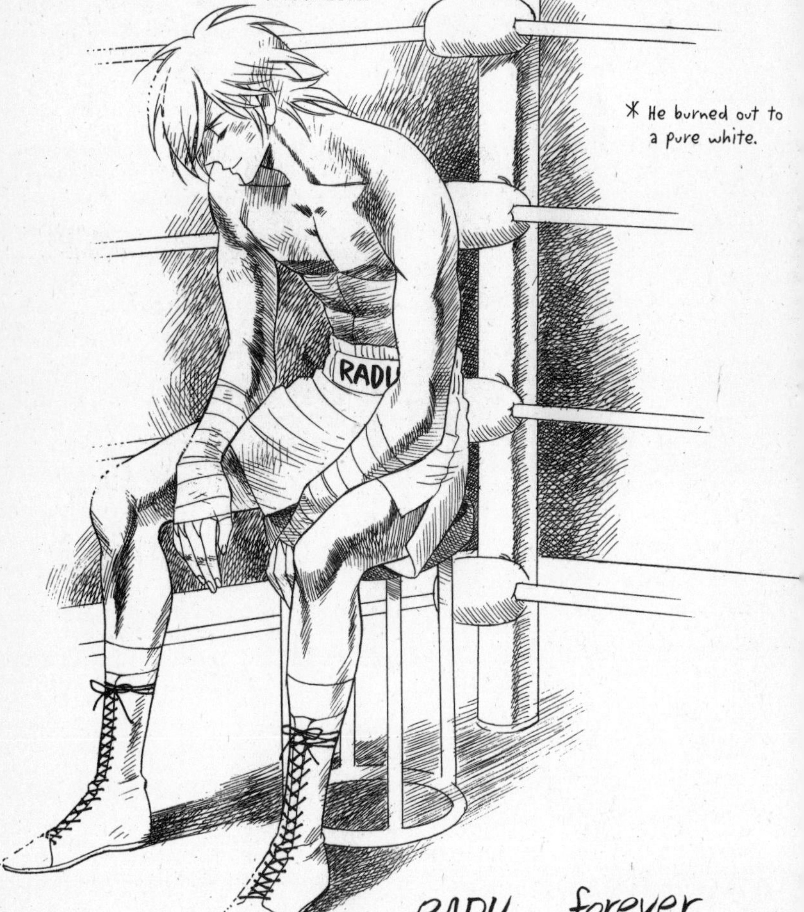
RADU
* He burned out to a pure white.
RADU forever

IN THE NEXT VOLUME OF

Caterina Sforza orders Abel and Esther to Istvan,
where the press swirls around Esther, who is
considered a Lady Saint for her role in saving the city.
But something terrible happens before Esther can
speak to the crowds on the anniversary of
the battle against Gyula.

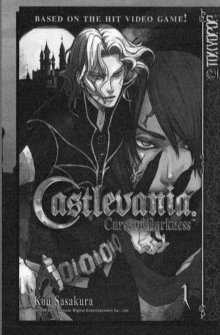

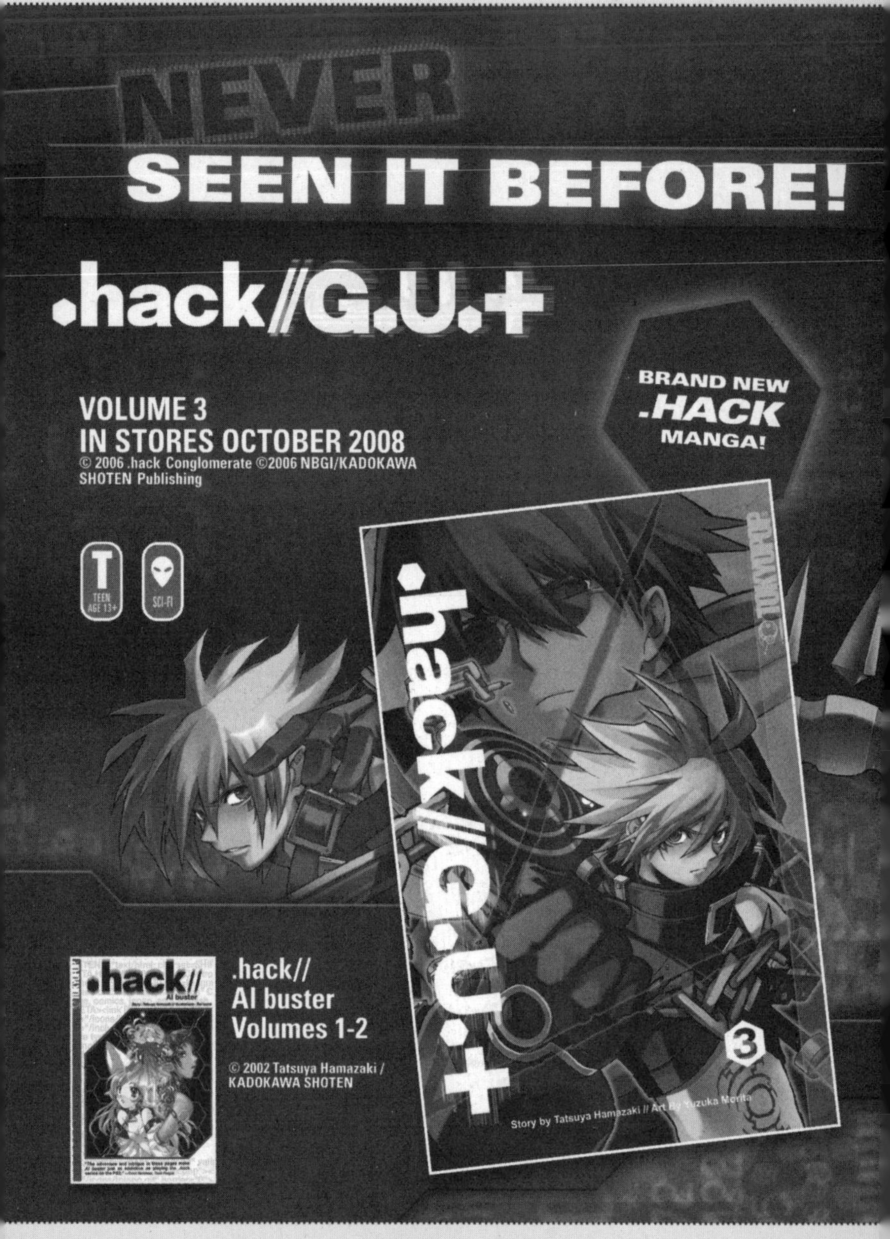
NEVER
SEEN IT BEFORE!
.hack//G.U.+
BRAND NEW .HACK MANGA!
VOLUME 3
IN STORES OCTOBER 2008
© 2006 .hack Conglomerate ©2006 NBGI/KADOKAWA SHOTEN Publishing
T TEEN AGE 13+
SCI-FI
.hack//G.U.+
3
Story by Tatsuya Hamazaki // Art By Yuzuka Morita
.hack//
AI buster
Volumes 1-2
© 2002 Tatsuya Hamazaki / KADOKAWA SHOTEN

INCLUDES A PREVIEW OF FRUITS BASKET VOL. 22 (MARCH 2009)

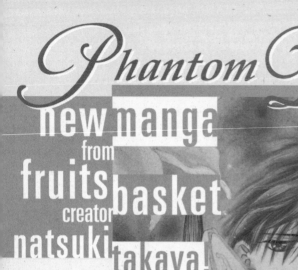

From the creative minds that brought you the first Princess Ai trilog
Princess Ai: The Prism of Midnight Dawn
Also Available: Limited time only! Special Edition with bonus Princess Ai DVD
The long-awaited Princess Ai sequel has arrived
Volume 1 in Stores December 2008!
Explore the Princess Ai world at www.TOKYOPOP.com/PrincessAi
© & TM TOKYOPOP Inc. and Kitty Radio, Ir

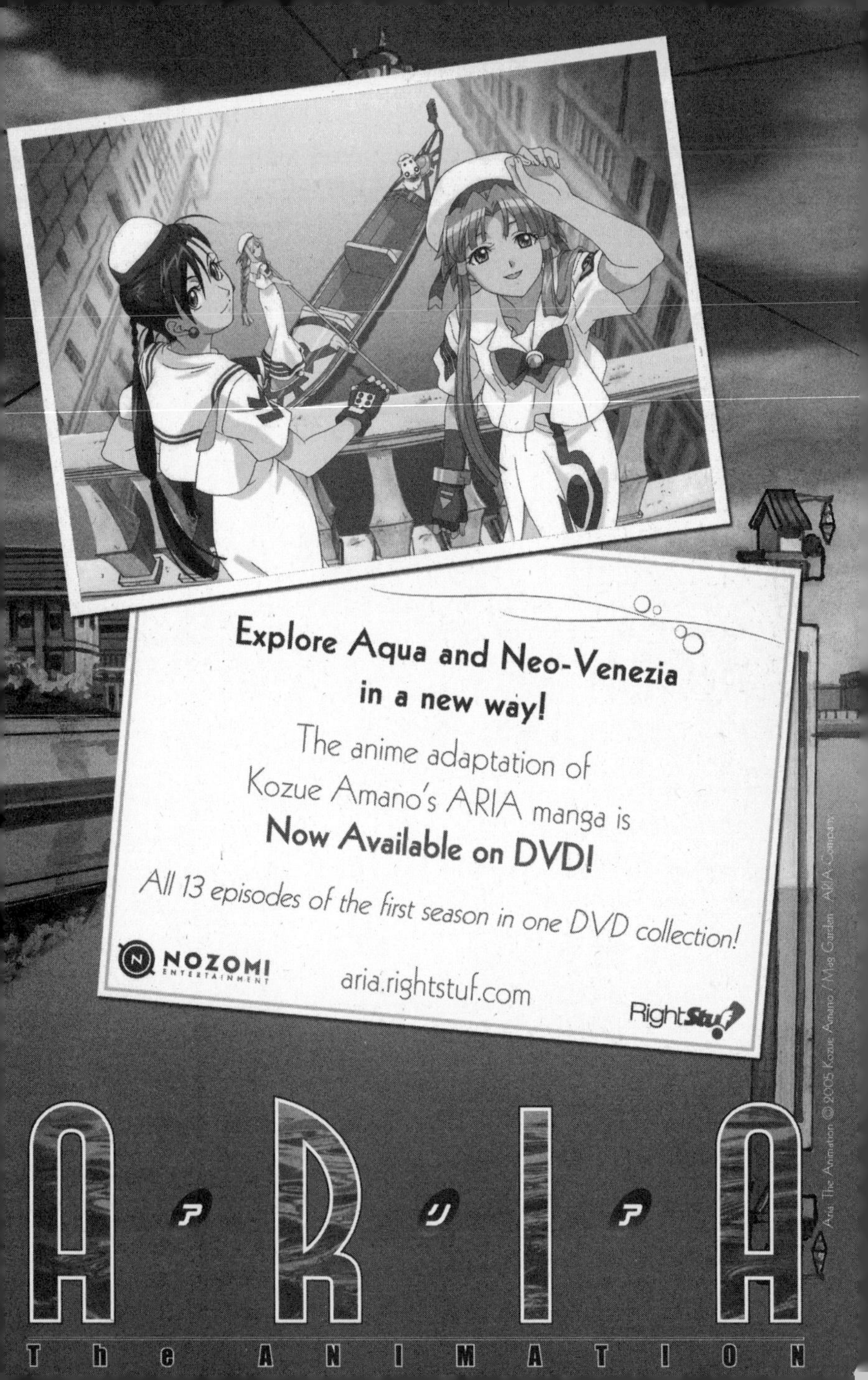

Explore Aqua and Neo-Venezia in a new way!
The anime adaptation of Kozue Amano's ARIA manga is
Now Available on DVD!
All 13 episodes of the first season in one DVD collection!
NOZOMI ENTERTAINMENT
aria.rightstuf.com
RightStuf
ARIA
アリア
The ANIMATION
Aria The Animation © 2005 Kozue Amano / Mag Garden · ARIA Company

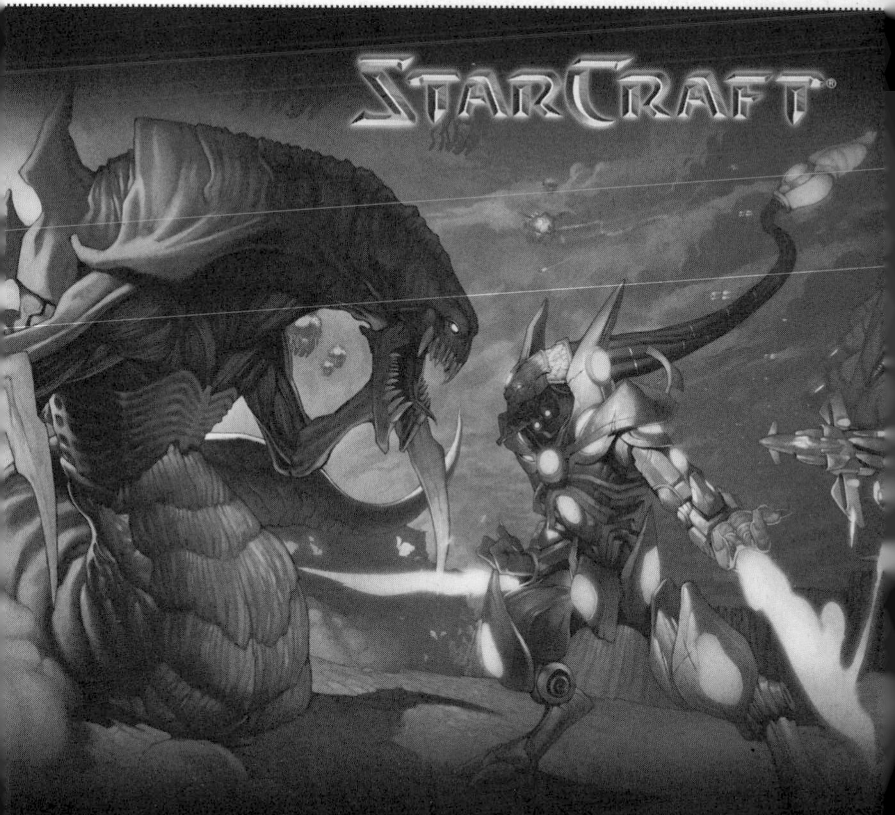
STARCRAFT®

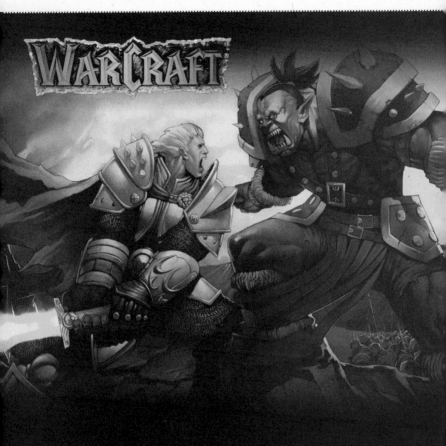

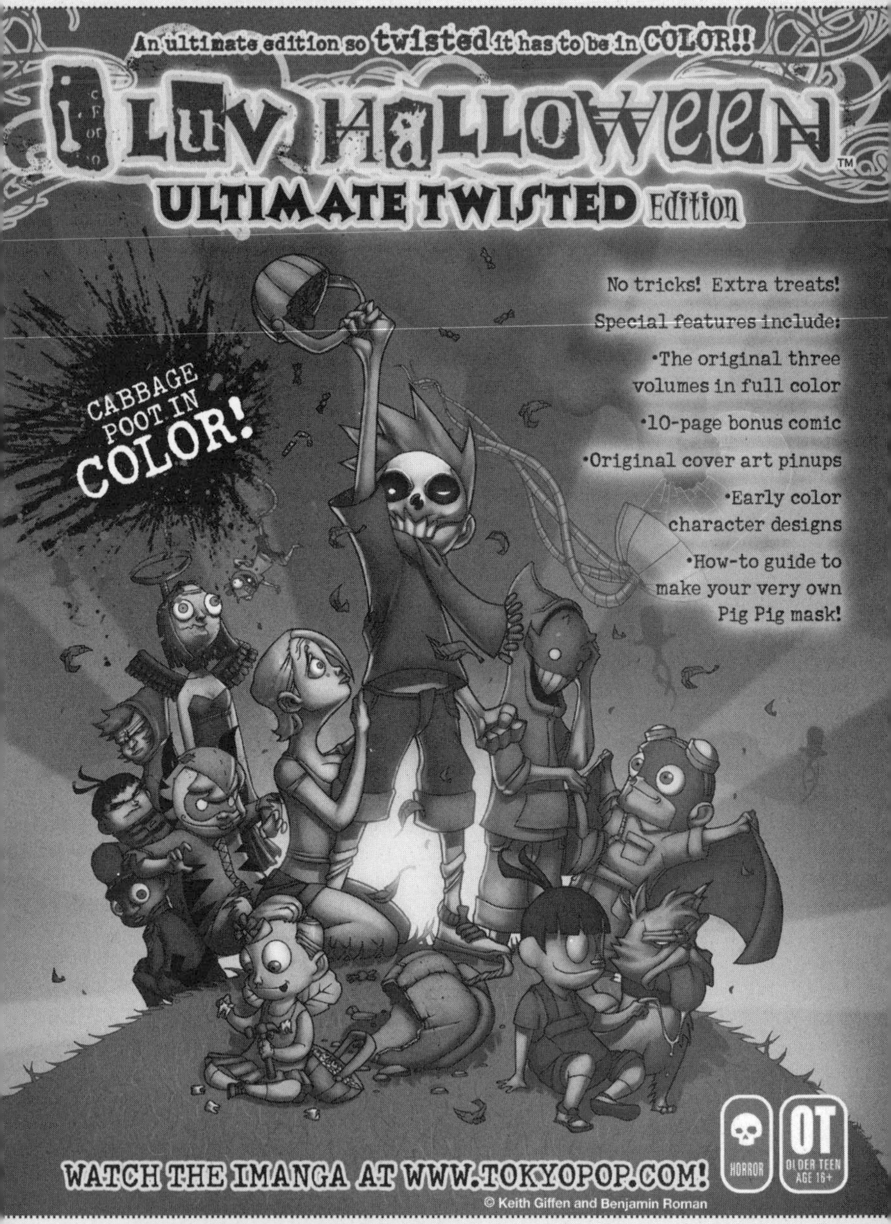
An ultimate edition so twisted it has to be in COLOR!!
I LUV HALLOWEEN™
ULTIMATE TWISTED Edition
No tricks! Extra treats!
Special features include:
•The original three volumes in full color
•10-page bonus comic
•Original cover art pinups
•Early color character designs
•How-to guide to make your very own Pig Pig mask!
CABBAGE POOT IN COLOR!
HORROR
OT OLDER TEEN AGE 16+
WATCH THE IMANGA AT WWW.TOKYOPOP.COM!
© Keith Giffen and Benjamin Roman

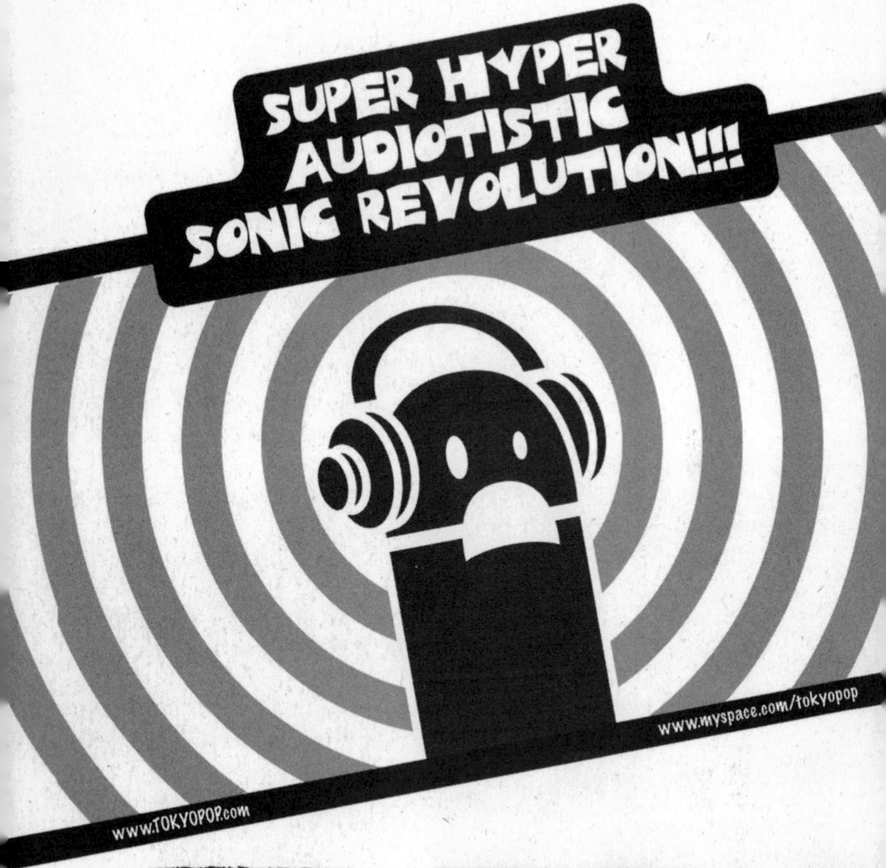
SUPER HYPER
AUDIOTISTIC
SONIC REVOLUTION!!!
www.myspace.com/tokyopop
www.TOKYOPOP.com

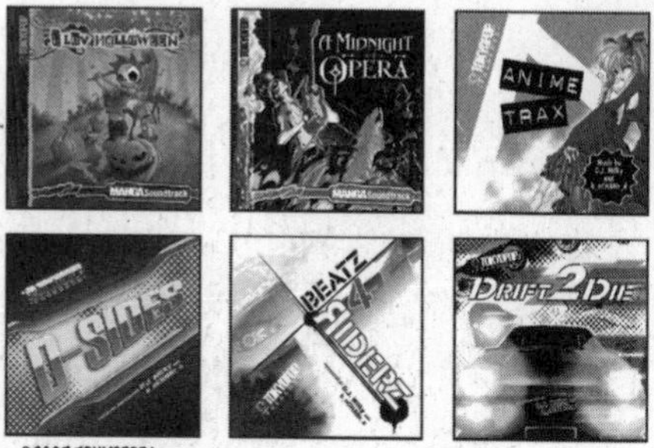
A MIDNIGHT OPERA
ANIME
TRAX
BEATZ 4 RIDERZ
DRIFT 2 DIE

STOP!

This is the back of the book.
You wouldn't want to spoil a great ending!

This book is printed "manga-style," in the authentic Japanese right-to-left format. Since none of the artwork has been flipped or altered, readers get to experience the story just as the creator intended. You've been asking for it, so TOKYOPOP® delivered: authentic, hot-off-the-press, and far more fun!

DIRECTIONS

If this is your first time reading manga-style, here's a quick guide to help you understand how it works.

It's easy... just start in the top right panel and follow the numbers. Have fun, and look for more 100% authentic manga from TOKYOPOP®!